Anti-Semitism:
A History

Anti-Semitism: A History

DAN COHN-SHERBOK

SUTTON PUBLISHING

First published in the United Kingdom in 2002 by
Sutton Publishing Limited · Phoenix Mill
Thrupp · Stroud · Gloucestershire · GL5 2BU

British Library Cataloguing in Publication Data
A catalogue record for this book is available from the British Library.

ISBN 0-7509-2492-6

For my mother

Typeset in 11/14.5pt Sabon.
Typesetting and origination by
Sutton Publishing Limited.
Printed and bound in England by
J.H. Haynes & Co. Ltd, Sparkford.

Contents

Acknowledgements

I would like to acknowledge my indebtedness to Léon Poliakov's multi-volume *History of Anti-Semitism*, which served as a source of information and source material used throughout this study, as well as these other works: Roberto Finzi, *Anti-Semitism*; Edward Flannery, *The Anguish of the Jews*; Graham Keith, *Hatred without a Cause*; Albert Lindemann, *Anti-Semitism before the Holocaust*; Rosemary Radford Ruether, *Faith and Fratricide*; Lionel Steiman, *Paths to Genocide*; Joshua Trachtenberg, *Jewish Magic and Superstition*; Robert Wistrich, *Anti-semitism*. I would also like to thank Christopher Feeney and his colleagues for their support and encouragement.

Preface

In an interview given to Al-Jazeera Arab television in 1998, the Arab terrorist Osama bin Laden chillingly castigated America and the Jewish people and encouraged Muslims to wage a holy war against the enemies of Islam: 'Our duty,' he declared, 'is to incite the *jihad* against America, Israel and their allies. . . . With the grace of God we have established [common cause] with a large number of our brothers in the International Islamic Front to confront Jews and the Crusaders. We believe that the affairs of many of those are moving in the right direction and have the ability to move widely. We pray to God to grant them victory and revenge on the Jews and Americans.'

Such sentiments reflect the attitude of many Muslims throughout the world who are bitterly opposed to the support that America has given to the Jewish state. The twenty-first century thus bears witness to the continuing hostility that has been expressed towards Jewry for nearly 4,000 years. Today, it is the peoples of the Islamic world who have become the proponents of rabid anti-Semitism; in the last century the Nazis sought to bring about the genocide of the Jewish people; in previous centuries, the Church attempted to eliminate Jewry through conversion, persecution and murder.

Why is it that the Jews have been so bitterly hated for nearly four millennia? In an earlier study, *The Crucified Jew*, I focused on the Christian roots of anti-Semitism. The aim of this volume is to answer this question by surveying the history of anti-Semitism from a more global perspective. As will be seen, numerous factors created a climate of Jew-hatred. Scripture records that the Jews were oppressed by the Egyptian Pharaoh; through Moses' deliverance the ancient Israelites escaped bondage, eventually settling in the land that God had promised to the Patriarchs. There they established a kingdom, but were subject to constant attack from their neighbours.

In the Graeco-Roman world, Jews were viewed as alien and xenophobic. In the Hellenistic world, the common view was that anything non-Greek was uncivilized. In this context Judaism was regarded with contempt. With the emergence of Christianity such hostility towards Jewry intensified. Drawing upon Hellenistic ideas that had penetrated the Jewish religion, Christianity absorbed pagan hostility to the Jewish people and utilized aspects of Pharisaic Judaism to distance itself from the faith from which it had evolved. Eventually, such anti-Jewish sentiment became an essential element of Christianity.

The New Testament served as a basis for the early Church's vilification of the Jews. According to the Church Fathers, the Jewish people are lawless and dissolute. Because of their rejection of Christ, the Jewish nation has been excluded from God's grace and is subject to his wrath. This *Adversos Judaeos* teaching of the early Church Fathers continued into the medieval period. During the Crusades Christian mobs massacred Jewish communities; Jews were charged with killing Christian children to use their blood for ritual purposes, blaspheming Christ and Christianity in their sacred literature, and causing the Black Death by poisoning wells. Throughout the Middle Ages Jews were detested, and the image of the satanic Jew became a central feature of Western iconography. Repeatedly, Jews were accused of satanic activities and viewed as a sub-species of the human race.

In the post-medieval period such negative stereotypes of the Jews became a central feature of Western European culture. In France Jews were depicted in the most terrible fashion. In England Jews were as detested as they were in Germany. Such Christian anti-Semitism was most forcibly expressed in Martin Luther's diatribes against German Jews. Elsewhere Jewish converts to Christianity became subject to the Inquisition. Initially tribunals were established in Spain to seek out those converts suspected of practising Judaism in secret; later the Inquisition spread to Portugal.

Jews living in Poland were also subject to assault. In the mid-seventeenth century a Cossack pogrom led by Bogdan Chmielnicki led to the death of thousands of Jews. When Polish territories were annexed to Russia in the nineteenth century the Christian population viewed their Jewish inhabitants with contempt, and eventually Jews were expelled from the villages where they lived. Such attitudes continued into the modern period, where traditional Christian prejudice was coupled with commercial interests. In Germany merchants alleged that Jewish trade would pollute the nation and undermine the economic vitality of the country while in France the French bourgeoisie resisted Jewish settlement, as did the British.

Even though eighteenth-century champions of the Enlightenment sought to ameliorate the conditions under which Jews lived, others attacked Jews on the basis of misconceived rationalist and scientific assumptions. In France Protestants influenced by Enlightenment ideas sought to counter such charges, but even they were unable to free themselves from traditional prejudice. In Germany the rise of a sense of national identity and self-confidence fuelled anti-Semitic feelings among various writers. At the beginning of the nineteenth century, Napoleon's summoning of the Sanhedrin was an attempt to improve Jewish life, but such steps were opposed by reactionaries who feared the consequences of such a policy.

During the twentieth century Jews were attacked for a number of reasons. In Germany Jews were denigrated in various racist publications; such an atmosphere led to the creation of political parties that were anti-Semitic in orientation. In France too anti-Jewish views were expressed by various writers, providing the background to the Dreyfus Affair. During this period vicious persecution in Russia drove many Jews to emigrate, while others sought to improve their position in society through revolutionary activities. In the years prior to the First World War Jews became scapegoats for the ills afflicting European countries. In Germany polemicists protested against the malevolent influence of Jewry. In Russia anti-Semites accused Jews of espionage and collaboration with the enemy; with the onset of the revolution, Jews were also charged with fomenting insurrection against authority. In Britain Jews were accused of international conspiracy; across the Atlantic, in the United States, a number of writers criticized Jews for their revolutionary attitudes as well as their alleged quest to dominate world affairs.

Such Judaeophobia serves as the background to the rise of Nazism. According to Hitler, the Jews constituted a vile race intent on seizing control of political, social and economic affairs. On the basis of Nazi racism, grounded in the writings of earlier German thinkers, the Jewish community was subject to a series of restrictive measures and eventual plans for its extermination. Throughout this period the Nazis sought to bring about the total destruction of the Jewish nation. This terrible mission having failed to quench the flame of Judaism, in the post-Holocaust world Jews became intent on protecting themselves from future forms of violence by creating a homeland in Palestine. While, contrary to Zionist aspirations, the creation of the State of Israel has fuelled Arab hatred of Jewry, Israel has served as a bulwark against modern manifestations of anti-Semitism that continue to threaten Jewish survival in the contemporary world.

Thus, for nearly 4,000 years the Jewish people has been subject to prejudice, persecution and murder. The motives for such antipathy have been religious, economic, political and social. Even though numerous attempts have been made to curtail such Judaeophobia, anti-Semitism continues to exist in new forms. Is there no end to humanity's longest hatred? Arguably this grim and unrelenting chronicle of Jewish misery confirms the biblical prophecy that Israel has been and will continue to be God's suffering servant through the centuries, afflicted by many and led to the slaughter.

ONE

Jews in the Ancient World

The story of Jewish suffering opens with the Hebrew Scriptures, which record the history of anti-Jewish sentiment beginning with the events of the Exodus. As the centuries passed, the Jewish nation endured repeated calamities, yet it was only in Hellenistic times that antipathy towards Jews and Judaism was fiercely expressed by both political leaders and authors. Such animosity continued throughout the Graeco-Roman period, and was crystallized in the writings of prominent figures of the age.

BIBLICAL HOSTILITY TO JEWS IN ANCIENT TIMES

The Hebrew Bible recounts the earliest known instance of hostility to the Jews in Pharaoh's persecution of the Jewish population prior to the Exodus. According to the Book of Exodus, Pharaoh expressed concern at the growing numbers and potential disloyalty of the Jewish population living in Egypt:

> Now there arose a new king over Egypt, who did not know Joseph. And he said to his people, 'Behold the people of Israel are too many and too mighty for us. Come let us deal shrewdly with them, lest they multiply, and if war befall us, they join our enemies and fight against us and escape from the land.' (Exodus 1:8–10)

Even though the Egyptians mistrusted the Jews, the Jewish community grew in strength, which caused dread among the Egyptians. Eventually, Pharaoh resolved to kill all first-born sons. Speaking to the Hebrew midwives, he declared:

> When you serve as midwives to the Hebrew women, and see them upon the birthstool, if it is a son, you shall kill him; but if it is a daughter, she shall live. (Exodus 1:16)

However, the midwives feared God's wrath and did not comply, allowing the male children to live. As a consequence, the Pharaoh condemned all the people:

> Every son that is born to the Hebrews you shall cast it into the Nile, but you shall let every daughter live. (Exodus 1:22)

Here the motive for such hostility was not racial prejudice, economic envy or disdain of Jewish ways; rather Scripture states that the Pharaoh acted out of fear for his own nation.

Later when the Jewish people had established itself in its own land, the country divided into two kingdoms – Israel in the north and Judah in the south. During their history, both kingdoms were repeatedly attacked by surrounding nations. In the tenth century BCE, for example, the aggressor who threatened the nation was Shoshenk I, the first pharoah of the Twenty-second Dynasty, who invaded the land and forced Rehoboam, the southern king, to pay tribute. An inscription in the Temple of Amun at Thebes refers to this conquest. Shoshenk does not mention the capture of any towns in Judah, but he does refer to some cities in the northern kingdom. Another inscription found at Megiddo suggests that the Egyptian incursion must have enveloped most of the territory. In any event, it was not motivated by hatred of the Jewish population; rather the Egyptian king invaded the country as an act of conquest.

Similarly, in the eighth century BCE the Assyrian king Tiglath-Pileser III embarked on a policy of expansion during the reign of Menahem, King of Israel. Menahem's son Pekahiah held his throne for two years by paying tribute to the Assyrian ruler, but was overthrown by his rival Pekah. The new Israelite king formed an alliance with the king of Syria against the Assyrians. Together they attempted to persuade Jotham, King of Judah, to join them; when he refused they declared war on Judah. In the face of this danger, the southern prophet Isaiah declared to Ahaz, Jotham's successor, that this threat would come to naught: both Israel and Syria would collapse. But Ahaz was unconvinced. He attempted to placate the Assyrians and went to Damascus (which the Assyrians had just conquered) to pay homage to Tiglath-Pileser III. He returned with the plans for an altar to be erected in the Temple as a sign of Judah's submission.

In the northern kingdom, Pekah's position was weakened as the Assyrians pressed forward, and he was assassinated by Hoshea who surrendered to the

Assyrians. When Shalmaneser V replaced Tiglath-Pileser III, Egyptian forces were powerless to help, and Shalmaneser V conquered Israel's capital, Samaria, after a siege of two years. The annals of Shalmaneser's successor Sargon II record that 27,290 Israelites were deported as a result of this conquest, which marked the end of the northern kingdom. However, as in previous centuries, this onslaught against the Jews was not the result of Judaeophobia but the consequence of political expansion.

The same applies to the Babylonian conquest of the kingdom of Judah in 586 BCE. In the seventh century BCE, the Babylonians advanced against Assyria and captured all its main cities. Later, they made a final attempt to regain the town of Harran. Embroiling himself in this struggle Josiah, the southern king, tried to halt the Egyptian army that had been summoned by the Assyrians to come to their aid. In the ensuing battle Josiah was mortally wounded, and Judah came under the domination of Egypt. Eventually, however, the Assyrian empire collapsed and the Babylonians succeeded in conquering the Egyptians at Carchemish in 605 BCE. At this King Jehoiakim, who had been put in power by the Egyptians, transferred his allegiance to King Nebuchadnezzar II of Babylon.

When Babylon was defeated by Egypt several years later, Jehoiakim decided the time was ripe for rebellion. Nebuchadnezzar, however, quickly responded by invading the country and conquering Jerusalem. In this siege Jehoiakim was killed and replaced by his son Jehoiachin, who was taken prisoner. Along with other important citizens he was led into captivity, and the treasures of the palace and Temple were plundered. A new king, Zedekiah, was placed on the throne by Nebuchadnezzar in 597 BCE. The prophet Jeremiah counselled the king to accept Babylonian domination, but he was persuaded to join a rebellion led by Egypt. After a siege of eighteen months, Jerusalem was conquered; all the main buildings were destroyed, and Zedekiah was blinded and exiled to Babylonia. As had occurred centuries earlier in the north, the southern kingdom was overpowered by the might of Assyria. Here, then, in the history of ancient Israel, it is clear that the Jewish nation endured centuries of upheaval, oppression and conquest. Yet, such suffering was not due to animosity against the Jewish nation, but to the aims of foreign powers who engaged in a policy of expansion and conquest.

Nonetheless later events in Jewish history illustrate that foreign powers were disdainful of Jewish beliefs and customs. During the Hellenistic period, the kingdom of Judah was dominated by foreign powers. In 198 BCE the

Seleucid king, Antiochus III, defeated Scopus, the general of the Egyptian king, Ptolemy V. Initially Antiochus III had a positive attitude towards the Jews; he reduced their taxes and made a donation to the Temple. In time, however, he reversed these policies for economic reasons. In 190 BCE he was defeated in a battle against the Romans at Magnesia near Ephesus. By the terms of the ensuing peace treaty he was forced to hand over his territory in Asia Minor, the richest part of the empire. A year later Antiochus III was killed while robbing the Temple in Jerusalem to increase his revenue and was succeeded by his son Seleucus IV, who, in his turn, dispatched his chancellor Heliodorus to plunder the Jerusalem Temple.

Later in the second century BCE, Seleucus IV was murdered and succeeded by Antiochus IV Epiphanes. Jason, a member of the Oniad family, bribed Antiochus IV to make him High Priest and on his appointment to this position, Jason attempted to Hellenize Jerusalem. This involved the introduction of Greek games in which athletes competed naked – a sight shocking to traditional sensibilities. Many Jews found such changes abhorrent, and Jason was deposed. In 168 BCE Antiochus IV invaded Egypt, but this time he encountered the Romans, who drove back his onslaught.

In Jerusalem it was rumoured that Antiochus IV had been killed, and a rebellion took place. Antiochus IV, however, reacted speedily; he conquered Jerusalem and led off some of the people as slaves. In addition he banned circumcision, Sabbath observance and the reading of the Torah. He also decreed that the Temple be dedicated to the worship of the Greek god Zeus, pigs sacrificed on the altar, and that all people, including Jews, should be allowed to worship there. In response, many Jews were willing to die rather than violate their traditions. Eventually a guerrilla band led by a priest, Mattathias, and his five sons engaged in armed revolt; on Mattathias' death, this movement was spearheaded by his son Judas Maccabaeus. After a series of military engagements, the oppressive policies of the Seleucids were reversed. Jewish law was reinstated, and the Temple was restored and rededicated, an event subsequently commemorated by the festival of Hannukah. In this struggle, the Seleucids – unlike the Egyptians, Assyrians and Babylonians in previous centuries – were critical of the Jewish way of life, and in particular appear to have been disturbed by what they perceived as Jewish xenophobia and misanthropy. In their place they championed Hellenism as a superior civilization. In this respect, the Seleucids served as a model for future forms of anti-Semitism.

The antipathy towards Jews and the Jewish religion expressed by the Seleucids was indicative of the view of Hellenistic society in general. In the Graeco-Roman world Jews did not occupy positions of economic influence that aroused envy, as frequently occurred in subsequent centuries. Nor were they subject to racial persecution as in the Middle Ages and, most horrifically, in modern times. Instead, both Greeks and Romans objected to Jews on social grounds, giving rise to a general polemic against the Jews and their faith among classical writers such as Cicero, a Roman orator of the first century BCE.

In a famous speech *Pro Flacco*, delivered in 59 BCE, Cicero argues that the Jews represent an element within society which is contrary to the values of Rome. They are the embodiment of barbaric superstition. In his view, superstition is opposed to religion – religion is the essence of the political, cultural and spiritual ideals of ancient Rome. Because the Jews represent superstition, they stand for everything that opposes these values. Judaism, he continues, is inimical to the religion of Rome because it is incompatible with ancestral customs and institutions. In this diatribe he expresses contempt for the Jewish people, their behaviour and customs, and their growing influence in society, which he fears threatens the value-system of Rome.

In Egypt, where the Jewish community was particularly numerous, Jews frequently served as middlemen between rulers and the general populace. In this context Egyptian intellectuals relied on the biblical account in the Book of Exodus to castigate Jews who lived in their midst. According to the Hebrew Bible, the ancient Egyptians perished on account of Pharaoh's unwillingness to allow the Israelites to flee from Egypt – the ten plagues were sent by God to persuade him to relent. This biblical account provided the basis for anti-Jewish riots which took place in Alexandria in the first century CE, and stimulated anti-Jewish polemics in Egyptian literature of the period.

This diatribe was expressed in an alternative account of the Exodus, according to which the Jewish people were initially a diseased population that had married slaves. Their flight from Egypt was caused by the Egyptians themselves, who wished to be rid of these lepers. According to Egyptian tradition, the observance of the Sabbath was caused by the disease-ridden condition of the ancient Israelite population: Jews were only able to travel for six-day periods because they were so unwell. In the third century BCE similar stories were recounted by the Egyptian priest Manetho, and later repeated by such historians as Cheremona and Lysimachus of Alexandria and Apollonius Molon and Pompeius of Trogus.

Paralleling such contempt, Hellenistic society in general reacted against what was perceived as Jewish exclusivity and the particularistic character of the Jewish community. Jews were determined to live apart from their neighbours and largely refused to embrace Greek customs. In their opinion, the gods of the Greeks were false deities, and Greek culture was seen as unclean. As a consequence, the Jewish population and non-Jewish society lived in a state of constant tension. Nonetheless, Jews were protected by Rome. Even though most Jews were not granted citizenship, they were permitted to practise their faith. Another factor which mitigated pagan animosity to Judaism was the fact that Jewish thought in Palestine and the diaspora (outside the Holy Land) borrowed various Hellenistic features. This helped to diffuse what otherwise might have led to an outburst of anti-Jewish feeling.

When Hellenistic writers expressed hostility towards the Jewish populace, a number of Jewish apologists stressed that Greek thinkers such as Plato and Aristotle had learned about philosophical concepts from Moses. As a result, Judaism contains a higher and purer religious system than that which is found among Greeks and Romans. Convinced of the correctness of their beliefs, Jews attempted to convert gentiles to the true faith. Thus in the Graeco-Roman period Judaism was missionary in its outlook and sought to establish itself as a universal faith. Converts were viewed as having the same status as born-Jews, and in addition numerous sympathizers of Judaism, known as God-fearers, became active participants in synagogue worship. For such gentiles, it was necessary only to keep the Noachian laws – those given to Noah – rather than the entire corpus of Jewish law. Such righteous gentiles, together with faithful Jews, could be assured of entering the World-to-Come.

In the first century CE, the Jewish population rebelled against Roman domination. The first revolt occurred from 66 to 73 CE, but was crushed by Roman forces. In the next century, from 133 to 136 CE, the Jews again rebelled, and this second attempt was similarly put down. As a result, the Jewish community was viewed with suspicion and contempt. Such conflict, however, did not provoke widespread persecution of the Jewish population. Rather the Romans simply desired to create a social structure that would place each ethnic group, including the Jews, into an administrative relationship with the Roman authorities. Even though Jerusalem had been decimated and the Temple destroyed, the Roman government sought to cooperate with those Jews who lived in Rome. Yet despite such accommodation, most Romans viewed Jewish religious practices as mere superstitions, and they regarded Jewish laws, such as circumcision, dietary regulations and Sabbath observance, with disdain. Although such friction was continuous, Jewish and Roman leaders nevertheless attempted to establish a basis for coexistence.

Even though antagonism existed between Jews and pagans in the ancient world, there were some Jewish writers who absorbed elements of Hellenistic culture. By translating the philosophical currents of the Graeco-Roman world into a Jewish framework, these authors sought to reconcile the Jewish faith with Greek thought. Yet, paradoxically, this quest provided the basis for Christianity's eventual spiritualization of the Hebrew Bible and that religion's subsequent attitude of animosity towards Judaism.

The Hellenistic interpretation of the Hebrew Bible is illustrated most clearly in the writings of the first-century Jewish philosopher Philo, who produced a variety of philosophical treatises. In his view, God's creative power was initially manifest as the *Logos* or Word of God, a concept which unified the biblical Word of God with the Platonic concepts of the Ideal World and the Divine Mind.

For Philo, the *Logos* was expressed in Natural Law, which rules the cosmos and is found in all things. In this context the Torah should be seen as universal in scope. Yet the Torah is also a special revelation to the Jewish nation whose mission is to be a light to all peoples. Israel's task is to enlighten the world, to draw all nations to an acceptance of God's universal truth. In this sense the Torah should be understood as an expression of the path that all human beings need but which is possessed in its fullest manifestation by the Jews. Such ideas paved the way for the Christian belief in Christ and the *Logos*, as well as the doctrine of the Incarnation.

Such a universalistic conception of the Hebrew Bible gave rise to an allegorical interpretation of the commandments in Scripture. The Sabbath, for example, was perceived as the day on which the *Logos* emanated from God and served as the basis for the created order. For this reason the Sabbath was dedicated to the pursuit of spiritual wisdom. Similarly, ritual food laws were understood allegorically; they were conceived as signalling God's characteristics of mercy and cleanliness as opposed to violence. Only animals that exhibit benevolent attributes were fit for food, whereas animals that were violent in nature were forbidden. Further, circumcision was viewed as an allegory of cutting away illegitimate pleasures as well as the sin of pride.

Such spiritualization and universalization invested Jewish ritual with mystical significance. The letter of the law was not to be disregarded, and through this interpretation of Jewish law and institutions, Philo sought to establish a link between inner and outer meaning. In his opinion it is not possible to dispose of outward observance and still experience the inner meaning of the law. Rather, it is precisely the physical observances prescribed in the Torah that express the spiritual character of the Jewish faith. Thus Philo's allegorical interpretation was designed to demonstrate that God's decrees serve as the expressions of universal, spiritual truths.

Despite Philo's interpretation of the Torah, the Church Fathers utilized this spiritualizing tendency to distinguish between the spirit and the letter of the law. For Christians it became possible to observe a universal Law of Nature without taking into account the specific injunctions in the Bible. For these early followers of Christ, Jewish law was abrogated by the arrival of the Messiah. True sacrifice was therefore understood as the sacrifice of the heart through prayer and penitence. Further, authentic incense was understood as that which ascends towards Heaven through heartfelt prayer. Influenced by these Hellenistic notions, Judaism thus unintentionally paved the way for a separation between traditional Judaism and Christianity, a rift that was the inadvertent result of the quest to harmonize Jewish theology with Hellenistic categories of thought. Yet, instead of achieving their aim, writers such as Philo provided a justification for separating religiosity from ritual observance. Once Christianity had become a world religion, this transformation would have unforeseen and tragic consequences for the Jewish people.

The Hellenizing of Judaism as illustrated in Philo's writings, however, was not universally accepted within the Jewish community. In the second century BCE, for example, the actions of Antiochus Epiphanes IV provoked the wrath of pietists known as Hasidim who urged the nation to return to upholding the ideals of Torah Judaism. Subsequently various sectarian groups carried on this tradition. Many Jews anxiously awaited the coming of the Messiah who would fulfil all previous biblical expectations of the redemption of their nation. Under God's dominion, it was believed, the reign of evil powers would end and Israel would be saved.

Anticipating these momentous events, various Palestinian Jewish sects viewed themselves as true heirs of the covenant. The Samaritans regarded themselves as the inheritors of God's revelation. Situated on Mount Gerizim, they strictly observed biblical law, rejecting the interpretation of Scripture expounded by official Judaism. In their view, Moses was the sole prophet of Israel who would return as the Messiah and bring about a restoration of the Jewish people. Believing themselves to be the true keepers of the Torah and the sanctuary, they stressed that all Israel would in time return to their form of belief and practice in the messianic age.

Another sect of this era were the *Nazaraioi* living in Jordan who embraced various types of ascetic practice; abstaining from meat as well as Temple sacrifice, they observed the Sabbath, practised circumcision and strictly followed other Jewish customs. Like the Samaritans, they viewed themselves as the true representatives of patriarchal times.

The Essenes were a third Jewish sect that flourished during the Graeco-Roman period, claiming to possess the true Zadokite priesthood as well as the correct Jewish calendar. Opposed to the Temple cult in Jerusalem, they adopted eschatological doctrines concerning Davidic and Aaronic Messiahs who would undertake both kingly and priestly functions in a reconstituted Israel. In their view, a Mosaic prophet would serve as a forerunner to these messianic personages. Critical of the Jewish establishment in Jerusalem, they envisaged the present as an era of darkness presided over by the powers of Belial.

A fourth Jewish sect active in the Hellenistic world were the Pharisees – in all likelihood descendants of the Hasidim of the Maccabean period. Like the Essenes, they wished to attain perfection by separating from other Jews in order to observe Jewish law. It was their aim to set a high standard of religious practice; congregating in the synagogue, they sought to lead the nation back to the covenant. According to Pharisaic doctrine, they were the true inheritors of ancient Israel.

In different ways these various sects sought to call the people to dedication to God's covenant. In their opinion, the Jewish people had abandoned God's law, and a conversion of the heart was now required to restore the community to its previous situation. Proclaiming this message, these groups proposed a new interpretation of Israel, one no longer based exclusively on birth, but rather on conversion and commitment. Among a number of these sects, those who were persuaded of the truth of this vision had to undergo ritual immersion in the same manner as gentiles who converted to the Jewish faith.

The central feature of these sectarian movements was their conviction that the true Israel must be distinguished from those who had abandoned the Jewish way of life. Jews who remained loyal to the tradition constituted a spiritual community who, having undergone conversion of the heart, would triumph against the forces of darkness. In the final apocalyptic battle, they would be victorious. Official Judaism, however, was perceived as no longer part of the covenant. Those who supported established institutions were like gentiles. Filled with messianic longing, these sectarians saw themselves as living in the last days, awaiting the unfolding of God's plan for his people.

It was in such a milieu that the Christian faith developed as a sectarian messianic Jewish movement. Drawing on Jewish apocalyptic imagery, the early Church believed that their Teacher of Righteousness was the long-awaited Messiah. Vindicated through his resurrection, Jesus was understood as having ascended to heaven, where he sits on the right hand of the Father. According to the early Church, it is through Jesus' ministry and death that all peoples can attain forgiveness and salvation. Sectarian Judaism of the Graeco-Roman world thus paved the way for the Christian doctrine of the transformation of history through God's Anointed One.

Together with other groups, early Christians believed themselves to be the true Israel, a concept that provided the basis for the emergence of Judaeophobia within the Church. The absolutist claims made by the Church about Jesus' redemption as promised in Scripture were set alongside Jewish blindness and stubbornness. Jewish existence was thereby negated, and the Jewish faith was understood as a stage on the way to Christianity rather than as an authentic religious tradition. In this way Jewish sectarianism inadvertently provided the basis for the repudiation of traditional Judaism through the Christian proclamation of the good news of Christ's message and ministry.

Another important development in the ancient world also served to undermine traditional Judaism. The quest to assimilate Hellenistic patterns of thought to the Jewish tradition led to the development of gnostic doctrine. Drawing on Greek philosophy, oriental religions and the Hebrew Bible, various gnostic groups argued that the Supreme Divine Being must be distinguished from the demiurge who is responsible for creation and involved in the material world. Advocating a form of dualism, the members of these sects maintained that the world is ruled by two opposing heavenly powers, generally viewed as male and female.

The Supreme First Principle was conceived among gnostics also as an all-good Deity; the Creator Demiurge, however, was viewed as imperfect.

According to some Christian gnostics, the First Principle should be identified with the New Testament 'God of Love', whereas the secondary creator was equated with Old Testament law. In opposition to Genesis 1:31 ('And God saw everything that he had made, and behold, it was very good'), the gnostics believed that the universe is the result of a primordial fall. Further, they stated that the soul was created to be in exile in a lower, evil world into which it had fallen – the only hope of return was through the acquisition of secret knowledge (*gnosis*). Some sects also maintained that liberation from the material world could only occur by abandoning law.

Within Judaism at the end of the Second Temple Period, such gnostic ideas became part of the teaching of sectarian sects including the Essenes. Common both to Gnosticism and the Dead Sea Scrolls is the view of esoteric knowledge as a redemptive factor by which humans are able to bridge the abyss separating the human from the divine. Thus the War Scrolls of the Essene community teach that members of the sect are to be those who hear the glorious voice and see holy angels. The literature of this sect also adopted the dualistic principle of God (light) and the principle of evil (darkness).

Such ideas, which emerged within Judaism and spread beyond Jewish society, constitute a third source of anti-Judaism. Although dualisitic theories were rejected by Christian orthodoxy in the second century CE, the earliest Christians in Alexandria as well as in the Palestinian Church were Gnostic-Essenic in orientation, and this type of Christianity eventually penetrated into Western Christendom. By the fourth century CE, it had become the dominant form of Christian spirituality, despite the biblical belief in the goodness of creation. In this way, Hellenistic Jewish thought inadvertently planted in Christian soil the seeds of doctrines which were later used to undermine Judaism itself.

Pharisaic Judaism also laid the framework for the emergence of antipathy towards the Jewish tradition. According to Pharisaic doctrine, the Oral Law was part of God's revelation to Moses on Mount Sinai. By promulgating laws based on the 613 commandments contained in the Torah, this scholarly class provided a means of emancipating the Jewish people from a cultic system of Judaism based on Temple worship. The oral tradition served as a mechanism for coping with the changed circumstances and fortunes of the Jewish people in exile.

The new formulation of the Jewish faith in Hellenistic and Roman times embraced Greek thought in a number of respects. The Pharisees translated their concept of the Jewish nation into a form that Jews could transport with them no matter where they lived. Pharisaic Judaism also embraced the concept of a spiritual Jew whose life was regulated according to the covenant. Such a notion transcended ethnic descent and gave rise to the belief in the true Israel – those whose lives were structured by divine law. The obligation to serve God was thus incumbent upon all born-Jews, but it was also a viable option for gentiles. As a result, conversion to Judaism became a possibility as never before. Those who embraced the Jewish faith were to be regarded as the home born. Hence Pharisaic Judaism opened the way to missionary activities and a universalization of the Jewish faith. Moreover, linked to this stance was the Pharisaic belief that righteous pagans who kept the Noachide commandments (a limited number of ethical and ritual obligations) could enter into the World-to-Come.

Pharisaism also adopted an historical stance that emancipated Jews from involvement with both tribe and homeland. Just as a Jew could live a religious life without land, political autonomy or the Temple, so Jews were not to be overly concerned with the events of human history. What is of central importance is the spiritual significance of past events. For this reason, Jewish exegetes were at liberty to engage in speculation about the biblical text in order to extract the spiritual significance of past events for its application in the present.

Regarding messianic teaching, the Pharisees preserved central tenets such as belief in the resurrection of the dead and in the Hereafter. Nonetheless, these ideas were formulated in terms of obedience to law. Following the messianic age, those who had led righteous lives governed by the Torah would enter into *Gan Eden* (Heaven) whereas those who had violated the covenant would be confined to *Gehinnom* (Hell). Such an eschatological vision enabled the Jewish community to remain hopeful of future glory amidst the calamities of history and the loss of the Holy Land.

As far as God's presence was concerned, the Pharisees further maintained that after the destruction of the Temple, the *Shekhinah* (God's Presence) followed his people into exile. Thus God ceased to be localized in the Temple; rather, he was available to Jews everywhere. In this context, the Pharisees believed that the exile itself was due to Israel's sinfulness. What was now required was adherence to the Torah. As a consequence of their waywardness, God had driven the people from their ancient homeland. In anticipation of this disaster, the Pharisees located their centre at Jamnia outside Jerusalem, where Pharisaic scholars met to carry out the interpretation of Jewish law.

The destruction of Jerusalem and the Second Temple in 70 CE thus became for the Pharisees a means of transforming the Jewish faith. Although overwhelmed by this tragedy, they nevertheless created a framework for Jewish survival in the diaspora. This revolution provided Jews with a constitution independent of the previous structure of a national faith, and through this reformulation the nation was freed from previous institutions and political boundaries. It had become a universal people with a transportable heritage. Yet, paradoxically, it was by adopting this very concept of universalism and spiritualization that the early Christian community was also encouraged to seek converts from among Jews and gentiles. With the dissolution of the nation, the Christian community claimed for itself the role of being a light to the nations. It regarded itself – rather than the Jews – as the true Israel, the authentic inheritor of the biblical tradition. For the Church, Judaism was an obsolete faith, rejected by God because of its rejection of Christ. It was Christianity that had now become the spiritual fulfilment of the Hebrew Scriptures.

JUDAEOPHOBIA AND JEWISH MYTH

As we have seen, Scripture records hostility to the Jews from the beginnings of the Hebrew nation. According to the Bible, Pharaoh feared the Jews and sought their destruction; on his instruction, first-born sons were to be killed. While it is impossible to know whether such events ever took place, the story of the Exodus has served as a central orienting event in the life and thought of the Jewish people throughout its history. Every year at the Passover ritual meal, the *Seder*, Jews recount the narrative of the exodus from Egypt. Early in the service, referring to the unleavened bread, the leader proclaims:

> This is the bread of affliction that our fathers ate in the land of Egypt. All who hunger, let them come and eat: all who are in need let them come and celebrate the Passover. Now we are here – next year we shall be in the land of Israel; now we are slaves – next year, we shall be free men.

The *matzoh*, the unleavened bread, thus symbolizes persecution and oppression. As the *Seder* unfolds, the story of Jewish suffering is repeatedly emphasized. Quoting from the Book of Exodus, the Passover *Haggadah* relates:

And it came to pass in process of time, that the king of Egypt died; and the children of Israel sighed by reason of their bondage. And God heard their groaning, and God remembered his covenant with Abraham, with Isaac, and with Jacob. . . . And the Lord said, 'I have surely seen the affliction of my people, which are in Egypt, and have heard their cry by reason of their taskmasters; for I know their sorrows.'

The Passover symbols further stress the suffering of God's people. The bitter herb, for example, is eaten because 'the Egyptians embittered the life of our ancestors in Egypt. And they made their lives bitter with hard bondage, in mortar and in brick, and in all manner of service in the field; all their service, wherein they made them serve, was with rigour.'

In these passages, the myth of Jewish oppression is paramount, and this theme integrates the events that allegedly took place in ancient Egypt. Whether the Jews were in fact persecuted by the Egyptians, the theme of Jewish suffering has given shape to Jewish consciousness for nearly 4,000 years – a motif that is reinforced in the celebration of other festivals, which highlight both tragedy and triumph.

Of central importance in the Jewish calendar is *Tishah Ba'av*, a fast that commemorates the day on which the First Temple was destroyed by Nebuchadnezzar and the Second Temple by Titus. According to the Talmud, the destruction of the Temple took place on 9 Av, and all subsequent major catastrophes that happened around that time were ascribed to that day. This day is traditionally observed as a fast; there is a ban on bathing, shaving and wearing leather shoes, and it is customary not to work or sit on ordinary chairs before midday. The essential characteristics of the liturgy include the reading of the Book of Lamentations in the evening service and the recital of dirges composed not only in commemoration of the events of 9 Av, but also in memory of the calamities that occurred throughout Jewish history.

In many synagogues, congregants sit on the floor or on low benches and read these dirges by dim candlelight as signs of mourning. In some synagogues the curtain over the ark is removed, and among some Sephardi congregations a black curtain covers the ark. It is also customary to visit the cemetery during the day. All these observances are designed to stress the perilous situation of the Jews throughout their history, and to reflect on the tragedy of the Jewish past. By recalling their history of persecution and suffering, the theme of continuing Judaeophobia is integrated into the life of the nation.

Another important festival in the Jewish calendar emphasizes victory over Israel's enemies – the festival of Purim adds a further mythological dimension to the belief in the Jewish people's continual suffering, but at the same time depicts Israel's ultimate triumph. The Book of Esther deals with the Jewish community in the town of Susa, the Persian capital during the reign of King Xerxes in the fifth century BCE. According to some scholars the book was written in the second century BCE; other scholars date it much earlier because of the number of Persian loan words contained in the text as well as its oriental atmosphere. In any event, the book no doubt reflects attitudes towards the Jews in the period of the Second Temple.

Once Esther had become the consort of King Ahasuerus, her uncle Mordecai discovered a plot to destroy the Jewish people. Haman, the chief adviser to the king, was outraged that Mordecai would not bow down to him and declared to the king:

> There is a certain people scattered abroad and dispersed among the peoples in all the provinces of your kingdom; their laws are different from those of every other people, and they do not keep the king's laws, so that it is not for the king's profit to tolerate them. If it pleases the king, let it be decreed that they be destroyed. (Esther 3:8–9)

Here the Jews are portrayed as an alien people, determined to observe their own customs. But, as the Book of Esther relates, Haman's scheming was foiled, and the Jews protected by royal decree. At the king's request secretaries wrote to all the governors of all the provinces where Jews lived, granting them permission to defend themselves from attack. To commemorate this victory over the nation's enemies, the festival of Purim was inaugurated. In mythological terms, Haman personifies all of Israel's enemies through the ages who have sought the destruction of the Jewish nation.

The theme of suffering and triumph is reiterated at Hannukah. This festival is celebrated for eight days and commemorates the victory of the Maccabees over the Seleucids in the second century BCE. At this time the Maccabees engaged in a military struggle with the Seleucids who had desecrated the Temple. After a three-year struggle, from 165 to 163 BCE, the Maccabees under Judas Maccabaeus conquered Jerusalem and rebuilt the altar. According to Talmudic legend, one day's worth of oil miraculously kept the menorah (the eight-branched candelabrum) burning in the Temple for eight days. The central observance of Hannukah is the kindling of the festive lamp or candles on each of the eight nights – symbolically this Festival of Lights represents the triumph of light over darkness. The message is that the Jewish people will ultimately overcome their enemies.

A further mythological dimension to Jewish persecution relates to the account of the birth of Jacob (symbolically the Jew) and Esau (symbolically the non-Jew). In this, the twins are described as already warring in the womb; later Jacob tricked Esau out of his blessing from their aged and blind father. Esau was the first born and Isaac's favourite; when he discovered what his brother had done, he was outraged. Fearing for his life, Jacob fled, and a lasting hatred was sealed with symbolic implications for their offspring.

In rabbinic sources this story has evoked a wide range of interpretations. Repeatedly, Esau has been symbolically and genetically linked to opponents of Israel, ranging from the Edomites (Esau's direct descendants) to the Romans. Unlike Jacob, who is contemplative and cunning, Esau is depicted as a warrior and hunter, brutal and barbarous. Hence, from the beginning of Israel's history a distinction is drawn between Jew and gentile, and this biblical tale thus adds to the collective memory of Jewish suffering.

This tradition of Jewish persecution and suffering embedded in the biblical narrative and commemorated in Jewish observance forms the background to an understanding of Jewish consciousness concerning the origins and nature of hostility to the Jewish people as it evolved through history. As we have noted, when Jews occupied their own country, they were subject to attack from foreign powers, yet this was not due to hatred of the Jewish nation – the development of hostility to Jews *per se* occurred in the diaspora when Jews dwelt among other peoples. As late as the fifth century BCE, the Greek historian Herodotus ignored the Jews altogether, an omission which suggests that until then they had evoked little adverse reaction from those among whom they dwelled.

In the early references to Jews in the fourth and third centuries BCE, one can discern little negativity. However, a notable exception to such general tolerance was the destruction of the temple in the Elephantine colony in about 410 BCE. Possibly this was an act inspired by political motives: the Jewish garrison stationed there had been sent by the Persians and naturally aroused Egyptian antipathy to these Persian representatives. In addition, the Jewish practice of sacrificing animals appears to have infuriated Egyptian priests, who worshipped the ram as sacred.

In the Hellenistic world, attitudes towards the Jews hardened. With the consolidation of Hellenistic culture, the Jews were increasingly perceived as alien. Distancing themselves from the majority population, Jews viewed Jerusalem as their holy city, and regarded the invisible God of Scripture as Lord of the universe. Setting themselves apart, they regarded their host countries as profane and their fellow citizens as religiously blind. Living in a self-imposed ghetto, they segregated themselves from the rest of society. Not surprisingly, such attitudes provoked resentment and fear, giving rise to venomous depictions of Jews and their religion.

Later, Seleucids such as Antiochus Epiphanes IV continued this tradition of hostility to Judaism in his assault against Jewish customs. Setting themselves against the Hellenizing process, the Maccabees championed Jewish civilization, and established themselves as rulers over their own people. However, under Roman rule, the Jewish community once again repeatedly came under attack in literary works of this period by such writers as Poseidonius, a Stoic philosopher and historian, who echoed Manetho's description of Israel's expulsion from Egypt as lepers. During this period, the rhetorician Apollonius Molon composed a diatribe against the Jews, repeating earlier charges that the Jews are atheists, hate strangers and observe superstitious practices. Again, Apion, an Alexandrian rhetorician, attacked the Jews in his *History of Egypt*. Not only are the Jews misanthropic, he argues, but they engage in sedition. Continuing this tradition of anti-Semitism, Cicero criticized Jewish ethnocentrism and religious intransigence, while Tacitus bitterly attacked Jewish institutions as sinister and shameful.

Graeco-Roman antipathy thus serves as the background for the emergence of Christian hostility towards the Jewish nation. Nonetheless, it was only when Christianity emerged in the first century CE that Jews came to be viewed as contemptible and demonic. In their advocacy of anti-Jewish attitudes, Christian theologians drew upon Hellenistic ideas that had penetrated the Jewish faith. Within Hellenistic Judaism the Torah was interpreted allegorically, and such a conception was transformed by the Church into a justification for separating religious meaning from ritual observance. Revivalist movements also provided a source for the Christian conviction that Judaism constituted the fulfilment of biblical teaching. Further, Gnosticism, which grew out of the attempt to harmonize

Hellenistic ideas with the Jewish tradition, endorsed the Christian denigration of the God of the Old Testament. Finally, the Pharisaic spiritualization and universalization of Judaism intensified the Christian determination that the good news of Scripture should be spread to all peoples. Christianity thereby utilized features inherent in Judaism in the Graeco-Roman world to shape its own identity and distance itself from the faith from which it had originated.

TWO

Judaeophobia in the New Testament

As we have seen, hatred of the Jewish faith did not originate with the emergence of Christianity; rather, Judaeophobia was common in Hellenized society. Yet anti-Jewish sentiment, which was prevalent in the Graeco-Roman world, intensified within the Christian community. Jesus' messiahship was understood as ushering in a new era in which the true Israel would become a light to the nations. Christian animosity was fuelled by the Gospel writers, who depicted Jesus attacking the leaders of the nation. Further, the Church taught that what was now required was circumcision of the heart rather than obedience to the law. In proclaiming the good news, Paul emphasized that the Hebrew people had been rejected by God; Christ is the true eternal Temple in opposition to the earthly cult in Jerusalem. Such a contrast is also to be found in the Fourth Gospel, which differentiates between the spiritual universe of Christianity and a fallen world represented by the Jews.

ANTI-JUDAISM IN THE NEW TESTAMENT

While we cannot know with certainty what Jesus actually said, the Synoptic Gospels (Matthew, Mark and Luke) record many of his utterances, which reflect first-century Jewish thought. His view of divorce, for example, accords with the teaching of the sage Shammai; his understanding of the Sabbath being made for man rather than man for the Sabbath was a common attitude among the Pharisees; his preoccupation with intention as opposed to action was also a familiar theme. Nonetheless, there were important differences between his teaching and that of Pharisaic sages. Jesus' concern for ethical behaviour was linked to messianic redemption. Convinced of the imminent coming of the Kingdom of God, he repeatedly urged his hearers to repent. Inclusion in this realm demanded adherence to God's covenant.

According to the Gospels, Jesus saw himself as the long-awaited Messiah. Hence, when he entered Jerusalem prior to his crucifixion he believed that his proclamation of the Kingdom would usher in a new era of human history. However, rather than triumphing in glory, Jesus was killed like a criminal – for his disciples this event served as the ultimate test of faith. They did not abandon hope; instead they trusted in their Lord, who appeared to them as the Risen Christ. Initially he was active in their midst, but later ascended to heaven to sit at the right hand of the Father.

For the disciples, Jesus was the dying Messiah. Appealing to the Suffering Servant passages in Isaiah, they saw Jesus as fulfilling this prophecy. The Servant is depicted 'as despised and rejected by men; a man of sorrows, and acquainted with grief; and as one from whom men hide their faces, he was despised, and we esteemed him not. Surely he has borne our griefs and carried our sorrows; yet we esteemed him stricken, smitten by God and afflicted. But he was wounded for our transgressions, he was bruised for our iniquities; upon him was the chastisement that made us whole, and with his stripes we are healed' (Isaiah 53:3–6). Prior to his death Jesus linked his destiny to this prophecy, and his disciples aligned this vision with the Psalmist's description of the suffering and glory of the Messiah in Psalm 22, his prayer for deliverance in Psalm 69, and his rule over the whole earth in Psalm 18. In addition, Psalm 110 served as the basis for their conviction that the Messianic King would sit at God's right hand until his enemies were conquered.

In portraying Jesus' ministry, Daniel 7 provided an image of a glorious figure who would appear with God on Judgment Day:

> Behold with the clouds of heaven there came one like a son of man . . . to him was given dominion and glory and kingdom that all peoples, nations, and languages should serve him. (Daniel 7:13–14)

These biblical passages were viewed as predicting a future Redeemer who would be rejected, suffer, die, be resurrected and reign in glory (Mark 12:35–7; Matthew 22:41–5; Acts 2:34–5).

For the early Christians, it was the Jewish leaders who were the enemies referred to in the Psalms: they had led the suffering prophet to his death. But Jesus was the Son of Man of whom it was recorded that he would be rejected and suffer. This was the treatment meted out by the Jewish establishment. Until such a time as God will disclose himself to all people, salvation would be reserved for those who acknowledge Christ; these are the individuals whom God will redeem in the last days. Jesus, they asserted through the words of the Psalmist, was 'the stone whom the builders rejected', but had 'become the head of the corner' (Psalm 118). As Isaiah prophesied: he was the stone that would 'become a rock of stumbling to both houses of Israel' (Isaiah 8:14). Yet, as Isaiah declared, the same stone is a sure foundation of his people (Isaiah 28:16). Citing the prophecy of Daniel, Jesus was perceived as the stone who will disperse God's enemies on the last day and become 'a great mountain which will fill the entire earth' (Daniel 2:34–5).

In this light, it is the Church – rather than the synagogue – which possesses the correct interpretation of Scripture. Armed with the good news, Jesus' disciples set out to spread the message to Israel. Yet the nation refused to listen; only a few were drawn into the new community of Christian believers. The Jewish people did not heed Jesus' message of repentance: this was the faithless, hard-hearted Israel unable to respond to God's revelation in Christ. Paradoxically, however, it is the unrighteous of the nation who will enter into the Kingdom of God because of their trust in Christ: 'Truly I say to you, the tax collectors and the harlots go into the Kingdom of God before you' (Matthew 21:31).

The Christian faithful thus constituted a Jewish messianic sect whose adherents claimed to be the true Israel. According to the Gospel tradition, the followers of Christ castigated official Judaism, accusing it of sinfulness and treachery. The Gospel of Matthew refers to these unbelievers as hypocrites, blind fools and serpents; unbelievers who will be uprooted and thrown into the fire. The Church, on the other hand, was seen as the true plant of God. As the Gospel of John declares:

I am the vine, you are the branches. He who abides in me, and I in him, he it is that bears much fruit, for apart from me you can do nothing. If a man does not abide in me, he is cast forth as a branch and withers; and the branches are gathered, thrown into the fire and burned. (John 15:5–6)

Although New Testament scholars stress that the conflicts between Jesus and the leaders of the Jewish nation were in all likelihood interpolated into the New Testament by later Christians for polemical purposes, these confrontations reflect early Christian antipathy to Jewish sages. Linking himself to the tradition of prophetic protest, Jesus attacked the scribes and Pharisees. Critical of their hypocritical attitudes, he warned:

Beware of the scribes who like to go about in long robes, and to have salutations in the market places and the best seats in the synagogues and the place of honour at feasts, who devour widows' houses and for a pretence make long prayers. (Mark 12:38–40)

The Pharisees, Jesus stated, had betrayed God's purposes:

For the sake of your tradition you have made void the word of God. You hypocrites! Well did Isaiah prophesy of you when he said: 'This people honours me with their lips, but their heart is far from me; in vain do they worship me, teaching as doctrines the precepts of men.' (Matthew 15:6–9)

Again, in prophetic fashion, Jesus reproached the Pharisees for their rejection of God's commandments:

But woe to you Pharisees! for you tithe mint and rue and every herb, and neglect justice and the love of God; these you ought to have done, without neglecting the others. (Luke 11:42)

Repeatedly in the Gospels, Jesus is depicted as rejecting moribund, ritualized religious practices. For this reason, he renounced the Pharisaic interpretation of biblical law. In the Gospel of Matthew, for example, he defends his disciples for plucking grain on the Sabbath (Matthew 12:1–8). In this instance, the Pharisees were not concerned whether Jesus' disciples were hungry; their only interest was that the Sabbath law be observed. Replying to their rebuke, Jesus reminded them that David had transgressed the law that reserved the eating of the loaves of offering in the Temple to the priests. Moreover, on the Sabbath the Temple priests were allowed to perform their function without being accused of breaking the Sabbath. If they were permitted to do this, Jesus argued, then his disciples could do the same in the new Temple, which is Jesus himself. Jesus' aim here was to illustrate that his disciples' action could be defended by an appeal to Scripture. For Jesus, love must take precedence over law.

Another encounter between Jesus and the Pharisees concerned a paralytic present in the synagogue on the Sabbath (Matthew 12:9–14). Jesus was not dissuaded by the Pharisees' rebuke when he administered healing on the Sabbath, and replied:

What man of you, if he has one sheep and it falls into a pit on the Sabbath, will not lay hold of it and lift it out? Of how much more value is a man than a sheep? (Matthew 12:11–12)

In a similar confrontation, Jesus pointed out that an act of compassion and love must take precedence over Jewish legalistic prescriptions. Here Jesus healed a blind and dumb demoniac. When the Pharisees observed this, they said: 'It is only by Beelzebub, the prince of demons, that this man casts out demons' (Matthew 12:24). In response, Jesus stated that their conclusion was contradictory:

Every kingdom divided against itself is laid waste, and no city or house divided against itself will stand; and if Satan casts out Satan, he is divided against himself; how then will his kingdom stand? (Matthew 12:25–6)

Again in Matthew 15 Jesus further emphasized the iniquity of the leaders of the people. Jesus was in Galilee when he was approached by scribes and Pharisees from Jerusalem: 'Why do your disciples transgress the tradition of the elders?', they inquired, 'For they do not wash their hands when they eat.' In response, Jesus stated that religious impurity is located in the moral rather than the ritual sphere:

Not what goes into the mouth defiles a man, but what comes out of the mouth, this defiles a man. . . . Do you not see that whatever goes into the mouth passes into the stomach, and so passes on? But what comes out of the mouth proceeds from the heart, and this defiles a man. For out of the heart come evil thoughts, murder, adultery, fornication, theft, false witness, slander. These are what defile a man; but to eat with unwashed hands does not defile a man. (Matthew 15:11, 17–20)

In another speech in the Gospel of Matthew, Jesus summarized his condemnation of the hypocrisy and iniquity of the leaders of the Jewish people:

The scribes and Pharisees sit on Moses' seat; so practise and observe whatever they tell you, but not what they do; for they preach, but do not practise. They bind heavy burdens, hard to bear, and lay them on men's shoulders; but they themselves will not move them with their finger. . . . Woe to you scribes and

Pharisees, hypocrites! for you are like whitewashed tombs, which outwardly appear beautiful, but within they are full of dead men's bones and all uncleanness. (Matthew 23:1–4, 27)

Such condemnation of hypocrisy and unrighteousness was based on the conviction that the leaders of the Jewish nation had directed the people away from God's true intention. Jesus is said to have attacked those who claimed to hold the keys to the Kingdom but refused entrance to others. This challenge to the false religion of Israel became a rallying cry for Christians, with Jesus' criticism of the leaders of the people serving to justify the Christian denunciation of both the Jews and the Jewish faith through the centuries.

For the Christian community, Jesus' words appeared to support the view that the law had been abrogated. In Acts 7 Stephen declared that from the time of Moses, the people of Israel had turned from worshipping God. For this reason the covenant that was originally designed for the nation had been withheld until Jesus' coming. Mosaic law thus never represented God's true intention for Israel since what God had wished to give his people had been nullified by their disobedience. However, the true covenant was now made available through a new prophet. Further, Stephen argued that God does not dwell in the Temple but fills the cosmos:

Yet the Most High does not dwell in houses made with hands; as the prophet says, 'Heaven is my throne, and earth my footstool. What house will you build for me, says the Lord, or what is the place of my rest?' (Acts 7:48–9)

While the early Church did contain a number of Jews who insisted that all converts must be fully observant, Hellenizers in sympathy with Stephen stressed that salvation was no longer dependent on the observance of Jewish ritual. Rather it is attained solely through faith in Christ. Only his followers constitute God's chosen people. All others are outside the covenant. From this standpoint, the Church alone possesses the correct interpretation of Scripture. Salvation now exists as the fulfilment of Scripture as predicted by the prophets. Christianity is thus not a new patch put on an old garment, or a new wine poured into old bottles, but needs a new garment and a new wine (Luke 5:36–9).

Given this understanding of law and salvation, the Church sought to bring the Gospel to the gentile world. The Christian message was for all who had ears to hear. By the second decade of the Christian era, it was acknowledged that God was carving out a new people for Himself. Since Jews continued to remain faithful to the old covenant, they were rejected; in their place a new Israel had been created. This notion is reflected in the New Testament by the frequent contrasts drawn between unbelieving Jews and committed gentiles. The leaders of the Jewish nation are depicted as rejecting and killing Jesus, whereas the first believer was a Roman centurion (Mark 15:39). The Good Samaritan is compared with the faithless Jew (Luke 10:33). The gentiles will come from all places to sit at the messianic banquet, whereas the sons of the Kingdom will be cast into outer darkness.

The parable of the wedding feast (Matthew 22:1–14; Luke 14:16–24) emphasizes God's rejection of Jewry. When the guests who were invited – the observant Jews – refuse to attend, the king's (God's) messengers go out a second and third time to gather the rabble (the unrighteous and the gentiles). Thus unrepentant Israel is rejected in favour of the gentiles, who were previously outside the convenant. For Matthew, those who were originally invited were not simply too busy, as those described in Luke. They 'seized the servants, treated them shamefully and killed them' (Matthew 22:6). In response the king grew angry, destroyed the murderers, and burned their city (Matthew 22:7). Further, once the wedding hall was filled with guests, the king threw out a man who was not wearing a wedding garment (Matthew 22:11). In this parable Matthew emphasizes that God will punish the Jews for their lack of repentance and welcome faithful gentiles into the covenant.

The belief that Israel not only rejected the Gospel but also attempted to kill God's messengers is a frequent theme in the New Testament. The Synoptic Gospels minimize the Romans' part in Christ's death; instead the elders, the chief priests and the scribes play a dominant role. Similarly, blame for the deaths of Jesus' disciples is attributed to the Jewish authorities, a conviction which serves as the basis of the parable of the vineyard (Mark 12:1–12; Matthew 21:33–46; Luke 20:9–10). Here the vineyard owner (God) puts his vineyard (Israel) into the hands of the tenants (Jews). At times he sends his servants (the prophets) to gather his share of the produce. However, the tenants attack and kill them. Eventually the owner sends his son, but he is also killed in order that the tenants can assert squatters' rights. Yet since they are owner tenants, he will come and destroy them and give the vineyard to others.

In Matthew's Gospel the belief that the Jews murdered the prophets engendered hostility toward the Jewish population:

> Woe to you scribes and Pharisees, hypocrites! For you build the tombs of the
> prophets and adorn the monuments of the righteous, saying, 'If we had lived
> in the days of our fathers, we would not have taken part with them in
> shedding the blood of the prophets.' Thus you witness against yourselves that
> you are sons of those who murdered the prophets. Fill up, then, the measure
> of your fathers. You serpents, you brood of vipers, how are you to escape
> being sentenced to hell? (Matthew 23:29–33)

These accusations demonstrate that by the second decade of its mission, the Church had come to believe that the Jews had been not only implicated in but were mainly responsible for the deaths of Christ and his disciples.

Paul makes no distinction between the circumcised and the uncircumcised – both Jews and gentiles are in the same situation before God. In Paul's view, as traditionally interpreted, the Torah is identical in content with natural law. In this respect both Jews and gentiles know God's will and are equally sinful. Yet since the Jew possesses God's revelation, he is aware of his inadequacies. In his fallen state he witnesses to the power of sin.

Since Jews and gentiles belong to fallen humanity as represented by the Old Adam, salvation is obtainable only through a new covenant based on Christ. Through the coming of the Messiah human beings are able to attain a transformed nature that provides for spiritual authenticity. This transformation brings to an end all presumptions of special rights and privileges; hence confidence in such practices as dietary laws, observance of festivals, new moons and Sabbaths must be set aside:

> Therefore let no one pass judgment on you in questions of food and drink or
> with regard to a festival or a new moon or a Sabbath. These are only a
> shadow of what is to come; but the substance belongs to Christ. (Colossians
> 2:16–17)

In Paul's view, what is required instead is circumcision of the heart. This is possible only through the power of Christ which does away with the Old Adam. Obedience is not possible under the Mosaic covenant; rather, a new covenant including baptism is now required. Through baptism it is possible to put off the body of flesh and be raised with Christ (Colossians 2:11–12). Only this new covenant can provide the power to become a living law when God's commands are written on the tablets of the human heart (2 Corinthians 3:3).

The distinction between these two types of circumcision is elaborated in Paul's discussion of Abraham's children. When Abraham was uncircumcised, God gave him the promise of salvation. Hence Abraham is the father of those who seek to achieve righteousness through faith rather than law. Abraham is thus the father of spiritual Israel, descended by faith in the promises given to him rather than through physical lineage. It is Christ who is the true heir: 'Abraham "believed God, and it was reckoned to him as righteousness". So you see that it is men of faith who are the sons of Abraham' (Galatians 3:6–7).

For Paul the reign of the Torah is synonymous with the domination of demonic powers. According to the law, the people were subject to the elemental spirits of the universe, but through Jesus' death and resurrection, they have become free sons of God:

> Formerly, when you did not know God, you were in bondage to beings that by nature are no gods; but now that you have come to know God, or rather to be known by God, how can you turn back again to the weak and beggarly elemental spirits, whose slaves you want to be once more? (Galatians 4:8–10)

In his description of the two covenants Paul offers an allegorical interpretation of the two wives of Abraham. Hagar and her progeny symbolize the era of slavery, whereas Sarah and her children belong to the period of freedom. The followers of Christ are the children of Sarah. However, those who adhere to the Mosaic covenant are seen as sons and daughters of Hagar. In Paul's estimation, Hagar and her children represent Mount Sinai, while those who believe in Christ are part of spiritual Jerusalem. 'We brethren, like Isaac,' he writes,

> are children of promise. . . . Cast out the slave and her son; for the son of the slave shall not inherit with the son of the free woman. (Galatians 4:28,30)

Thus the Church has not simply superseded Judaism. Rather, the two faiths are opposed to each other. Judaism belongs to the realm of fallen Adam, but Christianity fulfils the divine promises recorded in Scripture.

Those who belong to the Mosaic covenant will be cast out, but the children of the new covenant will be saved in Christ. Paul's diatribe against the Jews is thus a rejection of the Jewish tradition. The Mosaic covenant belongs to an apostate people. Yet God's true covenant was given before the revelation on Mount Sinai and will be fulfilled with the advent of the messianic age. Only those who belong to this spiritual community will be vouchsafed the divine promises contained in Scripture.

In Romans 9–11 Paul argues that the true Israel is this community; it is the Israel of the promise as opposed to the Israel based on descent. Only a remnant from the Jewish people is intended for salvation, and there is a divine purpose to be found in the reluctance of the Jewish community to accept Jesus as Christ. They have been hardened by God so that the gentiles will be ushered in. But as soon as this ingathering occurs, God will turn their hearts and Christ will return to complete the work of salvation.

In the Epistle to the Hebrews a contrast is made between the new and old covenants. The new covenant supersedes the old: it contains the true meaning of what is anticipated in the Mosaic covenant. Here Judaism is viewed as mutable, whereas the Christian message is eternal. For the author of Hebrews, the Son of God is superior to the angels who revealed the old covenant; the Christian message, however, is spoken by Christ:

> In these last days he [God] has spoken to us by a Son, whom he appointed the heir of all things, through whom he created the world. (Hebrews 1:2)

The Torah is therefore only a portent of what is to come. All the great figures of the Bible testified to the coming of Christ. These individuals lived in anticipation of God's promises:

> All these, though well attested by their faith, did not receive what was promised, since God had foreseen something better for us, that apart from us they should not be made perfect. (Hebrews 11:39–40)

Moreover, since the ancient Israelites rebelled against Moses, they were not allowed to gain true rest. Such a promise was not to be found in the land of Canaan, but in the Kingdom of God. The true people of God shall proceed into this eschatological rest, whereas the rebellious nation of the covenant will be refused entry:

And to whom did he swear that they should never enter his rest, to those who were disobedient? So we see that they were unable to enter because of unbelief. (Hebrews 3:18–19)

Concerning the Temple, the author contends that Melchizedek symbolizes the true type of eternal priest of Christ in opposition to the Levite priesthood, who are mortal. Cultic sacrifices in the Temple provide no permanent forgiveness, whereas forgiveness offered through Christ's sacrifice is once and for all:

He has no need, like those high priests, to offer sacrifices daily, first for his own sins and then for those of the people; he did this once for all when he offered up himself. (Hebrews 7:27)

Temple sacrifice thus belongs to the temporal sphere, which is passing away. Its sanctuary was only a copy of the heavenly sanctuary. As the eternal high priest, Christ offers a means of reconciliation.

In the Fourth Gospel such a repudiation of Judaism was conceived as an antithesis between a fulfilled spiritual universe of Christ and a fallen world of darkness represented by the Jewish people. Jesus is the spiritual Temple in contrast to the Jewish Temple which will be destroyed (John 2:13–22). Jesus is the spiritual water of eternal life, rather than the physical water of Jacob's well (John 4:6–15). Jesus is the bread of truth as opposed to the manna of the wilderness that did not last (John 6:41–58).

Only those who know Christ can know God, and apart from the knowledge of Christ there is no knowledge of God – 'I am the way, and the truth, and the life: no one comes to the Father but by me' (John 14:6). Unlike the followers of Christ, the Jews are unbelievers who see and yet fail to believe. They are the incarnation of the false principle of a fallen world. Belonging to alienated existence, their reaction to the Son of God is to plot his death. The Jews are thus of the devil:

You are of your father, the devil, and your will is to do your father's desires. He was a murderer from the beginning, and has nothing to do with the truth, because there is no truth in him. When he lies, he speaks according to his own nature, for he is a liar and the father of lies. . . . The reason why you do not hear them [God's revealed words in Jesus] is because you are not of God. (John 8: 44,47)

According to the Fourth Gospel, Jesus is God's 'I Am', identified as the true path to the Father. Because of Jesus' claims, the Jews sought to kill him, and when they turned him over to the Roman authorities they asserted that he must die because of his blasphemy:

> When the chief priests and the officers saw him, they cried out: 'Crucify him, crucify him! . . . We have a law, and by that law he ought to die, because he has made himself the Son of God'. (John 19:6–7)

In this account Pilate refused to try Jesus under Roman law, and handed him over to the Jews. Thus, according to this way of reasoning, the Jews rather than the Roman authorities are responsible for his death. In John chapter 15 the writer asserts that as Jesus is in the Father, and the Father is in him, so his disciples abide in Jesus and he in them. The Jews, on the other hand, represent the demonic order; as they sought to kill Jesus, so they will seek to do the same to all his disciples.

JEWS, CHRISTIANS AND THE BIBLICAL HERITAGE

As we have seen, the New Testament appears to sow the seeds of later anti-Semitism. But is this a correct interpretation of Scripture? Nearly 40 years ago Jules Isaac, a French Jewish historian who had lost most of his family in the Holocaust, argued in his *Jesus and Israel* and *The Teaching of Contempt* that the Church has been largely responsible for the growth of anti-Semitism through the centuries. However, he did not point to the New Testament as the source of such antipathy towards Judaism and the Jewish nation. Rather, he claimed that Christians had misconstrued their own Scriptures.

This early view, however, has been disputed by a number of modern Christian writers, such as Rosemary Radford Ruether, who in *Faith and Fratricide* maintains that there is no way to exonerate the New Testament from the charge of anti-Judaism. Rather, she argues that hostility to the Jewish faith has been an essential element of Christian teaching from New Testament times to the present. This is so even though Jesus, his disciples, Paul and many of those who belonged to the early Church were Jewish by origin. According to Reuther, bitter rivalry set Judaism and Christianity against one another at the outset, and gave rise to animosity against the traditional Jewish establishment. From its inception, she argues, Christianity was inevitably bound to clash with traditional Judaism because of the claims made for Jesus: the concepts of man as God, of Jesus as the Messiah, and of the Trinity were totally incompatible with the Jewish belief in a single, omnipotent Creator.

Other contemporary Christian scholars, however, have argued against this interpretation of the New Testament on several grounds. First, they point out that in the first century CE the Jewish faith was pluralistic in character. Hence, if the New Testament attacks different expressions of religion among the Jews, this can be paralleled within rabbinic sources from the same period. On this basis, it makes little sense to view the New Testament as anti-Judaistic; rather, Scripture affirms the beliefs about Jesus as true Judaism in opposition to other forms of Judaism that existed during this period.

Second, it is vital to read the New Testament in its historical context. On this view, the Christian scriptures should be seen as responses of the early Church to problems faced by the Christian community in the early stages of its history. The presentation of the good news is therefore tempered by the aims of the authors of the Synoptic Gospels and the Fourth Gospel, Paul and the author of the Epistle to the Hebrews. In all cases, the Church sought to defend its conception of God's purposes. In this context, passages which express hostility to the Jews should be understood in a social context, rather than perceived as denunciations of the religion from which Christianity emerged. The New Testament should be read as an early document in the history of the Church, rather than as containing vehement criticism of the Jewish faith. In this light, some scholars have urged that a new translation of the New Testament be made from which passages damaging to the Jewish people be removed. This would provide a return to the essential teaching of Christ, eliminating those elements which are inessential and harmful to Jewish–Christian encounter.

Third, it is pointed out that the murder of Jesus is simply an extension of a Jewish practice whereby God's true prophets were frequently killed by their own kinsmen. Moses, for example, was nearly stoned to death by the people whom he had led out of Egypt (Exodus 17:4; Numbers 14:10). Elijah, too, complained that his own people, and not simply Queen Jezebel, wished to kill him. Thus, it is a mistake to believe that the New Testament seeks to place permanent blame on the Jewish people for Jesus' crucifixion.

Fourth, with regard to John's Gospel, it is alleged that the author was not hostile to Jews in general but to the corrupt leaders of the nation. The section of the Gospel from chapter 5 to chapter 10 describes an extended

controversy between Jesus and the Jewish leaders in Jerusalem. Here it is
not the Jews *per se* but rather leading Jewish figures who are castigated.
The Gospel of John thus poses the question whether these figures can
honestly reflect Judaism, rather than attacking Judaism itself. It is therefore
a mistake to interpret John 8:44 ('You belong to your father, the devil, and
you want to carry out your father's desire. He was a murderer from the
beginning, not holding to the truth, for there is no truth in him. When he
lies, he speaks his native language, for he is a liar and the father of lies') as
a charge against the entire nation. Rather, the author is engaged in an intra-
Jewish polemic against specific individuals.

Finally, there has been a concerted attempt to exonerate Paul from the
charge that he showed contempt for the Jewish faith. Some scholars
contend that Paul misunderstood or possibly distorted the Judaism of his
own time in making a case against Judaism. Others stress that Paul was
concerned exclusively with the relationship of gentiles to the Torah; thus he
does not deal with the question of Jewish observance of the law because it
is irrelevant to his concerns. Alternatively, it has been proposed that Paul's
opposition to Judaism was a stand against Jewish nationalism rather than
Jewish legalism. On this view, Paul was not attacking the law, but rather a
view that insisted on treating the law as a boundary around Israel, which
marked Jew off from gentile and restricted God's promise to the Jewish
nation.

Whatever one makes of this debate, there is no question that the Synoptic
Gospels, the Fourth Gospel and Paul's epistles have been used by the
Church to foster anti-Semitism through the ages. Through the centuries,
Christian theologians were intent on using Scripture as a basis for vilifying
the Jews – repeatedly Christian writers cited the biblical text in their
denunciation of the Jewish nation and the Jewish religion. This fearful
legacy has in recent years caused a growing number of Christians to
distance themselves from anti-Semitic charges based on scriptural texts.

With regard to the Jewishness of Jesus, for example, a number of
Christian scholars have been anxious to emphasize Jesus' connections with
his ancestral faith. In this quest these writers have stressed the importance
of dispelling the stereotyped pictures of first-century Judaism as portrayed
in the Gospels. Rather, the Jewish tradition should be understood in terms
of God's covenant with Abraham. In this light the law should be seen as a
gift, with Pharisaic Judaism as the logical continuation of God's
relationship with his chosen people.

As a product of the early Church, the Gospels reflect the disputes between the followers of Jesus and the Jewish community. Nonetheless, it is evident that Jesus had strong affinities with the Pharisees. His emphasis on reinterpreting the oral law is reminiscent of rabbinic teaching. Like the Pharisees he stressed the importance of love, adhered to belief in the resurrection, and rigorously observed Jewish festivals. Although Jesus did not follow all Pharisaic prescriptions, his departure from strict Pharisaism may simply have been a reflection of internal disputes among the Pharisees themselves.

With regard to scriptural claims that God's covenant with the Jews has been superseded by his covenant with the New Israel, there has been a concerted effort to stress the continuing validity of God's covenant with the Jews. According to some contemporary Christian scholars, both Judaism and Christianity are complementary aspects of the same divine purpose. Thus the eschatological significance of Jesus' salvific work must be understood as a future event – even for Christians Jesus is not yet the Messiah. Messianic fulfilment is not a present reality, but rather a mission. God's single covenant is new after the Christ event only in that it embraces both Jews and gentiles. In this light, the Church can be seen as a community of gentiles who have been drawn to worship God and bring knowledge of him to the nations. The Church and the Synagogue are therefore bound together in one covenant. Other Christian writers have formulated a two-covenant theory to deal with this issue. In their view, God has bound himself to both nations through a double covenant.

Concerning the scriptural injunction to draw others to Christ, some contemporary Christians are determined to reorient such activity. One approach to Christian outreach focuses on the distinction between proselytism as opposed to witness. While the quest to win converts from Judaism characterized previous Christian attitudes, Christian witness is currently understood as a sharing of religious experience. Such a reinterpretation of Christian mission is based on the recognition of God's presence among the Jews, a shift in perspective grounded in the conviction that a God of love could not allow the Jewish people to wallow in ignorance and darkness; as the providential Lord of history, God must provide a means of salvation for all people. In this light, according to current Christian exegesis, Judaism should be seen as an authentic religious expression, a shift in Christian perception that calls for a thorough-going reassessment of biblical teaching.

Today, then, there is a growing recognition that the roots of anti-Semitism can be traced back to New Testament teaching. Regardless of whether the Gospels and Paul's epistles are inherently anti-Jewish, there is no doubt that the Church has used Scripture as a framework for its teaching of contempt. Ways are now being sought to transcend this legacy of Christian anti-Semitism. Both the Roman Catholic and Protestant Churches have issued decrees condemning anti-Semitism, and Christians have been encouraged to understand Jesus in a Jewish context. God's continuing covenant with the Jewish people has also been recognized, and Christian mission has been largely curtailed. Further, Judaism has been affirmed as a valid tradition, and many Christians have come to accept a measure of responsibility for the Holocaust, given the Church's teaching about the Jews from New Testament times to the modern age.

THREE

The Early Church and Anti-Judaism

According to the early Church Fathers, the Jews were guilty of indecency: the Jewish nation is a lawless and dissolute people. Hence, all future promises apply solely to the Church. On the basis of Scripture, Christians scholars sought to demonstrate that the conflict between the Church and the Synagogue was prefigured in the Bible. Because of their rejection of Christ, Jews have continually been subject to God's wrath. Hence, it is Christians rather than Jews who constitute the elect; this is the fulfilment of the messianic vision of the ingathering of all people to Zion. As the religion of the Roman Empire, Christianity served as the vehicle for bringing God's redemption to all human beings. The Jews, on the other hand, suffer rejection and misery because of their unwillingness to accept Jesus as Christ. The Jewish nation is destined to wander in exile, and Jewish law has been superseded through Christ's death and resurrection. It is the Christian faith that offers salvation to the world.

JUDAISM AND CHRISTIANITY
Following New Testament teaching, the early Church Fathers developed an *Adversos Judaeos* tradition that flourished from the second to the sixth centuries. This malevolent polemic against the Jews is found in treatises, sermons and discourses as well as other types of literature which seek to illustrate that the Jews were rejected by God. Such hostility was always based on the now familiar claim that the Jews had refused to accept Jesus as Messiah and Saviour. For the Church Fathers, this was not an act of apostasy; instead the Jews had always been an apostate nation. Abraham, Isaac and Jacob – as ancestors of the Church – were righteous individuals; however, with the Egyptian sojourn the ancient Hebrews engaged in various types of evil acts. The aim of Mosaic legislation was to curtail such depravity. Hence, all the crimes in Scripture are said by Christian commentators to mirror the Israelites' corrupt lifestyle. In his writings, the fourth-century Christian theologian and preacher John Chrysostom, Bishop

of Constantinople, asserted that Jews in Egypt built a brothel, made love to barbarians and worshipped foreign gods. Here there was a radical departure from the earlier Graeco-Roman teaching about the Jews in Egypt. Instead of being depicted as a diseased nation, early Church Fathers maintained that the people suffered from moral depravity.

After the Israelites had escaped from Egyptian captivity, they assumed their idolatrous ways during their sojourn in the desert. According to the Fathers of the early Church, the Hebrews' worship of the Golden Calf was typical of their faithlessness. Thus the fourth-century Latin poet Prudentius wrote in *Apotheosis* that such worship was due to the deafness of the Jews to God's word. By giving over their earings to be melted down to form a golden idol, they had impaired their hearing. All their trappings, he wrote, have vanished from their ears and gone to fashion a cast head of Baal, robbing their ears of the honour.

In the Promised Land, the nation continued their idolatrous behaviour. The third-century African Church Father Tertullian wrote in his *An Answer to the Jew*, that according to Scripture the Jewish people forsook God and did degrading service to idols. They abandoned God and prostrated themselves before images. In later times when kings ruled over them, they worshipped calves and enslaved themselves to the Canaanite god Baal. In the fourth century, the Syrian exegete and ecclesiastical writer Ephrem in *Rhythm against the Jews* also accused the Jews of idolatry, contending that the persecution of Christ was prefigured in previous times. What was the iniquity of the Jewish people? he asked. They dishonoured the King and his Son. The King was dishonoured in the wilderness and the King's Son in Jerusalem. The Father was exchanged for the calf, and the Son was exchanged for a thief.

In early Christian sources, the Jews were also accused of blaspheming against God's nature, resisting his spirit, and engaging in sensual excess. Again, in *Eight Orations against the Jews*, John Chrysostom linked such behaviour with the rejection of God. As an animal when it has been fattened by getting all it wants to eat, he wrote, grows stubborn and hard to manage, so it was with the Jewish people. They were reduced by gluttony and drunkenness to a state of utter depravity. In such a state they would not accept Christ. In contrast with Christian asceticism, Jews indulged in vices of the flesh. For Ephrem the synagogue was personified as a harlot. According to the fourth-century Syrian Church Father Aphrahat in his *Demonstrations against the Jews*, Jerusalem was equated with Sodom and Gomorrah. The eighth-century Greek Father John Damascene proclaimed in *On the Sabbath, against the Jews*, that the Sabbath was given to the Jews because of their grossness and propensity for material possessions.

Further, a number of polemicists stated that the Jews were guilty of infanticide. John Chrysostom, for example, portrayed the ancient Hebrews as debauchers and idolators who sacrificed their sons and daughters to demons and ate their own children. Such practices justified God's rejection of the Jewish people. In the third century, in his *Expository Treatise against the Jews*, the Roman ecclesiastical writer Hippolytus summarized their fall from grace. Why was the Temple made desolate, he asked. Was it because of their worship of the Golden Calf? Was it because of their idolatry? Was it because the prophets' blood had been spilled? Was it because of the Jewish people's adultery and fornication? These were not the reason, he stated, because pardon was always open to them. Rather, it was because they killed the Son who is coeternal with the Father.

Moreover, previous crimes which had characterized the ancient Hebrews were viewed to have continued to the present day. Just as Jews were responsible in previous centuries for their sins, so they were equally guilty of iniquity in contemporary circumstances. In his sermons John Chrysostom emphasized that the Jews continued to be a lawless and dissolute people, destined to evoke God's wrath. With venom, he attacked the Jewish community of his own age. The synagogue, he stated, is not only a whorehouse and a theatre, it is also a den of thieves and a haunt of wild animals. The Jews have no conception of spiritual things; rather they live for the lower nature. They are no better than pigs or goats, and they live by the rule of debauchery. For Chrysostom and others, the Jews are not human beings; they are demons incarnate who had been cast off by God into utter darkness.

According to early Church Fathers, prophetic denunciations in Scripture against iniquity applied to the Jewish people; however, all future promises relate to adherents of the true Church. Given this interpretation, Scripture bears witness to a catalogue of Jewish sins. In his *Tract against the Jews*, the fourth-century theologian Augustine, Bishop of Hippo maintained that the Jewish nation is incapable of understanding the true nature of the Bible: they believe the divine promises apply to the Jewish people. But, Augustine asserted, the Jews are the enemies of God. When the prophets declared that God has cut off the House of Israel, these pronouncements refer to the

Jews. When Israel is described positively, these statements apply to the Christian Church.

Viewed thus, both apostate Jews and the universal Church were anticipated in the Hebrew bible. Those who are righteous belong to the Christian community. The Jews, however, are the enemies referred to in the Psalms and the Suffering Servant passages in Isaiah. In formulating this view, Christian scholars understood the account of Jacob and Esau as prefiguring these two religious groups. Genesis declares that 'When her [Rebekah's] days to be delivered were fulfilled, behold, there were twins in her womb . . . and two peoples, born of you, shall be divided; the one shall be stronger than the other, the elder shall serve the younger' (Genesis 25:23–4). Here 'the elder' refers to the Jews who will serve 'the younger' (the Church).

In *Contra Judaeos*, the fifth-century theologian Maximinus formulated a series of similar rivalries which prefigure Jewish–Christian conflict. Heading this list was Cain, who personifies the Jewish people, whereas Abel (who was murdered by Cain) represents Christ. Similarly, Tertullian argued that God rejected the blood sacrifices of the law (Jewish sacrifice) in place of the spiritual worship of the Church. In Aphrahat's writings the passage from John 8:44, 'Your father was a murderer from the beginning', was identified with Cain. Ephrem also identified the Jews with Cain. The glory that was with the people of Israel, he stated, has passed from them, and they now stand among the nations as ashamed as Cain was of his murderous deed. In the fourth century, Prudentius argued that the Jew was the murderous brother who now wanders over the face of the earth. From place to place, he wrote, the homeless Jew wanders in ever-shifting exile. Since the time when he was torn from the abode of his fathers, he has been suffering the penalty for murder. His hands are stained with the blood of Christ whom he denied.

This antithesis was also applied to the two wives of Abraham, Sarah and Hagar, as well as to Jacob's two wives, Rachel and Leah. Like Paul, who viewed the children of Sarah as the true Christian Israel whereas Hagar was identified with the Jews, Augustine stated that the Jews are a carnal people compared with the Christians, who are spiritual in nature. Hagar was the fallen Jerusalem, bound in servitude to Sarah's offspring. A parallel analogy was drawn in the third century by Cyprian, Bishop of Carthage in his *Three Books of the Testimonies against the Jews* where he argued that Jacob received two wives. The elder was Leah with weak eyes who represented the Synagogue; the younger, beautiful daughter Rachel represented the Church, who although initially barren brought forth Joseph, who himself is a type of Christ.

According to patristic tradition, the Church is the bride of God. But Israel is a harlot -- she has been given a bill of divorce and sent away. In his *Rhythm against the Jews*, Ephrem graphically represented this divorce. She – Israel – despised the voice of the prophets as well as the preaching of the Apostles. Thus he (God) wrote and delivered to her the bill of divorce. He took the veil from her head; he stripped her of her ornaments; he took the necklace from her neck and took away her bracelets and armlets. As if she were an adulteress and harlot, he drove her out and sent her forth from his chamber.

Referring to Hosea's preaching in Hosea 2:2 ('For she is not my wife, and I am not her husband – that she put away her harlotry from her face, and her adultery from between her breasts'), he stated that Israel has played the whore and Judah has committed adultery. However, the Christian community is the holy and faithful people who have cleaved to the Lord. Such imagery emphasized that God's promises no longer apply to the Jews. Divorced from the message of forgiveness and hope, the Jewish people have been rejected and subjected to God's wrath.

Given this teaching about sinful Israel, the early Church maintained that the Christian community had now taken the place of the Jews. This was not simply a substitution, but rather the new Israel was perceived as preordained in Scripture. The prophets insisted that the election of the Jewish nation was only provisional. The covenant thus has been inherited and fulfilled by those who accept Jesus as Messiah and Lord. In the past, biblical heroes and prophets prepared the way for this event, yet from the beginning the Jewish people continually refused to accept God. Christians, on the other hand, constitute a community of believers.

In presenting this view, the Church Fathers appealed to Paul's doctrine that the true sons of Abraham are those who are justified by faith. Hence, the descendants of Abraham are not the Jews, but the gentiles. As the fifth-century theologian Isaac of Antioch declared in *Homilies against the Jews*, the uncircumcised gentiles have taken Israel's place. Circumcision has thus ceased to be the mark of election. Rather, figuratively speaking, circumcision was a seal on a bag that has been kept for the true inheritors of this treasure. However, neither the seal nor the bag serve any purpose, and the Jewish community has become the possessor of only an empty container. Abraham, he wrote, was stamped like a vessel because of the treasure that was in him. And the seal continued because of the treasure that was in the Jews. But now the treasure has come forth, and it is safeguarded by the Christian community.

As in the New Testament, patristic literature interpreted those passages describing Israel as a light to the nations as prophecies about the Church. Conversely, scriptural passages concerning sinful Israel were understood as referring to Israel's rejection by God. The Psalms, for example, promised the rule of a Davidic king over the nations; such texts were presumed to refer to Christ. The nations to be conquered and converted are the gentiles. Texts such as Psalms 2:7–8 ('Thou art my son, this day I have begotten thee; ask of me and I will give the nations as thy inheritance') were read as God's decree to Christ that he would inherit the gentile Church. Prophetic texts concerning God's faithful people were also understood as referring to the gentile Church: 'Many and strong peoples shall adhere to the Lord (Zechariah 2:11), and in 'Those who are not my people I shall call my people' (Hosea 2:23).

Following New Testament teaching, the Church Fathers also maintained that the election of gentiles is the culmination of the messianic vision of the ingathering of the nations to Zion: according to Ephrem, the good news of Christ's redemption shall flow from Zion. God's gates will be opened with joy, he wrote, and gentiles shall enter into Zion and become an elect people. The Lord shall reign over Zion, and many peoples shall come and worship in Jerusalem. The Jews, however, will be rejected and despair.

Once Christianity became the faith of the Roman Empire, the concept of divine election was understood in political terms and the Roman Empire came to be identified with the reign of the Messiah. As John Chrysostom explained, Christendom should be identified with Christ's domination over the world. Everywhere paganism is defeated by the Church, and this victory is presaged by Christ's victory over demons. With all humanity united in Christ, brotherhood and peace hold sway. In *Oration on Constantine*, Eusebius, Bishop of Caesarea in the fourth century asserts that as knowledge of God and the doctrine of Christ was made known to all humanity, so the Roman Empire held dominion throughout the world. Thus by God's express desire, the Roman Empire and the doctrine of Christian piety sprang up for the benefit of all people.

In contrast with this vision of the universal Church, the Jewish dispersion was understood as a result of divine wrath. Persecuted Christians, on the other hand, were viewed as God's beloved servants; they were to be loved because they suffered for Christ. But Christians were to despise those who rejected Christ and killed him. As Chrysostom declared, the martyrs especially hate the Jews since they love so deeply the one who was crucified by them. The Jews declared that his blood be on us and on our children, while the martyrs shed their own blood for God's Anointed.

The Jews have thus been rejected because of their faithlessness. According to patristic tradition, the Jewish nation is therefore destined to suffer numerous calamities. Because of their refusal to accept Christ, they were cast out and despised. In his *Demonstrations of the Gospel*, Eusebius declared that because of their impiety, their kingdom was utterly destroyed, the Torah abrogated, and ancient worship uprooted. Their royal city, he wrote, was burned with fire, and the holy altar consumed with flames. In this process, the Jewish community was dispersed among the nations with no hope of any cessation of evil. The Jews were thus misguided in continuing to observe the Jewish legal system since the Temple, the priesthood and the sacrificial system have disappeared.

For Christians, however, non-cultic worship is the culmination of the spiritual development predicted by the prophet Malachi: 'Oh, that there were one among you who would shut the doors, that you might not kindle fire upon my altar in vain! I have no pleasure in you, says the Lord of hosts, and I will not accept an offering from your hand' (Malachi 1:10). Identifying Judaism with cultic observance in the Holy Land, Christians viewed the destruction of the Temple as a sign of God's disfavour. The Jewish people had been exiled, and the observance of ancient festivals outside the Holy Land was perceived as a violation of God's law. In the light of this teaching, Chrysostom denounced synagogue worship; to go there, he stated, was no better than visiting a brothel, a robbers' den or any indecent place.

In their writings, the Church Fathers utilized the Book of Daniel to illustrate that the Jews were to endure various captivities. Both the Egyptian and Babylonian captivities were limited in time, but there will be no future liberation from exile due to the Jewish refusal to accept Christ. No Messiah will deliver them from their wandering. As the third-century Roman theologian Hippolytus explained in his *Expository Treatise against the Jews*, the Jews wander as in the night, and stumble on places with no roads. They fall headlong because of their rejection of the Redeemer. They will not be bound to four hundred and thirty years servitude in Egypt, or seventy years in Babylonia, but their plight will last for ever.

Similarly, John Chrysostom argued that the Jews will be crucified throughout history because they crucified Christ. It is because they stretched out their hand against Christ and spilled his precious blood, that there is now no restoration, mercy or defence. This is why they are punished now more severely than ever in the past. Again, in *Demonstrations of the Gospel*, Eusebius contended that the rejection of the Jews was due to their own hard-heartedness. Because they did not hearken to Christ's words, they have suffered ruin. They neither received the law of Christ, nor were they able to keep the commandments of Moses. Thus they fell under the divine curse: they were exiled from Jerusalem, which was destroyed, and where alone it is permitted for them to celebrate with Mosaic music.

Some writers interpreted the rite of Jewish circumcision as the mark of Cain. Thus the second-century Christian apologist Justin Martyr wrote in *Dialogue with Trypho* that circumcision, according to the flesh, was given for a sign that Jews might suffer, that the land may be desolate, the cities burned with fires. The Jews, he continued, are wanderers, homeless and reviled by both God and human beings. They cannot be saved, and Jewish misery thus bears testimony to God's anger which has befallen this hard-hearted nation. The only hope for the Jews is to recognize that the Christian community constitutes the true Israel and join the Church. In this regard, Augustine argues following Paul's teaching in Romans 9–11 that Jews must repent of the errors of their ways and embrace the true faith. It is only by becoming followers of the risen Christ that salvation is possible.

Hence, according to the Church Fathers, Jewish law and the Temple cult are intrinsically unworthy and have become obsolete in the light of Christ's redemption. Christians are under no obligation to keep biblical prescriptions. In his *Epistle*, the third-century theologian Diognetus emphasized that Jewish practices have no efficacy. Those who believe they can offer God acceptable sacrifices with blood and fat and holocausts, he wrote, are nothing more than fools who show the same devotion to deaf idols. Is it not ridiculous, he asked, to boast of a mutilation of the flesh as a sign of being chosen, as though they are particularly beloved of God. Christians are right, he continued, to keep away from such error.

In patristic literature, the concept of a pre-Mosaic religion plays an important role. For Eusebius, during the pre-Mosaic era human beings were naturally virtuous. The patriarchs were therefore not Jews, but simply members of the human race who were virtuous without being bound by law. In place of a legalistic code, they were motivated by the law of conscience. This spiritual religion has now become available to all peoples through Christ. It is not a new covenant. Rather, it is the restoration of the original religion of the patriarchal period. Within this framework, the Ten Commandments should be understood as the basic law of God, whereas Mosaic legislation is temporary in nature and given only to the Jews.

Legislation in the Five Books of Moses is therefore designed for an intermediate period: from Moses to Christ. It is of an inferior status to patriarchal faith. Its purpose is punitive rather than redemptive, and was designed to elevate the Jews from the state of moral decay into which they had fallen in Egypt. As Chrysostom remarked, this is what God did: he saw the Jews raving mad, choking themselves in their lust for sacrifices, and ready to succumb to idolatry if this desire were not fulfilled. For this reason, sacrifice was allowed. Similarly, the Sabbath was instituted to curb the Jews' lust for material gain. Further, circumcision was prescribed to separate the Jews from those who engaged in idolatrous practices.

However, Jewish law has been superseded by a new dispensation. Christians now are the true keepers of God's law of inward obedience and dedication. In place of Moses, Christ has become the new lawgiver. By following scriptural legislation, the Jewish nation has misconstrued God's real intention, acted against his will, and become a lawless people. Christians, on the other hand, are liberated from the law and are thereby able to discover its inner meaning. Through repentance, they have 'circumcised' the heart. As Isaac of Antioch declared, Joshua's stone knives, by which God commanded him to circumcise the people of Israel a second time, signify the circumcision of Jesus; this symbolizes a circumcision of the heart of Christians rather than the flesh. Dietary laws are similarly dealt with: they were initially given to Israel to restrain them from gluttony, but their real meaning is internal.

In like fashion, cultic observances were understood as irrelevant. In support of this view, the Church cited numerous prophetic statements condemning formal worship:

I hate, I despise your feasts, and I take no delight in your solemn assemblies. (Amos 5:21)

What to me is the multitude of your sacrifices, says the Lord; I have enough of burnt offerings. . . . Incense is an abomination to me. I cannot endure your new moons and Sabbaths and assemblies. (Isaiah 1:11–13)

Temple sacrifice thus does not fulfil God's will, and the destruction of the Temple confirmed this judgment. As John Chrysostom explained, after permitting Jews to offer sacrifices, God did not allow them to do so anywhere other than in Jerusalem. Then after they had offered sacrifices for a short period, he destroyed the city. Thus, by demolishing Jerusalem, God intended to lead the Jews away from this practice in spite of their desires.

What is now required is the sacrifice of the heart. Hence, Christian worship takes the place of cultic observance. The true faith consists of the spiritual Temple of the Holy Spirit found in each believer and also within the body of the Church. As far as the priesthood is concerned, the priests of Christ are superior to the Aaronite priesthood and the Eucharist is identified with the spiritual worship of bread and wine offered by Melchizedek. For John Chrysostom, the priests of Melchizedek have now taken over the role of those who regulated activities in the Temple. If perfection had been attainable through the Levitical priesthood, he wrote, there would be no further need for a priest to arise after the order of Melchizedek (Hebrews 7:11) rather than the one after the order of Aaron. On this view, the former priesthood had come to an end and a different one – much better and more sublime – had been introduced in its place.

In preaching this message, the Fathers stressed that they possessed the correct understanding of the Bible. The Jewish nation, however, is blind to its true meaning. They are incapable of seeing the implication of God's word. This is due in part to Jewish literalism, since Jews are unable to discern the inner meaning of Scripture. As the second-century theologian Irenaeus, Bishop of Lyons declared, the Jews departed from God, not simply in their unwillingness to receive his word, but by imagining that they could know the Father apart by himself. They believed they could know him without the Son; in this way they are ignorant of that God who spoke in human shape to Abraham and again to Moses.

For the Church Fathers, Christ is the incarnation of God's word – it is he whom the Jews have never known since they have preferred the exegesis of the Scribes and Pharisees as opposed to the direct word of Scripture. Rabbinic hermeneutics therefore constitutes the veil over the scriptural text. It induces blindness and leads the Jews astray. According to Augustine, Jewry is a carnal people that belong to the lower level of existence. Jewish teachings and customs are useless; they belong to Israel after the flesh in contrast to spiritual Israel, the Church. All that is Jewish has been set aside now that Christ has arrived.

CHRISTIAN ANTI-SEMITISM

As we have observed, the seeds of Christian hostility to the Jews were sown in the New Testament. But why did such animosity evolve into a ferocious diatribe against the Jewish nation? It appears that such hostility was motivated by the desire to differentiate faith in Christ from the Jewish heritage. Seeing itself as the fulfilment of Israel, the Church believed it was the true inheritor of God's promises. Jesus, the long awaited Messiah, had called on his followers to go and make disciples of all nations. Initially the Synagogue had regarded Jesus and his disciples with suspicion. But later, with the growth of Christianity, conflict between Christian believers and the Jewish community became increasingly intense. By the time of the Jewish rebellion from Rome between 66 and 70 CE, Christians had departed for Pella for the duration of the war. To Jews, this act was perceived as disloyalty, a deliberate dissociation from Judaism.

For the followers of Jesus, the destruction of Jerusalem and the Temple were understood as a punishment from God for the Jewish rejection of Christ. Aware of Christian hatred, Jewish leaders introduced a malediction against Christians which was included into the *Shomneh Esreh* prayer:

> May the *minim* (heretics) perish in an instant; may they be effaced from the Book of Life and not be counted among the just.

In addition, the Sanhedrin sent letters to Jews living in the diaspora concerning this new prayer and the correct attitude to be adopted towards the followers of Christ. Three Church Fathers – Justin in the second century, and Eusebius and Jerome in the fourth century – indicate the nature of this correspondence. As they explain, the Sanhedrin viewed Jesus as a false Messiah whose body was stolen by his disciples who then pretended that he was resurrected: these individuals preached that he is the Son of God. According to the Sanhedrin, Jews should have no contact with such persons.

As time passed, the separation between Church and Synagogue became final. As a result, patristic literature of the first century reflects the growing Christian animosity towards Jews and Judaism. The Didache, an early Christian manual on morals and Church practice, for example, warns Christians that they should not fast with hypocrites, possibly referring to Judaizers in the Church as well as the Jewish leadership in synagogues. The *Letter of Barnabas* is less ambiguous. Resorting to allegorical interpretation, it seeks to demonstrate how Jews have misunderstood the Hebrew bible by ignoring those sections that prefigure Christ and the Church. The Jews, the letter states, have lost the covenant for ever.

In the same century, Ignatius, Bishop of Antioch, corresponded with gentile communities, warning against Judaizing. In his view, there was no need for the disciples of Christ to observe the obsolete practices of Judaism. In the second century the Christian apologist Justin reiterated the theme of Jewish hate, alleging that Jews repeatedly persecute and slander Christians. During the same period Tertullian, the African Church Father, called the synagogues of his day 'fountains of persecution of Christians'. According to the third-century Alexandrian biblical critic, exegete and theologian Origen, Jews falsely accuse Christians of cannibalistic practices and sensual orgies. These and other writers also complained that Jews abuse the person of Christ. Justin, for example, related that Jews laugh, curse and insult Jesus.

It appears that some of these charges levelled against the Jewish community during the first few centuries of the Church had some basis in fact. Faced with such Christian antipathy, rabbinic authorities regarded Christianity as a formidable enemy. Rabbi Tarphon, for example, invoked a curse upon himself if he did not burn Christian Scriptures regardless of the fact that they contain God's name. Christians, he asserted, were worse than heathens.

As relations between Jews and Christians deteriorated, the Church launched an offensive against its Jewish neighbours. No century was more decisive for division between Church and Synagogue than the fourth. In the fourth century when the Roman emperor Constantine embraced the Christian faith, the Church was accorded a position of eminence and power within the Roman Empire. As a consequence, the imperial government was able to impose restrictive measures against the Jewish population. By the end of the fourth century, the civil status of Jewry had been undermined. Despised by the state, Jews were increasingly subject to anti-Jewish polemic.

In this context defenders of the Church inveighed against the Jewish community. Developing the themes of earlier Christian polemicists, they sought to demonstrate the perversity of the Jewish people: in their view, the Jew was an obdurate unbeliever who had been cast off by God, and punished for his hard-heartedness. In the first half of the fourth century Eusebius, Bishop of Caesarea, composed two volumes of Church history based on the distinction between Hebrews and Jews. The Hebrews, he argued, were primitive Christians; the Jews, however, were an unworthy people for whom Jewish law was necessary. In a similar vein, in the same century Hilary, Bishop of Poitiers reinterpreted history to demonstrate that the Jews were a perverse people, despised by God.

In the same century the Syrian apologist Aphrahats warned against Judaizing practices, and another Syrian Ephrem included contemptuous references to Judaism in his liturgical hymns. Similarly, Cyril, Bishop of Jerusalem denounced the Jews as did Epiphanius, Bishop of Salamis who in his study of Judaeo-Christian heresies denounced the Herodians as real Jews because of their dishonesty. Later in the century Gregory of Nyssa described the Jews as slayers of Christ, adversaries of grace, enemies of their fathers' faith, advocates of the devil, a brood of vipers, slanderers, scoffers, sinners, wicked men and haters of goodness. In like manner, the biblical scholar Jerome described Jews as serpents, haters of men and Judases.

The pre-eminent critic of Judaism in the fourth century was John Chrysostom, Bishop of Constantinople, who, as we have seen, engaged in a venomous attack on Jewry in a series of sermons preached in Antioch. In his view, Jews were lustful, rapacious, greedy and perfidious. They are inveterate murderers, destroyers, and possessed of the devil whose debauchery and drunkenness have given them the manners of the pig and goat. They know only one thing: to satisfy their gullets, get drunk, and kill and maim one another. They have surpassed the ferocity of wild beats, since they murder their offspring and immolate them to the devil. According to Chrysostom, the synagogue is a theatre, a house of prostitution, and domicile of the devil. Indeed, Jews worship the devil; their rites are criminal and impure, their religion a disease.

The Jews are degenerate, he asserted, because they assassinated Christ – this supreme crime is unforgivable. Hence, there is no expiation possible, no indulgence or pardon. Divine vengeance is without end, and the Jewish nation will forever remain without their Temple. It is God's will, he states, that the Jews be dispersed and abandoned. Henceforth, Jews will live under the yoke of eternal servitude. God hates the Jews and on the Day of Judgment, he will say: 'Depart from me, for you have had intercourse with my murderers'. Thus, it is the duty of Christians to hate the Jews.

Although less vehement than Chrysostom, Augustine, Bishop of Hippo, was at a loss to understand Jewish unbelief. In his view, Judaism as practised since Christ is a corruption. The Jews, he continues, bear guilt for the death of the Saviour. In one of his sermons he declared that the Jews held Christ; they insulted him; they bound him; they crowned him with thorns; they dishonoured him; they scourged him; they heaped abuses on him; they hung him upon a tree; they pierced him with a lance. Nonetheless, the survival of the Jews was providential – they are witnesses of evil and of Christian truth. Like Cain, they carry a sign of disobedience. Yet, the Christian has a duty to preach to this dissolute people, to bring them to Christ.

Such denunciations of Jewry were accompanied in the fourth and fifth centuries by a series of legislative measures taken by both the Church and the empire – these laws were a concrete reflection of patristic teaching about the Jews. At the beginning of the century the Council of Elivra in Spain forbade intermarriage between Jews and Christians except where the Jewish partner had converted to Christianity. The Council of Antioch (341) prohibited Christians from celebrating Passover with Jews. The Council of Laodicea (434–81) forbade Christians from keeping the Jewish Sabbath or from receiving gifts of unleavened bread from Jews.

These edicts were followed by the *Codex Theodosianus*, a compilation of law issued from the time of Constantine, which was promulgated in 438. Although this codex does guarantee certain rights to the Jewish population, it bans conversion to Judaism as well as the circumcision of slaves of Jewish owners. In addition, the codex bars Jews from public functions, administrative posts and the legal profession. Marriages to Jews were also prohibited. Throughout this codex there are numerous insulting references to the Jewish faith – Judaism is referred to as a wicked sect, and Jews are described as abominable.

Such a context of rivalry and hatred inevitably led to repeated outbreaks of hostility between Jews and Christians during the first few centuries of the Church. In the third century in Alexandria, Jews joined Arians in riots against Athanasius. During Julian's reign, from 361 to 363, Jews aided pagans who rebelled against Christian control. Later they took part in the Persian persecutions of Shapur II when Archbishop Simeon of Ctesiphon was killed. According to the historian Socrates, Jews in Imnestar seized a boy during the Purim celebration, and fatally attacked him. Under the patriarchate of Cyril in *c.* 414, Jews in Alexandria killed a number of Christians; the next day encouraged by Cyril, Christians attacked local synagogues and killed those Jews whom they could find.

During this period Christians repeatedly attacked synagogues. In 388, for example, a Christian mob led by the bishop burned the synagogue in Mesopotamia; in Ipasa in Africa, the synagogue was seized and turned into a church; in Rome the synagogue was destroyed; at Antioch, the tomb of the Maccabees was converted into a church; in Edessa, a synagogue was seized; in Magona, Minorca, a riot broke out leading to the burning of a synagogue; in Palestine a group of monks under Barsauma attacked synagogues and massacred Jews.

By the fifth century, the status of Jews had been transformed. In the eyes of the Church, the Jew was regarded as a representative of Satan – an obstinate unbeliever, subject to God's wrath. Christian anti-Judaism had thus been accorded offical approval by the Church. Jewish souls could be saved, but only if they embraced Christ. Yet, those who remained obdurate were lost forever. The growth of Christian anti-Semitism from New Testament times was thus rooted in the conflict between these two rival faiths, both seeing themselves as the true Israel: both religions laid claim to being God's chosen people, the recipients of his revelation. Yet now that Christianity had become the religion of the empire, Jews were defenceless against the Christian onslaught.

FOUR

Medieval Anti-Judaism

During the Middle Ages Christian hostility to the Jews was a constant feature. During the Crusades Jews were massacred throughout western Europe, and the populace continually attacked those who remained loyal to the Jewish faith. Such animosity, embedded initially in New Testament teaching and later developed by the Church Fathers, was intensified by various charges levelled at the Jewish population. Throughout this period Jews were accused of murdering Christian children to use their blood for ritual purposes, of blaspheming Christ in the Talmud, and of bringing about the Black Death. Those who perished in such Christian onslaughts died as martyrs to the Jewish heritage, assured of divine reward in a hereafter.

CONTINUING CHRISTIAN HOSTILITY

On the basis of such claims for Jewish depravity and perfidy made by the Church Fathers in the early history of Christianity, Christians in the Middle Ages continued to vilify both Jews and Judaism. Although little is know about Jewish–Christian relations in the Roman period, in subsequent centuries church councils were anxious to promulgate decrees governing contact between Christians and Jews. As we have seen, the Church issued a series of decrees regarding the Jewish community, such as the *Codex Theodosianus*, promulgated in 438, and the *Justinian Code*, issued in 529, which denied Jews various rights. According to church officials, Christians were to be careful to avoid the pernicious influence of Jewry.

In the ninth century Archbishop Agobard of Lyons penned a number of anti-Jewish epistles in which he expressed alarm about contact with Jews. No matter how kindly we treat them, he wrote, we do not succeed in drawing them to the true faith. Rather, he continued, when Christians share food with them, they are often seduced by the Jewish faith. Some ignorant Christians claim that the Jews preach better than the priests; others celebrate the Sabbath with them. Labourers and peasants are thereby inveigled into a sea of errors and regard the Jews as the only people of God. With anger, Agobard complained that Jews also spread venomous stories about Jesus, the Virgin Mary and the apostles. As a consequence, Agobard recommended various remedies to protect Christians from the Jews. Twenty years later his successor Amolon reiterated these exhortations: no Christian, he believed, should serve Jews either in cities or villages, or eat their food or drink their liquors.

Yet, despite the vehemence of such protests, Christians had not at this stage accused the Jews of diabolical acts including profaning the Host, ritual murder and poisoning wells. Hence it appears that anti-Jewish propaganda in the ninth century had not reached the virulence of later anti-Semitism. Rather, it seems that Judaism had managed to attract a number of Christian believers. As a result prosperous communities emerged in Champagne, Lorraine and elsewhere, and Jews were granted a broad autonomy to administer their affairs. During this period Talmudic scholarship flourished along the banks of the Rhine and the Seine. In Troyes, the Jewish scholar Rashi composed commentaries on the Bible and Talmud. In general Jews mixed freely with the Christian population.

However, after the year 1000 rumours began to circulate about the 'prince of Babylon', who, at the instigation of the Jews, had destroyed the Holy Sepulchre in Jerusalem, persecuted Christians in the Holy Land and caused the patriarch of Jerusalem to be beheaded. As a result, princes, bishops and townsfolk sought revenge. In Rouen, Orléans, Limoges, Mainz and elsewhere Jews were converted by force, massacred, or expelled. At the end of the century, Pope Urban II at the Council of Clermont-Ferrand preached the First Crusade. As Christian knights, monks and commoners set out for the Holy Land, they launched an onslaught against Jewish infidels living in Christian lands.

In the Rhineland, where Jews were gathered in large communities, the most horrific massacre took place. On 3 May 1096 the first pogrom occurred at Speyer; when news of this event reached Worms Jews sought refuge in the palace of Bishop Adalbert or remained in their own homes. According to the chronicler Solomon bar Simeon, Jews caught hiding in the episcopal palace were put to the sword. Dying as martyrs, mothers killed their children, then fathers slaughtered their sons. All accepted the divine verdict, assured of reward in the hereafter. As they died a terrible death, they recited the ancient *Shema* prayer: 'Hear, O Israel, the Lord our God, the Lord is one.' Christians then stripped them naked and dragged them off except for those few who accepted baptism. In two days over eight hundred innocent victims were slain.

Several days later the Jews of Mainz were similarly attacked. According to the Christian chronicler, Albert of Aix, about seven hundred Jews died in this massacre. Initially they sought to defend themselves against forces far superior to their own. But aware of the hopelessness of their situation, the Jews took arms against their wives, children, mothers and sisters and killed each other so as not to fall into the hands of their enemies.

Even though bishops and noblemen, who benefited from their financial acumen, were anxious to protect the Jewish population in cities where they were under threat, thousands of Jews lost their lives at the hands of the mobs. Yet, despite these massacres, European Jewry resumed its former existence in the decades that followed. But in 1146 Pope Eugenius III and St Bernard of Clairvaux preached a new Crusade that led to further outbreaks of violence against Jewry. Again, Jewish communities in Cologne, Speyer, Mainz and Würzburg in Germany, and Carentan, Ramerupt and Sully in France were attacked. Later in the twelfth century the Third Crusade led to massacres in London, York, Norwich, Stamford and Lynn. Twenty years afterwards similar persecutions took place in the Midi during the Albigensian Crusade.

In 1236 when a further Crusade was proposed, fuelled by religious fervour, massacres took place in western France, England and Spain. In the next century such fanaticism led to uprisings in an abortive Crusade of 1309 in Cologne, the Low Countries and Brabant. This was followed by the Shepherds' Crusade in the Midi in 1320 which provoked outbreaks of anti-Jewish violence in Bordeaux, Toulouse, Albi and Spain. In general, such assaults followed the same pattern – looting of Jewish property, flight, failure to protect their Jewish citizens by local princes, fortresses taken by assault, mass suicide of the innocent Jewish victims.

During the eleventh century a number of chroniclers described the massacres of Jews by Christian crusaders. One anonymous chronicler writing a journal in his monastery in Prague succinctly commented that there was a massacre and Jews were baptised. In Würzburg an annalist stated that an enormous host coming from all regions and nations took up arms on their journey to Jerusalem and forced Jews to be baptised, massacring thousands who refused. Near Mainz over a thousand men, women and children were slaughtered. Commenting on the devastation that took place in Worms, the monk Bernold declared that the Jews were tempted by the devil, and killed themselves in the bishop's palace. Again, the chronicler Fruitolf stated that the crusaders killed or enforced baptism on the Jewish inhabitants of the villages through which they passed; yet, he continued, some Jews returned to the faith of their ancestors, just as dogs return to their own vomit.

Despite these reactions, there were some chroniclers prepared to deplore such massacres. The monk Hugon, for example, noted that the clergy were hostile to such acts of violence, a number of ecclesiastics even issuing sentences of excommunication on those who were involved, while various princes threatened retribution on their Christian subjects in an attempt to curtail similar onslaughts. In an anonymous Saxon chronicle, the author depicted those crusaders who devastated Jewry as the enemies of mankind. It was pitiful, he wrote, to see the heaps of bodies that were carried out of Mainz on carts.

Although public opinion was divided about the justice of the massacres, these events tended to inflame popular hostility towards the Jewish population. As a result, the massacres of 1096 marked the beginning of the deterioration of the status of European Jewry, a situation reflected in the religious literature of this period in which Jews were depicted in the most negative terms. For example, in the *Miracle de Saint Hildefonse* Jews are described as more bestial than naked beasts; they are hated by God, and therefore everyone must hate them. Conversely, in another text by the same author, *Les Miracles de Nôtre Dame*, a Jewish child touched by grace is described as wiser and much lovelier than all the other Jews; similarly, the wife of a rich Jew who embraces the Christian faith is described as brave and charitable.

A number of literary works of this period condemn Judaism and advocate conversion to Christianity. Thus in *Desputaison de la Sainte Église et de la Synagogue*, a Jew describes his desire to convert. Our foolish hope, he declares, was in vain, and expectation has deceived us as we waited for one who did not come. But the Messiah *has* come. Thus, he proclaims, 'I shall be baptised, and renounce my wicked sect.'

The Crusades and their aftermath thus brought into focus Christian contempt for those Jews who stubbornly clung to their ancient faith. In Christian eyes, they were villainous figures, descendants of the perfidious Jews depicted in the New Testament, the people castigated by the Church Fathers. Their only salvation lay in renouncing Judaism and embracing Christianity, either willingly or through forced conversion.

As a consequence of the passions unleashed against the Jews during the Crusades, by the twelfth century the Jewish community was charged with committing murder for ritual purposes. During the middle of the century Jews were accused specifically of killing Christian children and using their blood in the preparation of unleavened bread for Passover. The first case of ritual murder allegedly occurred in 1144 in Norwich, England. The body of a young apprentice was discovered in the woods on Good Friday, and a rumour spread that he had been murdered by the Jewish population in imitation of Christ's Passion. According to the accusers, the murder had been planned in advance by a group of rabbis who had met in Narbonne. Although the authorities gave no credence to this accusation and the sheriff attempted to protect the Jewish community, riots took place resulting in the death of a prominent Jew. These events gave rise to a local cult, and the relics of the murdered child, William of Norwich, became the object of pilgrimages.

In a parallel incident, in 1147 the body of a Christian was found in Würzburg during the preaching of the Second Crusade. Immediately the Jews in the city were accused of his murder, and several were tracked down and killed. Some years later a different charge was levelled at Jews, this time involving the alleged profanation of the Host. Describing these events, the chonicler of Liège, Jean d'Outremeuse wrote that at Cologne the son of a converted Jew went to church on Easter Day, where he received the Host; he took it in his mouth and then bore it to his house. There he became afraid, and in his distress made a hole in the earth and buried it. Eventually a priest came along, opened the hole, and found the shape of a child, which he intended to take to the church. But before he could do so, a great light came from the sky, and the child was borne up to heaven.

Although accusations of ritual murder were still relatively rare during this period, by the end of the century they had become more frequent. In 1171 at Blois, thirty-eight Jews were burned at the stake after a trial. In 1191 at Bray-sur-Seine, the number of victims reached a hundred. In the thirteenth century, numerous cases occurred. Eventually the emperor Frederick II convened a group of dignitaries to determine the truth of this allegation. Priests and prelates found the issue so vexing that they were unable to reach a decision, and the emperor then turned to converted Jews for a response. Converts from the cities of the empire travelled to his court and pronounced that there was nothing in the Hebrew Bible or the Talmud to support the claim that Jews used blood for such purposes. Rather, as they pointed out, Jewish law forbids such an act. As a result of this investigation, the emperor acquitted Jewry of this charge. Later, in 1247, Innocent IV issued a bull concerning this issue.

According to Innocent IV, the Bible enjoins Jews not to kill and forbids them to touch a dead body at Passover. Hence, they are wrongly accused of using the heart of a murdered child at Passover: such an action would be contrary to Jewish law. It is thus a mistake to accuse Jews of ritual murder when a corpse is found and deprive them of trial and judgment. In such a case, it is a mockery of justice when they are stripped of their belongings, starved, imprisoned and tortured. Yet despite such a pronouncement, accusations of ritual murder and the profanation of the Host nevertheless continued to circulate. In 1272 another papal bull was promulgated to stem such hostility. According to this bull (issued by Pope Gregory X), Christians fabricate false charges against Jews to provoke hatred and violence.

Although such decrees were designed to protect the Jewish population from attack, some Christians actively pursued the Jews. In Brussels, for example, the Jewish community was accused of profaning the Host in 1370 and about twenty Jews perished at the stake. Similarly, in 1473 a case of ritual murder was reported at Trent in the Tyrol, and nine Jews were arrested, tortured and executed. Subsequently, trials of Jews took place in Austria and Italy, resulting in expulsions and *autos-da-fé*.

During this period, Jews were thus victimized by Christians for allegedly perpetrating horrendous acts even though Church authorities had decreed that they were not responsible for such terrible deeds. By libelling the Jews in this fashion, the Jewish community was depicted as sadistic, thirsting for Christian blood. Predictably, such charges served only to inflame the passions of the masses, encouraging them to view Jews as evil monsters, intent on seeking revenge against their Christian neighbours.

In the face of such animosity towards Jewry, the Church issued two important decrees regarding the status of the Jewish population. In 1215 the Fourth Lateran Council declared that Jews of both sexes must be distinguished from other peoples by their garments. Moreover, Jews were forbidden to show themselves in public during Holy Week. Those who violated these laws would be punished by the secular powers. Enforcement of these provisions varied from country to country.

In France a circular badge of yellow cloth was worn, possibly in the form of a coin, a symbol of the Jews' perceived eagerness for money. The aim was to provide a humiliating and visible means of differentiating Jew from gentile. Between 1215 and 1370 twelve councils and nine royal decrees insisted on strict observance of this law. Philip the Fair made the badge a source of revenue; in 1297 the proceeds from the sale of these badges were fifty *livres tournois* from the Jews of Paris, and a hundred from Champagne. When King John the Good recalled the Jews to France after their exile, he ordered that the badge should be half red and half white, whereas the yellow used previously had symbolized wickedness and jealousy.

Throughout Europe measures were enacted to ensure that Jews were easily distinguishable from Christian subjects. In Germany a special kind of hat was worn rather than the badge. In 1267 the Council of Vienna deplored Jewish laxness in observing this decree. Texts from the fourteenth and fifteenth centuries refer to this hat as red and yellow, but in the following centuries a badge took its place. In Poland Jews had to wear a pointed green hat. In England they wore a series of strips of cloth sewn across the chest, often in the shape of the Tablets of the Law. In Spain and Italy a badge was ordered to be worn. In the fourteenth century it was common for artists to represent Jews, including figures from the Hebrew Bible, wearing such distinguishing marks. These various forms of garment impressed on the minds of gentiles the differences between Christians and Jews, encouraging them to view Jews as a different species.

During this period the Inquisition, under the control of the Dominicans, was charged with the responsibility of exposing heretical views. Anxious to uproot all heresies, the Dominicans took a special interest in the Jewish population. At the beginning of the thirteenth century, these protectors of orthodoxy were particularly agitated at the spread of Aristotelian ideas, which had exerted a profound influence on Christian thought through Arabic writings and translations of Greek philosophical texts. In 1210 and 1215 the Church, to curtail what it saw as the dissemination of heretical ideas about nature and existence, forbade the teaching of Aristotle's *Physics* and *Metaphysics*; in 1228 Pope Gregory IX deplored any contact with Greek philosophy. In the Jewish world similar hostility was expressed by the Jewish establishment towards Aristotelianism, and Maimonides' *Guide for the Perplexed*, which was based on Aristotelian ideas, was burned. Such antipathy towards philosophical speculation provoked two rabbis, Solomon ben Abraham and Jonah Gerondi, to ask why the Church did not concern itself with the writings of Maimonides, the author of impious works which, they believed, corrupted Jewish scholars. Since the Church was uprooting Christian heresies, they stated, why not uproot Jewish ones as well and order the burning of these wicked books?

As a consequence of such entreaties, the Inquisition took a special interest in Jewish religious texts, especially the Talmud. A Jewish apostate who had become a Dominican brother of La Rochelle, Nicholas Donin, went to Rome and informed Gregory IX that the Talmud was an immoral book and offensive to Christianity. In response, the pope urged the kings of France, England, Castile and Aragon as well as various bishops to investigate this claim. In France, Louis IX initiated such an examination and throughout the country copies of the Talmud were confiscated. In 1240 a debate took place in Paris between important scholars including Eudes de Châteauroux, Chancellor of the Sorbonne and Nicholas Donin on the Christian side, and Yehiel of Paris and Moses of Coucy on the Jewish side.

According to the Jewish account of this disputation, Donin argued that the Talmud contains various blasphemies against Jesus. Turning to other charges, Donin claimed that the Talmud permits Jews to spill the blood of gentiles. Donin then turned to passages in the Talmud that discriminate against gentiles. Jewish scholars countered such charges with quotations from Jewish sources, endeavouring to illustrate that, on the contrary, Judaism espouses a tolerant attitude towards Christians and Christianity. This dialogue between Donin and Yehiel was, however, not a real disputation but rather an interrogation in which Yehiel was given little scope to explain Jewish teaching about the status of non-Jews. As a result, the Talmud was condemned and burned. In 1248 a second commission, headed by the Dominican Albert the Great, confirmed the verdict of the first debate, arousing further animosity towards the Jewish population. In France the *Desputaison de la Sainte Église et de la Synagogue* dating from the same period concerned the 1240 controversy. According to the author, the Jews are poisoners of both the body and the mind.

Another important factor in the persecution of medieval Jewry was the hostility engendered by Jewish usury. In Carolingian Europe Jews acted as tradesmen; they were noteworthy in being the only merchants who maintained contact with the Orient. Then, from the tenth century onwards Venetians and Byzantines, followed by the Lombards, appeared in market fairs of Champagne and Flanders. During this period the economy was almost exclusively concerned with the barter of goods; commercial exchange involving money was rare. By the twelfth century, trade routes to Asia were opened to Europeans; as a result various types of products including spices, foodstuffs and luxury goods were carried by ship rather than by land, making them increasingly accessible. At the same time, cities began to develop and an exchange economy took the place of the economy of barter.

In such a milieu Christian merchants gradually replaced Jewish traders, a change largely driven by the massacres of the Middle Ages. Deeply shaken by this onslaught, Jews began to turn their property into possessions that could easily be converted in times of danger to gold or silver. Such legal tender was rare during this period, and their requirement for it led to the role of the Jew as moneylender. The tendency towards moneylending as the particular occupation of the Jew was initially opposed by rabbinic authorities, but later was viewed as inevitable. Just before the First Crusade, the biblical exegete and talmudic scholar Rashi condemned such a practice, while a century later the rabbis declared that no loans should be made to gentiles if it was possible to earn one's living in another way; however, if a Jew possesses neither fields nor vines, the lending of money at interest to non-Jews was necessary and therefore authorized.

The practice of usury, however, made the situation of the Jewish population increasingly perilous. In response to threats to their security, Jewish communities frequently sought the protection of princes, petitioning charters that afforded them temporary security while making them reliant on their good will. In this way, Jews became totally dependent on their protectors. As the British jurist Henry de Bracton stated, the Jew can have nothing of his own – all that he acquires becomes the property of the king. In this way the Jews live for others rather than for themselves. This medieval image of the Jew as moneylender contributed significantly to the negative stereotype of the Jew, a demonic figure preoccupied with finance.

In England, Jews arrived after the Norman Conquest and in the absence of local competition they became a tightly knit class of financiers. From the beginning they associated closely with the kings, handing on to royalty the notes of defaulting debtors in return for a share of the money due. In time a number of Jewish moneylenders became rich by advancing money to the aristocracy as well as the clergy. By the end of the twelfth century, Jews had created a monopoly, which was controlled by the Exchequer of the Jews: as a result, all transactions of loans took place in the presence of royal officials.

However, by the thirteenth century Jewish moneylending in England underwent a considerable decline, which was foreshadowed by King John's extortions during his conflict with foreign enemies and rebellious barons. In 1210 he demanded an enormous contribution from his Jewish subjects, which they were unable to meet. In response, he arrested a number of Jews including the wealthy Abraham of Bristol whose teeth were extracted one by one until he committed suicide. This was followed by expulsions of the Jewish population, followed by their readmittance. Finally, in 1290, the Jews were officially expelled from the country.

In France, a number of Jews similarly became rich through moneylending. However, with the accession of Philip II, Jewish life underwent a dramatic change. After becoming king, he had all the Jews arrested, releasing them only after they paid a ransom of 15,000 silver marks. Then he annulled all their credits except for a fifth share, which he took over. Finally, he ordered their general expulsion. In 1198, however, he decided to recall the Jews. Subsequently, Louis VIII extended the concept of personal authority over the Jews to the entire country; as a result, Jewish communities could be expelled or recalled according to the whim of the ruling powers. Jews were impoverished by both expulsions and confiscations of their property. In 1230, for example, the decree of Melun denied the validity of any debts owed to Jews; henceforth they could lend only to peasants, artisans and the poor whereas high finance passed over to the Caorsins and Lombards. Nonetheless, when in the early thirteenth century Jews were expelled by Philip IV, this caused an outcry on the part of those who depended on Jewish usury, and they were called back to France in 1315.

Unlike their coreligionists in England and France, German Jews were under the general protection afforded by the emperor. This relationship began during the period of the First Crusade, and gradually found expression in the concept of 'serfs of the imperial chamber' mentioned in a Golden Bull promulgated in 1236 by Frederick II, which cleared Jews of the accusation of ritual murder. Yet, despite such protection, Jews during the Middle Ages perceived their own existence as precarious, dependent on the good will of Christian neighbours whose passion was easily aroused against aliens living in their midst.

In the next century Jews were accused of bringing about the Black Death that ravished Europe from 1347 to 1350. According to Boccaccio's account of this event, in cities the population fell sick in their thousands; without care and aid, nearly all victims died. Eventually, he continued, the plague reached the point where no further notice was taken of a dying man than of cattle. Nor were villages spared from this scourge. Lacking the aid of a physician, poor and wretched farmers perished along with their families by day and night, on their farms or isolated homesteads, on the roads or in the fields. When this occurred, the people abandoned their customs; they no longer had any concern for their affairs or for themselves.

This calamity was the last in the chain of events adversely affecting the Jewish population. As medieval scholars relate, the plague was perceived as an unfavourable conjuction of the planets or a pollution of the air and poisoning of the waters. For the ordinary population, however, it was understood as a divine punishment, or the act of Satan who was in league with the Jews. In Savoy, for example, it was rumoured that a man named Jacob Pascal of Toledo allegedly distributed deadly drugs to coreligionists in Chambéry. On the order of Duke Amadeus of Savoy, Jews were arrested at Thonon, Chillion, Le Châtelard, and after being tortured, confessed to this crime.

From Savoy the legend spread to Switzerland, and trials followed by executions took place in Bern, Zurich, and near Lake Constance. Some of the consuls of Bern then wrote to German cities to warn them of this dreadful act. However, in Germany princes and magistrates sought to protect the Jews, and in September 1348 Pope Clement VI published a bull pointing out that Jews had died of the plague just as had Christians. Further, he indicated that the epidemic also broke out in regions where there was no Jewish population. Hence, there was no reason to charge the Jewish community with this crime.

Despite such observations, the German populace massacred Jews in Colmar, Worms, Oppenheim, Frankfurt, Erfurt, Cologne and Hanover. Moreover, Jews were also attacked for religious reasons. Bands of penitents, the flagellants, wandered from city to city, mortifying themselves to obtain the remission of sin. Leading an austere life and singing hymns, they travelled throughout Germany and France; their public exhibitions frequently led to a massacre of the local Jewish population. In the words of the chronicler Jean d'Outremeuse, cities were full of these individuals, who declared that their rites were more significant than the ceremonies of the priests and clerics. When these flagellants travelled through the countryside, it was commonly said that the plague came from the Jews and that they had poisoned wells and springs to destroy Christendom. As a consequence, there was a mass uprising against the Jewish population; they were put to death and burned in all the regions where the flagellants were to be found.

In Germany it was widely alleged that the Jewish community was largely immune from the plague: they did not perish from it, or they died in smaller numbers. Thus the chronicler Conrad von Megenberg reported that in many wells, bags filled with poison were discovered, and as a result of such accusations countless Jews were massacred in the Rhineland, in Franconia and in all the German countries. Yet, he himself was uncertain whether the Jews were responsible for this disaster. Vienna, he noted, contained a large Jewish population and so many Jews died there they were forced to enlarge the Jewish cemetery and purchase two more buildings. Surely, he stated, it would have been very stupid to poison themselves.

In fact, throughout Germany most major Jewish communities were devastated by the plague; indeed, the German Jewish population was so overwhelmed by this tragedy that in subsequent years a number of cities such as Speyer invited Jews to live in their midst with promises of protection and security, as did the Archbishop of Mainz. A codex published during this period, the *Meissener Rechtsbuch*, stipulates conditions favourable to the Jews: their synagogues and cemeteries are to be well protected, and Christians must aid them in the event of attack. Similarly, in France where expulsions and recalls had taken place throughout the century, the Jews were recalled by John II in 1361 under more favourable conditions. Eventually the Jewish population in these areas was renewed and Jewish fortunes revived.

The massacres of this period and those of previous centuries traumatized Jewish communities. Some of their reactions were incorporated into the Jewish liturgy; others served as the basis of religous chants (*selihot* and *kinot*) in the synagogue. In various chronicles of these centuries, animosity towards Jews was expressed in the most vehement terms. Thus, the chronicler Solomon bar Simeon recounted how the pope rose up and urged fellow Christians to unite to conquer the city of Jerusalem; en route they massacred Jewish communities, and so Solomon called for revenge. Similarly, the chronicler Eliezer ben Nathan declared: 'Strike our wretched neighbours sevenfold, punish them, O Lord, as they have deserved! Cause them distress and suffering, send them thy curse, destroy them!'

In addition, literary works of this period exhorted God to exhibit his divine justice against the Jewish people's enemies. Thus, in a poem about the martyrdom of Isaac, chatelain of Troyes, and his family who were tried for ritual murder, the author appealed to God for justice. Sinners have come for Isaac Cohen, he wrote. He says: 'What do you want of me? For God I will die. As priest, I will offer him the sacrifice of my body.' When he is held fast and told to convert to Christianity, he replies that he will not leave

God. Eventually he is thrust into a slow fire, and he prays to God beseeching divine vengeance on his foes. Determined to remain loyal to the faith of their ancestors, those who died in this terrible way cried out to God for revenge. Hatred and faithfulness were thus intermingled in the blood and tears of those who perished during this century of suffering.

THE MEDIEVAL ASSAULT

Embracing the negative stereotypes of Jews as expressed in the writings of the Church Fathers, the Church embarked on a sustained onslaught against the Jews throughout the Middle Ages. Under Islam, however, the Jewish population fared much better. In the sixth and seventh centuries the Arabs of the Arabian peninsula were polytheists living in nomadic tribes or settled in urban centres. At the beginning of the seventh century Muhammad, a caravan merchant from Mecca, denounced such paganism as a perversion of God's will. In the first phase of his preaching he stressed that biblical figures such as Abraham and Moses had been sent by God to warn humankind to abandon idolatry. Those who rejected this message were destroyed except for Jews and Christians who had transmitted the revelations given them in the Torah and the Gospels. Initially, Muhammad hoped to convert Jews to this new faith, but the Jewish community refused to recognize him as a true prophet. This rejection led Muhammad to denounce the Jewish nation. According to Muhammad, the Jews distorted Allah's message, and their Scripture contains falsehoods. Islam is thus superior to Judaism, and Muhammad is conceived as the last and decisive apostle of God. Judaism is therefore a legitimate but incomplete religious system.

By 626 two Jewish tribes had been expelled from Medina and a third had been exterminated, except for women and children, who were enslaved. In 628 Muslims conquered the Jewish oasis of Khaybar to the north; there Jews were subsequently permitted to remain if they gave half their produce as a tribute to the Muslims. By 644 Syria, Palestine, Egypt, Iraq and Persia were occupied by Muslim soldiers. During the following century the Abbasid caliphate was at its height – the Islamic post-scriptural oral tradition was formed, and Muslim jurisprudence, philosophy, theology and science flourished.

At first widespread conversion to Islam was not encouraged: Jews along with Christians were recognized as Peoples of the Book and were guaranteed religious toleration, judicial autonomy and exemption from military service. In return they were required to accept the supremacy of the Islamic state. This arrangement was formally codified by the Pact of Omar dating from about 800. According to this treaty, Jews were restricted in a number of spheres: they were not allowed to build new houses of worship, make converts, carry weapons or ride horses. In addition, they were required to wear distinctive clothing and pay a yearly poll tax. Jewish farmers were also obliged to pay a land tax consisting of a portion of their produce. Under these conditions, Jewish life nevertheless prospered.

Under Christendom, however, the situation was vastly different. Initially the Church sought to protect the rights of the Jewish population. Thus in the sixth century Pope Gregory I insisted that the legal rights of Jews were to be respected even though he exhorted bishops actively to engage in proselytizing. Yet, despite such tolerance, in his sermons Gregory depicted the Jews as perverse unbelievers. In Spain, the Third Council of Toledo of 589 forbade Jews from owning Christian slaves, marrying Christian women, or holding public office. In the seventh century King Sisebut of Spain gave the Jews an ultimatum – they must either be baptised or go into exile. After Sisebut's death, a council presided over by St Isidore in the presence of King Sisinand ruled that force must not be used in baptism, but those who had received the sacrament must remain Christians and avoid relations with unbaptised Jews. In cases where the children of baptised Jews had themselves been baptised, they were to be taken from their parents to receive a Christian education.

Later in the seventh century the Spanish King Recesswinth denounced Judaism before the Eighth Council of Toledo as an abominable and detestable faith. As a consequence, it was agreed that the country should be rid of all unbelievers and blasphemers. Although the council did not pass new regulations, the king formulated a body of laws which stripped Judaism of its rights. All Jews were forced to sign a lengthy oath which rendered the observance of Jewish law impossible. Violators of this decree were to be burned or stoned and Christians were warned against aiding or protecting Jews. Later, the ninth Toledan council of 655 ruled that baptised Jews must spend all Jewish and Christian festivals in the presence of a bishop.

Subsequently King Erwig of Spain enacted twenty-eight laws that severely constrained Jewish existence, and towards the end of the century, King Egica decreed that Jews must abandon commerce and surrender all property acquired from Christians. In 694 the seventeenth council accused

Jews of conspiracy, reduced them to slavery, banned all Jewish rites, and ordered Jewish children above the age of seven to be taken and reared as Christians.

In France various councils during the sixth and early seventh centuries legislated regarding Jewish–Christian relations, prohibiting mixed marriages, preventing Jews from eating with Christians, and Judaizing. In addition, Jews were barred from public office and from holding positions of authority. Repeatedly, attempts were made to enforce conversion such as the Frankish King Dagobert had perpetrated in the seventh century.

During the Carolingian period, however, the situation of Jewry underwent considerable change. In Charlemagne's reign in the eighth century Jewish status improved, a development that came to fruition in the reign of Louis the Pious in the ninth century when he granted Jews letters of protection. During his reign was established the position of *Magister Judaeorum* whose function was to guarantee Jewish rights.

Such tolerance, however, led to a profound reaction. As we have seen, Agobard, Archbishop of Lyons, was deeply concerned about the implication of allowing social relations between Jews and Christians and incensed about the favours the emperor had bestowed upon the Jews. In his writings he condemned the Jews because of what he held to be their superstitious practices and blasphemy and complained about the sacriligeous charges they made about the Christian faith. Jews were accused of cursing Christ, vaunting their royal favours before Christians, effecting a change of the market day from Saturday so adversely affecting worship, building synagogues, stealing Christian children and selling them to Arabs. In a letter to the Bishop of Narbonne, he charged Jews with seducing Christian women and concluded by describing Jews as accursed and covered with malediction which, he claimed, had penetrated them as water in their entrails and oil in their bones. They are, he continued, cursed in the city and cursed in the country, cursed in their coming in and in their going out.

Echoing such sentiments, his successor Amulo wrote a letter, *Liber Contra Judaeos*, which describes Jewish belief as detestable and goes on to demonstrate the fallen state of Jewry on the basis of Scripture, Church councils, and the writings of the Church Fathers. Jews were charged with blasphemies against Christianity, and Jewish tax collectors were accused of seeking to influence impoverished Christians to convert.

Thus the seeds of hostility towards the Jews sown in the New Testament and nurtured in the writings of the Church Fathers reached their fruition during the first millennium of the history of Christianity. Yet, the Crusade of 1096 marked a central turning point in the history of Jewish–Christian relations. Peasants, monks, knights and nobles set off in their thousands to free the Holy Land from the Muslim infidels; en route they turned against the Jews. Typical was the reaction of crusaders from Rouen, as reported by the chronicler Guibert of Nogent who declared: 'We desire to combat the enemies of God in the East; but we have under our eyes the Jews, a race more inimical to God than all the others.'

Along the Rhine crusaders urged on by preachers such as Peter the Hermit and Count Emicho offered Jews the option of conversion or death. Rather than undergo baptism, many Jews committed suicide; typically, Jewish parents killed their own children and then themselves to sanctify God's name. As the crusaders made their way east, massacres took place at Trier, Neuss and Ratisbon, and in cities along the Rhine and the Danube, in Bohemia and then in Prague. Finally, in Jerusalem in 1099 the soldiers of Godfrey of Bouillon discovered Jews assembled in a synagogue and set it ablaze. From January to July 1096 it is estimated that about 10,000 Jews died in this onslaught. In the wake of this slaughter, a cult of martyrdom was instituted whereby Jews who gave up their lives to sanctify God's name were revered by the community, and recollection of their sacrifice came to be incorporated in the synagogue service.

In 1146 the Second Crusade brought about the same suffering, though on a smaller scale because of the intervention of Emperor Conrad III, Louis VII, as well as the bishops. In this instance, economic motives were added to religious fervour. As we have observed, Jews were involved in moneylending, evoking antipathy from both clergy and laity. Pope Eugenius III who initiated the Crusade suggested to princes that crusaders should be absolved of their debts to Jews. In France, Jewish debts were cancelled without accompanying violence; in Germany, however, a French monk Radulph went about preaching that Jews were enemies of God and should be persecuted. The mobs aroused by such inflammatory rhetoric were responsible for the deaths of many Jews. When Archbishop Henry of Mainz called upon St Bernard for help in restraining these Christians, he agreed that Jews should not be harmed but neither should they collect interest on crusaders' debts. Yet, not all clerics agreed with St Bernard. Peter of Cluny, for example, wrote Louis VII a letter urging the king to punish the Jews for their infidelity. They defile Christ and Christians, he wrote. The Crusade should be financed from their monies. Even though they should not be killed, they should be made to suffer fearful torments and be prepared for ignominy, for an existence worse than death.

In this milieu, the imperial protection of the Jews that we have observed served to enslave the Jewish population and increased their vulnerability. The Crown viewed them as serfs of the imperial chamber (*servi camerae*). Even though this status was intended to provide a means of protection, it became a device for enriching the monarchy. Living a marginal existence in a feudal system, Jews became increasingly dependent on the whims of their overlords. Jewish rights were temporary and could be withdrawn at any time. Hence, Jews were treated like property that could be bought, loaned and sold.

By the end of the twelfth century a number of Jews engaged in moneylending, exacerbating their precarious position in society. Understandably, those who were compelled to pay high rates of interest were bitterly resentful of those who lent them money. Though protected by princes, Jews were subject to repeated outbursts of hostility. When the anger of the mob reached its height, kings often abandoned their Jews rather than face the wrath of their Christian subjects. By the end of the thirteenth century, Jews were expelled from France, England and most of Germany, resulting in the cancellation of debts. In this way economic motives were combined with religious fervour directed at so-called Christ-killers and those who debased the Christian faith.

Jews were also subject to accusations of murder that further inflamed the Christian population. Indeed, the charge of ritual murder became a constant feature of the Middle Ages. Beginning in the twelfth century in Norwich, the accusation spread to other English towns including Gloucester, Bury St Edmunds, Bristol and Winchester, and to Würzburg in Germany during the Second Crusade. At the same time, Jews were accused of desecrating the Host in Belitz, also in Germany. This charge was continually repeated, often prior to an onslaught against local Jews. In time, the harassment of Jews became so serious that both the emperor and pope convened a group of Jewish converts to investigate the charge of ritual murder. In his Golden Bull, the emperor prohibited this accusation, and in 1247 Pope Innocent IV also issued a bull exonerating Judaism from this charge. Yet, despite such interventions, it was widely believed that Jewish communities were guilty of such crimes, and alleged victims became objects of popular devotion.

As we have noted, religious feeling in the Middle Ages was also provoked by charges made against the Talmud. Opponents of Judaism, including

Jewish converts such as Nicholas Donin, sought to demonstrate that the Talmud was offensive to Christian sensibilities. When church commissions ruled against this sacred text, cartloads of copies of the Talmud were burned. Subsequently, many popes reiterated this condemnation. Such public trials of the Talmud contributed to the poisoning of Jewish–Christian relations during this period.

In the fourteenth century, animosity towards the Jewish population reached even greater heights when Jewry was condemned for causing the Black Death. For Jews, this event was a tragedy of the most serious magnitude. Throughout Europe, Jews were subject to assault by the Christian populace, who believed that by poisoning wells Jews sought to destroy Christian civilization. In southern France, the entire population of a town was burned. From there this allegation spread to northern Spain, to Switzerland and then into Bavaria, along the Rhine, into eastern Germany, and to Belgium, Poland and Austria. Frequently, local town councils put their Jews on trial. When confessions were obtained under torture, Jews were subject to increasing violence. Again, economic motives played a significant role in this onslaught. Confiscations of debts and property followed the death of Jews residing throughout Europe. Religious motives were ever present. During this period flagellants roamed throughout Germany and France, stirring up negative feelings towards Jewry. Over two hundred communities were destroyed in this assault.

Hence, we can see that Jews in the Middle Ages living under Christians were subject to the most terrible calamities. They were hated by their Christian neighbours, and charged with the most heinous crimes. Even though a number of Christian leaders sought to protect the Jewish population from attack, Jewish suffering increased with the onset of the Crusades. In addition, Jews were frequently accused of killing Christian children and were also charged with blaspheming the Christian faith in the Talmud. As a result, this sacred text was cast into the flames. Further, Jews were blamed for causing the Black Death by poisoning wells. Yet, despite such an onslaught, many Jewish martyrs went to their deaths confident that their tormentors would be punished eternally for their sins.

FIVE

The Demonic Stereotype of the Jew

During the Middle Ages, the negative stereotype of the Jew came to be incorporated into Western folklore. Jewry was continually depicted as possessing the attributes of the Devil. As the personification of evil, Jews were viewed as a sub-species of the human race. In addition, they were seen as sorcerers, able to work magic against the Christian population, a belief that served as the basis for the charge that Jews killed Christian children and used their blood for ritual purposes. Because of such allegations, the populace attacked Jews in their pursuit of demons, and in such onslaughts thousands of innocent victims lost their lives.

THE DEVIL AND THE JEWS

Throughout the Middle Ages, antipathy towards the Jewish populace was a central feature of Christian literary and artistic compositions. In all literary genres, including satires, legends and ballads, Jews were ridiculed and portrayed in the most hideous manner. In a French satire of the fourteenth century, for example, a Parisian Jew is depicted as falling into a public latrine. When other Jews came to his aid, he begged them not to pull him out. 'Today is the Sabbath,' he cried out. 'Wait till tomorrow, so as not to violate our law.' They agreed and departed. When this incident was related to King Louis IX, he ordered his men to prevent the Jews from removing their coreligionist from the latrine on the Lord's Day. 'He has observed the Sabbath,' he stated. 'He will observe the Lord's Day as well.' But when the men came to rescue him on Monday, they discovered he had died.

After the Black Death, there were hardly any Jews left in the Low Countries, but many works were written in which they are mentioned. Some poems referred to the case of profaned Hosts in Sainte–Gudute in 1370; other described a ritual murder, where Jews were portrayed as 'wicked and cruel as dogs. Brutally they seized the child; threw him down and trampled him. . . . The filthy Jews, stinking dogs, inflicted several wounds with daggers and knives.' In England, Jews were expelled in 1290;

nonetheless, various literary works refer to their iniquity. In about 1255 the story of ritual murder appeared, giving rise to twenty different versions of a ballad entitled 'Sir Hugh or the Jew's Daughter'. In the latter half of the fourteenth century, Geoffrey Chaucer incorporated the theme of ritual murder in his *Prioress's Tale*. In Italy the theme of a pound of flesh connected with a merciless creditor was transformed into a story, *Il Pecorone*, by the Florentine author Ser Giovanni Fiorentino – this work later inspiring Shakespeare's *Merchant of Venice*.

These motifs were also to be found in religious drama which inspired further anti-Jewish sentiment. In scenes from the New Testament presented in the vernacular Jews were portrayed in the most terrible fashion. Repeatedly, playwrights sought to emphasize the greatness of Christianity in contrast with the pitiful nature of Judaism. Frequently Jews are described in these plays in the vilest terms: 'false Jews', 'false thieves', 'wicked and felonious Jews', 'perverse Jews', 'disloyal Jews', 'traitorous Jews', 'false and perverse nation', 'false and cursed race'.

As a result of such characterization, it became acceptable to portray sadism on the stage, including torture and rape. In some cases miracle plays ended with a final scene in which Jerusalem was destroyed by the Romans: having become a Christian, Titus conquers Jerusalem and burns the city to avenge the Virgin Mary. In other plays, the scene is contemporary. Thus in *Mistère de la saincte hostie*, a Jewish usurer forces a Christian debtor to give him a piece of the consecrated Host. He then attacks it; the Host bleeds but remains intact. Witnessing this miracle, the Jew's wife and children are touched by grace, denounce the Jew, and plead to be converted. The Jew subsequently also asks for baptism, but instead is condemned. He dies calling for 'his book', and utters imprecations: 'O Devil, I feel I am burning; Devils, devils burn and flame; I flare and flame in every limb; I perish now in fire and flame; My body, mind and soul burn now and fiercely consume; Devils come speedily, and carry me off from this ordeal.'

Accounts of miracles concerning the Holy Virgin have been preserved from this period which describe the profaning Jew. In addition, mystery plays dramatizing the Passion evoked strong reactions from audiences. In the German mystery play, *Alsfelder Passionspiel*, for example, two devils plot the betrayal of Jesus. The play unfolds with the dealings between Judas and the Jews. The payment of thirty pieces of silver is agreed, although each party seeks to cheat the other. During the Crucifixion itself Caiaphas says to Jesus: 'Take off your clothes. . . . Lie down on the Cross; and stretch out

your feet and arms.' One of the executioners then asks for three heavy
nails, a hammer and tongs. He orders that Jesus' hands and feet be bound
and that he be laid out along the Cross. The play continues with Christ's
sufferings while the Jews present rejoice and mock him.

In a French mystery play, *Mistère de la Resurrection de Notre-Seigneur,
Jésus-Crist*, it is the Jews themselves who are made to inflict sufferings on
Christ. One of the torturers comments: 'See the blood streaming; And how
his whole face is covered.' Another adds: 'Here, false and bloody man;
I pity not your pain, more than that of a vile trickster; That nothing avails,
he is so low'; and another: 'Let us play at pulling out his beard, that it is
too long anyway.' A bystander states: 'I have torn at him so hard, that the
flesh has come away too.' One of those involved in this torment is made to
exclaim: 'See what a clump this is, that I pull away as if it were lard.' In
contrast to these perfidious Jews, Pilate expresses his disapproval: 'His
martyrdom so displeases me,' he states, 'that I can scarcely endure to see it.
Yet regard these Jewish lords, watching what this man endures. See the pain
that overcomes him. He bears the worst of all evils.' Inevitably, such
frightful depictions had a powerful effect on the assembled crowds,
inflaming their hatred against the Jewish populace living in their midst.

The animosity between Christian and Jew as portrayed in such scenes
finds its counterpart in the architecture of the Middle Ages. Repeatedly, the
Church was represented as a resplendent virgin compared to the Synagogue
which was depicted as a fallen widow, depictions that appeared on
numerous tympana (as on the tympanum at Strasbourg Cathedral) and
stained-glass windows. In many cases the two rival personifications were
presented symmetrically, while in later examples Christ is flanked on one
side by the Roman centurion Longinus who, at the foot of the Cross, was
blinded by true faith; on the other side is the Synagogue, which bears a
sponge soaked in vinegar in an attempt to poison Christ's wounds.

At the end of the fourteenth century, Italian artists also identified the
Jews with scorpions. In paintings and frescoes, this creature appears on
standards, shields and tunics of the Jews. German painters of this period
associated the image of the sow with Jews, giving them suck and
fornicating with them. One of these depictions is described by Martin
Luther in his pamphlet *Vom Schem Hamephoras*: 'Here in Wittenberg, on
our church, a sow is carved in stone. Some young piglets and some Jews are
suckling her; behind the sow is a rabbi. He raises the sow's right leg, with
his left hand he pulls out his member, leans over, and diligently

contemplates, behind the member, the Talmud, as if he desired to learn something very subtle and special from it.'

In the fifteenth century, witch-hunting flourished in the mountainous regions of Savoy, Switzerland and Germany. In 1484 Pope Innocent VIII observed in his bull *Summis Desiderantes* that the Teutonic territories were filled with representatives of the Devil. The German inquisitors Sprenger and Institoris published a tract, *Malleus Maleficarum*, and inquisitors held trials throughout the land. During this period, Christians suspected one another of being Satan's agents, and the Devil was increasingly understood as an individualized person who roamed the earth in search of victims. Possessing horns, talons, a tail, and wearing a goat's beard, this evil black figure gave off a strong odour. The Devil was everywhere working evil, sowing hatred, pronouncing spells, and possessing individuals. His chief agent on earth was the witch, a woman of impurity, weakness and temptation.

In line with this description of the Devil and the demonic realm, Christians came to believe that the Jews united in their persons the attributes of the Devil and those of the witch. Depicted as having horns, tails and the beard of a goat, they were said to emit a terrible odour (*foetor judaïcus*). They were thus perceived as possessing extraordinary powers, while at the same time they were depicted as weak and sickly, suffering from overwhelming afflictions that only Christian blood could cure. Further, they were seen as born misshapen, haemorrhoidal; in addition both men and women were said to be afflicted with menses. In short, for the masses the Jew was understood as less than human, possessing all the attributes of evil.

Such imagery is reflected in the accusations of ritual murder made against the Jewish community in Trnava, Slovakia, at the end of the fifteenth century. The traditions of the Jews, it was alleged, explain that Christian blood is an excellent means to cure the wound produced by circumcision. This blood permits them to prepare a dish that wakens mutual love. Suffering from menstruation, both men and women have noticed that the blood of a Christian constitutes an excellent remedy against affliction. Finally, by virtue of an ancient and secret commandment, Jews are obliged to offer yearly sacrifices of Christian blood.

Hence, throughout the Middle Ages, Jews were seen as personifying evil. Dabbling in the occult, they were associated with Satan and the demonic realm. Often they were depicted as the Devil himself; alternatively, they were seen as agents of Satan. It is not surprising, therefore, that the Jewish community was relegated to a sub-species of humanity and butchered without any sense of guilt. As vermin of the earth, polluters of blood, they were considered a contagion on the body of Christian Europe.

Throughout the Middle Ages, Christians viewed Jews as sorcerers, able to cast spells against their enemies. Since the Devil was perceived as the source of such power, Jews were viewed as his earthly associates. As a result, the Christian masses attacked the Jewish population, believing that Jews were able to work magic against them. In September 1189, for example, an onslaught took place against Jews living in London fuelled by such belief. At the occasion of the coronation of Richard I, a Jewish delegation brought gifts and pledges of allegiance to the king. However, when they were accused of casting spells against him, they were driven from the palace and attacked by crowds. This incident was followed by repeated attacks on the Jewish population throughout the country.

In the mind of Christians, every Jewish act was conceived as a demonic device for working magic against gentiles. Hence, in Paris at the beginning of the thirteenth century, the custom of casting earth behind one after a funeral evoked a charge of sorcery. Again, the practice of washing hands when returning from the cemetery aroused similar suspicions. Responding to such charges, the rabbinic establishment suspended a number of Jewish practices. In this atmosphere of suspicion, the *mezuzah* (a piece of parchment fixed to a doorpost and inscribed with biblical passages) was viewed with fear: because of the danger of Christian retribution Jews in the Rhineland were compelled to cover them. As a thirteenth-century writer commented: Christians act out of malice; they stick knives into *mezuzah* openings and cut up the parchment. In some cases Christian officials actually used the *mezuzah* for magical purposes. At the end of the fourteenth century, for example, the Bishop of Salzburg asked a Jew to give him a *mezuzah* to affix to the gate of his palace as a talisman.

In the field of medicine, Jewish doctors were also believed to work magic, and were often called upon by Christians to perform miracles even though such a practice was condemned by popes and synods. According to tradition, demons were viewed as responsible for disease, and magic was therefore seen as an effective cure. When the ministrations of Jewish physicians proved successful, these individuals were respected and feared. However, if the patient died, the doctor was held accountable for murder, a charge linked to the generalized belief that Jews sought to poison Christians. Physicians in particular were accused of this crime, but Jews in general were regarded as guilty as well.

So widespread was this belief that in 1550, when the Polish king Sigismund Augustus demanded of Ivan IV that he allow Lithuanian Jews into Russia to help the economy, Ivan replied that it would not be advisable to permit Jews to come with their goods to Russia because they would import poisonous herbs into the realm. Similarly, in the same century Martin Luther speculated that if the Jews could kill Christians, they would gladly do so. Indeed, he continued, those who profess to be physicians were often responsible for such deaths. Because they are knowledgeable about medicine, Jewish physicians can administer poison to a patient that will kill him in an hour, or in ten or twenty years, as the physician chooses. Not surprisingly, such attitudes had led to the massacre of thousands of Jews in the previous century when the Jewish population was accused of bringing about the Black Death.

A further charge levelled against Jewry was that sorcery was practised in connection with the Eucharist. The Christian doctrine of transubstantiation meant that the mutilation of the Host was conceived as a heinous crime. According to various accounts, Jews attacked the Host in different ways. In addition, some reports related that Jews created an image of Christ from wax, and through their magic art transmitted various tortures to both Jesus and his followers. It was alleged that such sympathetic magic was also used to inflict suffering on Church leaders. Hence in 1066 the Jews of Trier were accused of having formed a wax image of Bishop Eberhard which was baptised by a priest whom the Jews bribed and was later burned on the Sabbath. It was alleged that as a result the bishop became ill and died.

The accusation of ritual murder was also linked to Jewish sorcery. During the Middle Ages a wide range of occult remedies specified the use of human flesh, blood, entrails, hands and fingers. In addition, menstrual blood was considered especially efficacious. In the light of such practices, the Jews were accused of using Christian blood for magical purposes. One of the earliest references to this practice was made by Thomas of Cantimpre in the thirteenth century, in which he alleged that Christian blood was used by Jews to cure haemorrhages. In 1235 the Jews of Fulda were charged with killing five children and confessed that they did so to obtain their blood for healing. In Matthew Paris' account of the murder of Hugh of Lincoln by Jews in 1255, the allegation was made that the intention was to use his bowels for divination. At the beginning of the fifteenth century the city Council of Freiburg requested that Jews be expelled from the city because the Jewish community periodically murdered a Christian child. These examples illustrate that the suspicion of magic lay behind the charge of ritual murder: the notion of using blood to make Passover matzah was a later refinement of this accusation.

During the Inquisition, gentiles who were brought before tribunals confessed to a wide range of magical practices: the adoration of Satan, the desecration of the Host as well as other consecrated objects, the sacrifice of infants, cannibalism, and the use of human ingredients in various salves and potions. In addition, they confessed to creating wax images baptised in their names and to the crime of poisoning. This catalogue of crimes served as the background to the charges levelled against Jews during the Middle Ages. The Jews were an alien, strange and mysterious people with whom the majority of Christians had little contact. It is not surprising, therefore, that the Jewish nation was regarded as guilty of the most heinous and diabolical practices.

Even though the legend of Jews as sorcerers was a Christian invention, it is true that Jews did conduct a range of magical practices throughout the Middle Ages. From the geonic period in the sixth century CE Jews engaged in such practices based on mystical and Gnostic sources. Those who practised magic were familiar with various methods of inducing disease and death, arousing and quenching passion, and employing demons for various purposes. As in the Christian community, Jews believed that sorcerers could alter their shape and assume the forms of wolves, hares, donkeys and cats as well as transform their victims into animals. Further, it was widely believed that the soul of a magician could travel to distant places and then return to his body.

In such an atmosphere, where hatred and mistrust and fear were constants, the concept of a witch became a central preoccupation. In various thirteenth-century sources, witches are depicted as having dishevelled hair, flying at night, and feeding on the blood and flesh of infants and adults. Accompanied by demons in the form of animals who carry out their designs, they cause havoc and instil fear in their victims. Thus Menahem Ziyuni, in his commentary on the Bible written in 1430, observed that there are both men and women who possess demonic attributes; they smear their body with secret oil and fly off over seas, rivers, forests and brooks. Since they must return home by sunrise, their flight follows a predefined course. Anyone who trespasses upon their meeting place is likely to suffer harm.

Even though Jews were interested in magical practices, they were excluded from the gentile fraternity of sorcerers and witches. The witch-cults blasphemed various Church rites in their own ritual, and such observances would have had little meaning for Jews. Moreover, demonic practices of this period were based on Satanic worship, whereas Jewish magic functioned in the context of the Jewish faith, which excluded any association with God's arch-enemy. Medieval Jewish magic instead focused on the power of good, which was invoked by calling on the names of God and the angelic powers. Jewish magic was thus rooted in the Jewish tradition and exhibited none of the anti-Church elements fundamental to Christian magic. In general Jewish magicians were God-fearing, pious individuals who were faithful to the tradition. Within the ranks of Jewish wonder-workers were scholarly individuals who had received a thorough training in Hebrew and Aramaic as well as rabbinic literature. Such study enabled them to invoke God's names in order to bring about magical cures. Jewish women, too, served as magicians, healers of wounds, and makers of love-potions.

While Jews are known to have worked sympathetic magic during the Middle Ages, it appears not to have been intended to harm or kill anyone. Instead, it was commonly employed to force thieves to return stolen objects. In such cases, the image of a suspected thief was drawn on a wall, and nails were struck into it in order to force him to confess. Another use of this procedure was to arouse passion. In a fifteenth-century work in Hebrew and Yiddish, instructions were given to take virgin wax and make a female figure with the sex organs clearly delineated to resemble those of the person in mind. The figure should then be buried and covered, so that its limbs remained unbroken, and left for twenty-four hours. The object should then be retrieved and reburied, this time under leaves, great care being taken to ensure that no one witness this act. It should then be covered with a stone so that it does not break. When the object is disinterred, it should be dipped carefully in water three times, first in the name of Michael, second in the name of Gabriel, and third in the name of Raphael. It should then be immersed in urine and dried before being pierced in the heart with a new needle to arouse passion.

Another popular magical device was the amulet, which was worn on the body or attached to objects and animals. Jewish amulets generally consisted of written texts or objects such as herbs, foxes' tails, and stones. A Talmudic amulet widely used in the Middle Ages was a stone which was believed to prevent miscarriage. In a related practice, a person born with a caul was instructed to wear an amulet at all times as a protection against the demonic realm. In later centuries it became common to hang a piece of the *Aphikomen* (part of the unleavened bread eaten during Passover) in the home or to carry it in a pouch as protection against evil spirits. In other cases, a metal plate was inscribed with the letter *heh* (a symbol of the Tetragramaton, a Hebrew name of God). Written amulets were also used to protect a person from the evil eye and evil spirits.

These examples illustrate the pervasiveness of Jewish magic and superstition during the Middle Ages. Yet even though sorcery became an important aspect of medieval Jewish life, it had a fundamentally different character from that which was claimed by Christians who accused the Jewish population of nefarious activities. Jews never saw themselves as agents of the Devil. Instead, Jewish practices were designed to protect the community from evil. Thus, it was a mistake to view Jews as demonic figures with evil designs on the Christian population.

Nonetheless, believing in the demonic power of the Jewish people a number of clergy encouraged the persecution of the Jews. Thus the fifteenth-century preaching friar and miracle worker, Vincent Ferrer, journeyed throughout France and Spain seeking to win converts. Leading a band of flagellants, he went to synagogues where he urged worshippers to accept Christ. This scourge of the Jews persecuted Jewish communities throughout Spain. In Toledo, for example, he and his followers burst into a synagogue, expelled the congregation, and renamed the place the Church of the Immaculate Virgin. Another tormentor was the Inquisitor John of Capistrano, who travelled throughout Italy and Germany preaching about death, Hell and punishment. Initiating a campaign against Jews, he threatened princes who protected local communities. From 1453 to 1454 he conducted a series of ritual murder trials that resulted in the hapless victims being burnt at the stake.

Another leading figure and scourge of the Jews in this period was Bernardino of Siena, who encouraged a devotion to the Holy Name of Jesus, who believed that Jews conspired against Christians through usury and that Jewish doctors sought to ruin their health. His successor, Bernardino of Feltre, was equally scathing of the Jews. 'They bleed the poor to death and grow fat on their substance,' he stated, 'and I who live on the bread of the poor shall I then be mute as a dog before outraged charity? Dogs bark to protect those who feed them, and I, who am fed by the poor, shall I see them robbed of what belongs to them and keep silent? Dogs bark for their masters; shall I not bark for Christ?'

In the view of the Christian community, the Devil's hand was seen at work in the activities of the Jewish nation. The Jew stalked Europe, seeking Christians as his prey. In this environment of suspicion and hatred, Jewish doctors in particular were perceived as agents of the Devil. As we have noted, they were repeatedly cast as evil magicians, and consequently condemned by the Church. In the thirteenth century, for example, the Council of Béziers prohibited Christians from employing Jewish physicians on pain of excommunication. This prohibition was repeated by the Councils of Albi (1254) and Vienne (1267), and by a decree of the University of Paris (1301). Hence, even at the risk of one's life, it was forbidden to resort to Jewish medicine.

To forswear the assistance of Jewish medicine was not simply an act of abstinence but one of prudence since it was alleged that Jewish doctors sought to worsen the condition of Christian patients. In this context, it was claimed that Charles the Bald (Charles I), Hugh Capet, and even the Emperor Charlemagne were the victims of Jewish doctors. According to the Vienna Faculty of Medicine, the private code of Jewish doctors required them to murder one patient in ten. Thus Jewish physicians and usurers were seen as united in a common quest to rob Christians of their well-being. The Jew in the Middle Ages was therefore conceived as the demonic counterpart of the Christian saints; in the mythology of the Middle Ages Jews came to symbolize all that is evil and impure.

In the light of this conception of the Jew-Devil, Jews were depicted in chronicles of the period as predators who sought to destroy the entire life of the gentile communities in which they lived. Hated by their neighbours, Jewish people turned inwards and formed their own closed worlds. However, despite such isolation, they were unable to protect themselves from Christian persecution and massacre. When faced with the choice between death and conversion, many went to their deaths as martyrs. During the Black Death, it was reported by first-hand observers that they met their deaths dancing and singing, as gay as if they were on their way to a wedding. Neither mother nor father would convert, for the sake of their children. Instead, when they saw the burning fire, women and children leapt into it while singing.

In some cases Jews committed collective martyrdom for the sake of God's name rather than die at the hands of their Christian oppressors. Those who met their deaths in this way were convinced that they would be reunited with their loved ones in a future life. Suffering was thus diminished by the promise of heavenly reward. Rabbi Meir of Rothenburg counselled: 'Whosoever has taken the firm decision to remain loyal to his faith and to die, if he must, a martyr, does not feel the sufferings of torture. Whether he be stoned or burnt, buried alive or hanged, he remains without feeling, no moan escapes from his lips.' For those who faced death, the cult of the martyrs was an inspiration.

Some Jews, however, were unable to endure such a fate and converted instead. Yet subsequently many wished to return to the faith of their forefathers. For these apostates, there remained hope, as the fifteenth-century Talmudist Israel Isserlein explained. 'We must remember,' he wrote, 'that he who returns to Judaism imposes upon himself a continual penitence, for he turns his back upon the advantages and felicities from which he benefited as a Christian, and assumes the sufferings and persecutions which the Jew needs must endure. He did not have to bear this burden while he was a Christian, and in truth his fault is expiated when he assumes it of his own free will, with the sole purpose of again becoming a member of the Jewish community.'

All aspects of Jewish communal life reflect the atmosphere of suffering and misery undergone by generations of Jews during this dark period of their history. Traditionally once a year Jews observed the festival of Purim with gaiety, a religious act that afforded them the opportunity to celebrate victory over their oppressors in ancient times. Yet, even this annual celebration was forbidden by Christian authorities, and the ceremony was limited to a symbolic stamping accompanied by noises during the reading of the Scroll of Esther. On other days, amusements were often severely restricted. The secular theatre was forbidden, and card games were played only in exceptional circumstances. All ornamentation as well as gaiety in clothing were proscribed; instead, both men and women wore black or grey garments. In these and other ways the joyfulness of Jewish life was overshadowed by a sense of hopelessness and despair.

This period of misfortune was marked at the end of the Middle Ages by the transformation of Jewish quarters into ghettos with locked gates. Behind the ghetto walls, Jews withdrew into themselves, continually fearful of Christian hostility. Accused of sorcery and black magic, branded as agents of the Devil, Jews were imprisoned from the outside world. In this way gentiles believed they could be protected from the evil influence of Jews who sought to undermine their neighbours and destroy the fabric of Christendom.

THE SATANIC JEW

In previous centuries, the image of the Jew in the New Testament had provided the basis for Christian hostility. Jews were perceived as Christ-killers, and Judaism was viewed as the old covenant that had been superseded by a new dispensation. In the eyes of the Church, the Jews were guilty of carnality and spiritual blindness. As the enemies of God, they were being punished by being forced to live in exile and in degrading conditions. Yet they were not to be killed. In seeking to make sense of the continuing existence of the Jewish people, Christian theologians portrayed Jewry as a silent witness to Christian truth and as a group that would eventually convert to Christ at the end of time.

Such a conception was enshrined in papal thinking, as is evidenced in a letter from Pope Innocent III to the Count of Nevers written in 1208: 'So that Cain might be a wanderer and a fugitive over the earth,' he wrote, 'and yet not be killed by anyone, the Lord set a mark on him by making his head to shake. Thus, the Jews, against whom the blood of Christ calls out, although they ought to be killed . . . yet they had to be scattered over the earth as wanderers until their countenance be filled with shame and they seek the name of the Lord Jesus Christ.'

However, as time passed there developed a far more sinister concept of the Jew, which frequently led to violent measures against the Jewish populace undertaken by both rulers and the Christian masses. The Jew was not simply the denier of Christian truth; rather, he was satanic in nature. The connection between Jews and Satan was taken so far that Jews were thought to possess physical characteristics which aligned them with the Devil. They were perceived as having horns, tails and the beard of a goat, and could be recognized by their noxious smell, the *foetor judaïcus*. By the late medieval period, Jews were thus seen as different from the rest of humanity not only in their religious beliefs and practices, but also in terms of their physical characteristics. This demonic stereotype of the Jew laid the foundations for Nazi racial anti-Semitism in which metaphors of disease were combined with satanic personifications of the Jewish nation.

Given such imagery, it is not surprising that Christians believed Jews to be involved in a wide range of villainous activities. As satanic predators, they continually sought to destroy Christendom. Looking back over the charges brought against the Jewish populace, the claim that Jews engaged in ritual murder stems from the belief that Jews were murderers, agents of the Devil, and lacked any moral scruples. As we have seen, Jews were repeatedly accused of murdering Christian children to use their bodies for healing or magical purposes. Beginning in the twelfth century in Norwich, Jews were thought to murder Christian children to deride the death of Christ. As time passed, accusations of ritual murder multiplied in England, France and Germany. Invariably, such a charge was based on the link between the demonic realm and Jewish intentions.

The same background and rationale applies to the charge of Host desecration: repeatedly Jews were accused of stealing the consecrated Host in order to assault it and thereby torture Christ. This slander arose out of Christian belief in transubstantiation, the change whereby the actual body and blood of Christ are present in the consecrated Host and wine. Such a doctrine had been confirmed at the Fourth Lateran Council of 1215 and, as a result, the Eucharist had acquired a concrete character, and in its honour the feast of Corpus Christi became an official festival of the Church. In this light, the charge of Host desecration took on the same character as the ritual murder libel. In both cases, it was believed that Jews were agents of a dark satanic realm, instructed to carry out the Devil's wishes. Inevitably such a notion could only inspire horror and revulsion, thereby providing a pretext for massacres of the Jewish population.

The prevalence of such popular demonology also helps to explain Christian attitudes to the Talmud. As we have noted, the first confiscation and burning of the Talmud was due to the interference of Nicholas Donin, a Jewish convert to Christianity. At a public disputation in Paris, Donin pointed to numerous references in this rabbinic text which were offensive to Christian sensibilities. In scattered references, the Talmud refers contemptuously to *minim* (heretics) and *goyim* (non-Jews); in other passages Jesus is referred to in an insulting fashion. These and other negative portrayals of the Christian faith were regarded as the product of Jewish animosity towards Christianity. This, too, was the Devil's work. As a consequence, wagon loads containing thousands of volumes of the Talmud were consigned to the flames in the manner of heretics. In Christian eyes, the Talmud, which inspired the demonic desire to denigrate the true faith, was to suffer the same torment as Jews who lost their lives in the Christian onslaught.

Christian charges against the Jews concerning their responsibility for the Black Death should similarly be understood within this context. Just as Jews were intent on killing Christian children, stabbing the Host and desecrating Christianity, so they wished to poison Christian Europe. Again, this was the Devil's plan. For three years, between 1348 and 1350, Jewish communities were devastated by Christians who blamed them for this tragedy. Who else but the anti-Christ could have brought about this terrible plague? Confessions to this crime, extracted by torture, revealed that Jews allegedly used a mixture of lizards, spiders, frogs, human hearts and sacred Hosts to poison wells throughout Europe. This claim first gained credence in southern France where the entire Jewish community was burned; from there the rumour spread to northern Spain, Switzerland, Bavaria, the Rhineland, eastern Germany and then to Belgium, Poland and Austria. In some cases the local population put Jews on trial in advance of suffering their own outbreak of the plague; in most cases the pattern was the same: Jews were accused, tried, tortured, confessed, and then burned at the stake.

Given the Christian conviction that the actions of the Jews against the gentile population were carried out to fulfil their satanic role, Christian Europe was intent on expelling this alien people. By ridding Europe of its Jewish population, Christians were ensuring that Satan's evil influence would be curtailed. By the end of the thirteenth century, Jews had been expelled from France, England and most of Germany. Yet, it should be noted that motives other than the purely religious were implicated in the treatment of Jews during this tumultuous period. It is unquestionable that many of the massacres as well as expulsions that occurred throughout the Middle Ages were motivated by economic considerations. When Jews were killed or removed from their dwellings by force, debts owed to creditors were cancelled. In this way, debtors were able to rescue their situation by eliminating the cause of their financial distress.

Notwithstanding the indisputable fact that economic considerations played a significant role in the treatment meted out to the Jewish population, Christian anti-Semitism stemmed largely from the conception of the Jew as the demonic agent of Satan. As we have noted, the various charges levelled against the Jews during this period were the result of such a conception. Yet, historians of the Middle Ages repeatedly emphasize that there was no substance to the various allegations made against Jews. Regarding the blood accusation libel, for instance, scholars note that it would have been inconceivable for Jews to murder children and use their blood for ritual purposes given the halakhic prohibition against consuming blood. Further, the fact that various papal bulls exculpated Jews of this charge lends support to the view that such an allegation was simply the result of animosity and misunderstanding.

With regard to desecration of the Host, historians similarly claim that such actions would have been inconceivable. The spread of this rumour, they argue, was based entirely on hallucinatory fantasy. Jews would not have behaved in this way since they did not accept the doctrine of transubstantiation. Given that no credence was given to the Christian view that the consecrated Host was in fact Christ's body, it would have made no sense for Jews to stamp on the Host or drive nails into it, believing that in so doing they were actually torturing Christ. When 'bleeding Hosts' were discovered and held as evidence of such desecration, it is far more likely that such disfiguration was simply caused by a fungoid organism or other natural causes.

Again, historians of the period are anxious to dismiss the charge that Jews sought to kill their neighbours by poisoning wells. In 1348 Pope Clement VI issued a bull which called into question this allegation, and chroniclers of the period noted that since many Jews succumbed to the plague it is ridiculous to think that Jews would have poisoned themselves. Rather, bubonic plague was spread by rats – hence Jews were entirely blameless. Confessions obtained through torture do not in any way constitute proof of Jewish involvement.

It must be asked, however, if Jews were in fact totally innocent of the heinous and horrific crimes attributed to them. In all likelihood, such charges were grotesque fantasies. Yet, it is not impossible that isolated individuals, overwhelmed by hatred, actually did engage in these practices. It is conceivable, for example, that some Jews did steal the Host and disfigure it, believing that by committing such sacrilege they were avenging themselves on their enemies. Likewise, it is not impossible that there were Jews who did murder Christian children out of revenge for the loss of Jewish lives. There is no historical evidence that these incidents took place, but such actions would be consonant with the prayers of Jews during this period for divine vengeance, such as that of the chronicler Solomon bar Simeon who proclaimed: 'O God of vengeance, O Lord God of vengeance, appear! It is for thee that we have let ourselves be slaughtered every day. Return sevenfold the wrongs of neighbours so that they may curse you! Before our very eyes let the nations be punished for the blood of thy servants that they have shed.'

SIX

Jew-hatred in Western Europe

In the fourteenth century Jewry was expelled from France; nonetheless, stereotypical images of the Jews in the popular imagination, in church teaching and as represented in art and architecture continued to fuel hostility and contempt for the Jewish nation. In catechisms, lives of Jesus and canticles the Jewish people were portrayed as demonic in character. In addition, tracts denouncing Jews as tools of Satan circulated throughout the country. Similarly, in England Jews were vilified even though the Jewish community had been expelled in 1290. German Jews were also detested during the post-medieval period – hostility most powerfully expressed by Martin Luther in a series of diatribes. These publications were followed by numerous tracts which denigrated both Jews and Judaism. Hence, even though court Jews occupied important roles in Germany, the Jewish masses continued to experience considerable adversity.

JEWRY IN POST-MEDIEVAL EUROPE

In France the expulsions of the Jewish population during the fourteenth century ensured the removal of Jewry from most French territory. Nonetheless, at the beginning of the sixteenth century groups of Marranos – Jews who had converted to Christianity but secretly practised Judaism – were found in Bayonne, Rouen, Nantes and Bordeaux. Yet, even though Jews had largely disappeared from French life, the negative image of the Jew persisted in society. As in medieval times, Jews were viewed as rapacious usurers, anxious to gain money by shady dealings, and the figure of Judas in the New Testament was associated in the public mind with deviousness and treachery.

These stereotypes were sustained and strengthened within the home where children were initiated into the Christian faith. There they were taught of the alien people who had infected French society and were guilty of committing the most heinous crime: the murder of Christ. In parish schools the catechism was taught; in it Jews were presented as wicked and deceitful. Typical of such catechisms was that of Abbé Fleury, which over the course of two centuries went through more than one hundred and fifty editions. In it a series of questions was asked about the Jews: 'Did Jesus have enemies? – Yes, the carnal Jews. To what point did the hatred of Jesus' enemies go? – To the point of causing him death. Who was it who promised to hand him over? – Judas Iscariot. Why was this city [Jerusalem] treated in this way? – For having caused the death of Jesus. What became of the Jews? – They were reduced to servitude and scattered throughout the world. What has become of them since? – They are still in the same state. For how long? – For seventeen years.'

Within this context, Judas was conceived as symbolic of the Jewish people, and Jews were viewed as agents of Satan. Moreover, in the lives of Jesus and the saints as well as in accounts of pilgrimages, Jewry was presented in the most terrible manner. In a typical depiction of the life of Christ from the fifteenth century, Jews are portrayed as malicious torturers of Christ: 'Some insulted him; others, with the backs of their hands, struck his noble and gentle mouth; others spat into his face . . . others tore out his beard or pulled at his hair, and thus trampled under their accursed feet the Lord of the angels. . . . And still spitting into his noble countenance, they struck his head with a stick, so that the thorns of his crown sank into his head and made the blood flow down his cheeks and over his forehead. . . . Pilate commanded that in this shameful and inhuman state he be led before all the Jewish people, who had remained outside in order not to sully themselves on the day of the Sabbath. But these accursed sons of the Devil, all cried out with one voice: "Take him away, take him away, crucify him. . . ."'

During this period the medieval accusations of blood libel and desecration of the Host were also current, and in various texts Jews were presented as inhuman in character. They were described as 'a monstrous people, having neither hearth nor home, without a country and of all countries; one of the most fortunate in the world, now the evil spirit and the detestation of the world: wretched, scorned by all, having become, in their wretchedness, by a curse, the mockery of even the most moderate.' Some writers stressed that they are to be punished for their iniquity: 'Death in sin, death with sin, death even, as it often happens, by sin. . . . That is God's most terrible weapon in the arsenal of his wrath; that is what the Son of God threatens the Jews with today.'

Such hatred of the Jew was also inflamed by canticles, such as that composed in the seventeenth century by Grignon de Montfort, which was based on a medieval mystery of the Passion. Its bloody imagery was designed to evoke bitter animosity towards the race that had tortured and killed the Saviour of humanity. Jesus is flagellated as an innocent victim: 'He is covered with wounds; his blood flows in rivulets; overwhelmed with bruises; his flesh falls in strips.' He is then crowned in thorns: 'He is crowned with thorns; with blows of a stick; everyone makes faces at him; shrieking like a demon; this cruel crown pierces his skull; the brain oozes out; with blood and sweat.' Jesus is then crucified: 'This insolent rabble; again tears everything from him; his poor bloody robe; sticks everywhere to his skin.' A refrain recounts his misery: 'O cruel savagery! His limbs are broken; his flesh is all bruised; his nerves are laid bare.' Finally Jesus is buried: 'O abominable sinners; it is done, Jesus is dead; we are all guilty; what is our fate to be? It is for us, O sinners; that he died in such pain.' Such imagery was designed to provoke audiences to fury even in the virtual absence of Jews from French society.

Despite such anti-Jewish sentiment, no onslaught took place against the Jewish population in France during the period of the Reformation. This was largely due to the fact that Protestants, rather than Jews, were then the target of Catholic hostility and contempt. Nonetheless, in the seventeenth century, an incident concerning the Guild of the Fripiers (old clothes dealers) provoked considerable anger towards Jewry. When the guild members were on guard duty, they passed the Church of St Eustache. A young bystander, John Bourgeois, the son of a merchant, mocked them saying: 'There go the gentlemen from the synagogue.' In response, the men of the guild attacked him. Later, a complaint was lodged against the Fripiers by John Bourgeois and one of them was arrested. Determined to avenge this act, the young man was set upon and killed by the Fripiers.

As a result of this outrage, political pamphlets were distributed that discussed this incident, attributing Jewish descent to the Fripiers. Initially, prose tracts were published, such as *A monitory letter published by all the parishes of the City of Paris, against the Jews of the Synagogue: A simple and true account of the cruel murder and horrible massacre committed on 26 August 1652*, and *A scrutiny of the life of the Jews, of their religion, trade and associations*. One of these tracts declared: 'There is no one who does not know that the Jews are the opprobrium of all nations and have been so for sixteen hundred years and more. . . . Their customs show their malediction no less than their bondage. There is no one who does not know that they have no other profession in life than usury, and that their false witnesses and their infamous practices have shown corruption the world over.'

Other tracts contained verse denunciations of the Jews reminiscent of medieval Christian tracts: 'Infamous murderers, detestable nation; abhorred by men, everywhere rejected. Must you today renew the effort of your horrid cruelties, which put to death the God by whom we live?' Other such works accused the Jews of demonic practices: 'Demons from hell, race of the Jews, detestable men, more accursed than Lucifer, and more wicked than all the devils, cruel tigers, be gone, unworthy as you are to live among us, when you thirst so for blood.' As in previous centuries, these pamphleteers linked current religious themes with contemporary events.

In other texts, remedies were suggested for dealing with this villainous people, recalling the medieval practice of expulsion as well as the differentiation of Jews from gentiles: 'Cast out from our walls people of such evil ways. Or, by the king's command, make them wear a sign that distinguishes them from Christians, and sets them among the dogs.' Another text proposes that they should be hanged: 'Let them be seen, hands and feet bound, those of their horde following closely the footsteps of him whom they laid low by a death all too cruel. Let them be seen on the scaffold with no favour, grace or pardon.'

It was also suggested that Jews be castrated so that the Jewish race be eliminated: 'I believe it is more fitting that the steel arrange matters differently. And that there be removed from them entirely that member which in them is already imperfect. In order that in punishment of their vice, they may survive their torment, and that according to our just desires, their name here on earth perish with them.'

These texts demonstrate the intense anti-Jewish feeling that persisted into the post-medieval period. Profoundly influenced by Christian motifs of previous centuries, the authors of these pamphlets continued to lay the charge of deicide against the Jewish community, viewing the Jewish nation as corrupt and dangerous. Even though a number of French humanists of this period advocated a more tolerant policy, prejudice was rampant and anti-Jewish stereotypes continued to perpetuate the demonic image of the Jew. Even such a sympathetic figure as Blaise Pascal, who admired the sincerity of Jews, observed: 'It is a wonderful thing, and worthy of particular attention, to see this Jewish people existing so many years, always in misery, for it is necessary as a proof of Jesus Christ, both that they should continue to exist, and that they should be miserable because they crucified him; and though to be in misery and to exist are contradictory, they nevertheless still exist in spite of their misery.'

Turning to England, the Jewish community was expelled in 1290 but there is evidence that non-baptised Jews entered London illegally in the fourteenth and fifteenth centuries. In 1498 Henry VII took an oath not to allow Jews into his dominions, a decision that was observed by his successors. However, in 1540 a Marrano colony was established in London, only to be dispersed two years later. Subsequently in the sixteenth century Henry VIII consulted Italian rabbis concerning his desire to divorce Catherine of Aragon, who had previously married his elder brother, Arthur, Prince of Wales. The king had hoped that the biblical view concerning levirate marriage might allow him to obtain a divorce. Such contact led to an interest in Hebrew studies in England, and several converts from the continent served as tutors to Christians.

In the seventeenth century a number of Puritans converted to Judaism; others insisted that Jews should be permitted to settle again in England. Once the monarchy was overthrown and Oliver Cromwell acceded to power, the issue became more pressing, particularly since a small ex-Marrano colony had been established in London. Determined that Jews be allowed to resettle in England, a Dutch rabbi, Manesseh ben Israel, met Cromwell, and a special commission consisting of clerics and representatives of the City of London was appointed to consider the proposal. Even though Cromwell was well disposed to the idea, this suggestion provoked considerable opposition.

An opponent of this plan, William Prynne, expressed considerable alarm at the possible re-entry of Jews into the country. In a pamphlet, *A short Demurrer to the Jews' long discontinued Remitter into England*, he described the general agitation about this scheme:

As I kept on my way . . . in Lincolns-Inne Fields, passing by seven or eight maimed soldiers on stilts, who begged me; I heard them say aloud one to another, 'We must now all turn Jews, and there will be nothing left for the poor.' And not far from them another company of poor people, just at Lincolns Inne back gate, cried aloud to each other: 'They are all turned Devils already, and now we must all turn Jews.' Which unexpected concurrent providences and speeches, made such an impression on my spirit, that before I could take my rest that night, I perused most of the passages in our English Histories concerning the Jews' carriage in England, with some of their misdemeanours in other parts, to refresh my memory.

As the debate continued, Cromwell faced considerable resistance from various quarters: representatives of the clergy feared that society would be adversely affected by subversive views; London merchants were suspicious of Jewish competition. As time passed, public opinion, which was aroused by Prynne, became increasingly ill-disposed. At a public hearing a hostile crowd pressed into the stands. Eventually Cromwell ended discussion in a speech mocking his adversaries. In an account of the occasion, Sir Paul Rycant reported that Cromwell first reminded the ministers that the Scriptures announced the conversion of the Jews, and that there was only one means to this end: preaching. The Jews must therefore be permitted to live where the true Gospel was preached. Then he conceded that the Jews were the meanest and the most despised of all peoples. 'So be it,' he declared. 'But in that case, what becomes of your fears? Can you really be afraid', he asked, 'that this contemptible and despised people should be able to prevail in trade and credit over the merchants of England . . . ?' Matters then remained as they were and Jews were not officially allowed to resettle. Nonetheless, the Marrano colony in London was permitted to expand in numbers and construct its own place of worship.

As was the case in England, in post-medieval Germany Jews were detested. Thus in 1477 a burgher, Peter Schwartz, explained in terms reminiscent of previous centuries why they suffered persecution throughout the country: 'The Jews have been punished severely from time to time. But they do not suffer innocently. They suffer because of their wickedness, because they cheat people and ruin whole countries by their usury and secret murders, as everyone knows. That is why they are so persecuted, and not innocently. There is no people more wicked, more cunning, more avaricious, more impudent, more troublesome, more venomous, more wrathful, more deceptive, and more ignominious.'

Echoing such hostility, the scholar Johann Reuchlin criticized the Jews in more traditional Christian terms: 'Every day, they outrage, blaspheme, and sully God, in the person of His Son, the true Messiah Jesus Christ. They call him a sinner, a sorcerer, a criminal. They treat the sainted Virgin Mary as a witch and a fury. They call the apostles and disciples heretics. They regard us Christians as stupid pagans.' Theologians, who enveighed against Jewish usury, suggested that Jews be put to work.

During this period a converted Jew, Johannes Pfefferkorn, composed a pamphlet, *Der Judenspiegel*, demanding the suppression of the Talmud, and obtained consent from Emperor Maximilian to seize and destroy all copies of this work. Even though he was critical of Jewry, Reuchlin defended Jewish sources and sought to show that the Talmud and kabbalistic texts support the truths of Christianity. This conflict led to a widespread debate between Christian humanists and others, and all European men of letters sided with Reuchlin.

Paradoxically, however, their condemnation of Pfefferkorn was couched in anti-Semitic terms. As one of Reuchlin's supporters, Ulrich von Hutten, stated: 'Germany could not have produced such a monster [Pfefferkorn]. His parents are Jews, and he remains such, even if he plunged his unworthy body into the baptism of Christ.' According to the Dutch scholar Erasmus, 'Pfefferkorn is revealed to be a true Jew. . . . He appears quite typical of his race. His ancestors attacked Christ only, whereas he has attacked many worthy and eminent men. He could render no better service to his coreligionists than by betraying Christendom, hypocritically claiming to have become a Christian. . . . This half-Jew has done more harm to Christendom than all the Jews together.'

During this period, there were few gentiles who championed the Jews. Martin Luther was a notable exception. Initially he condemned the persecution of Jewry and instead encouraged tolerance. Concerning the controversy between Reuchlin and Pfefferkorn, he was critical of the confiscation of the Talmud and rabbinic sources. In a pamphlet, *That Christ Was Born a Jew*, he expressed sympathy for Judaism and the Jewish people.

However, when his early missionary efforts failed to draw Jews to Christ, he grew increasingly hostile, and in 1542 he published a tract, *Against the Jews and their Lies*, in which he attacked the Jewish nation for their mercenary nature. 'The Jews,' he stated, 'being foreigners should possess nothing, and what they do possess should be ours. For they do not work, and we do not give them presents. Nonetheless, they keep our money and our goods and have become our masters in our own country and in the dispersion. When a thief steals ten guelders, he is hanged; but when a Jew steals ten barrels of gold through his usury, he is prouder than the Lord himself!'

For Luther, the Jews are an unwanted pestilence, and were therefore repeatedly expelled from the countries in which they lived. 'No one wants them,' he wrote. 'The countryside and the roads are open to them; they may return to their country when they wish; we shall gladly give them presents to get rid of them, for they are a heavy burden on us, a scourge, a pestilence, and misfortune for our country. This is proved by the fact that they have often been expelled by force: from France . . . where they had a downy nest; recently from Spain . . . their chosen roost; and even this year from Bohemia, where, in Prague, they had another cherished nest; finally, in my own lifetime, from Ratisbon, Magdeburg, and from many other places.'

Repeating previous religion-based allegations against the Jews, Luther stressed that they are the most contemptible of all peoples: 'Know, O adored Christ, and make no mistake, that aside from the Devil, you have no enemy more venomous, more desperate, more bitter, than a true Jew who truly seeks to be a Jew.' Those who tolerate them will incur great loss: 'Whoever wishes to accept venomous serpents, desperate enemies of the Lord, and to honour them, to let himself be robbed, pillaged, corrupted, and cursed by them, need only turn to the Jews.'

On a practical level, Luther proposed a number of measures against this alien nation. 'Their synagogues,' he wrote, 'should be set on fire, and whatever does not burn up should be covered or spread over with dirt so that no one may ever be able to see a cinder or stone of it.' All this should be accomplished for the sake of the faith: 'This ought to be done for the honour of God and of Christianity in order that God may see that we are Christians, and that we have not wittingly tolerated or approved of such public lying, cursing and blaspheming of his Son and his Christians.'

Fearful of the pernicious influence of the Jewish community and the Jewish tradition, Luther argued that Jews should be denied their homes and religious literature and instruction: 'Their homes should likewise be broken down and destroyed. For they perpetrate the same things there that they do in their synagogues . . . they should be deprived of their prayerbooks and Talmud in which idolatry, lies, cursing and blasphemy are taught . . . their rabbis must be forbidden under threat of death to teach any more.'

Luther was also concerned with Jewish livelihoods: 'Passport and travelling privileges should be absolutely forbidden to the Jews. . . . They ought to be stopped from usury. . . . Let the young and strong Jews and Jewesses be given the flail, the axe, the hoe, the spade, the distaff, and spindle, and let them earn their bread by the sweat of their brow.' In conclusion, he stated: 'To sum up, dear princes and nobles who have Jews in your domains, if this advice of mine does not suit you, then find a better one so that you may all be free of this insufferable devilish burden – the Jews.'

Several months later, Luther published *Vom Schem Hamephoras* in which he attacked the Jews for their unwillingness to embrace Christ. Repeating medieval charges about the nature of Jewry, he wrote: 'It is as easy to convert the Jew as to convert the Devil.' And he stated, 'A Jew, a Jewish heart, are hard as stone, as iron, as the Devil himself. In short, they are children of the Devil, condemned to the flames of hell.'

For Luther, it was justifiable to inveigh against this despicable nation given their satanic character: 'Perhaps some merciful and holy soul among us Christians will be of the opinion that I am too rough with these poor and pitiable Jews, mocking and deriding them. O Lord, I am much too feeble to mock such devils. I would do so, but they are much stronger than I am in raillery, and they have a God who is a past master in this art; he is called the Devil and the wicked spirit.'

Reflecting on the reasons why Jews are so skilful, Luther used imagery drawn from the New Testament to indicate their perfidious nature: 'I cannot understand how they manage to be so skilful, unless I think that when Judas Iscariot hanged himself, his guts burst and emptied. Perhaps the Jews sent their servants with plates of silver and pots of gold to gather up Judas' piss and other treasures, and then they ate and drank his offal, and thereby acquired eyes so piercing that they discover in the Scriptures commentaries that neither Matthew nor Isaiah himself found there, not to mention the rest of us cursed *goyim*.'

Repeatedly, Luther argued that Jews are in league with the Devil, and should therefore be despised: 'I cannot understand it except by admitting that they have transformed God into the Devil, or rather into a servant of the Devil, accomplishing all the evil the Devil desires, corrupting unhappy souls, and raging against himself. In short, the Jews are worse than the devils. O God, my beloved father and creator, have pity on me who, in self-defence, must speak so scandalously of thy divine and eternal Majesty, against thy wicked enemies, the devils and the Jews.'

When faced with anti-Jewish sentiment in the sixteenth century, Yosel of Rosheim sought to protect the rights of his coreligionists by interceding with the government. He was successful in preventing the expulsion of Hungarian and Bohemian Jews, and he convened a rabbinical conference that adopted a code of ethics regulating commerce about which he stated: 'I shall cause this programme to be observed if the authorities do what is necessary to let us live in peace, to put an end to the expulsions, to permit us to move about, and to curtail their bloody accusations. For we too are human beings, created by almighty God to live beside you on the earth.'

During the next century German Jewish communities followed the traditional Jewish way of life with court Jews playing a major role in state

affairs. In each royal and princely court there was a Jewish auxiliary.
Emperor Leopold, for example, summoned Samuel Oppenheimer from
Heidelberg, giving him responsibility for provisioning the army. A letter
composed by Oppenheimer and sent to a dignitary of the court illustrates
the nature of his undertakings: 'As long as I lived in Vienna', he wrote, 'I
provisioned almost every year, the two armies engaged against the French
and the Turks, supplying flour, oats, horses and money for recruits, as well
as munitions, powder, lead, cannon, artillery, wagons, horses, and oxen.'
Wherever they were employed, these court Jews administered finances,
provisioned armies, raised money, provided precious stones and textiles to
the court, founded new industries and established manufacturing
enterprises.

   In return for such necessary activities, both royalty and nobility
maintained social contact with these individuals. Thus Glückel von Hameln
was able to describe social relations between court Jews and their
employers. Of a marriage of court Jews with royalty in attendance, she
wrote: 'When the couple was standing under the canopy it appeared that,
in the confusion, someone had forgotten to write the *Ketubah* [marriage
contract]. What was to be done? All the nobles and the young princes were
already there and ready to watch the ceremony. The rabbi then said that the
groom must furnish a surety and promise to write the *Ketubah* immediately
after the marriage. And he read aloud the *Ketubah* from a book.' Following
the nuptial blessing, the nobles were led into the festival hall of Elias Cleve,
which was hung with gilded leather. There was a great table in the centre
which was covered with delicacies. The nobles were then treated according
to their rank.

   These court Jews were at the pinnacle of the Jewish social hierarchy,
forming an elite class. However, the vast majority of Jews continued to live
in simplicity, often enduring considerable persecution. In Frankfurt, for
example, Jews were compelled to wear a distinctive symbol and were
forbidden to linger in the streets. Further, they were forbidden to walk in
pairs, use certain streets, or appear during Christian festivals. In the city of
Hamburg, the number of guests allowed to attend a wedding banquet was
limited, as were the types of presents to be given and the food served. Later,
in 1726, the Court of Vienna declared that only the eldest son of a Jewish
family could marry within the law; the other sons were obliged to remain
bachelors. This policy was adopted in Bohemia and Moravia, and later in
Prussia, the Palatinate and Alsace.

The printing press became a crucially important invention of this age, making it possible to popularize various works on Judaism that denigrated the Jewish faith and the Jewish nation. By the eighteenth century, nearly a thousand such publications were in circulation including missionary treatises designed to convert gentiles, as well as tracts designed for the Jewish population. In addition, studies of Jewish customs and tracts dealing with the Jewish problem were written, some of which appeared to the Jewish population as anti-Semitic. There were also polemical works including *The Enemy of the Jews; The Scourge of the Jews; Jewish Practices, a Study of their impious Life; A Brief Catalogue of the Horrible Jewish Blasphemies; The Inflamed Poison of the Dragons and the Furious Bile of the Serpents;* and *The Jewish Baths, in which is publicly shown the secret practices and Jewish knavishness, how they drink the blood of Christians, as well as their bitter sweat.*

Reaffirming the medieval myth of the wandering Jew, *The Brief Account and Description of a Jew Named Ahasuerus* was published in 1602 and went into numerous translations. Thus originated the myth of the wandering Jew who witnessed the Crucifixion, and was condemned by Jesus to wander endlessly until the time of the Last Judgement. Moreover, a number of studies were published which sought to demonstrate that anti-Christian heresies and blasphemies existed within Jewish sources. I.A. Eisenmenger's *Judaism Unmasked, a True and Accurate Report*, a further example of this trend in the seventeenth century, contributed to the perpetuation of this malignant story. After it was published, the intervention of the Jewish community led to its suppression although a second edition was nevertheless published in 1711. Despite such antipathy, German Jewry was not subjected to the violent outbursts of modern times.

THE REFORMATION AND THE HOLOCAUST

During the Middle Ages Christendom had been unified by both belief and practice. However, the Protestant Reformation of the sixteenth century led to the disintegration of the medieval world-view. With Luther's rejection of papal authority, the Church's order was undermined. This call to reform the existing order was taken up by princes, serfs, merchants and peasants. The Hundred Years' War resulted in the transformation of feudalism into a new system. The Reformation thus had a progressive impact on Western society and culture, and it might be expected that this upheaval would have resulted in the amelioration of the lot of the Jewish community.

As we have seen, however, the Jewish population did not benefit from this quest to return the Church to its biblical foundation. Although it might have been expected that humanistic ideals would animate Christian consciousness, leading humanists did not embrace principles of liberation and tolerance. Even such figures as Johannes Reuchlin did not champion the Jewish cause although he was respectful of rabbinic sources. Instead of demanding their freedom of expression, he was convinced that the plight of the Jewish community was a punishment for their rejection of Christ and he looked forward to their eventual conversion. Even Erasmus was bitterly critical of the Jews, fearing that the revival of Hebrew learning might lead to the revival of the Jewish faith.

Because society was inherently Christian, the Jews continued to be perceived as a threat. Although tolerance was a Christian virtue, it did not extend to the Jewish community. Thus, even though humanists revived interest in the Hebrew language, they remained loyal to the tradition of Judaeophobia which animated Christian life through the Middle Ages. Pre-eminent among the enemies of the Jewish tradition was Martin Luther, whose primary impulse was to convert the Jewish nation. When this effort failed, his rhetoric paralleled that of the early Church Fathers who denounced both Judaism and the Jewish nation. Drawing on the stereotypes of the past, Luther condemned the Jews as agents of Satan as well as instigators of social and economic corruption.

Luther initially issued a strong statement in defence of the Jews: *That Jesus Christ Was Born a Jew*. In this work Luther addressed the Church's policy towards the Jews, urging that Christians adopt a brotherly attitude to their Jewish neighbours since Jesus was a Jew and so that they might convert to the true faith. Previously, he stated, the Jews had been mistreated by church leaders: 'They have dealt with the Jews,' he stated, 'as if they were dogs rather than human beings; they have done little else than deride them and seize their property. When they baptise them they show them nothing of Christian doctrine or life, but only subject them to popishness or mockery.'

Luther, however, believed that such attitudes should be rejected if the Church were to be successful in drawing Jews to Christ. 'If we really want to help them, we must be guided in our dealings with them not by the papal law but by the law of Christian love. We must receive them cordially, and permit them to trade and work with us, that they may have occasion and opportunity to associate with us, hear our Christian teaching, and witness our Christian life.' For Luther, the Jews did not constitute a threat to Christian life. Indeed, he viewed the Jewish community in a positive light.

Eventually, however, Luther completely reversed this policy of defending the Jewish community. In the 1540s he came to believe that the Church was living in the last days – his major objective was to ensure that the Gospel witness would be maintained. For Luther, there was an unholy Satanic alliance embracing the pope, heretics, Turks and Jews. Hence, he had no reason to express toleration of the Jewish populace. By this stage Luther believed he could discern the dangerous influence of Jews in society – in 1538 he received confirmation and elaboration of rumours that throughout Christendom Christians were having themselves circumcised and were following Jewish observances. Some had even become convinced that the Messiah was yet to come.

Further, Luther was persuaded that Jews blasphemed Christ and sought to destroy Christian civilization. Influenced by a work written by a Jewish apostate, Anthony Margaritha, in which he alleged that Jews daily ask God to destroy the Roman Empire, uproot all Christian authorities and, through letter manipulation, curse Christ, Luther was convinced that Jews slander the very things which Christians regard as precious. Bitterly he criticized 'the lies, the blasphemy, the defamation, and the curses which the mad Jews indulge in so freely and wantonly against the person of our Lord Jesus Christ, his dear mother, all Christians, all authority, and ourselves'.

In this altered context, Luther virulently attacked Jewry in his later tract *On the Jews and their Lies*. As we noted, in this work he criticized Jews for their association with the Devil. In his view, Jewry does not constitute a specific race; rather its adherents are condemned because they carry out the work of the Devil. In combating this alien nation, Luther saw himself as engaged in a struggle with Satan. Thus, Luther's anti-Semitism has little in common with the racist anti-Semitism of later centuries. Nonetheless, the Judaeophobia of the Reformation period and the racist policies of the Nazis exist on the same historical continuum. For the Nazis, Luther was perceived as a great anti-Semite, and his fame was exploited for their nefarious purposes. In 1938, for example, a German bishop justified mass violence against German Jews by invoking Luther's writings. And after the Second World War, a number of historians traced the essentials of Nazi racism back to Luther.

Viewed from this perspective, it cannot be denied that there are important parallels between Luther's stance and the policies of the Nazis.

As we have seen, when he asked what was to be done with Jews living in German lands, Luther replied that their synagogues should be set on fire, and that whatever does not burn should be covered or spread over with dirt so that no one may ever be able to see a cinder or stone of it. During the Holocaust, such a policy was repeatedly put into practice by the Germans, not for religious but for racial reasons. During *Kristallnacht* in 1938 in Leipzig, for example, the American Consul David Buffum reported: 'Three synagoges in Leipzig were fired simultaneously by incendiary bombs and all sacred objects and records desecrated or destroyed, in most cases hurled through the windows and burned in the streets.'

This was a scene repeated throughout the country. In Höngen, for instance, a nephew of the local butcher recalled:

After a while, the Storm Troopers were joined by people who were not in uniform; and suddenly, with one loud cry of 'Down with the Jews', the gathering outside produced axes and heavy sledgehammers. They advanced towards the little synagogue which stood in Michael's own meadow, opposite his house. They burst the door open, and a whole crowd, by now shouting and laughing, stormed into the little House of God. Michael, standing behind the tightly drawn curtains, saw how the crowd tore the Holy Ark wide open; and three men who had smashed the ark threw the Scrolls of the Law of Moses out. . . . Men had climbed on to the roof of the synagogue and were hurling the tiles down, others were cutting the cross-beams as soon as they were bare of cover.

Continuing his diatribe against Jewry, Luther declared that the homes of Jews should likewise be destroyed. During the Nazi regime such a policy became a central feature of the assault against the Jewish nation. Again, during *Kristallnacht* Jewish property and homes were devastated. As Buffum observed:

The shattering of shop windows, looting of stores and dwellings of Jews which began in the early hours of 10 November 1938 was hailed subsequently in the Nazi press as a 'spontaneous wave of righteous indignation throughout Germany' as a result of the cowardly Jewish murder of the Third Secretary vom Rath in the German Embassy at Paris.

Not only did Luther advocate the destruction of Jewish property and places of worship, he recommended that Jews be deprived of their religious sources. Repeatedly during the Nazi campaign, German troops denigrated Jewish objects of worship. During the attack against Poland, for example, Jews were compelled to treat Jewish ritual objects with a lack of respect. Frequently German troops forced Jews to scrub lavatories with their prayer shawls. An eye-witness to the destruction of books in a rabbinical academy in Lublin recalled:

> We threw the huge Talmudic library out of the building and carried the books to the market place, where we set fire to them. The fire lasted twenty hours.

Concluding his attack, Luther called upon princes to rid their lands of a Jewish presence. For Luther, the aim was to eliminate this demonic element from their midst, and in propounding such a solution he believed he was acting in the best interests of the Christian population. The Jews – as deniers of Christ – were an embarrassment and nuisance. Despite his valiant efforts, this stiff-necked people refused to convert to the true faith.

Like Luther, Hitler viewed the presence of the Jew as a pernicious influence in society. Yet Hitler was not motivated by Christian principles. Instead, he considered that the Jews polluted society because of their racial character. The only solution to this racial problem was extermination. In a speech given to the Reichstag in 1939, Hitler declared:

> Today I will once more be a prophet! If the international Jewish financiers in and outside Europe should succeed in plunging the nations once more into a world war, the result will not be the Bolshevizing of the earth, and thus the victory of Jewry, but the annihilation of the Jewish race in Europe.

The links, then, between Luther and Hitler are not tenuous – despite their differences, they regarded Jewry as an undesirable pestilence in European society. Both sought to rid Germany of their presence. Hence, Luther's influence on the course of history in the twentieth century is unmistakable. While Hitler and his executioners acted out of racial rather than religious motives, the image of the Jew, which had evolved throughout Christian history and was perpetuated by Luther, served as the framework for Nazi demonology.

SEVEN

The Jews in Spain

Throughout the Middle Ages Jewry flourished in Spain, yet by the end of the fourteenth century the Jewish community had come to be regarded with suspicion and contempt. A large number embraced the Christian faith in order to escape attack. This change resulted in the disintegration of Jewish communal life. In the next century the Church embarked on a new form of persecution: the Inquisition, which was established under Ferdinand and Isabella. Determined to root out heresy within the Church, the inquisitors sought to purge *conversos* – Jewish Christians who were suspected of practising Jewish customs. Throughout Spain tribunals were created that used torture to extract confessions from the guilty. Those who refused to confess were burned at the stake. Finally, in 1492 the entire Jewish population was expelled from the country.

THE RISE AND FALL OF SPANISH JEWRY

In the Middle Ages Jews in Spain attained a high level of cultural achievement. In the tenth-century Spanish royal court the Ummayad caliphs employed the Jewish statesman Hasdai ibn Shaprut as court physician, administrator and diplomat. In addition he acted as head of the Jewish community and patron of Jewish scholarship. Cordova, the capital of the Ummayad caliphate, became a vibrant centre of Jewish civilization, attracting poets, grammarians and *yeshivah* students from throughout the diaspora. In later centuries Jewish theologians, philosophers and mystics made major contributions to learning.

By the fourteenth century, however, anti-Jewish hostility had spread across the Iberian Peninsula resulting in massacres in most Spanish villages. In 1321 the Shepherds' Crusade had devastating consequences for Spanish Jewish communities, and two decades later Jews were accused of bringing about the Black Death. From 1355 to 1366 civil war was waged in Castile between King Pedro the Cruel and his bastard brother Henry of Trastamara. Because most Castilian Jews were loyal to the king, Henry referred to Pedro as the

'Judaized king' who was controlled by the Jews. Eventually, it was rumoured that this Judaized figure was in reality a Jew who had been substituted for Pedro at the time of his birth, and was thus more illegitimate than Henry himself. As the community became ravaged by the war, the Jewish populace was seen as the cause of the social upheaval that was taking place.

Once Henry was victorious, the Cortes (legislature) met in Burgos and demanded that measures should be taken against the Jews. As the Jewish question became a burning issue of the day, the Cortes of Toro explained why the kingdom was in turmoil: 'Because of the great liberty and power accorded to the enemies of the faith, especially the Jews, in our whole kingdom, in the royal household as well as in the houses of the knights, the squires, and the nobles, and because of the high offices and the great honours which they enjoy, all Christians are forced to obey them and fear them and bow deeply to them, so that the councils of all the cities and of all places and all people are captives of the Jews and subjugated to them.' Jews, it continued, are an evil influence on society, enemies of the true faith: 'The Jews, evil and rash men, enemies of God and of all of Christianity, cause numerous evils and sow corruption with impunity, so that the greater part of our kingdom is tyrannized and ruined by the Jews, in contempt of the Christians and our Catholic faith.'

What was to be done to remedy such a situation? The Cortes of Toro demanded that there should be no Jewish officials or tax-collectors. Jews should be required to wear a distinctive insignia. They should be prohibited from riding on horseback and dressing luxuriously. All Jewish names should be changed if they were Christian in character. The degradation of the Jews during this period is reflected in numerous literary works. Chancellor Lopez de Ayala, for example, accused the Jews of being bloodsuckers in his satire, *Rimado de Palacios*: 'Here come the Jews all alike, and present their detailed writings, to drink the blood of the poor people, promising jewels and gifts to the courtiers.'

In the latter half of the fourteenth century, anti-Jewish legislation was instituted in Castile. Nonetheless, unlike Jews in other European lands, the Jewish populace did not turn inward behind ghetto walls. Rather, many Jews converted to Christianity as a solution to their plight. Hence, in 1380 a Cortes petition noted that Jews and Jewesses who had embraced the Christian faith needed to be protected from the Jewish community. In the same year the anguished Rabbi Shemtov Shaprut reflected that 'many of our coreligionists are abandoning our ranks and pursuing us with their arguments, trying to prove the truth of their faith to us with the aid of verses of the Holy Scripture and of the Talmud.' Thus Christian persecution of Spanish Jews resulted in apostasy rather than martyrdom. Paradoxically, this step eventually led to greater hostility and bloodshed once the Inquisition embarked on a quest to root out backsliding Jews who ostensibly became followers of Christ.

At the end of the Middle Ages, Seville had become the richest city in Spain. During this period the archdeacon of Ecija, Ferrant Martinez, had been inciting Christians against the Jewish community there. Even though he was ordered by the king to refrain from such agitation, he paid no attention, and for twelve years he preached anti-Semitic sermons, encouraging fellow Christians to expel Jews from the cities and to destroy their synagogues. Once Juan I, king of Castile and Barroso, had died, the Archbishop of Seville intensified his campaign against Jewry. On 6 June 1391 the Jewish section of Seville was attacked; the majority converted and the rest were massacred. In the same month assaults against the Jews took place in the other Andalusian and Castilian cities, eventually reaching Aragon and Catalonia.

Even though a number of rulers attempted to intervene to curtail such riots, their efforts were in vain. Throughout the country mobs murdered Jews and pillaged their property, believing they were acting in consonance with God's will. Even though some Jews remained loyal to their ancestral faith, in the face of such unmitigated aggression others accepted baptism, including a number of rabbis. Seeking to explain such an act of apostasy, Joshua Halorki, who later joined the ranks of those who embraced the Christian faith, adopting the name Jeronimo de Santa Fé, described the motives of these Jewish converts. In a letter to the rabbi of Burgos, Solomon Halevi, who had become a Christian, Halorki asked:

Did you perchance lust after riches and honours? Or did the study of philosophy cause you to change so radically and to regard the proofs of faith as vanity and delusion, so that you therefore turned to things more apt to gratify the body and satisfy the intellect without fear and anxiety and apprehension? Or when you beheld the doom of our homeland, the multitude of afflictions that have recently befallen us, which ruined and destroyed us . . . did it then seem to you that the name of Israel would be remembered no more? Or perhaps the secrets of prophecy have been revealed to you and the principles of faith . . . and you saw that our fathers had inherited falsehood . . . and you chose what is true and established?

In the midst of this religious turmoil, Spanish Jewry divided into two opposing groups: traditionalists viewed Jewish apostates with horror; they were traitors who had abandoned their people. Converts, however, regarded religious Jews with disdain: they were a constant reproach to their new way of life. Nonetheless, both groups were bound together by familial ties, and converts continued to live in their previous homes and carry on their trades as before.

However, in some cases these new Christians (*conversos*) became ardent persecutors of their former coreligionists. Hence, in July 1392 Henry III wrote to the municipal authorities of Burgos about the local Jews: 'The Jews of your *aljama* (community) have informed me that when they were attacked they left their homes in fear of death and took refuge in the houses of the best of you, where they live today in your safe custody, not daring to return to their houses in the *aljama*, for fear that certain Jews who now have become Christians will persecute them and do them harm.'

Two years later, *conversos* in Perpignan, southern France, incited hatred against local Jews, preventing them from returning to their homes. In some instances these converts turned over the assets of the Jewish community to the Church. In Jerez, for example, *conversos* donated the community's property to the Bursar of the Dominican monastery because of the benefits that they received from him. Similarly, in Lerida the synagogue became a church and was dedicated to St Mary of the Miracles.

Deeply troubled by such apostasy, the rabbi of Barcelona, Hasdai Crescas, struggled to rebuild Spanish Jewry with the help of the king and queen of Aragon. In 1393 he was given authority to create new *aljamas* in Barcelona and Valencia. In pursuit of this aim, tax exemptions were granted to all Jews in the cities of Aragon, an amnesty was granted to those who had sought refuge abroad, and a new constitution was drafted to protect the Jewish population. Crescas himself composed tracts attacking philosophical theology, which he regarded as undermining the Jewish community, as well as anti-Christian treatises.

Despite such efforts, Spanish Jewry continued to decline. This was due in part to the missionary activities of preachers such as Vincent Ferrer. In his sermons, which Jews were compelled to attend, he stressed that Jesus and the Virgin Mary were Jews. In his opinion God did not want conversion by force. Rather, he stressed, it should be obtained voluntarily. 'The apostles,' he wrote, 'who conquered the world carried neither lance nor knife. The Christians should not kill the Jews with knives, but with their words.'

Travelling through Aragon, Castile and Gascony, Ferrer preached against the Jews, and as a result mobs of Christians attempted to convert the Jewish population by all available means, despite Ferrer's words of caution. In 1412 he succeeded in having the Statute of Valladolid passed. This forbade Jews from providing food for Christians, prefacing their names with the title 'Don', changing their place of residence, cutting their hair, and shaving their beards. Jews were also forced to wear simple clothing which displayed a badge of Jewish identity.

During this period Pope Benedict XIII summoned the Disputation of Tortosa in an effort to bring about mass conversion. Christianity was championed by the apostate Joshua Halorki (Jeronimo de Santa Fé) who was opposed by fourteen distinguished Jewish scholars of Aragon. The point at issue in this debate was whether the Talmud supported the view that the Messiah had appeared in the person of Christ. The Disputation attracted an enormous audience including numbers of Jews who at the close of each session confessed that they had been convinced by Halorki's arguments. As a consequence, 3,000 Jews converted to Christianity from 1413 to 1414.

Even though the *aljamas* underwent a considerable decline, Spanish Jewry experienced a period of tranquillity at the beginning of the fifteenth century. Two bulls promulgated in 1421 and the next year by Pope Martin V decreed that forced baptism should not be perceived as a proper form of conversion to Christianity; in addition, Jewish persecution was condemned. Under such newly favourable conditions, a number of Jews who had been forcibly converted sought to embrace Judaism; this could be accomplished by settling in North Africa or Portugal. However, such an option was not open to all Jews, and those who remained in Spain baptised their children.

These *conversos* remained aloof from the Christian community; some were circumcised as adults. Such a return to the Jewish faith was encouraged by the Fall of Constantinople in 1453 – this victory by the Turks was seen by many *conversos* as anticipating the fall of Edom and the deliverance of Israel. Hence, in Valencia a group of *conversos*, believing that the Messiah had just appeared on a mountain near the Bosporus, desired to emigrate to Turkey. As one of these converted Jews explained:

The blind *goys* [non-Jews] do not see that after we have been subject to them, our God will now see to it that we dominate them. Our God has promised that we will go to Turkey. We have heard that the Anti-Christ is coming; they say that the Turk is he, that he will destroy the Christian churches and will turn them into stables for the beasts and that he will bring honour and reverence to the Jews and the synagogues.

Some of these Jews successfully reached Constantinople; others were preparing to join them when they were stopped by the Aragon Inquisition in 1461. In any event, those Jews who practised Judaism in secret were haunted by a sense of self-reproach since they could not live in accordance with Jewish law. Overcome by remorse, their prayers expressed a strong sense of guilt:

Lord, I have failed Thee by my meanness and my unworthiness, ruled by my evilness and by my treason in spite of myself. Thou, who has visited me in true justice and hast cherished me like a son, see how I have fallen in a tribulation so great and so perilous, from which I cannot arise or escape. Knowing my guilt, I turn to Thee, Lord, repentant, sighing and weeping, as a son turns to his father, begging Thy holy mercy for forgiveness, that Thou mayest raise me from the great torment and the great tribulation into which I have fallen.

In order to escape from their allegiance to Christianity, a number of *conversos* sought to de-Christianize themselves by following bizarre practices, including fastening a crucifix to their buttocks, or destroying statues of Jesus. Others simply rationalized their lifestyle. Thus the statesman and jurist Pedro de la Caballería responded to a Jewish scholar who asked how he could justify becoming a Christian by pointing out the advantages of such a new identity. 'Imbecile,' he said, 'with the Jewish Torah what more could I have ever been than a rabbi? Now, thanks to the "little hanged one" I have been given all sorts of honours. I am in command of the whole city of Saragossa, and I make it tremble. What is there to keep me from fasting at *Yom Kippur* and observing your holidays if I feel like it? When I was a Jew, I did not dare observe the Sabbath and now I do anything I want.'

Other *conversos* became fervent atheists. A number of them formed a conventicle known to have existed at Medina del Campo; they possessed various Jewish texts revealing the secrets of the past, what Abraham, Jesus and Mohammad were, and the spirit that animated these three so-called imposters. Adamant in their beliefs, they attempted to recruit proselytes to whom they taught that the Gospels were nothing but deceit and fraud. Not surprisingly these deniers of the faith were denounced by both the Jewish and the Christian establishments.

There were, however, a number of *conversos* who became devout Christians, including bishops and church officials of Jewish descent. As Fernán Pérez de Guzmán testified:

> I am going to put forward certain reasons to counter the opinion of those who, without distinction or difference, absolutely condemn the nation of New Christian converts of today, saying that they are not Christians and that their conversion was neither good nor useful . . . I believe that among them are people who are good and devoted, for the following reasons: first, I believe in the virtue of the holy baptismal water, which cannot be sprinkled and lavished without any result; second, I have known and I know good *conversos*, who of their own free will lead an austere life in the religious orders; third, I have seen them work and wear themselves out in the monasteries, reforming dissolute and corrupt orders.

However, even those *conversos* who had become committed Christians were unable to escape their Jewish origins. Thus the poet Antonio de Montoro remarked to Queen Isabella: 'I have said the Credo; I have prayed to the pot of fat pork, I have heard the Masses and I have prayed, and still I have not been able to wipe out the lineaments of the confession. I have prayed with devotion, and I have counted the beads. But I have never been able to lose the name of a common old Jew.'

Within Christian circles, these apostates were despised because of their racial origins even though they had embraced Christianity. Thus Andrés Bernáldez, chaplain to an inquisitor, remarked:

> They never lose their Jewish way of eating, preparing their meat dishes with onions and garlic and cooking them in oil, which they use in place of lard, so that they will not have to eat pork fat; and oil with meat is something which gives the breath a very bad odour; and their houses and their doorways smell very bad because of this way of cooking, and they themselves attribute their Jewish odour to these dishes.

Such antipathy towards Jews was enshrined in official church documents. Thus in 1499 city officials in Toledo gave a lengthy enumeration of the crimes of *conversos*:

We declare that all the said *conversos*, descendants of the perverse line of the Jews . . . in reason of the above mentioned heresies and other offences, insults, seditions and crimes committed by them up to this time, should therefore be held as disgraceful, unfit, inept and unworthy of holding any office and public and private benefit in said city of Toledo and in its lands . . . to give witness and faith as public notaries or as witnesses . . . to have domain over Old Christians in the holy Catholic faith.

As time passed the Inquisition came into full force. One of its main aims was to purge *conversos* who were suspected of living secretly as Jews. In 1478 a papal bull was promulgated that created the Castilian Inquisition; several years later the first tribunal was established in Seville. Once the Inquisition was formally instituted, the tribunal requested that heretics confess to their crimes. This 'Edict of Grace' lasted for thirty days – those who came forward were obliged to denounce all other Judaizers. In compensation, they were spared torture and imprisonment. They atoned by flagellation, wearing the *sambenito*, and confiscation of their possessions. In addition, they were barred from holding office, practising a profession, or wearing formal dress.

The next stage of the inquisitorial process involved the naming of suspects. An edict was issued which outlined various ways that such individuals could be recognized. Judaizers, it explained, celebrated Jewish festivals, kept the dietary laws, consumed meat during Lent, omitted the phrase 'Glory be to the Father, and to the Son, and to the Holy Ghost' at the end of psalms, and cooked with oil. Once suspects were identified, the Inquisitors attempted to extract a confession. To achieve this end, various tortures were used, interspersed with kind words such as, 'I pity you, when I see you so abused and with a lost soul. . . . So do not assume the sin of others . . . admit the truth to me, for, as you see, I already know everything. . . . In order that I may be able to pardon you and free you soon, tell me who led you to this error.'

Those who confessed their sins were spared; those who persisted in denying the accusations made against them were burned at the stake. In this quest to root out Christian heresy, there were even some who praised the executions of innocent victims. In the sixteenth century, for example, Francesco Pegna declared that such persons died as martyrs for the faith: 'If an innocent is unjustly condemned, he has no reason to complain about the Church's sentence, which is based on sufficient proof, and what is hidden cannot be judged. If false witnesses have caused him to be condemned, he should accept the sentence with resignation, and rejoice in dying for truth.' Even though thousands of Jews died in this way, the majority of those who appeared before the Inquisition sought to be reconciled to the Church and were sentenced to imprisonment after having their property taken away and undergoing various humiliations. In addition, their children and grand-children were forbidden to wear gold or silver or to hold either public or ecclesiastical offices.

In Seville, where the first tribunal took place, the majority of *conversos* hoped to placate the Inquisitors through acts of dedication to the faith as well as offerings and gifts. The rich *converso* Mesa, for example, had the central place of atonement decorated with statues of the prophets. Nonetheless, for seven years the Inquisition purged 5,000 individuals who were punished and accepted reconciliation with the Church. Some seven hundred others were branded as heretics and burned at the stake. In 1483 Tomas de Torquemada became Inquisitor for all Spain, and tribunals were set up throughout the country. In Aragon popular uprisings against the Inquisition occurred; in Saragossa an attempt was made to assassinate the Inquisitor Pedro de Arbues. From 1486 to 1490, about 4,850 *conversos* were reconciled to the Church, and less than two hundred burned.

King Ferdinand championed the cause of the Inquisition even though he was acutely aware of the financial implications for Spain. In response to the municipal authorities of Barcelona who expressed concern at the economic crisis brought about by the Inquisition, he stated: 'Before consenting to the establishment of the Inquisition in the cities of our kingdom, we considered the harm this could cause craftsmen and commerce. But in our great zeal for our holy faith, we have placed the service of the Lord well above all our other interests.' Ironically, however, the Inquisition compelled many Jewish *conversos* to readopt the Jewish faith. In their distress they appealed to the God of their fathers. Defying Christ and Christianity, they declaimed the *Shema* ('Hear, O Israel, the Lord our God, the Lord is One') as they met their death. Some Catholics were so horrified by the Inquisition that they converted to Judaism.

Jews who had never undergone baptism were often caught up in this conflict. The Inquisitors imposed the duty of identifying Judaizing *conversos*, and charges were frequently brought against those who sought to convince baptised kinsmen to keep Jewish practices. Further, those who supported the return of *conversos* to Judaism were indicted. Jews were also accused of acting with *conversos* in committing ritual murder. Thus, in 1490 six Jews and five *conversos* of La Guardia were charged with attempting to bring about the destruction of Christendom through black magic. According to the accusation made against Yuce Franco, one of those on trial:

> His soul embittered and depraved, he went in good company with several others to crucify a Christian child on a Good Friday, in the same fashion, with the same animosity and cruelty as his forefathers had for our Saviour Jesus Christ, tearing his flesh, beating him and spitting in his face, covering him with wounds, crushing him with blows, and turning to ridicule our holy Faith. . . . He mixed his heart with a consecrated Host. With this mixture, Yuce Franco and the others expected that the Christian religion would be overturned and destroyed, so that the Jews would possess all the property which belongs to the Catholics, that their race would grow and multiply while that of the faithful Christians would be extirpated for ever.

During the Inquisition, torture was frequently used to extract confessions. When this was achieved, the Inquisitors were satisfied. However, the innocent suffered more than those who remained loyal to Judaism in secret. Typical of the procedures used by the Inquisitors was the case of Elviro del Campo who was accused by the authorities of Judaizing. As the report concerning her trial explains: 'She was carried to the torture chamber and told to tell the truth when she said that she had nothing to say. She was ordered to be stripped and again admonished, but was silent.' Eventually she was stripped and declared her innocence. Yet, fearing what would occur next, she pleaded with the Inquisitors, 'Señores,' she declared, 'I have done all that is said of me and I bear false witness against myself, for I do not want to see myself in such trouble; Please God, I have done nothing.'

Undeterred, the Inquisitors told her not to bring false testimony against herself, but to tell the truth. Her arms were then tied. She said: 'I have told the truth: what have I to tell?' She was again told to tell the truth and stated: 'I have told the truth and have nothing more to tell.' One cord was applied to her arms and twisted. She was then admonished to tell the truth, but again said she had nothing to tell. She then screamed and said, 'I have done all they say.'

The torture then increased in intensity, and more turns of the cord were applied. She cried, 'Loosen me a little that I may remember what I have to tell. I don't know what I have done; I did not eat pork for it makes me sick; I have done everything; loosen me and I will tell the truth.' Another turn of the cord was ordered, and she was told to explain in detail what she had done. She said: 'What am I expected to tell? I did everything – loosen me for I don't remember what I have to tell.' In agony, she cried out: 'Don't you see what a weak woman I am? Oh! Oh! my arms are breaking.'

Once a sixteenth turn of the cord had taken place, she was set upon the rack. Distraught, she cried: 'Señores, why will you not tell me what I have to say? Señor, put me on the ground – have I not said that I did it all?' She was then again instructed to explain everything. She said: 'I don't remember – take me away – I did what the witnesses say.' She was then told to relate in detail what the witnesses had said. She stated: 'Señor, remind me of what I did not know – Señores, have mercy upon me – Let me go for God's sake – They have no pity on me – I did it – take me from here and I will remember what I cannot here.'

In Spain, and later in Portugal, the judicial sentence of the Inquisitors following such torture was passed in public in the presence of dignitaries and crowds. At these ceremonies, known as *autos da fé*, sermons were preached; the earliest took place in 1481, and they continued until the nineteenth century. In all, the total of those who appeared to be charged numbered hundreds of thousands. Over 30,000 suffered the death penalty. However, the burning of heretics did not occur during the *auto da fé* – those found guilty were handed over to the secular authorities who were responsible for their execution at the place of burning.

Such treatment of the Jewish community ended with expulsion. On 31 March 1492, Ferdinand and Isabella signed the Edict of Expulsion that sealed the fate of Spanish Jewry:

> We have been informed by the Inquisitors, and by other persons, that the mingling of Jews and Christians leads to the worst evils. The Jews try their best to seduce the [New Christians], and their children, bringing them books of Jewish prayers, telling them of the days of Jewish holidays, procuring unleavened bread for them at Passover, instructing them on the dietary prohibitions, and persuading them to follow the Law of Moses. In consequence, our holy Catholic faith is debased and humbled. We have thus arrived at the conclusion that the only efficacious means to put an end to these evils consists in the definitive breaking of all relations between Jews and Christians, and this can only be obtained by their expulsion from our kingdom.

Once this decree was promulgated, Jews were given four months to liquidate their businesses and sell their property, but they were forbidden to export money or precious metals. Although the Jewish community sought to have this edict overturned, their attempts were unsuccessful. Only a last minute baptism would save them, and during the weeks preceding the mass exodus Spanish clergy embarked on a missionary campaign. As an observer at Segovia remarked: 'As the time approached, the Jews left their houses and scattered in the fields, hoping for a postponement. The Jewish cemetery was full of these miserable people. Some people of our city, concerned for the salvation of their souls, took advantage of the occasion to preach sermons and demonstrate to them their blind lack of belief, in face of so much evidence and so many centuries of calamities.'

As a Jewish witness related, such an attempt to convert Jewry was frequently successful: 'Numerous Jews, great and small, and even rabbis, remained in the country, preferring to change their Law to that of the God of the country. At their head was the rabbi Abraham Seneor, rabbi of all the Spanish communities, with his sons and all his relatives and many thousands of other Jews. Only a segment of the Spanish rabbis preferred martyrdom and left.' Nonetheless, such acts of baptism, even that of the celebrated court rabbi Abraham Seneor who was converted in the presence of the king and queen, were not followed by all Jews. It appears that nearly 150,000 of them went into exile.

The atmosphere of such a massive departure is described by the chaplain to the Inquisitor General: 'In a few months, the Jews sold all they could; they would barter a house for a donkey and a vineyard for a small piece of cloth or linen. Before leaving, they married off all their children of more than twelve years, so that each girl had the protection of a husband. . . . Then, trusting in the blind hope that God would lead them to the Promised Land, they left their homes, great and small, old and young, on foot, on horseback, on asses or other beasts or in wagons, some falling, others rising, some dying, others being born, others falling sick.'

Another account by Barthelemy Seneraga, a Genoese chronicler, emphasizes the plight of those who had now become homeless:

It was a sad sight to see. The majority were exhausted by hunger and thirst. . . . One would have said that they were ghosts: pale, shrunken, hollow-eyed, one would have thought them dead if they had not moved from time to time. A great number of them died on the pier in a place which was set aside for them not far from the market. . . . Their sufferings would seem praiseworthy for anyone who is of our religion, but they are not without cruelty if we consider them not as animals, but as human beings, created by God in his image.

CHRISTIANITY AND SPANISH RACISM

Under Muslim rule Jews prospered during the eleventh and twelfth centuries in Spain. During this period Jewish culture and learning flourished, and major contributions were made to Jewish theology, philosophy and mysticism. However, with the emergence of the Almohades who were fanatical missionaries, many Jews migrated to the north to join their coreligionists in the Christian kingdoms of Castile, Aragon, Leon, Portugal and Navarre. The largest number settled in Toledo, the capital of Castile, where a series of kings, beginning with Ferdinand I, granted them equal rights and employed them in their courts. Under these conditions, Jews continued to prosper.

By the end of the eleventh century, Gregory VII cautioned Alphonso VI not to allow Jews to rule over Christians. Nonetheless, Jews were readily absorbed into society, and under Alphonso VIII, they fought together with their Christian neighbours against the Almohades. Despite such integration, Jews did suffer attacks by the crusaders in the latters' quest to wrest control of southern Spain from Muslim rulers. As the *Reconquistia* continued into the thirteenth century, only Granada was left in Muslim hands. Under such conditions, an attempt was made to enforce the anti-Jewish legislation of Innocent III and the Lateran Councils.

Jews in Castile, however, refused to wear the badge. Although the Church objected to any form of leniency, the Council of Valladolid was content that Jews should not wear the same tunic as the clergy. In Aragon, the badge caused less of a controversy since Jews wore their own distinctive clothing. In short, Spanish Jewry – unlike their coreligionists in other European countries – did not suffer the same indignities. Considered the king's 'serfs', a number amassed great wealth.

The Church, however, was not content that the Jewish population should remain loyal to their ancestral traditions. In Aragon, a major missionary effort was directed at the Jewish community, and James I envisaged the ultimate conversion of all Jews and Arabs in his realm. In this quest, he was aided by the Dominicans who taught Hebrew and Arabic in their seminaries. Pre-eminent among such missionaries was Raymond Penaforte, the Dominican confessor to the king who had converted Pablo Christiani. This Dominican brother was authorized to preach in Jewish synagogues, and in 1263 a disputation took place between Christiani and Nachmanides. As a consequence, Christiani denounced the Talmud to Clement IV and was successful in ensuring that Jewish religious texts were scrutinized for anti-Christian references. During the next century, Jews in Aragon – along with Jewish communities in other lands – were accused of spreading the Black Death and attacked.

Elsewhere in Spain conditions varied. In Navarre, which bordered on France, economic constraints were imposed in 1284, and Jews suffered from considerable hostility. In 1328 the Franciscan friar, Peter Olligen, provoked massacres in Estella and elsewhere, resulting in the death of thousands of Jews. In Castile, however, a series of kings supported Jews, protecting them from Christian antipathy. Jews frequently served the kings in various capacities. Under Alphonso X in the thirteenth century, for example, Jews were granted lands and mosques for synagogues, and aided in the creation of astronomical tables. During his rule Jewish culture, particularly in the spheres of philosophical speculation and talmudic study, underwent considerable development. Later under Ferdinand IV, a number of Jews were prominent in the court.

Not surprisingly, such prosperity evoked a hostile response among nobles, clergy and the general population. The Cortes (legislature) was opposed to usury, and imposed heavy taxation including the cancellation of debts to Jews. Acceding to this demand Alphonso XI agreed that one fourth of their credits should be cancelled and forbade usury. In addition, church councils promulgated restrictive legislation, limiting Jewish freedoms. Placing blame for their poverty on courtly financiers, the masses became increasingly angered by the affluence of those Jews living in their midst.

As we have seen, during the fourteenth century Jews in Spain became embroiled in political controversy. When Jews rallied to the side of King Pedro, the king was referred to as a 'Judaized king' and a rumour was spread that he was the bastard son of a Jewish woman. After his death, Jews suffered under his brother Henry of Trastamara. Throughout Spain oppressive measures were imposed including the wearing of the badge. The clergy, particularly Dominican friars, spoke harshly about the attitudes of Jewry, and as a result of such increased hostility a number of Jews embraced the Christian faith.

Pre-eminent among clerics who engaged in active missionizing was Ferrant Martinez, an archdeacon in Seville. At the latter part of the century he had waged a campaign against Judaism and the affluence of influential Jews. Despite being rebuked by the Crown and the archbishop, he persisted in his activities, which resulted in a pogrom against the Jewish quarter in Seville when, several months later, a mob broke into this section killing 4,000 Jews. From Seville, such violence spread through Spain, resulting in the death of approximately 50,000 Jews and the mass conversion of nearly three times that number.

As a consequence, the number of Jewish converts to Christianity increased. Initially the Inquisition was directed at these *conversos*, many of whom had embraced the Christian faith against their will. Not surprisingly, many of these converts had also not broken with their ancestral faith. Living outwardly as Christians, they continued to observe various Jewish practices in secret. Some, regretting their baptism, followed Jewish customs awaiting the time when they might re-embrace Judaism publicly: occasionally these Jews observed rites of de-Christianization. Others, aware of the advantages of their new station, maintained relationships with their Jewish neighbours while seeking to improve their position in society.

Although such individuals were regarded with contempt by the Jewish establishment, official Jewish policy was lenient towards apostates. *Anusim* (forced ones) were regarded as Jews, and in accordance with the view of Rashi and Rabbi Gershom of Mainz, they could be reinstated without punishment or embarrassment. The Church, however, adopted a much harsher policy. Baptisms – even under duress – were deemed valid. As Innocent III declared: 'Whoever is led to Christianity by violence, by fear and torture . . . receives the imprint of Christianity and can be forced to observe the Christian faith.'

In the fifteenth century children of *conversos* followed the pattern of their parents and continued to live as Christians while secretly observing Jewish practices. Contemptuous of such hypocrisy, both clergy and laity deplored such duplicity and branded the *conversos* 'Marranos' (swine). Throughout Spain preachers condemned these New Christians. Eventually the reaction against Marranos reached such an intensity that they were attacked in 1440 when they attempted to collect governmental taxes. Two years later the Franciscan friar Alphonso de Spina published *Fortalitium Fidei* in which he repeated libels against Jews in general as well as against the Marrano community in particular.

In the public mind anti-Semitism and hatred of the Marranos were fused, and it was believed that hereditary Jewishness was responsible for the evils inflicted upon Spanish society. Even if Jews were baptised, they had *mala sangre* (bad blood). This belief gave rise to a form of Spanish racism based on *limpieza de sangre* (purity of blood). Judaism hence ceased to be a religious problem. Meanwhile the attacks on Marranos continued, culminating in the onslaught against *conversos* which took place in 1473 to 1474.

Determined to deal with this problem, the Inquisition turned its attention to these Christian converts. The Inquisitorial tribunal was founded in the thirteenth century by the Holy See to combat the Albigensian heresy (doctrine of radical dualism as between good and evil); later it was introduced into Aragon. Although practising Jews were exempt from the Inquisition, Marranos were not: deemed Christian heretics, they became a central focus of its activities. When in 1479 Ferdinand and Isabella brought together Castile and Aragon, Tomas de Torquemada, the queen's confessor, besought the sovereigns to introduce the tribunal into a unified Spain. In 1480 Sixtus IV granted this request, and Marranos were arrested and brought before the Inquisitors. Under Torquemada's administration, the Marrano community lived in terror.

As we have seen, elaborate regulations were formulated to detect Judaizers. Various clues were sought, and the faithful were obliged to denounce suspects. In addition, rabbis were encouraged to impose excommunication on the faithful for failure to denounce their coreligionists. Thirty days of grace were given for self-denunciation, which was followed by torture to obtain confessions. Paradoxically, the Inquisition evoked a determined response from many Marranos who tenaciously clung to their ancestral faith. According to a Jewish chronicler of the period, it was possible to observe from towers throughout Spain smokeless chimneys of Marranos who scrupulously observed the Jewish prohibition against lighting a fire on the Sabbath. Some of these faithful individuals went to their deaths reciting the ancient *Shema* prayer.

Faced with such determination, the Jewish community expressed fraternal sympathy for these apostates. Such bonds between Marranos and the Jewish community enraged the Inquisitors; eventually Torquemada sought the expulsion of all Jews from the kingdom. When he approached civil and ecclesiastical authorities, he initially encountered reluctance. However, in 1490 Marranos were accused of plotting the overthrow of

Christianity by using a consecrated Host and crucifying a young boy. When a trial was held, the accused was burned. The public reaction to this event spurred Torquemada to continue with his plea for expulsion. Finally, in 1492, Ferdinand and Isabella conceded to his request, and all Jews were compelled to leave the realm.

The striking feature of the onslaught against both Marranos and practising Jews was the conviction that Jews – regardless of their religious beliefs – possess impurity of the blood. In the Spanish mind, there was no way by which individuals could free themselves from the taint of Jewish blood. As we have seen, in previous centuries the Church attacked the Jewish populace on religious grounds. Jews were perceived as demonic, not because of racial descent, but because of their beliefs. In Spain, traditional Christian anti-Semitism was transformed into ethnic prejudice. For this reason, it became necessary to rid the country of its Jewish inhabitants. Baptism, it was believed, could not rid Jews of their spiritual and cultural deficiencies.

Tragically, similar convictions, like this earliest form of the racial corruption type of anti-Semitism, fuelled hatred of the Jews in modern times. Like the Spanish in the early modern period, the Nazis were convinced of the racial inferiority of the Jewish nation. For Hitler, European civilization was threatened by the presence of Jews, just as Torquemada and others had feared for Christian civilization nearly five hundred years previously. For Hitler, the Jew could never become a German because he was racially and religiously distinct. The difference between Jews and Germans was so vast as to make the former inherently alien.

Comparing Jews with vermin, Hitler wrote in *Mein Kampf*, 'Was there any form of filth or profligacy, particularly in cultural life, without at least one Jew involved in it? If you cut even cautiously into such an abscess you found, like a maggot in a rotting body, often dazzled by the sudden light – a kike!' For Hitler, as for Torquemada, there could be only one solution to the Jewish problem: the elimination of the Jewish population. In 1492 the Jews were expelled *en masse*; under the Nazis the death camps served a similar purpose.

EIGHT

Marranos

As the Inquisition intensified its efforts to root out heresy in Spain, many Marranos fled to other countries. Some went to Portugal where they lived publicly as Christians while secretly observing Jewish customs. Following the events in Spain, the Portuguese Inquisition was created in 1536 and sought to discover Marranos wherever they resided. Other Marranos were compelled to find homes further afield. Both Turkey and Salonica constituted important Marrano refuges from oppression in the sixteenth century. Yet others emigrated to Antwerp, Venice, Ancona and Bordeaux. In the next century, Marranos settled in Amsterdam, Hamburg and London. In these centres many *conversos* returned to Judaism, yet they retained some of their former cultural characteristics. During this period a number of Marranos gained enormous political influence; such a one was the Duke of Naxos who acted on behalf of the Jewish community. Others awaited the coming of the Messiah who would lead them back to Zion. Some Marranos, however, broke away from traditional Judaism and advanced heterodox theories that unintentionally provoked anti-Jewish attitudes.

THE DISPERSAL OF THE MARRANOS
Seeking to escape the Spanish Inquisition, some Jews sought refuge in Portugal. Unlike their Spanish counterparts, these *conversos* imitated the Christian way of life, complying with Catholic rites and attending mass and confession. Nevertheless, they selectively observed various Jewish rituals such as Yom Kippur (the Day of Atonement) and Purim (Feast of Esther). In addition, they were comforted by various texts, such as the Prayer of Esther which became an important prayer for the Marrano communities: 'I whom you keep among the infidels, you know how much I hate their criminal feasts . . . this pomp to which I am condemned, this diadem in which I must appear. Alone and in secret I trample them under my feet.'

Marrano insecurity in the face of Christian persecution manifested itself in various messianic movements. In the sixteenth century, the adventurer David

Reubeni presented himself at the court of Pope Clement VII in 1524 as a representative of the Jewish kingdom of the East. Taking his claim seriously, the Pope referred him to the King of Portugal where he sailed in a ship flying the Jewish flag of his imaginary kingdom. In Portugal Marranos believed that their time of deliverance had arrived and were jubilant. In their frenzy they attacked the inquisitorial prison in Badajoz. One of those present, Diego Pires, became a Jew and took the name Salomon Molcho; when he joined Reubeni, they travelled throughout Europe encouraging messianic expectations. Eventually they were received at the court of Charles V, but ultimately were delivered to the Inquisition and burned at the stake.

In 1536 the Inquisition was established in Portugal, but unlike in Spain, it was accepted that the New Christians constituted an important element of the population despite their beliefs and practices. Hence King John III informed the Pope that the *converso* population greatly contributed to commerce and industry. They had served him well, and there was no reason to hate them, he declared. 'How can one dare to require me to cut the throats of my own flock?' he asked.

Despite such views, the Inquisition operated with fervour, and Marranos were tracked down throughout the country – in cities, villages, forests and mountains. As had occurred in Spain in the previous century, Jews went to their deaths bravely. Hence after burning twenty New Christians in 1542, the Inquisitor of Lisbon praised these martyrs for their fortitude: 'Nothing astonished me so much as to see the Lord give such steadfastness to the weakness of flesh; children attended the burnings of their parents and wives those of their husbands and no one heard them cry out or weep. They said farewell and blessed them as if they were parting to meet again the next day.'

Confronted with such an onslaught, a number of Marranos fled abroad; others, however, remained in Portugal where they continued to practise Judaism secretly. Yet, among these New Christians knowledge of Judaism declined, so that during an *auto da fé* held in 1705 the archbishop stated: 'Miserable relics of Judaism! Unfortunate fragments of the synagogue! Last vestiges of Judaea! Scandal for the Catholics, laughingstock of the Jews themselves! . . . You are the laughingstock of the Jews because you do not even know how to obey the law under which you live.' Even though the distinction between New and Old Christians was removed at the end of the eighteenth century, Marranism continued to survive. In Portugal Marranos continued to combine the outward display of Christian observances with secret observance of Jewish rites and festivals.

When Jews were expelled from Spain in 1492, thousands of them emigrated to Barbary, Turkey and the Christian territories where they were permitted to live. In the next two centuries, Marranos continued to settle in other lands. In some cases these departures were legal; in others they were the result of clandestine arrangements. Yet, in nearly all cases, they were facilitated by financial transactions. An example of such illicit emigration took place between 1609 and 1614 when a number of Portuguese crypto-Jews and Spanish *conversos* joined the Moriscos who had been expelled and crossed the Pyrenees.

In Turkey the Marranos were welcomed since considerable efforts had been made to attract them from the Iberian Peninsula ever since Constantinople had been conquered. As Rabbi Moses Capsali noted, Sultan Mohammed II proclaimed: 'Hear, descendants of the Hebrews who live in my country. Let each who desires it come to Constantinople, and let the remnant of your people find asylum here.' As Capsali reported, 'Throngs of Jews flocked to Constantinople from all directions. The sultan put homes at their disposal and they settled there.' In the words of the French ambassador d'Aramon: 'Constantinople is inhabited principally by Turks, then by an infinite number of Jews, that is, Marranos who were driven out of Spain, Portugal and Germany. They have taught the Turks every handicraft, and the majority of the shops belong to Jews.'

His contemporary Nicholas de Nicolay further remarked: 'Among [the Jews] are very excellent workers in all arts and manufactures, especially the Marranos who have recently been banished and chased from Spain and Portugal. To the great detriment and shame of Christianity, they have taught the Turks numerous inventions, artifices, and machines of war, such as how to make artillery, arquebuses, cannon powder, cannon balls, and other arms. Similarly, they have set up a printing shop, never before seen in these regions.'

Even more than Turkey, Salonica constituted a Marrano refuge in the sixteenth century. The rabbis there encouraged these refugees to become observant, yet the ordinary Jewish population viewed them with disapproval. Their ambiguous status caused considerable confusion. Many Marranos were unsure of their identity and vacillated between Judaism and Christianity. There were even those who returned to the Jewish faith, and were then overcome by a longing for Catholicism. Others embraced Islam and served in the military under the sultan.

Those Marranos who settled in new countries were driven by various factors. Some went to places where they could live freely as Jews; others were attracted by commercial and economic advantages. Hence, Marrano communities were established in Antwerp, Venice, Ancona, Solonica and Bordeaux in the sixteenth century and in Amsterdam, Hamburg and London in the next century. Conscious of the financial contributions these newcomers could make, various Christian governments granted them special privileges. However, wherever they went the Marranos retained their Spanish character and used Castilian written in either Latin or Hebrew to communicate with one another and in their publications.

Such communal identification evoked a feeling of disdain from German and Polish Jews. Hence, in a letter to Voltaire, himself critical of Jews and Judaism, Isaac de Pinto wrote:

> M. Voltaire cannot be ignorant of the scrupulous exactness of the Portuguese and Spanish Jews not to intermix in marriage, alliance, or any other way with the Jews of other nations. . . . Their variance with their other brethren is such that if a Portuguese Jew in England or Holland married a German Jewess, he would of course lose all his prerogatives, be no longer reckoned a member of their synagogue, forfeit all civil and ecclesiastical preferments, be absolutely divorced from the body of the nation, and not even be buried with his Portuguese brethren. This is the cause of those distinctions and of that elevation of mind which is observed among them, and which even their brethren of other nations seem to acknowledge.

The cohesion that existed among Marranos meant that even when they returned to Judaism, they retained their former cultural characteristics. As de Pinto observed: 'They do not wear beards, and do not affect any distinction in their clothing. Those who are well off pursue elegance and ostentation to the same extent as the other nations of Europe, from whom they differ only in religion.' Not surprisingly, such attitudes often aroused criticism, such as that displayed by the preaching brother Labat who wrote of the Jews of Leghorn: 'They are free there, they do not wear any beard to distinguish them from the Christians. They are not confined to their neighbourhoods. They are rich; their business is extensive. Almost all have favours from the prince, and they are protected to the point where it is proverbial in Tuscany that it would be better to beat the Grand Duke than a Jew. This only makes them all the more odious to everyone else.'

Such condemnation, however, was not universal. Others viewed these displaced Jews more favourably. Thus the English navigator Thomas

This wall painting, excavated in 1932, depicts Ahasuerus and Esther enthroned, receiving a report of the number of Jews slain in Shushan. *(Beth Hatefutsoth Photo Archive, Tel Aviv)*

A fourteenth-century representation of the Israelites crossing the Red Sea as depicted in the Sarajevo Haggadah. *(Sarajevo National Museum/photo courtesy Beth Hatefutsoth Photo Archive, Tel Aviv)*

Emperor Justinian I, ruler of the eastern Roman Empire AD 527–65 and author of the Justinian code. He is shown preventing the desecration of a synagogue. *(Beth Hatefutsoth Photo Archive, Tel Aviv)*

A Christian mob attacks the Jews in the *Judengasse* and drives them out. This is a fourteenth-century German engraving. *(Beth Hatefutsoth Photo Archive, Tel Aviv)*

Anno 1475. am Grünen Donnerstag war das Kindlein Simeon
2 Jahr alt als es von den Juden ist umgebracht worden
Cet enfant nommé Simeon agé de 2 Ans fut tué par les Juifs,
le jour du Grand-Jeude de l'An 1475.

Diese Abbildung stehet zu Franckfurt am Mayn
am Brücken Thürn abgemahlt.
Ce portrait est peint sous la porte du pont de Francfort
sur le Mayn

Dieses ist
der Jüden Teuffel

Ju weih Rabb: Anschl au au Mausch au weih au au
O Veh Rabbi Anschel. au au Mauche o Veh au au.

Sauff Mauschi sauff die Milch friß du Rabbi den Dreck
es ist doch alle Zeit euer bestes Geschleck:
Bois Mauche bois ce lait Manges Juifs ces ordures:
Ces sont friands pour vous. de bonnes confitures.

An anti-Semitic drawing showing the Simon of Trent blood libel of 1475
and, below, the notorious Judensau libel. The circles on the clothing of the
protagonists denote their Jewishness. The text (originally German) has
been translated into French. (*Beth Hatefutsoth Photo Archive, Tel Aviv*)

This woodcut from Schedel's *Weltchronik* shows Jews being burned in fifteenth-century Germany. *(Beth Hatefutsoth Photo Archive, Tel Aviv)*

A Hungarian version of the blood libel, 1591. *(Beth Hatefutsoth Photo Archive, Tel Aviv)*

Martin Luther. Initially an apologist for the Jews, he later became one of their persecutors.
(Bildarchiv Foto Marburg/photo courtesy Beth Hatefutsoth Photo Archive, Tel Aviv)

Bogdan Chmielnicki, leader of the Cossacks, led the pogroms against Ukrainian Jews in 1648–9. He is branded as one of the most sinister oppressors of their people in the annals of Jewry. *(Beth Hatefutsoth Photo Archive, Tel Aviv)*

These Cossacks, led by Chmielnicki, are attacking the Jews in Tulchin. The Jews defended themselves with the help of some Polish citizens, who later betrayed them. *(Beth Hatefutsoth Photo Archive, Tel Aviv)*

Coryat wrote that the Jews of Venice were 'such goodly and proper men, that I said to my self our English proverb "To look like a Jew" is not true. For indeed I noticed some of them to be most elegant and sweet featured persons. I saw many Jewish women, whereof some were as beautiful as ever I saw, and so gorgeous in their apparel, jewels, chains of gold, and rings adorned with precious stones, that some of our English Countesses do scarce exceed them.' Thus the Marranos evoked a range of different responses from those among whom they lived. Spanish by origin, outwardly Christian, yet inwardly Jewish, they despised their fellow Jews. Such contradictions frequently led to crises of personal identity and loyalty to Judaism and the Jewish community.

Among the Marranos in the sixteenth century, the Mendes brothers exerted considerable influence. Living in Lisbon, Francisco Mendes established a company with his brother Diego Mendes in Antwerp that became the main spice importer for northern Europe. Not only did they provide funds for kings, they also transferred Marrano capital and property from Portugal to Flanders and then to Italy. Following their death, Francisco's widow Beatrice de Luna headed the firm and was joined by her nephew Juan Micas who was knighted by Charles V. According to contemporaries, he was described as civilized and elegant: 'He comported himself in humane and dignified fashion in all things . . . [He is a man who is] more fitting to be a Christian than a Jew.' According to another report, 'there are few persons of account in Spain, Italy or Flanders who are not personally acquainted with him.'

Once plans had been formulated for a marriage between Brianda de Luna, the daughter of Beatrice, and Juan Micas, the Mendes family travelled to Venice, eventually settling in Constantinople where they were welcomed by the sultan. There Juan Micas became Joseph Nasi, and his aunt Beatrice de Luna became Gracia Nasi. She devoted herself to pious works while Joseph became an influential figure in Ottoman foreign policy. Because of his extensive contacts and commercial ties, two sultans relied on him for advice.

When Joseph was introduced into the Ottoman court by the French ambassador to Rome, Seigneur de Lansac, he became a fervent enemy of France as a result of litigation concerning 150,000 ducats that he had lent to Henry II. According to a French report, this debt could be dispensed with if it were owed to a Marrano, 'for the laws of the kingdom do not permit Jews such as the said Joseph Nasi to do business or traffic in anything; but they order that all their goods be confiscated.' The logic of this position was that since Marranos deceived Christians by secretly engaging in Jewish observances, they deserved to be deceived by the non-payment of financial obligations. Eventually, however, Joseph persuaded the sultan to confiscate merchandise taken to the Levant under the French flag until the debt was paid.

The relationship between Joseph and the Crown of Spain was equally difficult. According to Philip II, Joseph was the originator of an anti-Christian plot. He was 'the one who contributes the most to the enterprises prejudicial to Christianity and who instigates them'. Nonetheless, in 1570 Joseph asked Philip for safe conduct for himself and others to return to Spain. He asked to be pardoned for following Jewish law. It is not clear whether he was serious in this admission, or whether such a statement was mere pretence. In any case, Joseph asked for exemptions from customs duties for goods he wished to import. Philip was inclined to accede to this request, and it became the subject of Spanish dispatches. In the end, however, it was not granted.

In addition to these activities, Joseph often acted on behalf of the Jewish people. When Pope Paul IV ordered that twenty-five Marranos be burned at the stake in Ancona in 1556, Joseph and Gracia Nasi organized a boycott of the port of Ancona. Earlier, during his stay in Italy, Joseph asked that Venice put an island at the disposal of homeless Marranos. In 1561 the sultan granted him the city of Tiberias and surrounding territory for a Jewish homeland, which he rebuilt despite the protest of the apostolic legate in Palestine who inveighed against 'the arrival of these vipers more deadly than those which haunt the ruins of the city'.

According to the French ambassador de Petremol, this enterpise was part of Joseph's plan to become king of the Jews. 'Nasi,' he stated, 'has received permission from the Grand Signior . . . to build a city on the shore of Lake Tiberias wherein Jews only are to live. In fact, he proposes to begin his achievement here by this renewal, having the intention so far as one can judge of proclaiming himself king of the Jews. This is why he is demanding from France so insistently.'

This project, however, was unsuccessful because of the lack of Jewish enthusiasm for the creation of a Jewish presence in the Holy Land. Few Jews came to settle in Tiberias. However, Joseph persisted in his plans to create a Jewish state, and in 1566 the new sultan Selim II gave him the island of Naxos and made him duke. In 1570 he encouraged Selim II to declare war on Venice. This campaign began with the conquest of Cyprus over which

Joseph had hoped to rule as king. However, that plan was never realized and in 1579 Joseph died, rich but without having attained this ambition.

So great was Joseph's fame that he exerted a strong impact on the Christian conception of the Jew in the years after his death. Used by the playwright as his model in Christopher Marlowe's *Jew of Malta*, Joseph's persona contributed to the creation of the character Shylock in Shakespeare's *Merchant of Venice*. In this play the highly unsympathetic Venetian moneylender does business with Christians despite their antipathy to him. Protesting against their hatred of him as a Jew, he stated: 'I am a Jew. Hath not a Jew eyes? hath not a Jew hands, organs, dimensions, senses, affections, passions? . . . If you prick us, do we not bleed? if you tickle us, do we not laugh? If you poison us, do we not die? and if you wrong us, shall we not seek revenge?' These words were devised to combat the centuries-old stereotype of the Jew as the demonic agent of the realm of darkness and evil.

For the Marrano community the belief in the coming of the Messiah was of central importance, and in the next century Jewish believers, including many Marranos, were certain that the advent of the Messiah was at hand. Against this background Shabbetai Tzevi, a self-proclaimed messianic king, brought about the transformation of Jewish life. Born in Smyrna into a Judaeo-Spanish family, he initially received a traditional Jewish education, only later embarking on a study of kabbalistic texts. In the 1650s he left Smyrna and travelled to various cities in Greece as well as to Constantinople and Jerusalem. Finally he joined a kabbalistic group in Cairo; there he came upon Nathan of Gaza who believed Shabbetai to be the Messiah. In 1665 his messiahship was proclaimed, and Nathan wrote to Jews throughout the diaspora beseeching them to repent and acknowledge Shabbetai Tzevi as their redeemer. Shabbetai, he explained, would take the sultan's crown, return the lost tribes, and bring about the period of messianic redemption. Throughout the Jewish world, rich and poor made preparations to leave for Palestine.

After a lengthy sojourn in Jerusalem, Shabbetai returned to Smyrna, where he met strong opposition from a number of local rabbis. He denounced the disbelievers and stated that he was the Anointed of the God of Jacob. This provoked a hysterical response; Jews fell in trances and had visions of him on a royal throne crowned as the King of Israel. In 1666 he journeyed to Constantinople, but was arrested and put in prison. Within a short time the prison became a messianic court, and Jews from various countries made their way to Constantinople. There they engaged in ascetic and messianic practices. Hymns were written in Shabbetai's honour, and new festivals were initiated. According to Nathan, who remained in Gaza, the alteration in Shabbetai's moods from illumination to withdrawal had kabbalistic significance: they symbolized his soul's struggle with demonic powers. At times he was imprisoned by the forces of evil, but at other moments he was able to vanquish them.

During this period Shabbetai met the Polish kabbalist Nehemiah ha-Kohen, who denounced him to the Turkish authorities. When Shabbetai was brought to court, he was given the choice between conversion and death. Faced with this alternative, he converted to Islam. Dismayed by such an act of apostasy, most of his followers ceased to believe in his messiahship, yet Shabbetai defended himself by claiming that he had become a Muslim in obedience to God's commands. Some of his followers accepted this explanation and continued to believe that the messianic age was imminent. Some thought it was not Shabbetai who had become a Muslim, but rather a phantom who had taken on his appearance. Others cited biblical and rabbinical texts to justify his action. Nathan explained that the messianic role involved taking on the humiliation of being portrayed as a traitor.

Subsequently Nathan visited Shabbetai in the Balkans, then travelled to Rome where he performed secret rites to bring about the end of the papacy. Meanwhile Shabbetai remained in Adrianople and Constantinople, where he lived both as a Muslim and as a Jew. In 1672 he was deported to Albania, where he taught his own kabbalistic theories to a group of supporters. After his death two years later, Nathan declared that Shabbetai had ascended to the supernatural world. A number of groups continued in their belief that Shabbetai was the Messiah, including the Dissidents (*Doenmeh*) who practised Islam publicly, but secretly adhered to their own traditions. Like the Marranos, these individuals lived openly as members of another religious tradition, while privately adhering to Judaism. Marrying among themselves, they eventually evolved into antinomian sub-groups which violated Jewish sexual law and asserted the divinity of Shabbetai and their leader, Baruchiah Russo. In Italy a number of secret Shabbetean groups followed halakhic practices. Shabbetean missionaries also spread their beliefs in Eastern Europe during the late seventeenth and early eighteenth centuries.

In the eighteenth century, the most important Shabbetean group was led by Jacob Frank, who was influenced by the *Doenmeh*. Believing himself to be the incarnation of Shabbetai, Frank proclaimed that he was the second person of the Trinity, and became the leader of a circle of disciples who indulged in licentious orgies. In the 1750s disputations took place between traditionalists and the Frankists. Later Frank expressed his willingness to become a Christian, but he desired to maintain his own group. Even though this request was refused by church leaders, Frank and his followers were baptised. The clergy, however, became aware that Frank's trinitarian beliefs were not consistent with Christian doctrine, and he was imprisoned for thirteen years. Frank then lived in Germany, where he practised a variant of the Shabbetean tradition. These events added to the general antipathy towards Jewry in the early modern period.

By the seventeenth century Amsterdam had the largest Marrano community in Europe. There they created a book industry, published translations of the Bible for Protestant use, and produced a Jewish newspaper, *Gazeta de Amsterdam*. Although their former apostasy was a source of guilt, it was difficult for many to resume a traditional Jewish lifestyle. As a consequence, there was considerable debate about practice and belief within the Marrano community.

Pre-eminent among the descendants of the Marranos who participated in these discussions was Baruch Spinoza. Born in Amsterdam, he was exposed to Hebrew, the Bible and the Talmud as well as medieval Jewish philosophy; subsequently, he engaged in the study of natural science and contemporary philosophy. At the age of twenty-three, he was questioned by the leaders of the Amsterdam Jewish community about his religious beliefs, and offered a stipend if he would remain silent and conform to Jewish practice. When he refused to comply, he was excommunicated.

The rabbinic proclamation declared:

The chiefs of the council make known to you that having long known of evil opinions and acts of Baruch de Spinoza, they have endeavoured by various means and promises to turn him from evil ways. Not only being unable to find any remedy, but on the contrary receiving every day more information about the abominable heresies practised and taught by him, and about the monstrous acts committed by him, having this from many trustworthy witnesses who have deposed and borne witness on all this in the presence of said Spinoza, who has been convicted; all this having been examined in the presence of the rabbis, the council decided, with the advice of the rabbis, that the said Spinoza should be excommunicated and cut off from the Nation of Israel.

For the rest of his life, Spinoza lived in various towns in Holland where he supported himself by grinding and polishing optical lenses. During this period he attracted a wide circle of admirers and was offered a professorship at the University of Heidelberg in 1673, which he declined. In 1661 he began work on his *Tractatus Theologico-Politicus*; his *Ethics* appeared posthumously. Starting from the heterodox views expressed within the Marrano community, Spinoza developed a critique of Judaism and supernatural religion in the *Tractatus*. Insisting that religious beliefs should be judged only on the basis of reason, he rejected the belief that Moses received the Torah on Mount Sinai and the possibility of prophecy.

In his writings, Spinoza made a number of critical observations about the Jewish concept of peoplehood. Rejecting the belief that Jews are God's chosen people, he criticized the prerogatives accorded to the Jewish community:

> He who thinks that his blessedness is increased by the fact that he is better off, or happier and more fortunate, than the rest of mankind, knows nothing of true happiness and blessedness, and the pleasure he derives from such thoughts, unless merely childish, arises only from spite and malice. . . . The man who is pleased by such thoughts is pleased by the misfortune of another; he is therefore spiteful and wicked, and knows nothing either of true wisdom or the peace of mind which true living involves.

For Spinoza, it was not a miracle that the Jewish people had endured through the centuries. Rather, it was due in large part to their desire to separate themselves from other people. Yet by doing so the Jewish nation evoked hatred from those among whom they lived:

> As for the fact that they have survived their dispersion and the loss of their state for so many years, there is nothing miraculous in that, since they incurred universal hatred by cutting themselves off completely from all other peoples; and not only by practising a form of worship opposed to that of the rest, but also by preserving the mark of circumcision with such devoutness. Hence the patriotism of the Jews was not only patriotism but piety, and it was so fostered by their daily ritual that it must have become second nature. . . . And this must have inspired in the Jews continued and ineradicable hatred, for a hatred which springs from great devotion or piety, and is itself believed to be pious, is undoubtedly greater and more persistent than any other. And

the common reason for the continued growth of hatred, i.e., the fact that it is returned, was also present; for the gentiles must have regarded the Jews with the most bitter hatred.

Spinoza's heterodoxy originated in an environment in which the Marranos' apostasy and subsequent return to Judaism caused confusion and resentment. Not surprisingly, traditional Jewish belief came under threat as Marranos struggled to harmonize Jewish teaching with human reason. Unintentionally, Spinoza's anti-Jewish rhetoric provided the basis for later anti-Semitism; his observations about the Hebrew Scriptures, ceremonial law and Jewish doctrine were used by Christians to denigrate Judaism and the Jewish nation.

THE INQUISITION AND MARRANO DISPERSAL

The activities of the Inquisition traumatized the Jewish communities of Spain and Portugal. Determined to root out heresy, the Inquisitors directed their attention to the New Christians. Their primary function was to demonstrate and prove heresy as well as punish offences. In any district it was the Inquisitor's task to bring all suspects before the tribunal, and it was the duty of both the clergy and laity to expose those suspected of harbouring dangerous views. In all cases the trail began when a person was denounced and arrested for heresy or for the merest suspicion of it. In contrast with other legal procedures, witnesses were kept secret. The Inquisitor assumed that the family and immediate neighbours of a suspect were also under suspicion.

Denunciations were frequently anonymous, and the summons to court was followed by a ten-to-fifteen-day period of grace during which the accused was expected to recant. If he failed to do so, he was arrested and tried. Witnesses were heard first, and those who spoke in defence of the suspect came under suspicion of heresy themselves. All witnesses spoke under oath. Trials were often short. Since it was not always easy to obtain a confession, Pope Innocent IV issued a bull, *Ad Extirpanda*, which permitted torture. The bull was based on the *Codex Justinianus*, which stipulated that torture could be used in cases of *crimen laesae maiestatis* (lèse-majesté) or treason, and hence sanctioned the use of torture where royal majesty was threatened.

The forms of torture were broadly the same as those used in the Middle Ages. Unlike secular courts, the main purpose of the Inquisition was to extract a confesson of guilt, not to kill the accused. Having confessed, a subject could then be given a suitable sentence, which varied in type. In cases of calumny, the accused was forced to retract and was rehabilitated. Coming under slight suspicion of heresy also necessitated retraction and penance, but punishment was more severe in cases of serious suspicion. But even here the life of the accused was spared. In cases of very great suspicion, however, suspects were condemned to wear a yellow cross in public for a fixed period, or they could be required to exhibit themselves to public view at the church door on feast days. In some cases they would be imprisoned for any period up to life. However, such penalties applied only if the accused expressed their willingness to recant. If they refused, they were turned over to the secular authorities.

The death penalty was issued only in cases of public or secret heresy. Those who were found guilty of heresy on more than one occasion could be sentenced to death even if they recanted. In such cases the Inquisitor assumed that former acts of repentance had no substance. Further, anyone who was suspected of recanting simply to avoid the death penalty automatically incurred this punishment. If the person accused repented of heresy but was not sufficiently penitent, he could be sentenced to life imprisonment. Such punishment was incredibly horrible: the prisoner was isolated from the outside world, often in chains. If the death sentence were passed, the judge pronounced this judgment in prison. The Church disowned the heretic, and the prisoner was surrendered to the prison authorities for execution. At the place of execution, the Inquisitor would preach a short sermon while the fire was prepared; if the person under sentence were a member of the clergy, he was deprived of ordination and condemned, and surrendered to the secular powers before the sentence was carried out. In most cases these executions were public events; the convicted prisoners were dressed in the heretics' robes of shame, and led through the streets or brought on a cart to the place of execution.

Faced with this frightful danger, New Christians fled in terror. Initially *conversos* of Jewish origin began to leave Spain following the mass conversions of 1391, and later Portugal after the forced conversions of 1497. The waves of emigration varied depending on circumstances. To stem this exodus, the Christian authorities in both countries issued regular decrees prohibiting emigration. Even the granting of permission to emigrate, which was purchased from Philip III in 1601 during the union of Spain and Portugal, was eventually rescinded.

Nonetheless, as we have seen, such proclamations were repeatedly evaded: Marranos left both countries clandestinely, or alternatively obtained permission to take trips abroad and never returned. There were even cases of Marranos leaving on the pretext of making a pilgrimage to Rome as a means of escape. However, once the authorities became aware of such plans they attempted to prevent the Marranos' departure. There are some cases where the highest authorities closed their eyes to such emigration, particularly where the skills of those wishing to leave were needed in other lands. Thus, thousands of Marranos left the Iberian Peninsula during the centuries when the Inquisition was in power.

It should be noted that not all New Christians who left Spain and Portugal practised Judaism in secret. Some were actually devout Christians and had no intention of reverting to Judaism. A number of these may simply have shared the general insecurity felt by all New Christians. Others possibly feared that they might be caught up in the Inquisition because of their connections with relatives or friends. In some cases, they may simply have wished to hide their Jewish origins, seeking to improve their lot in foreign lands.

Yet, there were large numbers of secret Jews, passionately devoted to the Jewish faith, who fled from oppression. In their quest to find a safe place where they would be able to live openly as Jews, they travelled to a wide variety of countries. The most natural places of refuge were Muslim lands since Muslims were the arch-enemies of the Christians, and the staunchly Catholic Spain and Portugal were particularly detested. By the end of the fourteenth century Morocco had become a haven of refuge, but in later centuries Marranos were attracted to the lands of the Ottoman Empire. In this regard the Ottoman sultan Bayazid II mocked King Ferdinand for impoverishing Spain by expelling the Jews, and numerous cities in the Ottoman Empire grew in numbers of these emigrés including Cairo, Jerusalem, Safed, Damascus, Constantinople and Salonica.

Next to Muslim countries, Protestant lands offered an important refuge for fleeing Marranos. As in Ottoman territory, here Catholics were detested, and the Inquisition was seen as a heinous and fearful institution since it was no more tolerant of Protestant heretics than of Marranos. In England, Hamburg and other German cities, Marranos lived as secret Jews before the Reformation, continuing that way of life long after these areas had broken with Rome since Protestant authorities were not willing to permit Jews to live in their midst. In Hamburg, for example, the settlement of Jews was not authorized until 1612. In England, Marranos settled in London and Bristol but were never officially recognized as Jews. Initially figures such as Manasseh ben Israel sought to secure formal recognition of the Jewish community, but their efforts were unsuccessful. However, when the Crown granted Jews an official charter of protection, such permission further facilitated the development of the Marrano community.

While Marranos settled in Amsterdam at the end of the sixteenth century, they had to wait until 1615 before Jewish settlement was officially allowed. Yet, the Marranos in Amsterdam differed from those in other Protestant countries since they openly practised Judaism from the time of their arrival. Such an open environment encouraged mass emigration and, as we have noted, Amsterdam became one of the most important Jewish centres in Europe. In addition, it also served as a refuge for oppressed Jews from other countries including France in 1615 and Eastern Europe after the Polish pogroms of 1648.

Not surprisingly, Catholic lands outside the control of Spain and Portugal did not offer as secure a haven as Ottoman or Protestant countries. Yet, because they were not under the control of the Inquisition of Spain and Portugal, they did provide a place of refuge; nonetheless, local authorities were not free from outside pressure and, as a result, Marranos were not free of danger. In Rome and Ancona, Marrano communities in the sixteenth century prospered under Clement VII, Paul III and Julius III. Under Paul IV they were even guaranteed that if accused of apostasy they would be subject only to papal authority, yet during this period they became subject to the Counter-Reformation and all protection was withdrawn. As a consequence, over twenty Judaizers were burned alive in 1556, twenty-six others were condemned to the galleys, and thirty others were freed only after paying a fine. It was only through the intervention of Gracia Nasi that the sultan at Constantinople was able to release all Marranos who were his subjects. Plans were made to boycott Ancona and transfer all the Marranos' former business to Pesarol, but the project failed and the Duke of Urbino expelled Marranos from his territory.

In Florence, it appears that there were some Marranos among the Spanish and Portuguese merchants who traded with Spain and the colonies. In Ferrara, the Marranos formed an important community by the sixteenth century, and they were protected by the dukes until 1581 when Duke Alfonso II allowed many of them to be arrested. Three were sent to Rome to be burned at the stake. In Venice in the fifteenth and sixteenth centuries

Marranos were permitted to settle, but were subject to decrees of expulsion. Later, however, Marranos were welcomed, and some theologians claimed that Judaizers were outside the jurisdiction of the Inquisition since they had been baptised by force. During this period Ferdinand II sought to attract Marranos to Pisa and Leghorn by issuing a charter in 1593 protecting them from persecution. Although few Jews settled in Pisa, Leghorn became a significant centre.

In France Marranos practised Catholicism for two centuries while secretly following Jewish customs. Even though they were referred to as 'New Christians', their loyalty to the Jewish faith was widely accepted. Living in their own quarters, they developed a system of schools as well as communal institutions. As time passed their link to Catholicism became increasingly tenuous, and in 1730 they were officially recognized as Jews. Marranos had also settled in the Aragonese territories of Sicily, Sardinia and Naples as well as in Habsburg territories, colonial territories in the Far East and the Americas. Frequently their position was insecure, particularly where the Inquisition wielded authority.

In these far-flung communities, Marranos were often able to play important roles in economic and social life. Such opportunities were important incentives for Marranos to continue living as secret Jews in Catholic lands, rather than practise Judaism publicly. In many cases these individuals were allowed to settle in foreign lands precisely because they played a major role in the economic life of the host country. As we have noted, some Marranos rose to prominence in international trade, banking and finance. In addition, they were actively engaged in large trading companies such as the Dutch East Indies and West Indies Companies. Further, a number of Marranos made contributions to manufacturing, handicrafts, armaments and shipbuilding. Others dealt in commodities including coral, sugar, tobacco and precious stones. Yet other Marranos were engaged in printing – by the end of the sixteenth century Venice had the leading press, and in the next century Amsterdam became the centre for publishing. Other cities, including Leghorn, Hamburg and London, had important presses, and printing in smaller places added to the dissemination of Jewish culture. Marrano writers, too, made a significant contribution to Jewish life.

NINE

Eastern European Anti-Semitism

Jews living in Poland initially played an important role in the economic affairs of the country. Unlike Jews living in western European lands, Jews in Poland enjoyed a degree of tolerance and were granted various privileges. Under these favourable conditions, the Jewish population created an elaborate structure of self-government and rabbinic learning flourished. However, the country was subject to Christian-inspired anti-Jewish outbreaks in the late medieval period, and in the seventeenth century Polish Jewry was attacked by Cossacks led by Bogdan Chmielnicki. In the next century the Hasidic movement revitalized Jewish life, but its unorthodox approach was severely condemned by the rabbinic establishment. As the community was torn by this internal conflict, Jewry was subject to repeated attack. In Russia Jews were initially prevented from settling in the country; with the annexation of Polish territories to Russia in the nineteenth century, the Jewish people were viewed by their neighbours with contempt and eventually expelled from the villages where they lived.

JEWS IN EASTERN EUROPE
The first Jews to live in the area between the Oder and the Dnieper appear to have come from the south-east, the Jewish kingdom of the Khazars, and Byzantium. Initially they played an important role in activities related to the circulation of merchandise and money. In this milieu, Jews gained considerable influence; indeed, according to legend, a Jew, Saul Wahl, temporarily became king of Poland.

By the mid-thirteenth century, King Boleslav V granted Polish Jewry a charter similar to that granted by German princes in previous centuries. As might be expected, such positive treatment evoked a hostile response from the clergy. From the second half of the thirteenth century, Polish ecclesiastical authorities issued legislation against the Jewish population, and in 1279 an attempt was made to impose the wearing of a Jewish insignia. In the following century, Jews were accused of ritual murder and profanation of the Host. In 1454 Casmir IV withdrew a number of privileges granted to the Jews, and thirty years later Jews were expelled from Warsaw. This was followed by their expulsion from Cracow and an attempt to expel them from Lithuania.

Despite the similarities between these events and the treatment of the Jewish community in western European lands during the Middle Ages, Polish Jewry did not endure the same degree of hardship as their fellow Jews in England, France, Germany and Spain. Throughout Poland, Jews were successful in gaining important economic positions, and thus were deeply rooted in the social and cultural fabric of the country; they were employed in a wide variety of trades and created important communal organizations. As the Papal Legate Commendoni observed in 1565: 'In these regions masses of Jews are to be found, who are not subject to the scorn they meet with elsewhere. They do not live in abasement and are not reduced to menial trades thereby. They own land, engage in commerce, study medicine and astronomy. They possess great wealth and are not only counted among respectable people but sometimes even dominate them. They wear no distinctive insignia, and are even permitted to bear arms. In short, they have all the rights of citizens.'

Unlike their coreligionists elsewhere, Polish Jews did not live in ghettos, nor were they restricted in their occupations. Instead, they were able to engage in all aspects of commerce and trade, administration, industrial management and agriculture. Some Polish Jewish bankers owned considerable lands; others served as stewards, tradesmen and commercial agents of Polish lords. Others imported wood, wheat, skins and furs. The majority worked as tradesmen, artisans, innkeepers, retail dealers or farmers.

As a result of this socio-economic pattern, Polish Jewry was able to create a form of local and national self-government. The basis of this system was the *kahal* (community), a geographical unit comprising Jews who lived in the city and the surrounding countryside. Each year electors selected the administrators of each *kahal*. These individuals were responsible for collecting taxes and customs, maintaining public order, organizing synagogue affairs and controlling the labour market. The *kahal* was also responsible for appointing the rabbi, who had authority over judicial affairs. Elected commissioners dealt with various charitable activities, including ransom of prisoners and care of the sick, elderly and needy. Burial societies were charged with burial of the dead.

The *kahal* was employed by the Polish authorities for the collection of taxes. It was usual to impose a single annual tax on all Jews, to be allocated among the various communities. From the sixteenth century, representatives of each *kahal* gathered in the spring at the Lublin fair, and the Yaroslav fair in the autumn – there they determined their quotas, adjudicated conflicts, and published laws and decrees. This federal body, which met bi-annually, was referred to as 'Council of the Four Nations'. Through this organizational structure the Polish Jewish community enjoyed considerable autonomy and independence from external influence.

The favourable conditions prevailing in Poland during this period encouraged the flowering of talmudic scholarship. Beginning in the late fifteenth century a number of outstanding authorities produced commentaries on talmudic law; within *yeshivot* (rabbinical academies) the methods of *pilpul* (dialectical study) and *hilluk* (differentiation and the reconciliation of differing opinions) were widely used. A seventeenth-century chronicle describes the nature of the educational system that prevailed throughout Poland:

> Each community maintained young men and provided for them a weekly allowance of money that they might study with the head of the academy. And for each young man they also maintained two boys to study under his guidance, so that he would orally discuss the *Gemara*, the commentaries of Rashi, and the *Tosafot*, which he had learned and thus he would gain experience in the subtlety of talmudic argumentation. The boys were provided with food from the community benevolent fund or from the public kitchen. If the community consisted of fifty householders it supported not less than thirty young men and boys. One young man and two boys would be assigned to one householder.

As a result of this system there was scarcely a household in all of Poland where the members did not occupy themselves with Jewish study. Either the head of the family, or his son, or his son-in-law, or one of the young men who ate with them was a scholar.

In each community great honour was accorded the head of the academy: 'His words were heard by rich and poor alike. None questioned his authority. Without him no one raised his hand or foot, and as he commanded so it came to be. In his hand he carried a stick and a lash, to smite and to flog, to punish and chastise transgressors, to institute ordinances, to establish safeguards, and to declare the forbidden. Nevertheless, everyone loved the head of the academy.'

During this period Polish rabbinic scholars were indirectly influenced by Renaissance humanism. Textual criticism was used to determine the precise reading of ancient texts and correct errors that had occurred during centuries of copying manuscripts. In addition, scholars collected and summarized the legal interpretations of eastern European and western European and oriental *halakhists* (legal experts). With the emergence of printing presses, rabbinic sources were made available to Jewish scholars within the *yeshivot*. In the discussions that took place the value of Joseph Caro's *Shulkhan Aruch* (Code of Jewish Law) was a major issue. Some authorities were disappointed that this code had become the central text for study in the *yeshivot* as well as a guide for rabbis. In their view, the adjudication of cases should be based on talmudic sources and the opinions of recent scholars. Nonetheless, the *Shulkhan Aruch* became the basis for rabbinic study since it contained the notes and commentaries of Polish scholars of the sixteenth and seventeenth centuries.

Even though Jewish life in Poland was relatively stable, the Jewish community was subject to anti-Semitic attack. In 1521 the proconsuls and consuls of Lvov wrote to their fellow consuls in Poznan criticizing Jewish merchants. 'The infidel Jews,' they stated, 'robbed us and our merchant citizens of almost all our sources of livelihood . . . they alone engage in commerce, go out to the small towns and villages, and do not permit anything to reach Christian hands.'

Nearly a century later, the author and Jew-hater Sebastian Miczynski castigated Jews for their commercial techniques. 'In Lvov, in Lublin, in Poznan and particularly Cracow,' he wrote, 'not to mention Vilna, Mohilev, Slutzk, Brest-Litovsk, Lutsk and elsewhere, the Jews have in almost every brick house five, ten, fifteen or sixteen shops. These shops are full of merchandise and all kinds of wares . . . they go to other countries from which they import sundry goods to Poland . . . when goods of any kind reach Poland the Jews quickly purchase everything. . . . In addition they export goods . . . to Hungary, to Moravia . . . and to other places. They trade in spices and in all kinds of grain, in honey and sugar, in milk products and other foodstuffs. There is scarcely any kind of goods, from the most expensive to the cheapest, in which the Jews do not trade. . . . They do not rest satisfied with sitting in shops and doing business. Some of them actually go round the market, the houses and the courtyards peddling their wares. . . . They entice . . . the buyers . . . and attract them to the Jewish shops promising them good bargains.'

The wide dissemination of such sentiments alleging the pernicious influence of Jews led to major calamity in the middle of the seventeenth century. In 1648 Bogdan Chmielnicki was elected hetman of the Cossacks and instigated an insurrection against the Polish gentry, which had previously oppressed Cossack peasants. 'Remember the insults of the Poles and the Jews, their favourite stewards and agents!', he proclaimed. As administrators of noblemen's estates, Jews were slaughtered in this revolt. Estates and manor houses were destroyed, and victims were flayed, burned alive and mutilated. Infants were murdered and cast into wells; women were cut open and sewn up again with live cats thrust into their wounds.

Chmielnicki's troops spread throughout all of south-eastern Poland, reaching the gates of Lvov, massacring Poles and Jews indiscriminately as they passed. Contemporary Jewish accounts depict the horrors of this massacre: 'These persons died cruel and bitter deaths. Some were skinned alive and their flesh was thrown to the dogs; some had their hands and limbs chopped off, and their bodies thrown on the highways only to be trampled by wagons and crushed by horses; some had wounds inflicted on them . . . some children were pierced by spears, roasted on the fire, and then brought to their mothers to be eaten.' In this onslaught thousands died in towns east of the Dnieper and elsewhere.

As the Cossacks advanced, the Polish king died and was succeeded by John Casimir who attempted to negotiate with the Cossacks who demanded an independent Ukrainian state. After several years of battle, Chmielnicki appealed to the Russian allies who invaded north-western Poland, but by the following year a Polish partisan movement drove back these invaders. Eventually, in 1667 Russia and Poland signed the Treaty of Andrusovo, which distributed the western Ukraine to Poland, and the eastern Ukraine and the Smolensk region to Russia.

During this period the Jewish population was decimated by various forces: the Cossacks and Ukrainian peasants viewed the Jews as representatives of the Polish aristocracy; the Russians, who did not allow Jews to settle in their lands, joined the Cossack hordes in this massacre; and the Polish partisans saw Jews as allied with the Swedes. Nearly a quarter of the entire Jewish population died in this attack, and thousands were ransomed from the Tartars in the slave markets of Constantinople.

Following this catastrophe, the Jewish community went into mourning. In 1650 the Council of the Four Nations proclaimed national mourning in memory of the first victims. Polish Jews were not allowed to wear silk or velvet garments for three years. An annual fast was instituted on the twentieth of *Sivan*, the anniversary of one of the first massacres perpetrated at Nemirov, where Jews died as martyrs rather than convert to Christianity. To commemorate these tragedies new elegies (*selihot* and *kinot*) were written and recited in synagogues following those that traditionally recall Jewish suffering during the Crusades.

In addition, Jews performed acts of penance, seeing in their misery the just retribution for their sins. As an appeal from the Council of the Four Nations in 1676 declared: 'Gravely have we sinned before our Lord. . . . Troubles increase daily, life becomes more difficult, our people has no importance among other peoples. It is even surprising that, despite all the disasters, we continue to survive. The only thing left for us to do is to unite in a single alliance and obey the commandments of God and the precepts of our pious teachers and leaders.'

Some Jews, however, left Poland and sought a safe haven in other lands; everywhere Jewish communities offered assistance. Renowned rabbis went into exile and were welcomed because of their learning. Some were itinerant sages, such as the talmudist Zevi Hirsch Ashkenazi, the son of a famous rabbi of Vilna, who lived variously in Budapest, Sarajevo, Vienna, Venice, Prague, Altona, Amsterdam and London, eventually returning to Lvov. Other scholars adopted a less itinerant lifestyle, and for some time occupied rabbinic posts particularly in Germany. Mass immigration to Hungary and Rumania took place too, and collections were made to support these newcomers as well as to ransom those Jews who had been sold into slavery.

As the century progressed, Jewish life in Poland became more insecure due to increasing political instability. Nonetheless, the Jewish community expanded in numbers during the seventeenth century. Approximately a third of Polish Jewry lived in the countryside in small groups where they were repeatedly subject to accusations of shedding Christian blood for ritual purposes. During this period a witness, Michael the Neophyte, a converted Jew who claimed to have been the former grand rabbi of Lithuania, swore on the crucifix that ritual murder was an absolute commandment of Judaism and that he himself had murdered Christian children. His writings, *Revelations of the Jewish Rites before God and the*

World, became the catechism of anti-Semites for the next two hundred years and more.

Further to the east, in the 1730s and 1740s Cossacks known as Haidemaks invaded the Ukraine, robbing and murdering Jews, and finally butchering the Jewish community of Uman in 1768. Throughout this period the Polish *kehillot* (Jewish communities) were heavily taxed, and often claims were made that the leaders of Jewry placed most of the tax burdens on the poor.

In Lithuania, however, Jewish life flourished, and Vilna became a major centre of Jewish scholarship. There Elijah ben Solomon Zalman, the Vilna Gaon, lectured to disciples and composed commentaries on the Bible, Mishnah, Talmud, *midrashim*, the *Sepher Yetsirah* (Book of Creation), *Zohar*, and the *Shulkhan Aruch*. Distancing himself from earlier eastern European scholars, he rejected the method of *hilluk* and focused instead on the simple meaning of the text. In addition, his interests encompassed secular fields of knowledge such as algebra, geometry, astronomy and geography. Uniquely, he stood out against the excesses of religious piety that began to have a major influence on Polish Jewry during the latter half of the eighteenth century.

In the wake of the massacres of the seventeenth century, many Polish Jews became increasingly critical of traditional Judaism, and through the development of Hasidism – a pietistic movement with its roots in the eighteenth century – were able to develop a new type of spirituality divorced from the world of rabbinic scholarship. The founder of this new movement was Israel ben Eleazer, known as the Baal Shem Tov or Besht. Born in southern Poland in 1700, he journeyed with his wife to the Carpathian Mountains; subsequently he travelled to Mezibozh where, according to Hasidic legend, he performed various miracles and instructed his disciples in Kabbalah. By the 1740s he had attracted a considerable number of disciples who passed on his teaching. After his death in 1760, one of his disciples became the leader of this sect, and subsequently Hasidism spread throughout eastern Europe: to Poland, the Ukraine, and Lithuania.

The success of Hasidism evoked a hostile response from rabbinic authorities. In particular, the rabbinic leadership of Vilna issued an edict of excommunication, and the Hasidim were charged with various heterodox activities, including permissiveness in their observance of the *mitzvot*, laxity in the study of the Torah, excess in prayer, and preference for a kabbalistic prayer book rather than the Ashkenazi *Siddur*. Pre-eminent among those who condemned the Hasidim was the Vilna Gaon who declared in a pastoral letter: 'You have already learned, our brothers in Israel, of this news that our fathers never dreamed of, which is that a suspect sect has appeared, known as Hasidim. . . . In praying, they utter dreadful alien cries, behave like madmen and explain their behaviour by saying that their spirits are wandering in distant worlds. They use painted prayer books and shriek so that the walls shake; heads down, feet in the air, they pray moving in a circle.'

Continuing this diatribe, the Vilna Gaon castigated the Hasidim for their attitude to traditional learning and suggested how members of this deviant group should be treated: 'They completely ignore the study of the holy Torah, and are not ashamed to say that it is useless to devote oneself to study and that one need not excessively deplore sins already committed. . . . That is why we write to our brothers in Israel . . . that they may prove their ardour by exterminating them, banishing and anathematizing them . . . so that there will not be even two such heretics left, for their suppression will be a benefit to the world.'

In some cases charges made against the Hasidim were even more serious, and puns on the term *hesed*, which can mean disgrace and crime, made it possible to accuse them of even more serious offences and debaucheries. As one opponent declared: 'Horror be upon me, who am obliged to hear what mysteries they have invented! Do they not thereby introduce impure thoughts into the Holy of Holies. Their prayer becomes a kind of dream, for it is only in dreams that man learns of his hidden desires. . . . And to repress such thoughts, the Hasidim utter deafening cries and in the course of prayer scream words that have no part in them.'

In later years the Hasidim and their opponents, the Mitnagdim, bitterly denounced one another. Relations deteriorated further when Jacob Joseph Polonnoye published a book critical of rabbinic Judaism: his work was burned, and in 1781 the Mitnagdim ordered that all relations with the Hasidim cease. By the end of the century the rabbinic establishment of Vilna denounced the Hasidim to the Russian government, leading to the arrest and imprisonment of several leaders. Yet despite such bitter criticism, the Hasidic movement was eventually given official recognition by the Russian and Austrian governments. With time, the movement divided into a variety of separate groups under the leadership of various individuals who passed on positions of authority to their descendants.

As the Jewish community was torn asunder by the rift concerning the legitimacy of this growing movement, Jews continued to suffer hostility. In the Ukraine and White Russia, Jews were attacked. In this milieu Basil Voshtchilo styled himself as Ataman Voshtchilo, grandson of Chmielnicki, grand hetman of the troops. Determined to exterminate Jewry and defend Christendom, he declared:

> In their petitions, the Jews claimed that I am fomenting disturbances and that I oppose the government with violence. This is a base lie. I have never had such an intention. I am a Christian. In this region, infidel Jews have not only deprived Christians of their means of existence, but they carry out aggressions, murders, robberies, and oppress the holy sacraments. Without their sanction and their written authorization for the priest, no newborn child can be baptised. They bewitch the pans, the lords of the nobility, and thereby gain their acquiescence. They rape Christian women and do many other things that are difficult even to list. Impelled by my fervour for the holy Christian faith, I have decided in company with other men of honour, to exterminate the cursed Jewish people . . .

In the fifteenth century the first Jews settled in Muscovy during the reign of Ivan III. In about 1470, a Jew, Skharia, arrived in Novgorod, ingratiated himself with the clergy there, and convinced a number of them of the superiority of the Jewish tradition. As a consequence, Pope Dennis, Pope Alexis and several others converted to Judaism. Later a modified form of the religion was practised; although these Judaizers continued to revere Christ, they denied his divinity, and rejected the doctrine of the Trinity as well as burning icons. This heresy spread from Novgorod to Moscow and even penetrated the royal court.

Ivan III's favourite, Feodor Karitzin, and his daughter-in-law Helena joined this group. As a first-hand chronicler reported, 'since the time when the Pravoslavic sun first shone in our country, there has never been such a heresy. In the home, in the streets, in the markets, clergy and laymen debated the faith and no longer trusted the teachings of the Prophets, the Apostles, and the Fathers of the Church; but on the arguments of the heretics, renegades of Christianity, sided in friendship with them and accepted instruction in Judaism.'

When he recognized the inherent dangers of this heresy, Ivan III intervened, and in 1504 the leaders of the movement were burned.

Nonetheless, their religious views were not suppressed, and they reappeared in the following centuries. So as to protect themselves from future Judaizing, the Muscovite authorities decided to isolate the Jewish community. Hence in 1526 Demitri Guerassimov declared: 'The Jews revolt us most of all, and the very mention of their name horrifies us. We do not permit them to enter our lands, for they are vile and evil-doing men.'

Later, when Ivan IV was urged by the Polish king Sigismund Augustus to permit several Jewish merchants to live in Moscow, he stated:

Apropos of what you write to persuade us to allow your Jews to enter our lands, we have already written several times, telling you of the vile actions of the Jews, who have turned our people away from Christ, introduced poisonous drugs into our state, and caused much hurt to our people. You should be ashamed, our brother, to write about them knowing their misdeeds all the while. In other states, too, they have done much evil, and for this have been expelled or put to death. We cannot permit the Jews to come into our state, for we do not wish to see evil here. We pray that God may permit the people of our country peace; without any disturbance. And you, our brother, should not write to us in the future concerning the Jews.

Such a resolute stance was maintained by his successors; however, in the seventeenth century, a number of converted Jews, some of whom practised Judaism in secret, were allowed to reside in Moscow, albeit unofficially; officially, they were forbidden to enter the city. Thus in 1698 Peter the Great said to the burgomaster of Amsterdam who requested that Jewish merchants be allowed to enter Moscow: 'You know, my friend, the character and customs of the Jews; you also know the Russians. I, too, know them both, and believe me: the time has not yet come to unite these two peoples. Tell the Jews that I thank them for their offers and I understand the advantages I might have derived from them, but I would have pitied them for having to live among the Russians.'

This policy of exclusion continued after his death and was followed by Empress Catherine I who published an order which proclaimed: 'The Jews of masculine sex and those of feminine sex who are found in the Ukraine and in other Russian cities are to be expelled at once behind the frontiers of Russia. Henceforth they will not be admitted into Russia upon a pretext, and a very close watch will be kept upon them in all places.'

Over the next two centuries, Jews entered Russia illegally or with permission from Poland and Lithuania. Occasionally they settled in border towns. During this period, Russian rulers issued decrees which prohibited the entry of Jewish merchants and treaties between Poland and Russia included such proscriptions. Nonetheless, small Jewish communities existed in the region of Smolensk. In 1742, Tsarina Elizabeth Petrovna expelled the few Jews living in the kingdom. In response the Senate sought to cancel this decree by pointing out the financial loss to the state it entailed, but the Tsarina declared that she did not wish to profit from the enemies of Christ.

Later, at the beginning of Catherine II's reign, the question of whether Jews might be permitted to enter Russia for economic reasons again became an issue. Although the Tsarina was inclined to accede to this request, she was compelled to give in to popular opinion. Despite such a setback, some Jews penetrated the territory, and the authorities did not disturb those living in territories conquered from Turkey in 1768. However, by the close of the century, hundreds of thousands of Jews came under the jurisdiction of the Tsarina as a consequence of the partition of Poland. Those Jews who lived in the regions annexed to Russia formed a distinct social class – many leased villages, flour mills, farms, inns and taverns. Others were merchants, shopkeepers and tradesmen. The rest worked as craftsmen for landowners and peasants. However, the economic position of those Jews residing in this region declined over time. After coming under Russian rule, many Jewish communities incurred considerable debt, and the burden of taxes forced large numbers to leave small towns and settle instead in villages or on the estates of noblemen.

With the annexation of the Polish territories in 1772, the Russian government viewed Jews in Russia as a serious problem which could only be solved through assimilation or expulsion. However, during the first fifty years of their incorporation, their status remained as it had been under Polish rule. In 1791 a decree was promulgated that stipulated that Jews had the right to live in territories annexed from Poland, and permitted their settlement in the uninhabited steppes of the Black Sea shore as well as in provinces to the east of the Dnieper. This region – the Pale of Settlement – took its final form with the annexation of Bessarabia in 1812. The total lands of the Pale extended from the Baltic to the Black Sea, consisting of an area of nearly a million square kilometres.

In the regions that had been annexed to Poland, Jews living in villages were blamed for the impoverished condition of the peasantry, and Jewish autonomy was viewed as undermining the Christian feudal structure of the country. As a result, the first Jewish Statute was issued in 1804, which stipulated various economic restrictions. After the promulgation of this decree, the expulsion of the Jewish population from villages began to occur, as did the settlement of Jews in southern Russia. In 1822 Jews were expelled from villages, and an unsucessful attempt was made to persuade Jews to embrace Christianity.

CATASTROPHE AND MESSIANISM

Unlike Western Christendom, where Jews repeatedly suffered oppression and persecution, Poland initially offered its Jewish population a significant degree of security. As we have seen, the Polish Jewish community flourished throughout the Middle Ages, encouraging the efflorescence of rabbinic learning. Yet generations of Ukrainian peasants viewed Jews as agents of Polish overlords and Christ-killers. To the Ukrainian, the Pole was an alien, yet Jews were worse: they were infidels who served alien conquerors.

The Chmielnicki rebellion was thus sparked by social, economic and religious motives and resulted in the destruction of hundreds of Jewish communities; it is probable that more than over 100,000 Jews were killed in this onslaught. From the Ukrainian nationalist perspective, this revolt was an early movement of liberation, and its leader was perceived as a national hero. In reality, Chmielnicki was the politically ambitious son of a minor aristocrat who had capitalized on the grievances of the peasants. His aim was to create an autonomous Ukraine; ten years after his death his plan came to nothing with Russia's annexation of eastern Ukraine.

Whatever the outcome, the Chmielnicki uprising was savage in character, and became a war of extermination against the Polish nobility and the Jewish community. The peasantry seized the opportunity to rid the country of an oppressive regime, and sought to avenge previous injustices. Not surprisingly, this catastrophe encouraged the Jewish masses to long for a messianic redeemer who would deliver them from their travails. The terrible devastation of Polish Jewry heightened the belief that the coming of the Messiah was close at hand.

Anti-Semitism and messianism were thus inextricably linked in the early modern period, providing the background for the arrival of the mystical Messiah, Shabbetai Tzevi. However, as we have seen, Shabbetai's conversion to Islam caused great consternation among his followers: many of his former disciples abandoned their belief in messianic redemption and left for their native lands. Nonetheless, not all of those who had accepted Shabbetai's messianic role deserted their leader, and Shabbetean groups flourished in Turkey, Italy and Poland where various figures claimed to be his legitimate successors. The largest circles of Shabbeteans in Turkey were located in Salonika, Smyrna and Constantinople.

In Constantinople the head of the Shabbeteans was Abraham Yakhini who died in 1682. In Smyrna, Abraham Cardozo played a leading role among the Shabbeteans after he left Tripoli in 1673, and later Tunis and Leghorn – there he joined a large circle of followers of Shabbetai including the rabbi and preacher Elijah ben Solomon, Abraham ha-Kohen Ittamari and the cantor David ben Israel Bonafoux. During this period Cardozo produced a wide range of literary works in which he expounded his interpretation of Shabbetean theology.

In his *Boker Avraham*, Cardozo argued that there is a difference between the God of the philosophers and the God of Israel who revealed himself to the Jewish people. In his view, the Jewish nation had been misled by the writings of such thinkers as Saadiah Gaon and Maimonides; only the teachers of the Talmud and the kabbalists have understood the true meaning of the Torah. However, with the coming of messianic redemption, a few elect individuals will be able to penetrate the divine mysteries as conceived by Shabbetai. For some time, Cardozo saw himself as the Messiah ben Joseph, the revealer of the true faith who must suffer before the advent of the Messiah ben David.

In Salonica, on the other hand, there existed a wide circle of believers in Shabbetai's teachings including Shabbetai's last wife, her father Joseph Filosof, and her brother Jacob Querido as well as several influential rabbis. After Nathan's death, those claiming to have visions of Shabbetai became increasingly common, leading to a mass conversion of some three hundred families who had become convinced they should follow Shabbetai's example. Along with these converts among Shabbetai's contemporaries, a new group led by Joseph Filosof and Solomon Florentin established a new sect, the *Doenmeh* who, as we previously noted, professed Islam in public but in private adhered to an heretical form of Judaism. Marrying among themselves, they were soon perceived as a distinct group by both Jews and Turks and developed into three sub-groups. Among these apostates, Baruchiah Russo created a further schism by teaching that the new messianic Torah called for a complete reversal of values, symbolized by an inversion of the thirty-six prohibitions of the

Torah into positive obligations. It appears that this sect also developed the view that Shabbetai was divine; later Baruchiah was also seen as a divine figure.

With the exception of the *Doenmeh*, most of Shabbetai's followers did not depart from the Jewish tradition. This was true of Ashkenazi Jewry as well. After Shabbetai's death, a number of Ashkenazi Shabbeteans speculated that Shabbetai was the Messiah ben Joseph rather than the King-Messiah. Pre-eminent among those who adopted this position was Mordecai Eisenstadt; together with his brother he travelled through Bohemia, southern Germany and northern Italy encouraging the masses not to lose faith in messianic redemption. During this period, various claimants for the role of Messiah ben Joseph also came forward. These messianic figures had an enormous impact on Jewry as far away as Italy, where Abraham Rovigo and his associates collected testimonies from various Polish visitors such as Hayyim ben Solomon from Kalisz (Hayyim Malakh). In 1691 he came to Italy to study the writings of Nathan, which were not available in Poland; after his return he disseminated Nathan's ideas among the Polish rabbis.

Subsequently Hayyim Malakh went to Adrianople, and became a spokesman for the more radical branch of the Shabbetean movement, joining forces with Judah Hasid from Shidlov. From 1696 to 1700 they became the leaders of the 'holy society of Rabbi Judah Hasid', a group consisting of hundreds of Shabbeteans who engaged in extreme asceticism and planned to emigrate to Palestine to wait for Shabbetai's second coming. Groups of these individuals travelled through Polish and German communities spreading Shabbetean doctrine.

The emigration of Shabbeteans to Jerusalem in 1700 signified a high point of Shabbetean activity. However, the movement suffered great disappointment in its earliest stages. Hasid died on his arrival in 1700, and dissension erupted between moderates and the more radical elements, led by Malakh, who were expelled. Yet, even the moderates were not able to settle in the Holy Land, and many returned to Germany, Austria and Poland. Many believers had expected Shabbetai's return in 1706; when this did not materialize, the movement was further weakened and driven underground.

In time Shabbeteanism divided into two different factions. The moderates provided literary works that reached a wide public who were unaware of the messianic convictions of their authors. The radicals, on the other hand, became increasingly active after Baruchiah had been proclaimed 'Swanto Señor' and an incarnation of the Shabbetean interpretation of the 'God of Israel'. Through emissaries from Salonika and Podolia, they circulated manuscripts and letters expounding their kabbalistic views. The circles of Hasidim in Poland prior to the emergence of the Baal Shem Tov were deeply influenced by Shabbetean doctrine.

The Frankist movement was the last stage in the development of Shabbeteanism. Born in Podolia, Jacob Frank was educated in Czernowitz and Sniatyn, living for several years in Bucharest. It appears that Frank associated at an early stage with the Shabbeteans connected with the radical wing of the movement. Accompanied by these teachers, he visited Salonika in 1753 and became involved with the *Doenmeh*. Later he journeyed to the grave of Nathan of Gaza as well as Adrianople and Smyrna. Eventually he emerged as the leader of the Shabbeteans in Poland where he was viewed by his followers as a reincarnation of the divine soul which had previously resided in Shabbetai and Baruchiah.

In 1755 Frank, accompanied by R. Mordecai and R. Nahman, spent time with his relatives in Korolewka; he then journeyed through the communities in Podolia, which contained Shabbetean groups. Although he was received enthusiastically by Shabbeteans, his appearance at Lanskroun caused widespread consternation when he was discovered conducting a Shabbetean ritual with his followers. His opponents claimed that a religious orgy was taking place similar to the rites practised by members of the Baruchiah sect in Podolia. Although Frank's followers were imprisoned, he was released because the authorities thought he was a Turkish subject. At the request of the local rabbis an enquiry was instituted in Satanow that examined the practices of the Shabbeteans.

Frank then crossed the Turkish border and was arrested in March 1756 but again allowed to go free. Subsequently he remained in Turkey where he became a convert to Islam. In June and August 1757 he made secret visits to Podolia to confer with his followers. When he appeared in Poland, he was regarded as the central figure for the Shabbetean community. The rabbinic authorities, however, were deeply troubled by the findings of the Satanow enquiry: it became clear that Shabbeteans transgressed various Jewish laws including sexual prohibitions of the Torah. The results of this examination were presented to a rabbinic assembly at Brody and confirmed at a session of the Council of the Four Lands. In Brody a *herem* (excommunication) was issued against the members of the sect, which led to widespread persecution of the Shabbeteans, particularly in Podolia. To protect themselves from such antagonism, Frank's followers put themselves under the protection of Bishop Dembowski of Kamieniec-Podolski. On Frank's advice, they stressed the beliefs they held in common with Christians; in addition, they issued anti-Jewish propaganda at the instigation of their Christian protectors.

After the Brody *herem* was issued, the Frankists asked Bishop Dembowski to hold a new enquiry into the affair that took place at Lanskroun and petitioned that a disputation be arranged between themselves and the rabbis. In June 1757 a confrontation took place at Kamieniec involving nineteen opponents of the Talmud with several rabbis from local communities. Later in the year Bishop Dembowski issued his decision in favour of the Frankists and imposed a series of penalties on the rabbis including a decree that the Talmud be burned, an act reminiscent of church decrees of the Middle Ages. However, after the bishop's death, the Frankists were persecuted by the Jewish community, causing many to flee to Turkey where they converted to Islam. Other Frankists turned to the political and ecclesiastical authorities for permission to follow their own faith.

As time passed, it became clear that Frank and his followers would need to be baptised and they requested that Archbishop Lubienski in Lvov receive them into the Church. In making this application, they expressed the wish to be allowed to live a separate existence. The Church, however, replied that no special privileges would be granted. In July 1759 a disputation took place in Lvov as a precondition to conversion; there leading rabbis and members of the Frankist sect debated a variety of theological topics as well as the blood libel charge. In September 1759 Frank was baptised, and by the end of 1760 in Lvov alone more than five hundred Frankists followed his example.

Despite such widespread conversion, the Church became increasingly suspicious of the Frankists. It appeared that the real object of their devotion was Frank as the living incarnation of God. In February 1760 Frank was arrested and an inquisition took place that resulted in his exile to the fortress of Czestochowa. Despite his absence, his followers organized themselves into a network of secret sects. From the end of 1760 Frank's disciples began to visit him; in time the conditions of his imprisonment were relaxed and from 1762 his wife was permitted to join him, and a group of followers was allowed to settle near the fortress.

During the period between Frank's apostasy and his death, a number of members of the movement gained great wealth, particularly in Warsaw where they built factories and were involved in masonic activities. A group of about fifty families settled in Bukovina after his death and became known as the Abrahamites. Other families in Moravia and Bohemia maintained close connections with the *Haskalah* (Jewish enlightenment), combining kabbalistic theories with the rationalistic outlook of the Enlightenment. Only occasionally did entire groups of Frankists convert to Christianity, but a large number of younger members who went to Offenbach were baptised.

The Cossack uprising in Poland thus had profound implications for the development of Jewish messianism in the early modern period. In the wake of this onslaught, Jews in Eastern Europe and elsewhere became convinced that these terrible events were the birth pangs of the messianic age. Placing their hopes in the false Messiah Shabbetai, they believed that the anointed redeemer would come to deliver the Jewish people from the hands of their oppressors. News of Shabbetai's messiahship caused great frenzy throughout the Jewish world. Following Nathan of Gaza's instructions, Jews repented of their deeds, and engaged in various forms of asceticism. However, Shabbetai's subsequent conversion to Islam caused widespread dismay, despite the emergence of a range of Shabbetean sects. For the vast majority of Jews such an act of apostasy was deeply dispiriting. After centuries of persecution and murder, it appeared that the Jewish nation was to endure yet more tragedy as God's suffering servant.

TEN

The Early Modern Period

The commercial interests of the bourgeoisie coupled with previous
Christian antipathy to the Jews evoked considerable hostility towards
Jewry in the early modern period. In Germany merchants complained about
the infidels living in their midst; in their view Jewish trade undermined the
economic life of the country and corrupted the native population. In France
similar attitudes were expressed: the bourgeoisie resisted Jewish settlement
despite the fact that Jews were perceived by the nobility as particularly
useful. In Britain, Jews were also subject to bitter criticism, and attempts to
simplify procedures for Jewish naturalization met with resistance. In
addition, there was considerable opposition to the suggestion that Jews
should possess land. However, in the United States Jews were able to gain a
broad measure of freedom. Nonetheless, despite various advances made in
the seventeenth and eighteenth centuries, Jewish life did not radically alter.
Stereotyped as alien, Jews were subject to repeated acts of discrimination
and persecution during this period.

JEWS IN EUROPE AND THE NEW WORLD

At the beginning of the early modern period from the sixteenth century, Jewish
economic progress was often in conflict with the aspirations of the
bourgeoisie. As a consequence, commercial aspirations were frequently
intermingled with traditional forms of Judaeophobia. Towards the end of the
seventeenth century the Jewish population of Vienna was expelled by Leopold
I, Emperor of Austria. At the start of his reign he had adopted a positive
attitude towards the Jewish community. However, in 1669 a series of disasters
overtook him: a fire occurred in the palace, the heir to the throne died, and the
empress miscarried.

As the empress's confessor explained, these events were a divine
warning about the Jewish population. Thus the emperor decreed the
expulsion of Jewry on 28 February 1670. Later, when the Prussian Great
Elector, Frederick William, was informed of this proclamation, he took

advantage of their exodus to invite thirty rich Jewish families to live in his state to help finance industry and trade. Jews were granted a special and irrevocable charter which declared that they were to possess rights and protections. Yet, not unpredictably, such an influx incited the enmity of the indigenous Christian merchants. In 1673, they complained: 'These infidels run from village to village, from town to town, offer this and take that, whereby they do not only dispose of their discarded and wretched goods and deceive the people with old rags, but they spoil all commerce and particularly the retail trade, especially in silver, brass, tea and copper.'

The inflammatory mix of Christian religious hostility and perceived thwarted economic interests resulted in an attack on the Jewish population which took place in the Prussian town of Halberstadt. The Jews living there had built a synagogue without obtaining official permission. In response, the Christian population attacked the synagogue. As a Jewish document of the period explains: 'these traders, accompanied by armed musketeers, burst into our synagogue, seized the windows and doors and partially broke them down and razed the whole building to the ground, destroyed and smashed everything, cut it into pieces and caused such violent tumult and confusion, fear and terror that we could not but think that we were to be cut down and chased away to the last man, and then when the mob came running up from every corner we had to have soldiers on guard day and night for our protection.'

The Prussian government instituted an investigation of this incident. In their defence the Halberstadt bourgeoisie stated that their act was justified because of the pernicious influence of the Jews: 'it is unfortunately drawn from experience what evil is caused to the Jews and their eternal damnation by the establishment of such seminaries, in which superstition and a perverted understanding of all divine prophecy and revelation as well as contempt for Christ and his holy word is inculcated from childhood onwards, and thus the way to their conversion is made more difficult and remote; also, this people nowhere grows more numerous than where they are permitted to exercise their damnable religion.'

Despite such animosity, princes and nobility continued to view Jews as providing substantial economic advantages even though they were perceived as a corrupt influence on the Christian nation. In this regard, Frederick William advised his son, the future Frederick the Great, how to treat the Jewish population. 'So far as the Jews are concerned,' he stated, there are unfortunately many in our hands who have no letters of protection from me. These you must chase out of the country for the Jews are a locust in a country and ruin the Christians. I ask you, issue no new letters of protection, even if they offer you much money . . . if you need something for your pleasure, then put all the Jews down for 20,000 to 30,000 thalers every three or four years, in addition to the protection money they must give you. You must squeeze them for they betrayed Jesus Christ, and must not trust them for the most honest Jew is an arch traitor and rogue.

During this period German Jews played an important role in the commercial life of the country. In Leipzig, 25 per cent of those participating at fairs in the eighteenth century were Jews; in Hamburg they were actively involved in trade; in Frankfurt, Jewry comprised 16 per cent of the total population. Confronted by these Jewish tradesmen at the end of the eighteenth century, Goethe caricatured their commercial interests in a poem: 'If you want to buy a suit, to the Jew run back/ Silver dishes, linen, tin – anything the households lack/ you will find the Jew has by him, taken as a pledge for loans/ Stolen goods, abducted items, with him make their happy homes/ Coats and trousers – what you will, he will sell it cheap/ The craftsmen can sell nothing. To the Jew all creep.'

In the literature of this period the traditional identification of Jews as swindlers was reinforced. Hence, Spener, the founder of Lutheran pietism, declared: 'As for the poor among them, whose number, as it is among the Christians, is always the largest, it is quite impossible for them to live without cunning and ruses for they, having only a few thaler capital, must turn this over through trade so that they can meet the needs of their family as best they may; so the wretched people can day and night think and rack their brains about nothing else than how to spend their miserable lives in cunning, intrigue, deception and theft.'

Jews had been expelled from France during the Middle Ages; this edict was renewed by Louis XIII in 1615. Nonetheless, Jews lived semi-clandestinely in the kingdom. By the eighteenth century the Jewish community was widely despised. Given such a pervasive sentiment, there was constant resistance to any suggestion that Jews be granted official permission to settle in specific towns. Thus in 1708, the minor clergy of Nancy protested to Duke Leopold of Lorraine concerning just such a plan:

As we are to lose within minutes what has always so happily distinguished us from the most flourishing kingdoms, and will we, like the nations surrounding us, be forced to mourn the deadly wounds that eternally contagious trade can inflict on a state and a religion? These are no vague alarms. . . . How many visions of ruined merchants, devastated fields, oppressed and penniless families rise up before our eyes! Will you grant to the Jews, the most mortal enemies of Jesus Christ, his Church and the Christian name, what you have so firmly refused to heretics who have forgotten nothing in order to settle in your states?

Later in the second half of the eighteenth century, the Jewish request for authorization to engage in commerce in Paris met a similar reaction. The guilds opposed this plan on the grounds of tradition, and 1765 the lawyer Maître Goulleau, who represented the merchants and traders of Paris, drafted a memorandum listing crimes and misdeeds allegedly committed by Jews ranging from unsociableness to ritual murder. In another lawsuit, the lawyer and polemicist Linguet stated: 'Habit, religion, policy, reason perhaps, or at least an instinct justified by many reasons, drives us to attach both scorn and aversion to the name of the Jews.' In a similar vein and from another social level, in 1789 the old-clothes-men of Montpellier castigated the Jews for their previous crimes, and recommended their segregation: 'There is no one who does not carry in his heart the conviction of the evil that the Jewish people does throughout the world. The Supreme Being, when he created nature, expressly wished this race to be confined to a specific area, and forbade it to communicate in any way with other nations.'

In general French anti-Semitism in the eighteenth century was based on Christian religious antipathy combined with commercial interest. Both factors evoked hostility and fear, as the Minister of State Malesherbes expressed to Louis XVI on the eve of the Revolution: 'There still exists in the hearts of most Christians a very strong hatred of the Jewish people, a hatred based on the memory of the crime of their ancestors and corroborated by the custom whereby Jews in every country engage in trade which the Christians regard as their downfall.'

Militant Judaeophobia was thus largely a bourgeois-Christian phenomenon. Only the nobility, whose position in society rested on birth, showed some sympathy towards the Jewish population. Thus Prince Charles de Ligne composed *Memoire sur les Juifs* in which he declared that

Jews are never drunk, always obedient, precise and attentive to ordinances, loyal subjects to the sovereign in times of revolt, never angry, united among themselves, sometimes hospitable, and charitable to their poor coreligionists. In this tract, he appealed for the emancipation of Jewry. 'And, lastly,' he wrote, 'the Israelites, while awaiting the impenetrable decrees of Providence on their obduracy in the matter of the wrongs of their ancestors, will at least be happy and useful in this world, and will cease to be the meanest people on earth. I well understand the origin of the horror the Jews inspire, but it is time this ended. Eighteen hundred years seems to me long enough for anger to persist.'

Devoid of bourgeois prejudice, priests of aristocratic origin occasionally sought to protect Jews in the realm. Thus the Abbé de la Varenne de Saint-Saulieu declared in a letter to the Lieutenant of the Paris police in 1744 on behalf of a Jewish prisoner: 'I have not forgotten that you told me that I seemed like a rabbi when I spoke to you of this affair; but when you hear that the Jew on whose behalf I am speaking has done at least as much good in the prison where he is as all the charitable offices, when he has been in good health, and that few prisoners have left it without feeling the effects of his liberality, you will probably no longer accuse me of Judaism, and I am even convinced that you will become as much of one [a rabbi] as me, and that your sense of justice will commit you to imitate the Lord who rewards even in this world the good faith of these miserable victims of their blindness.' Such philo-Semitism, however, was not representative of the nation as whole. Among the vast majority of the French populace, the Jews were perceived as a malevolent force within society, dangerous to the merchant classes and a threat to Christian values.

The Jewish community in England was expelled at the end of the thirteenth century. In the middle of the seventeenth century Oliver Cromwell sought to readmit Jews to the British Isles, but this proposal was met with fierce opposition. Nonetheless, he allowed a colony of rich ex-Marrano merchants to settle in London. Later, a number of these newcomers acted as financiers and political informants on Spanish affairs and in time London became one of the main centres of the Marrano dispersion. By the eighteenth century Jews of German and Polish descent joined their coreligionists so that at the turn of the nineteenth century the number of Jews living in Britain was between 20,000 and 25,000.

English merchants were not unduly anxious about the Jewish presence. Thus in 1712 the statesman and publicist Joseph Addison remarked: 'They are indeed so disseminated through all the trading parts of the world, that they become the instrument by which the most distant nations converse with one another, and by which mankind are knit together in a general correspondence. . . . They are like pegs and nails in a great building, which, though they are but little value in themselves are absolutely necessary to keep the whole frame together.'

Despite such general tolerance, Jews were nevertheless subject to virulent criticism at the hands of several contemporary writers. Hence, in one of his satires, Alexander Pope composed a prayer in which he pleaded to be protected from the Jewish population: 'Keep us we beseech thee, from the hands of such barbarous and cruel Jews, who albeit they abhor the blood of black-puddings, yet thirst they vehemently after the blood of the white ones. And that we may avoid such like calamities, may all good and well-disposed Christians be warned by these unhappy wretches' woeful example, to abominate the heinous sin of avarice.' Similarly, Jonathan Swift warned the English public to be on its guard against the perfidious Jews: 'What if the Jews should multiply and become a formidable party among us? Would the dissenters join in alliance with them likewise, because they agree already in some general principles, and because the Jews are allowed to be a stiffnecked and rebellious people?'

In the same century the government of the Duke of Newcastle submitted a Naturalization Bill to simplify procedures for allowing Jews to become naturalized and acquire land. Even though both the House of Lords and the Commons adopted the bill, it encountered strong opposition from the general public. Petitions were submitted from all sectors of society, defamatory inscriptions appeared on the streets, and pamphlets were issued warning against the settlement of the Jews and their ownership of property. One of the agitators even gave a detailed prediction of the sad state that would befall England: St Paul's Cathedral transformed into a synagogue, trade ruined by the observance of the Sabbath, a ban on pork, and a Christian Naturalization Bill rejected by the Great Sanhedrin.

As a consequence of these charges, the law was repealed after six months. Underlying this rejection was deep-seated prejudice against the Jews – widely entrenched medieval conceptions of the Satanic Jew polluting Christian society overcame all efforts to grant Jews full civil rights. However, such political opposition to Jewish emancipation led to greater solidarity within the Jewish community. From 1760 representatives of Ashkenazi congregations joined with the Sephardim to oversee matters of common interest. This brought about the formation of the London Committee of Deputies of British Jews (known as the Board of Deputies) which comprised representatives of provincial and colonial congregations.

In the next century important families came to play an increasingly significant role in Jewish affairs. During this period Jewish civil and political disabilities were not acute; Jews enjoyed a considerable degree of social emancipation and were subject to few commercial restrictions. Nonetheless, a number of native-born Jews were influenced by the example of Jewish emancipation in France and pressed for similar changes to take place in Britain. In 1829 there was intense agitation for legislation similar to that which resulted in Catholic emancipation. The cause was championed by Robert Grant and Thomas Babington Macaulay in the House of Commons and by the Duke of Sussex in the Lords. Such pressure led to the Jewish Emancipation Bill being passed by the House of Commons in 1833, but rejected in the Lords. Despite such a defeat, minor disabilities were removed by the Religious Opinions Relief Bill of 1846, and some ten years later the House of Commons and the Lords permitted Jews to formulate their own oath, thereby allowing Jews to become Members of Parliament.

On the other side of the Atlantic, the New World and in particular North America began to see the immigration of Jews fleeing persecution and seeking religious and civil liberties. In the middle of the seventeenth century Jews fleeing the Brazilian Inquisition settled in New York. During this period other Jews settled in Massachusetts, Connecticut, Virginia and Maryland. By the middle of the next century there were several thousand Jews living in the United States. Even though representatives of the colonial power or the local assemblies issued complaints about them, there was little overt hostility directed at these immigrants. Such political figures as James Adams even extolled the Judaism of the Hebrew Scriptures and linked Puritan religious values to the Bible. In spirit, he stated, the Puritans should be considered as Jews rather than Christians: 'Their God was the God of the Old Testament, their guides to conduct were the characteristics of the Old Testament.'

In line with Christian teaching, the Puritans sought to bring these Jews to Christ. Thus, the Puritan Cotton Mather celebrated every Jewish conversion and wrote a treatise on the subject. The founder of Methodism, John Wesley, learned Spanish when he resided in America so that he could better convert Jews of Sephardic origin. 'Some of them,' he stated, 'seem nearer the mind that was in Christ than many of those who call him Lord.' In the view of the Quaker William Penn, the Jews should be converted with kindness. Other writers were more sceptical, insisting that Jews would never be integrated into the societies in which they lived. Thus Ezra Stiles noted: 'I remark that providence seems to make everything to work for mortification to the Jews, and to prevent their incorporating into any nation; that thus they may continue as a distinct people. . . . [It] forbodes that the Jews will never become incorporated with the people of America, any more than in Europe, Asia and Africa.'

Nonetheless, America was characterized by a tolerance for the Jewish population that was reinforced by the communal commitment to clear land and create settlements in the New World. Religious egalitarianism was the result of common effort and dedication; in such a milieu, Jews were able to obtain civic and electoral rights during the colonial period. During the War of Independence, a number of Jews served as soldiers; by joining together with their fellow Americans, these patriots won admiration and respect. In this regard, George Washington, the first President of the United States, expressed the desire that Jews enjoy prosperity and safety on American soil: 'May the children of the stock of Abraham who dwell in this land continue to merit and enjoy the good will of the other inhabitants; while every one shall sit in safety under his own vine and fig tree and there shall be none to make him afraid.'

By the end of the eighteenth century such liberality was reinforced by the doctrines of liberty and brotherhood enshrined in the constitution, yet other factors also served to improve the position of Jewry in the United States. The existence of a large black community provoked the resentment of the white population, thereby deflecting potential hostility away from the Jews. In addition, waves of immigration brought to the American shores individuals who evoked animosity and xenophobia: all these foreign groups became targets of prejudice in place of the Jewish population.

In the post-Revolutionary period many Jews, especially in South Carolina, where Jews had prospered from the eighteenth century, were highly educated and cultured. Nonetheless, such attributes did not protect them from Judaeophobia, which tended to increase as Jews gained positions of prominence. In federalist papers Jews who entered politics and joined the Jeffersonians were vilified as 'democrats'; others who sought public office were attacked. Despite such attitudes, emancipation was encouraged in the New Republic. In 1787, the Northwest Ordinance guaranteed Jews the same rights as fellow citizens in all new states, and the next year the Constitution granted equality at federal level. By 1820 only seven of the original thirteen states granted Jewry full political recognition, but ultimately Jews were appointed or elected town councillors, judges of lower courts, and members of state legislatures.

By the first decades of the nineteenth century there were about 4,000 Jews in the United States, scattered throughout the country. In the years prior to the Civil War the Jewish population grew dramatically. In 1840 there were about 15,000 Jews; by 1860 the number had grown to 150,000. This vast increase was the result of immigration from German lands. In Bavaria many villages lost their Jewish population to the New World; from Prussian Poland there was a constant flow of immigrants. German Jews from Bohemia and Hungary also emigrated to the United States. During the 1850s this influx reached a peak due to economic recession and the repressive aftermath of the continental revolutions of 1848–9. In the New World these immigrants were able to obtain the freedoms denied them in their countries of origin. Between 1820 and 1860 American Jews also attained considerable social acceptance, and in several cities including Charleston, New York and Philadelphia a number of them entered political life. In this milieu overt anti-Semitism was uncommon, and conversion to Christianity was a rare occurrence despite the activities of missionary groups.

Although there were undoubted improvements in Jewish life in various countries during the early modern period, the majority of Jews in western Europe were still confined to a ghetto existence. Thus the Prince de Ligne characterized German Jews in stereotypical terms, reminiscent of Jewish life in the Middle Ages, as 'always sweating from running about selling in public squares and taverns; almost all hunchbacked, such dirty red or black beards, livid complexions, gaps in their teeth, long crooked noses, fearful, uncertain expressions, trembling hands, appalling frizzy hair; knees bare and pocked with red; long, pigeon-toed feet, hollow eyes, pointed chins.'

In their quest to earn a living, Jewry was subject to innumerable obstacles. As the apologist Zalkind-Hourwitz remarked:

Here you have the state of the Jews . . . those who run about the provinces may breathe freer air, but are no less wretched for it. Apart from the expense, the difficulties and the dangers inseparable from a wandering life, they are continually harassed by trade, customs and inspection officials and very often arrested by the mounted constabulary on the slightest suspicion: they are obliged to carry their dishes and meat around with them, those of other nations being forbidden them; this annoys the greedy and intolerant inn-keepers who make them pay very dearly for the little they sell them. As oppression makes them suspicious, as people are likewise prejudiced against them, and as moreover they have no fixed domicile, they can barely buy or sell at all except for ready cash.

As in previous centuries, Jews were often described in the most negative terms; repeatedly they were depicted as exuding a particular smell (*foetor judaïcus*) in contrast to the Christian odour of sanctity. This smell was seen as a sign of their depravity. Thus the English author John Toland remarked: 'Yet so strong is the force of prejudice, that I know a person, no fool in other instances, who laboured to persuade me, contrary to the evidence of his own and my eyes . . . that every Jew in the world had one eye remarkably less than the other, which silly notion he took from the mob. Others will gravely tell you, that they may be distinguished by a peculiar sort of smell.'

Not surprisingly, the Jewish community turned inwards as a result of such prejudice, despising those who denigrated them. According to Zalkind-Hourwitz, Jews inevitably viewed Christians with the same contempt:

What must the Jews think of the people who oppress them solely because of their religion, and treat as friends all who abjure it, that is to say cease to be Jews, without worrying if they become Christians, or if they are decent people; what, I say, must the Jews think of this behaviour? Behaviour which, in this enlightened century, they can no longer attribute either to fanaticism or bad policy. Are they not right in concluding from it that Christianity ordains it, or that Christians, even the most honest and enlightened, are less zealous about moral principles and their own religion, than hostile to Judaism, and consequently to God its author?

Determined to remain loyal to their ancestral faith, Jews mistrusted Christians and rejected their values. Convinced of its own superiority, Jewry held firmly to the belief that God had chosen the Jews as his special people. Devoted to the covenant, they adhered to the ancient laws and customs of the Jewish faith. In response, Christians reviled these aliens in their midst. Even such enlightened and assimilated Jews as Moses Mendelssohn recognized the antipathy of the gentile world. Remarking that he preferred to stay at home rather than venture out into the streets, Mendelssohn stated in a letter to a Benedictine monk: 'Everywhere in this so-called tolerant country I live so constricted a life, hemmed in on all sides by true intolerance, that for the sake of my children I must shut myself up the whole day in a silk factory.'

As Mendelssohn explained, he repeatedly discussed this state of affairs with his wife and children: '"Father," an innocent child asks, "what does this fellow have against us? Why do people throw stones after us? What have we done to them?" "Yes, father dear," another says, "they chase after us in the streets and abuse us: 'Jews! Jews!' Is it then such a reproach in people's eyes to be a Jew? And how does that hamper other people?" Oh, I close my eyes and sigh to myself: Men! Men! How have you come to this?'

During this period even the word 'Jew' had come to be invested with emotive power, evoking hatred and disgust. Hence, when seeking to illustrate the vices of the Dutch, the writer Montesquieu exclaimed: 'I do not think that . . . there had ever been Jews more Jewish than some of them.' Even though some defenders of Jewry sought to improve the condition of the Jewish population, they universally abided by the same meaning of the word: the Jew was only esteemed on condition that he was not a Jew. Hence, the age-old concept of the Jew as a demonic and evil force in society continued to animate the Christian consciousness and evoked considerable resistance to proposals for the acceptance of Jewry on equal terms.

REFORMATION AND BEYOND

It might be expected that the emergence of modernity would bring to an end previous centuries of Judaeophobia. This, however, was generally not the case. Even though the Reformation of the sixteenth century brought many of the doctrines of the medieval Church under scrutiny, this did not include the traditional Christian hostility towards Jews. As we have noted, initially a number of leading Jewish scholars welcomed the Reformation, suggesting that this religious advance heralded the coming of the Messiah: some were encouraged by Luther's tract *That Jesus Christ Was Born a Jew*. Yet Luther's subsequent writings provided further justification for hatred of the Jewish population. The implications of Luther's attack on Jewry were far-reaching. If Christians were convinced that Jews were guilty of heinous crimes, then they were obliged to ensure that the Jewish community be prevented from committing further abominable acts. In Hesse another reformer, Martin Bucer, sought to restrict Jews in religious as well as commercial spheres.

There were nonetheless some Reformers who adopted a more sympathetic attitude, even though they shared their coreligionists' contempt for Judaism and the Jewish nation. Justus Jonas, a companion of Luther, stressed the missionary dimension of Luther's views: in his opinion, Christians have a duty to lead Jews to Christ. Another Lutheran, Andreas Osiander, the preacher at the Church of St Lorenz at Nuremberg, produced a work that sought to refute the blood-libel charge. In his view, it was ludicrous to believe that Jews should murder children and then use their blood for ritual purposes. Jewish law, he pointed out, specifies that Jews are forbidden to kill any human being, or to make use of blood from animals, much less that of a human child. No Jew, he noted, had ever made such a claim about other Jews. The origins of this charge were due no doubt to the unsubstantiated claims of those whose children had died of neglect or unknown causes.

Other Reform teachers emphasized the total depravity of humankind: in their view, gentiles and Jews stood guilty before God. Thus, it would be a mistake to insist that the Jews were particularly villainous. The reformer John Calvin of Geneva, for example, argued that when Scripture spoke of the Jews and their sinfulness, the Jews were a symbol of all humanity. When Jesus spoke of the hypocrisy of Jews in building the sepulchres for the prophets they themselves had killed, Calvin noted that there was a contemporary parallel: 'The world, in general, while not daring to scorn God utterly or at least rise up against Him to His face, devises a means of worshipping God's shadow in place of God: just so it plays a game over the prophets.' Even though Christians might erect statues of Peter and other saints, their base treatment of the faithful in their own day illustrates how they would react if Peter were among them.

Unlike Luther, who believed that God's special relationship with the Jews had come to an end, Calvin maintained that God often had to judge Israel. However, this did not mean that God's covenant with the Jews had been broken. Commenting on the verse: 'His blood be on us and on our children' (Matthew 27:25), Calvin stated that even though God had avenged Jesus' death with fearful means, he had left a remnant so that the covenant would not be destroyed: 'God in their very treachery displays the constancy of his faith, and to show that his covenant was not struck with Abraham to no effect. He rescues those he freely elected from the general destruction. Thus his truth ever arises superior to all obstacles of human incredulity.'

During this period, it was widely believed in Reformation circles that there would be a large-scale conversion of the Jewish people. In light of this, Calvin's successor at Geneva, Theodore Beza, revived Luther's early view that Christian churches were largely responsible for the current unbelief among the Jews: 'Those who today call themselves Christians . . . are very certainly punished and will be in the future, because, solely under the guidance of wickedness and perversity, they have mistreated in every way these people, so holy in their forefathers, actually hardening them further [against Christianity] by setting before their eyes the example of an odious idolatry. As for myself, I gladly pray every day for the Jews.'

Beza then went on to acknowlege the justice of divine anger against the Jewish people, but he pleaded that Christ would remember his convenants: 'Grant that we [gentiles],' he prayed, 'may advance in thy grace, so that we may not be for them [the Jews] instruments of thy divine wrath, but that we may rather become capable, through the knowledge of thy words and the example of a holy life, of bringing them back into the true way by virtue of thy Holy Spirit, so that all nations and all peoples together may glorify thee for eternity.'

The early Reformers thus reformulated previous Christian teaching about the Jewish nation. For Luther, Jews were demonic in nature, exerting a pernicious influence on Christian society. Others, such as Calvin and Beza, despaired of the Jews' refusal to accept Christ, yet basing themselves on Scripture, anticipated the eventual conversion of the Jewish people. Despite this shift in attitude among a number of Christian thinkers, anti-Jewish agitation, which had led to a series of expulsions from the latter half of the fifteenth century, continued in intensity. Senior clergy as well as secular rulers were involved in frequent attacks on the Jewish population, and expulsions continued to the latter part of the sixteenth century.

There were, however, some Protestant figures who adopted a more positive appraisal of Judaism. The Huguenot scholar, Joseph Justus Scaliger, who served as Professor at the University of Leiden from 1593, argued that it was only possible to establish the true text and meaning of Scripture by gaining an understanding of rabbinic sources. Jews, he maintained, should be permitted to return to western Europe not simply because of their economic importance, but because of their learning. In his view, Christians could not bring Jews to Christ if they were ignorant of talmudic and post-biblical literature.

In the seventeenth century, there was a lively interest in Jewish learning in a number of Reformed circles. In general it was believed that the Church's future was bound up with the conversion of the Jews. Some even suggested that their conversion would not be an event towards the end of the age, but rather foreshadowed a time of blessing for the Church on earth. Such a notion arose out of intense Bible study, particularly in connection with the Book of Revelation, which was seen as offering a detailed account of church history from Pentecost to the Day of Judgment.

In England the Cambridge scholar Joseph Mede held that the future millennium would be inaugurated or shortly followed by the return of the Jews to Christ in their ancient land. In his view, the Jews would be converted in a supernatural manner. Other scholars believed that Revelation 13–19 contained a divine promise of the overthrow of the enemies of the Gospel, interpreted as both the papacy and the Turks. This would be preliminary to a period of latter-day glory for the Church, which would see the conversion of the Jews as part of the movement of the Spirit of God. Through this process the earthly kingdoms would submit to the Gospel so that they could be said to have become 'the kingdoms of our God and of his Christ'.

Even among those Reformers critical of millenarianism, there was a widespread belief in the conversion of the Jews. Hence Robert Baillie, one of the Scottish Commissioners to the Westminster Assembly, contended on the basis of Romans 11 that the Jews would eventually return to Christ. In the Netherlands, Protestant churches followed a similar line. In the marginal notes on Romans 11, the orthodox Reformed translators of the 1637 Dutch version of the Bible argued that the 'whole of Israel' in this epistle implies the fullness of the people of Israel 'according to the flesh'. Thus, they maintained that the Jewish nation would eventually acknowledge Christ as Lord.

Such a positive assessment of the role of Jewry in God's providential plan was counterbalanced during this period by the revival of medieval stereotypical literary and artistic representations of Jews as found in Marlowe's *The Jew of Malta* and Shakespeare's *The Merchant of Venice*. In addition, in 1594 Rodrigo Lopez, a Portuguese physician of Jewish descent, was convicted of attempting to poison Elizabeth I – not surprisingly, this event led to widespread fear and hostility. Nonetheless, as we have observed, the seventeenth century witnessed a movement for the readmission of Jews to England.

By the middle of the seventeenth century, as the country was suffering from civil war, it was suggested this tragedy was due to God's judgment for previous cruelty and indifference towards the Jewish people. Those who pleaded for Jewish readmission contended that if Jews were allowed to return to Britain, they would hear some of the best gospel preaching on earth. This, they went on, would surely lead to their conversion to Christ, creating a golden age for the Church. To these religious arguments were added economic and political concerns.

As part of this campaign Oliver Cromwell invited Menasseh ben Israel, an Amsterdam scholar and rabbi, to England to argue the case for the Jews to be readmitted to England. This visit, however, stirred up considerable opposition from numerous critics such as the pamphleteer William Prynne and other Puritans who were sceptical about the mass conversion of the Jews. In their view the reference to Israel in Romans 11:25f referred to the whole New Testament Church of both gentiles and Jews. Other Puritans adopted a more welcoming attitude. Edward Elton, for example, remarked that Christians ought 'not to hate the Jews (as many do) only because they are Jews, which name among many is so odious that they think they cannot call a man worse than to call him a Jew; but, beloved, this ought not to be so, for we are bound to love and to honour the Jews, as being the ancient people of God, to wish them well, and to be in earnest in prayer for their conversion.'

As we have seen, such sentiments were not widely shared; throughout Europe Jews were viewed with contempt and hostility. Such attitudes reached a climax with the publication of *Judaism Unmasked* by Johann Andreas Eisenmenger, Professor of Hebrew at Heidelberg. In his view, the best way to defend Christianity against the Jewish threat was to rehearse the traditional medieval charges against the Jews. This work illustrated that despite the changing attitudes brought about by the Reformation, deep-seated Judaeophobia persisted in the early modern period.

Undeterred by such an attack the Jewish community believed it could curtail the distribution of Eisenmenger's treatise. Enlisting the aid of the court Jew, Samson Wertheimer, as well as various German princes, they gained the support of the Emperor Leopold. Although the book was eventually published after Eisenmenger's death by permission of the King of Prussia, the emperors retained their ban on the book since it was perceived as prejudicial to the public and to the Christian religion. The early modern period thus witnessed the continuation of the long tradition of Christian anti-Semitism alongside a growing awareness of the need to improve the position of Jewry. Voices were ranged on different sides of this debate by leading figures of the Reformation. Yet even those Reformers who encouraged their coreligionists to adopt a more positive attitude towards the Jewish community shared many of the prejudices of previous ages. Basing themselves on Scripture, they prayed for the Jews' eventual conversion to the true faith. In this way, they hoped for the eventual elimination of the Jewish race, an aspiration shared centuries later by the Nazis, who sought to accomplish the same end but through very different means.

ELEVEN

The Enlightenment

The Reformation led to an increasing acceptance of Jews in the countries where they lived. Eventually English advocates of the Enlightenment argued that the condition of the Jewish community should be improved. Such a quest, however, was opposed by a number of writers who continued to vilify Jewry in terms reminiscent of an earlier age. In France Protestant propagandists sought to refute charges against the Jewish population. Yet, despite such progressive attitudes consonant with the spirit of a new rationalist and scientific age, these champions of Jewish emancipation were unable to divest themselves of traditional assumptions about Jewish guilt and divine retribution. Further, many of the major thinkers of the period encouraged Judaeophobia. In Germany an attempt was made to present Jews in a positive light, but here too the emergence of national self-confidence evoked a hostile response towards the Jewish population. In order to escape such growing antipathy, several Jewish followers of the Enlightenment divested themselves of the Jewish tradition, while others embraced the Christian faith in an attempt to improve their circumstances.

THE ENLIGHTENMENT AND THE JEWS
The consequences of the English Civil War and the rise of the commercial middle class led to cultural and economic development. Most English thinkers of the eighteenth century embraced Christian teaching, yet some writers sought to reconcile the faith with the new scientific spirit. In their view, religion must be rational and natural. According to John Toland, for example, the Fathers of the Church had corrupted true Christianity. He believed that the original form of the faith was that practised by the Ebionites: 'The true Christianity of the Jews was over-borne and destroyed by the more numerous gentiles who, not enduring the reasonableness and simplicity of the same, brought into it by degrees the peculiar expressions and mysteries of Heathenism, the abstruse doctrines and distinctions of

their Philosophers, an insupportable pontifical Hierarchy, and even the altars, offerings, the sacred rites and ceremonies of their Priests, though they would not so much as tolerate those of the Jews.'

Such positive attitudes led Toland to support Jewish immigration to Britain; in 1714 he published *Reasons for Naturalizing the Jews in Great Britain and Ireland* in which he vehemently opposed the xenophobic attitudes of his countrymen: 'The vulgar, I confess, are seldom pleased in any country with the coming in of foreigners among them: which proceeds, first, from their ignorance, that at the beginning they were such themselves; secondly, from their grudging at more persons sharing the same trades and business with them, which they call taking the bread out of their mouths; and thirdly, from their being deluded to this aversion by the artifice of those who design any change in the government.'

Such liberalism, however, was not typical of Christian free-thinkers of the period. Rather, those who were sceptical of traditional Christian doctrine blamed the Jews for the errors of the Church. In accordance with such thinking the mathematician William Whiston, for example, sought to integrate biblical chronology with astronomical time. Unable to achieve this end, he ascribed mathematical inconsistencies to the malevolent intention of Jewish scribes. In a work entitled *Towards Restoring the True Text of the Old Testament*, he stated that 'the Jews, about the beginning of the second century of the Gospel greatly altered and corrupted their Hebrew and Greek copies of the Old Testament . . . in many places, on purpose, out of opposition to Christianity.' In a similar vein, Matthew Tindal argued in *Christianity as Old as Creation: or the Gospel, a Republication of the Religion of Nature* that Christianity is the natural religion, which had been perverted by Moses.

Another figure of this period, Thomas Morgan, contended that Gnosticism is consonant with the teaching of Christ, and he ridiculed the idea that the Jews are God's chosen people:

> To imagine that a company of poor, contemptible Egyptianized slaves, who having been delivered from one yoke of priesthood, were now to be put under another; a people scarce known to the rest of mankind, and were never to mix or converse with them, but to be mewed up in a little bye corner of the earth; that such a people, under such circumstances, were intended in the divine counsel and wisdom, as a light to the gentiles, and the means of preserving and keeping up the true knowledge and worship of God in the world, and of

the true religion or way to salvation; this surely, is supposing what we speak with scorn, that God was as much disappointed of his end, and took as wrong measures to obtain it, as Moses himself.

With similar vehemence Pastor Woolston maintained that the world is full of stinking Jews. Drawing on previous teaching about the dangers of the Jewish presence, he wrote that

> the world, according to the Proverb, and common belief of mankind, may be said to stink with them. Hence Ammianus Marcellinus very appositely to the purpose before us, speaking of the Jews, calls them tumulating and stinking Jews. How this mark of infamy was first fixed upon the Jews, whether from any ill smell that proceeds from them, according to the common opinion, or otherwise. It is all one to the prophecy and type of them; and if their bodies neither do, or even did stink living, yet their blasphemies against Christ, their maledictions of his Church, and false glosses on Scripture, are enough to make their very name odious and abominable.

Such attacks on Jewry were based on the traditional conception of the Jew as a dark, demonic and polluting force. Even though these writers were critical of traditional Christian teaching, they targeted Jews as polluters of the faith. Enriched by the language of conventional anti-Jewish attitudes, they kept alive the anti-Semitism of previous centuries which they infused with contemporary concepts consonant with the scientific age.

In eighteenth-century France, anti-Jewish sentiments continued to be widespread, as reflected in the opinion of Mme de Sévigné who observed: 'The hatred felt for them [the Jews] is extraordinary. But from where does this stench which confounds all perfumes come from? It is probably that unbelief and ingratitude smells bad as virtue smells good. . . . I feel pity and horror for them, and I pray God with the Church that he remove from their eyes the veil which prevents them from seeing that Jesus Christ has come.' Despite such antipathy, an increasing number of individuals promoted the amelioration of the position of Jewry.

Among French Protestants such aspirations were pronounced, since they themselves had suffered similar disadvantages as a minority living in French society. The Calvinist historian, Jacques Basnage, for example, intended to write a history of the Jewish people beginning with the destruction of the Second Temple in the first century BCE – *Histoire des Juifs*. 'We are reporting accurately and faithfully everything we have been able to unearth which refers to the Jews', he wrote. 'The Christian ought not to find it strange that we very often exonerate the Jews from various crimes they are not guilty of, since justice demands it; and to accuse of injustice and violence those who have pursued justice is only to show bias.'

Basnage's aim had been to put an end to the false legends that had grown up about deicide, yet his theological upbringing prevented him from following through with this plan. 'How then did the daughter of Zion fall?' he asked. 'The validity of a definite event cannot be disputed. It is sufficient to turn one's eyes to the present wretchedness of the Jewish people to be convinced that God is angry with them, and that their sins deserve of the blindness which has made them rejected. . . . Instead of repenting of as black a crime as the crucifying of the Messiah, a spirit of sedition and revolt grew up. The Jews, when aroused, carried out terrible cruelties.'

However, even though Jews merited God's anger, Basnage believed the punishment they had endured through the centuries was excessive: 'If the punishment had fastened on the heads of the guilty, it would not be surprising; but it has passed from generation to generation, from century to century. Seventeen hundred years of wretchedness and captivity have flowed by, with no prospect of relief . . . this unfortunate nation can find almost nowhere on the whole earth where it can lay its head or set its feet. It passes through torrents of blood which it has shed, and does not perish.'

Such a picture of Jewry was also to be found among other Protestant writers of the period. In their theological reflections, they disputed the previous denigration of the Jewish nation. Marie Huber, a theologian from Geneva, depicted two righteous Jews in *Le Monde fou préféré au monde sage*, who feel drawn by the message of Christ, but are discouraged by Christian society because 'all Christians of whatsoever sect they may be, are very consistent in one respect. This is in the love of wealth, the insatiable desire to accumulate it; in this they are more Jewish than the Jews themselves.' One of her characters, Philo, commented: 'I want to get to know them; and although they are Jews, I will not be at all ashamed to take lessons from them on what constitutes the spirit of Christianity.'

Again, the Marquis Jean-Baptiste d'Argens was a Catholic by origin but under the influence of two Protestant pastors he attacked the established churches and praised the Jewish faith for approximating the true natural religion. In one of his *Lettres juives*, he wrote:

Everyone who is called a free-thinker here [in Paris], fashionable people, society ladies, only practise the religion of Nazareth externally; very few of them are really convinced at the bottom of their hearts. They are satisfied to believe in God; several think that the soul is immortal; many others, like the Sadducees, claim that it is subject to death. I regard these latter as people labouring under a misapprehension; as the former category, I do not know if we can deny them the title of Jews. They believe in God who created the universe, who rewards the good, and punishes the bad. What more do we believe? Is not this the whole of our religion except for a few ceremonies which our scholars and priests have prescribed for us?

Nonetheless, and in spite of such a conception, d'Argens endorsed the Christian idea that God had punished the Jews for their crimes. In another of his *Lettres*, he portrays an ex-rabbi who confesses the ritual crimes of the Jews and supports other earlier allegations made against the Jewish people:

When I think of the ills our father suffered, I am tempted to believe that they were guilty of some great crimes, knowledge of which has not come down to us; and I must confess to you that, if I was not as confident as I am of the truth of my religion, when I examine the ills which have overwhelmed us since the birth of Nazareanism, I would find it easy to believe that the prophecies had been fulfilled and that the God of Israel had abandoned his people, and chosen another. Is it possible . . . that the Divinity should expose a people to such great ills if they did not deserve them because of crimes which required such severe punishment?

Hence even though such enlightened writers as d'Argens and Basnage sought to defend the Jewish population from traditional Christian antipathy, they were unable to free themselves from religious presuppositions about the villainous character of Jews. Their view of Judaism was tinged by implicit assumptions about Jewish guilt and divine retribution.

Despite general animosity directed against the Jews, a number of French writers influenced by the Enlightenment advocated tolerance and understanding, and encouraged a more benevolent attitude towards the Jewish population. Montesquieu, in *L'Esprit des lois*, argued that Christian intolerance is the source of Jewish ills and the cause of their peculiar customs: 'Commerce,' he wrote, 'was transferred to a nation covered with infamy; and was soon ranked with the most shameful usury, with monopolies, with the levying of subsidies, and with all the dishonest means of acquiring wealth. The Jews, enriched by their exactions, were pillaged by the tyranny of princes; which pleased indeed, but did not ease the people.'

According to Montesquieu, Jews should be treated as Christians want others to treat them. As a Jew declares in Montesquieu's 'A Most Humble Remonstrance to the Inquisitors of Spain and Portugal': 'We conjure you, not by the mighty God whom both you and we serve, but by that Christ who, you tell us, took upon him a human form, to propose himself for an example for you to follow: we conjure you to behave to us, as he himself would behave was he upon earth.'

However, other writers of this period fostered hatred of the Jewish populace, and their works reflect ancient and medieval Christian vilifications of Jewry. In his *Profession de foi*, the influential thinker Voltaire contrasted his view of God with the Jewish conception found in the Hebrew Bible, making himself the arbiter of morality: 'The morals of theists are of necessity pure; since they always have the God of justice and purity before them, the God who does not descend upon the earth to order people to rob the Egyptians, to command Hosea to take a concubine in exchange for money and to live with an adulterous woman. Also one does not see us selling our wives like Abraham. We do not get drunk like Noah, and our sons do not insult the respectable member which gave them birth.'

In his *Dictionnaire philosophique*, Voltaire continued this diatribe, including thirty articles that attacked Jews, who are described variously as 'our masters and our enemies . . . whom we detest', and 'the most abominable people in the world'. According to Voltaire, the Jews are 'an ignorant and barbarous people who for a long time have combined the most sordid greed with the most detestable superstition and the most invincible hatred for all the peoples who tolerate them and enrich them'. Even though Christians are culpable of crimes against the Jewish nation, the Jews themselves are guilty as well: 'The only difference is that our priests have had you burned by laymen, and that your priests have always sacrificed human victims with their sacred hands.'

For Jean-Jacques Rousseau, tolerance should be granted to the beleaguered Jewish nation, and Moses should be respected. Yet, like Voltaire, he was horrified by the biblical concept of the Divine. 'If then it [the Divinity] teaches us what is absurd and unreasonable, if it inspires us with feelings of aversion for our fellows and terror for ourselves, if it paints us a God angry, jealous, vengeful, partial, hating men, a God of war and battles, ever ready to strike and to destroy, ever speaking of punishment and torment, boasting even of the punishment of the innocent, my heart would not be drawn towards this terrible God.' At times Rousseau also speaks of the Jew in conventional Christian terms as 'the vilest of peoples', 'the baseness of [this people], incapable of any virtue'.

The contributors to Diderot's *Encyclopédie* were also frequently contemptuous of the faith of their ancestors. The article on 'Hebraic [language]', for example, implicitly denigrates Jewry: 'It is not for us, blind mortals, to question Providence; also let us not ask it why it pleased it only to speak to the Jews in parables: why it has given them eyes so that they do not see, and ears so that they do not hear, and why of all the nations of antiquity it chose particularly the one whose head was hardest and coarsest.' In an article dealing with medicine, the author was contemptuous of Jews: 'the ancient Hebrews, stupid, superstitious, separated from other peoples, unversed in the study of physics, incapable of resorting to natural causes, attributed all their diseases to evil spirits . . . in a word, their ignorance of medicine caused them to turn to soothsayers, magicians, enchanters or finally to prophets.'

Another criticism of Jewish superstition was made by Nicholas Boulanger:

> The monarch, with the obdurate Jews and with all the other nations, was regarded less as a father and a God of peace than as an exterminating angel. The motive behind theocracy would therefore have been fear: this was also true of despotism. . . . The true God of the Hebrews was also obliged, because of their character, perpetually to threaten them. . . . The Judaic superstition which fancied that it could not pronounce the terrible name of Jehovah, which was also the great name of its monarch, in this was transmitted to us one of the conventions of this primitive theocracy.

A disciple of Voltaire, Pastor Polier de Bottens, was equally critical of Jewry. In an article on the Messiah, he castigated Jews for their view of Christ: 'If the Jews disputed Jesus Christ's role of Messiah and divinity, they have also neglected nothing to make him appear contemptible, to cast on his birth, his life and his death, all the ridicule and all the opprobrium that their cruel relentlessness against this divine Saviour and his heavenly doctrine could imagine.'

Other writers in the eighteenth century published anti-clerical polemics that were Judaeophobic. Nicholas Fréret was one such. In *La Moïsade*, he concludes with a curse on Moses and the Jewish nation. A contemporary of Fréret, Jean-Baptiste de Mirabaud, argued that the Jewish people had fallen into disrepute long before the curse of Christ: 'You will therefore see from this that, a long time before they had brought down upon themselves this curse, which is now regarded as the cause of their wretchedness, they were generally hated and generally despised in every country which knew them.' Hence, even though France in the Enlightenment championed the rights of humanity, many of the distinguished figures of this period embraced anti-Jewish sentiments of an earlier age. Their advocacy of reason and anti-clericalism was accompanied by a parallel contempt for Judaism and the Jewish nation.

The spirit of the Enlightenment was firmly rooted in Germany. In particular German pastors advanced ideas of science and progress, and revised their theology in the light of new biblical scholarship. Among these advocates of Enlightenment values, particular concern was addressed to the plight of the Jewish community. Such favourable attitudes were promoted by descendants of court Jews such as Aaron Salomon Gumpertz, a member of the Berlin Gumpertz dynasty, who asked the writer Gottsched for permission 'to come and graze under your wings, to suck the sweet milk of sciences . . . it is you whom we Germans have to thank for such varied intellectual writings'.

Among those writers who sought to improve the situation of German Jewry was the playwright Gotthold Ephraim Lessing. In *Die Juden* he depicts the noble character of a Jewish traveller who saves a baron and his daughter from bandits. In gratitude the baron offers him his daughter's hand. Unable to accept, the traveller declares that he is a Jew. This, the baron declares, is a cruel mischance. The traveller, who is intent on gaining acceptance in society, declares: 'This offer is in vain for the God of my fathers has given me more than I need. As sole reward all I ask is that in future you judge my people more kindly and do not generalize. I did not conceal myself from you because I am ashamed of my religion. No! But I saw that you looked favourably on me but unfavourably on my people. And a man's friendship, be he what he will, has always been inestimable to me.'

During this period other playwrights similarly presented Jews in a positive light, and Jews were a symbol of the struggle against prejudice. In reaction, some writers disputed such claims. Jews, they contended, were incapable of attaining noble qualities. Hence the theologian Johann David Michaelis argued in *Journal de Goettingen* that no Jew such as Lessing's traveller actually existed. In reply, Lessing stated that in fact there were such individuals, and he published a letter from the Jewish philosopher Moses Mendelssohn to illustrate his point: 'Is the cruel judgment of Michaelis justified? How shameful for the human race! And how shameful too for the author! Is it not enough for us that we must suffer the attacks of the cruel hatred that the Christians have for us, and must this injustice be justified by a slander?' He wrote:

> Let them continue to oppress us, let them allow us to live in subjection amidst free and happy citizens, let us be exposed to the scorn and contempt of the whole world; but do not let them try to challenge our virtue, the sole solace for unhappy souls, the sole comfort of the abandoned. . . . In general, certain human virtues are met with more frequently among Jews than Christians. Think of the unutterable horror that they have of murder. You cannot quote a single example of a Jew . . . having killed a man. How easily many a worthy Christian will kill a man for a simple insult. They say this is because of cowardice among the Jews. So be it! If cowardice spares human blood, then cowardice is a virtue.

During this controversy, the Swiss Pastor Lavater called on Mendelssohn to refute Christian doctrine, or if he were unable to do so, to embrace the Christian faith. Even though Mendelssohn did not issue a public reply, he communicated his views to the Duke of Brunswick. His reason, he stated, prevented him from accepting the mysteries of Christianity. Lavater's challenge was countered by the publication of Mendelssohn's *Jerusalem* in which he argued for a secular state in which the political and juridical rights of the churches would be abolished, as well as the judicial autonomy of Jewish communities. In this work Mendelssohn's main aim was to obtain civil rights for all Jews.

Once Mendelssohn died, the era of tolerance for the Jewish population came to an end. The revival of national self-confidence evoked considerable anti-Semitism, and a number of German thinkers of the period wrote disparagingly of the Jewish people. Following the opinions of such nationalist theologians as Michaelis, Immanuel Kant declared that Judaism is not a religion. Rather, he argued, it is merely 'a union of a number of people who, since they belonged to a particular stock, formed themselves into a commonwealth under purely political laws, and not into a Church'.

Describing the Jews as Palestinians, he inveighed against their dishonesty: 'The Palestinians living among us are, since their exile, because of the usurious spirit, not unjustifiably renowned for their deceitfulness, so far as the great majority is concerned. It does indeed seem disconcerting to conceive of a nation of usurers; but it is just as disconcerting to conceive of the notion of pure mercantilism, by far the largest part of which is bound together by a superstition recognized by the state in which they live and do not seek any civic honour. But they try to compensate for this lack of advantages by outwitting the people among whom they find shelter and even by deceiving each other.'

For Kant's disciple Johann Gottlieb Fichte, the expulsion of the Jews was the only means of protecting the German nation. 'To protect ourselves against them', he wrote, 'I see no other way than to conquer for them their promised land and see them all there. . . . But to give them civic rights – I see no means to do that except, one night, to cut off all their heads and give them new ones in which there would not be one Jewish idea.' Similar hostility was expressed by the philosopher Georg Wilhelm Hegel who 'saw in Jesus only the man, the Nazarene, the carpenter's son whose brothers and kinsfolk living among them; so much he was, and more he could not be, for he was only one like themselves, and they felt themselves to be nothing. The Jewish multitude was bound to wreck his attempt to give them consciousness of something divine, for faith is something divine, something great, [and] cannot make its home in a dunghill.'

At the end of the eighteenth century a number of wealthy Jews had integrated into the cultural circles of Berlin society. These individuals, who had assimilated into western culture, were highly critical of traditional orthodoxy. Advocating the principles of the Enlightenment, they sought to bring about a reform of Jewish life. Some of those who moved in these circles depicted the stultifying nature of traditional Jewish existence. The Jewish philosopher Solomon Maimon, for example, decried the narrow confines of Polish life that he had endured as a young boy:

> My life in Poland from my marriage to my emigration, which embraced the springtime of my existence, was a series of miseries with a lack of all facilities for the promotion of culture, and consequently an aimless application of my powers. . . . The general constitution of Poland at the time; the condition of

our people in it, who, like the poor ass with the double burden, are oppressed by their own ignorance and religious prejudices, as well as by the ignorance and prejudices of the ruling classes; the misfortunes of my own family – all these combined to hinder the course of my development and to check my natural disposition.

In order to improve these circumstances, reformers promoted a revision of educational methods. In their view, by this means Jews would be able to recognize the absurdity of traditional Jewish belief and observance. Typical of such modernists, the Kantian Bendavid condemned traditional practices. 'How long will the excesses of the senseless and shameless ceremonial law endure?' he asked. 'How long will the Jew continue to believe that the heavenly Father will reward him with a special crown for practising it?' For Bendavid the only salvation for the Jew was re-education, and to this end he established a school for Jews in which worship was conducted in German.

Other reformers celebrated the Jewish contribution to the Enlightenment. Hence Moses Herschel, a Jewish writer from Breslau, declared:

Thanks to our philosophical century, the age of barbarism has passed away, when one must expect a contemptuous grimace at the mention of the word Jew. The torch of philosophy also illumines with its beneficent light our Silesia, and divine tolerance has made itself at home there. The man who is capable and worthy, whatever his faith and religious opinions, can henceforth lay claim to the affection and respect of those who think differently; he is certain to benefit from it. The Christian and the Jew can love each other with a brotherly love, esteem each other, and honour each other.

Even though most of these Jews retained some vestige of their ancestral faith, others embraced Christianity. Among Moses Mendelssohn's descendants, his youngest son became a Christian, and Abraham, the father of Felix Mendelssohn, had his children converted. Bartholdy, his brother-in-law, explained why such change was necessary:

Do you think you have done something wrong in giving your children the religion which you think the better for them? It is a real tribute which you and we are all paying to your father's efforts for true enlightenment in general, and he would have acted like you have done for your children, perhaps as I have done, for my part. One can remain faithful to an oppressed, persecuted religion; one can force it on one's children in expectation of a life-long martyrdom – so long as one believes it to be the only religion that can save you. But if one no longer believes this; then it is barbarous.

Regarding Mendelssohn's daughters, Recha remained Jewish, while the youngest, Henrietta, founded a boarding school for Parisian society girls. The eldest sister Dorothea married a banker, but became attached to the writer Friedrich Schlegel and converted to Protestantism. This couple met at the Berlin Jewish salon held by Henriette Herz, who was famed for her beauty; in her old age, she described the nature of these Jewish salons:

> There was no mediation of a tradition, of a culture transmitting itself from generation to generation, keeping pace with the spirit and knowledge of the time; and also none of the prejudice formed by such a train of culture. The lavishness, the arrogance, the transcendence of accepted forms of expression are to be attributed to a similar nature of this spirit and the awareness of this in those women who embodied it. But it was undeniably very original, very powerful, very piquant, very exciting and frequently, with its astounding mobility, of great profundity.

Another salon of this period was held by Rahel Levin, who was anxious to escape from her Jewishness. Such an aspiration was a central obsession of her correspondence. In a letter to a childhood friend, David Veit, she stated: 'I have a strange fancy: it is as if some supramundane being, just as I was thrust into this world, plunged these words with a dagger into my heart: "Yes, have sensibility, see the world as few see it, be great and noble, nor can I take from you the faculty of eternal thinking. But I add one thing more: be a Jewess!" And now my life is a slow bleeding death.' In a letter to her brother, she commented: 'I do not forget this same for a single second. I drink it in water, I drink it in wine, I drink it with the air; in every breath, that is. . . . The Jew must be extirpated from us, that is the sacred truth, and it must be done even if life were uprooted in the process.' In 1814 she converted and married the Prussian diplomat and writer, August Varnhagen von Ense.

During this period a number of Jews attempted to overcome the confines of their Jewishness by collective conversion, yet they were not willing to abandon Judaism altogether. In 1799 under the leadership of David Friedlander, a follower of Mendelssohn, a group of enlightened Jews declared their willingness to submit to baptism as long as they were not obliged to accept traditional Christian dogma. This request was addressed to Pastor Wilhelm Teller of the Lutheran Consistory in Berlin, who responded that he would be willing to grant baptism, but only if certain conditions were fulfilled: 'To be a Christian you must at least accept the sacraments of baptism and communion and acknowledge the historical truth that Christ is the founder of the most sublime moral religion. It is possible to grant you freedom of religious opinions, which moreover differ with the Church itself, but not as far as the dogmas are concerned.' When this appeal was made public, numerous Christian objections were raised by such figures as the theologian Friedrich Schleiermacher, who charged the petitioners with hypocrisy, alleging that they were motivated by material concerns. Thus, even though the Enlightenment encouraged many Christians to seek the improvement of conditions under which the Jewish population lived, undercurrents of traditional anti-Semitism continued to flow beneath the surface of public life.

STEPS TOWARDS EMANCIPATION

The Protestant Reformation led to the disintegration of medieval Christendom. For the Jews, this religious upheaval had important implications. At first, it appeared that the benefits of humanism might bring about a fundamental change in perception of the Jewish population. Yet the seeds of toleration planted by the humanists failed to bring about such transformation. Even though such figures as Johannes Reuchlin fostered a positive assessment of Jewish sacred literature, this did not result in a revolution in the social, legal and political position of Jewry. During this period, both Protestants and Catholics continued to press for the conversion of the Jews.

Nonetheless, the tumultuous events of the early modern period intensified efforts to alleviate Jewish disabilities, culminating in the quest to free Jews from prejudice and persecution. The Enlightenment, which encouraged these changes, was rooted in the scientific advances made by such figures as Kepler, Galileo, Copernicus and Newton. Their astronomical and physical discoveries epitomized the rationalism and universalism of the age. Rather than depend on the certainties of religion, these empiricists championed free enquiry. Rejecting the traditional Christian doctrine of the inherent sinfulness of human beings, the Enlightenment viewed human nature as essentially rational, possessing the ability to choose between good and evil. According to this view, the purpose of the state was to forge an environment that would maximize human goodness.

Not only was the doctrine of original sin rejected, the Enlightenment fostered the view that human beings possess inalienable rights. In line with the philosopher John Locke's opinion, the framers of declarations in both France and America defined these rights as including life, liberty and property, although the authors of the American Declaration of Independence substituted 'the pursuit of happiness' for property.

As far as Jews were concerned, these ideas seemed to undermine previous assumptions about Jewish culpability. Enlightened thinkers rejected the traditional Christian assumption that only those who accepted Christ could be saved, offering instead the conception of a universal rational faculty as the definition of humanity. Even though the Enlightenment did not deny the existence of evil, it rejected the view that this was due to human nature; instead it held that people are reasonable by nature and capable of good. In addition, Enlightenment thinkers applied the criterion of social utility to all policies and institutions.

On this basis, Jews were perceived as entitled to human rights regardless of their religious inheritance and identity. Inevitably, questions were asked whose answers appeared obvious: if human beings are united through a universal rational faculty, what about the Jews? Are gentiles like them, and they like us? Should not there be a natural affinity between Jews and gentiles? If their behaviour is not desirable, or if they possess negative characteristics, is this because of external circumstances? Was it the conditions of the ghetto that corrupted the values of the Jewish nation?

Such questioning combined with the needs of the emerging modern state served as the background to a radical change in Jewish existence as manifest in the treatise *On the Civil Improvement of the Jews* by the Prussian historian Christian Wilhelm von Dohm. According to von Dohm, previous allegations about the corrupt character of Jews were well-founded. Yet he argued that moral corruption of the Jews was a consequence of the oppressed condition in which they had been compelled to live for centuries. If one changed this condition, he continued, then their character would be altered.

Jews were in need of improvement, von Dohm stated. Schools should be created which imparted the ideals and responsibilities of rational, enlightened society. The state would have to prevent such schools from teaching anti-social opinions; they should instead ensure that the Jew 'is taught to develop his reason by the clear light of knowledge . . . and that his heart is warmed by the principles of order, honesty, [and] love for all men'. Regarding the undesirable results of Jews being concentrated in commerce, von Dohm hoped that the removal of restricted entry to other occupations would encourage Jewry to engage in farming and skilled crafts.

Underlying these recommendations, then, was a burgeoning antipathy to the stereotypical conception of the medieval Jew. What differentiated von Dohm and other Christian exponents of Jewish enlightenment was their belief in the improvability of human beings. Unlike previous critics of the Jewish people, von Dohm did not believe that the Jewish character was inherently flawed; rather, Jews had been corrupted through historical and social circumstances. All this could be changed through human reason and the granting of full membership in society. The Jew could become a better citizen if he were made an equal citizen.

In the light of such a social philosophy, several eighteenth-century rulers attempted to improve their states by removing restrictions from all their subjects, including the Jews. Emperor Joseph II of Austria, for example, attempted to legislate the abolition of serfdom and implement a measure of public education in his territories. In 1782 an imperial Edict of Tolerance recognized the right of Jews to become naturalized subjects. This first decree of Jewish emancipation was part of the Habsburg effort to bring various subject nationalities and regions within the confines of the state.

Not all those who supported the principles of the Enlightenment, however, agreed with von Dohm's principles or the policies of the Austrian government. Some of their critics emphasized that the character of the Jews was more a result of their religious beliefs than of the environment in which they lived. In particular the doctrine that held that the Jews are God's chosen people was perceived as a fundamental barrier separating Jews from those among whom they lived. Further, Jewish support for Palestine was perceived as indicating that Jewry had divided loyalties. According to this view, Jews could never be true patriots of the countries in which they resided. Moreover, it was widely believed that Jews could never become soldiers because they lacked the physical attributes, and also because Judaism forbade fighting on the Sabbath and eating non-kosher food. Nor did they respect an oath as did gentiles.

In this debate about Jewish status, a number of Enlightenment figures such as Voltaire continued to focus on what they considered the intractable nature of the Jewish character. Unlike von Dohm, Voltaire believed that

Jews were inevitably and invariably corrupt because their constitution was rooted in an 'alien' nature. Even though the Jewish character needed improving, it could not be improved. Hence, although Voltaire's writing epitomized Enlightenment ideals, he nevertheless continued to perpetuate the negative picture of the Jew inherited from previous centuries. As he noted in his *Dictionnaire philosophique*, the Jews constituted 'an ignorant and barbarous people who for a long time have combined the most sordid greed with the most detestable superstition and the most invincible hatred for all peoples who tolerate them and enrich them'.

Here, then, we can clearly see earlier surface traces of an ideology that became characteristic of the Nazi regime. In the Middle Ages, it was widely accepted that the Jewish problem could be solved through conversion. However, for Voltaire no change in religious conviction could fundamentally alter the nature of the Jewish character. The Jews, he believed, were destructive, in contrast to their Christian neighbours. It is thought that Voltaire acquired such anti-Jewish sentiments through unhappy relations with Jewish businessmen; his dealings with Jews engaged in commerce evoked strong feelings of dislike. Yet, whatever the case, Voltaire's malice was indicative of the feelings of a number of Enlightenment figures who castigated Jews for what they believed to be their negative influence in society.

Despite the antipathy of such major figures, various writers of this period continued to champion Jewish rights. Pre-eminent among them was Lessing, the foremost exemplar of the Jewish enlightenment. As we noted, he sought to expose the prejudices of his contemporaries and in plays such as *The Jews* and *Nathan the Wise* portrayed the noble character of Jewry.

As we will see in the next chapter, the French National Assembly, sensitive to these social and political developments, passed the Declaration of the Rights of Man and the Citizen, proclaiming that all human beings are born free and equal in rights. Such rights were extended to men of property who became active citizens, in contrast with those less wealthy, who were viewed as passive and only granted civil rights. In addition, the Declaration also affirmed the citizenship of all Frenchmen and the equality of all citizens. In this way those who had previously been subjects of the king became equal citizens of the state. In view of these changes, the question was asked whether Jews should be citizens as well. Since they are human beings, the answer was obvious. But only after two years of debate did the supreme legislative body decide to extend these rights to Jews.

It might be assumed that the Jewish problem was solved by this legislative decision. However, even those advocates of ameliorating the plight of Jewry viewed the Jews as undesirable. Their condition, they believed, was the result of social circumstance. By altering these circumstances, the character of Jews could be improved. Opponents, however, insisted this was not so. During this debate, notebooks of grievances were collected for presentation to the National Assembly to aid the members in drafting a constitution.

Following the passage of the Declaration of Emancipation, a Jewish merchant and banker of Nancy, Berr Isaac Berr, addressed his coreligionists, declaring that God had chosen the French nation as the instrument of Jewish salvation. Nonetheless, he tempered his praise of the French, warning that Jews should not be too hard on gentiles who had not overcome their prejudices. They should be given a chance to catch up with the spirit of the age. At the same time, he cautioned Jews to do their best to make themselves useful and thereby deserve the esteem and friendship of their fellow citizens. What was necessary, he stressed, was re-education: Jews would need to learn French and alter both their speech and appearance. Implicit in his analysis of the Jewish condition was the assumption that it was the exclusion of Jews from trades and their continual persecution that had forced them to abandon the pursuit of secular knowledge. In his view, civic equality would permit Jews to abandon commerce and engage in a wider range of activities.

Assimilation, however, did not occur immediately. In Alsace, with a population of approximately 30,000 Jews constituting 80 per cent of the total Jewish community in France, the traditional occupations of peddling, cattle-trading and moneylending remained the primary occupations of its Jewish inhabitants. Such a lack of change was due largely to practical circumstances: economic transformation did not occur until major economic changes took place in this region. In contrast with Berr Isaac Berr and others, most Jews regarded the quest for emancipation with scepticism.

However, when Napoleon extended Jewish emancipation beyond the borders of France, thereby becoming the liberator of modern Jewry, Jews became enthusiastic about emancipationist ideals. Nonetheless, they continued to be reluctant to return to their ancestral homeland and create a Jewish presence in the Middle East. This was largely because the prediction of those who advanced Jewish emancipation had not been fulfilled. Instead, complaints were voiced about France's Jewish population. Rather than integrating into society, French Jews were becoming increasingly insular.

When Napoleon received complaints from Alsace about Jewish usury, he called a General Assembly of Jewish notables in France, presenting them with a series of questions concerning Jewish status. The replies were reassuring: Jews indicated that Judaism does not countenance or encourage practices that conflict with those of the French nation. Even in situations of conflict, the law of the land takes precedence over religious law. Nevertheless, Napoleon sought to have this reassurance confirmed by a body that spoke for the Jews of Europe and in 1807 a Great Sanhedrin convened in Paris.

Even though only a few communities outside France sent representatives to Paris, this body confirmed the Assembly's earlier views. The response to this gathering from the non-Jewish world was intensely hostile: rumours spread that it was evidence of a Jewish world conspiracy. In Russia, the Holy Synod of the Orthodox Church instructed priests to announce that summoning this body of Jewry was a sign that Napoleon saw himself as the messianic redeemer. The Synod published a manifesto denouncing the Paris Sanhedrin as the same tribunal that once condemned Christ to the Cross. In response, the Jewish community in Russia assured the Tsar's government that they had no desire for emancipation or to be part of Napoleon's plans.

A month after the convocation of the Great Sanhedrin, Napoleon dissolved this body, yet for many it reinforced theories of Jewish intentions to undermine Christendom. Nor were such fears allayed by Napoleon's plans to regulate Jewish affairs. Like the Protestant Consistory, which governed Protestants in France, the Jewish Assembly of Notables was retained in order to oversee Jewish communal affairs. In addition, Napoleon's 'Infamous Decree' of 1808 imposed severe restrictions on Jewish civil and commercial activities: the payment of debts to Jews was suspended; Jews were compelled to obtain a certificate of good conduct and a licence if they desired to engage in commercial activities; they were not allowed to change their residence except to take up agricultural activities; Jews were required to abandon Hebrew names and assume French family names; and immigration of Jews to France was limited. Even though such discriminatory legislation was due largely to public pressure, Napoleon himself shared such prejudice, and his reforms were designed to lead to the disappearance of French Jewry either through assimilation, intermarriage or emigration.

TWELVE

Jewish Emancipation

By the end of the eighteenth century advocates of Enlightenment ideals pressed for the amelioration of Jewish life. In France, with the advent of the Napoleonic age, important steps were taken to improve the conditions of the Jewish population. Despite objections to the summoning of the Great Sanhedrin, this event paved the way for Jewish emancipation. In Germany, Jewish religious reformers sought to modernize the traditional liturgy, despite the objections of the orthodox establishment. By the middle of the eighteenth century, Reform synagogues appeared throughout Germany. Nonetheless, such changes to Jewish existence led to the erosion of traditional Judaism and intensified Christian antipathy to the Jewish way of life. In Russia, Jewish advocates of the Enlightenment argued that assimilation was essential in contemporary society. Traditionalists, however, feared that these changes would undermine Torah Judaism. Such ambivalence was shared by the gentile community; although liberals pressed for equal rights, others feared the consequences of such a policy. By the end of the second decade of the nineteenth century, Jews were again subject to repeated outbursts of hostility reminiscent of previous ages.

THE EMANCIPATION OF JEWRY

As we noted in the last chapter, the emancipation of the Jews began at the end of the eighteenth century. Throughout Europe humanist ideals began to stir the consciousness of the Christian population. By 1782 the last remnants of Jewish legislation were abolished. Yet throughout France complaint books were composed, listing a wide range of grievances against the Jewish populace. The book of the clergy of Colmar, for example, portrayed Jews in the most negative terms and advised that only the eldest son should be permitted to marry:

> The Jews, by their harassment, their depredations, the greedy duplicity of which they daily offer such pernicious examples, being the first and foremost

cause of the poverty of the people, of the loss of all sense of industry, of the moral depravity in a class formerly renowned for that much vaunted Germanic faith . . . [for all these causes] only the eldest son of every Jewish family should in future be allowed to contract a marriage.

In Alsace the rural population attacked Jews, forcing thousands to seek refuge in Switzerland.

In 1789 the French Constituent Assembly had enfranchised Protestants; Jewry, however, were refused such rights and even advocates of emancipation agreed that the Jews constituted a fallen nation that needed reform. According to Robespierre, Jews needed regeneration: 'The Jews' vices are born of the degradation you have plunged them into; they will be good when they can find some advantage in so being!' Others, however, found the Jews incorrigible and argued against improving their lot. Despite such protests, the Constituent Assembly provided for the total emancipation of French Jewry on 27 September 1791.

In general the Jewish population did not express enthusiasm for the Revolution, but with the emergence of the Napoleonic era their lives underwent considerable change as did those of their coreligionists elsewhere in Europe. At the beginning of the nineteenth century, France assumed the role of protector and emancipator of Jews throughout Europe. In Napoleon's view, the Jews were 'an objectionable people, chicken-hearted and cruel'. 'They are caterpillars, grasshoppers, who ravage the countryside,' he declared. Such evil, he believed, 'primarily comes from the Talmud, where their true biblical traditions are found side by side with the most corrupt morality as soon as their relations with Christians are involved'.

Nonetheless, Napoleon also believed that Jews could be prevented from exerting a deleterious effect on society: 'I do not intend to rescue that race, which seems to have been the only one excluded from redemption from the curse with which it is smitten,' he stated, 'but I would like to put it in a position where it is unable to propagate the evil.' In his opinion, the remedy lay in the abolition of Jewry by dissolving it into Christianity. 'When one in every three marriages will be between a Jew and a Frenchman,' he contended, 'the Jew's blood will cease to have a specific character.'

In 1806 Napoleon summoned Jewish representatives to a General Assembly held in Paris to whom he addressed a series of questions about the Jewish attitude to France and the French, the authority of Jewish institutions, and the problem of usury and of Jewish occupations. The next year the Great Sanhedrin met, consisting of rabbis as well as leading Jewish figures, to give religious sanction to the Assembly's replies. In 1808 two edicts were enacted to regularize the position of French Jews. According to the first, a hierarchical organization of communities was to be established; all individual and communal Jewish affairs were to be concentrated in a central consistory in Paris. A second edict – the 'Infamous Decree' – imposed control over Jewish loans, introduced permits to engage in trade, forbade Jews to settle in other areas in north-east France, and prohibited the substitution by Jews of replacements for military service.

Even though these edicts provided the basis for Jewish emancipation, they imposed serious restrictions on French Jewry and ensured that the requirements took precedence over those of religion. The organization of consistories hired rabbis to ensure that Jews 'should regard military service as a sacred task, and they should inform them that during the period in which they dedicate themselves to service the Torah exempted them from observing Jewish religious injunctions which cannot be reconciled with it'. Such legislation was designed to foster assimilation, as the last paragraph of the 'Infamous Decree' makes clear:

> The instructions in this order will be implemented over a period of ten years in the hope that at the end of this period, under the influence of the various measures undertaken with regard to the Jews, there will no longer be any difference between them and other citizens of our Empire. But if, despite all this, our hope should be frustrated, implementation will be extended for whatever length of time seems appropriate.

However, once Napoleon was defeated, there was a vehement reaction against Jewish emancipation. In Italy Jews were forced to live in ghettos and deprived of their rights. German Jewry was treated similarly: in Frankfurt Jews were also forced to live in the ghetto, and in Lübeck a total expulsion took place. At the Congress of Vienna, the Germanic Federation discussed the Jewish question and agreed not to return to the conditions pertaining prior to Napoleon's conquest. Rather, it decided to discuss the means of achieving civil amelioration. During the debate, a number of states proposed granting Jews those rights accorded them by the French under Napoleon; most, however, were unwilling to maintain laws that had been forced upon them. Hence, paradoxically, the French quest to emancipate the Jews eventually led to a regression to previous attitudes towards both Jewry and the Jewish faith.

During the Napoleonic period Jews in German lands experienced considerable improvement in their way of life. In some areas, Jewish emancipation was fostered by French occupational authorities; elsewhere it was the result of the French example, or the influence of prominent Jews. In Seesen, Westphalia, for example, the communal leader Israel Jacobson promoted religious reform, founding a boarding school for boys in 1801. Later he created similar institutions throughout the kingdom. In these progressive institutions general subjects were taught by Christian teachers, while a Jewish instructor gave lessons about the Jewish faith. The consistory of which Jacobson was president also introduced various reforms to the service for worship including choral singing, hymns, and prayers in German.

Several years later Jacobson built a Reform synagogue alongside the school; the dedication service took place in the presence of Christian clergy and other dignitaries. In his address Jacobson explained why such changes had been introduced: 'Our ritual is still weighed down with religious customs which must be rightly offensive to reason as well as to our Christian friends. It desecrates the holiness of our religion and dishonours the reasonable man to place too great a value upon such customs; on the other hand he is greatly honoured if he can encourage himself and his friends to realize their dispensability.'

After Napoleon's defeat Jacobson settled in Berlin, where he founded the Berlin synagogue. In 1817 a Reform synagogue was established in Hamburg; various innovations were made to the liturgy, with the inclusion of prayers and sermons in German as well as choral singing and organ music. Defending such change, the Hamburg reformers justified their actions on the basis of Talmudic teaching. Two years later the community issued its own prayerbook, which excluded repetitions of the prayers as well as medieval poems. In addition some of the traditional prayers relating to Jewish nationalism and messianic redemption were omitted. Anxious to justify such alterations to the liturgy, Jacobson was instrumental in obtaining rabbinic opinions supporting the actions of the synagogue. The Hungarian rabbi Aaron Chorin, for example, maintained that it was permissible to modify the liturgy, hold services in a language comprehensible to the worshipper, and to accompany them with both organ and song.

Outraged by such reforms, the Orthodox establishment condemned the
Hamburg reformers. Thus Eleazer Fleckeles, a member of the Beth Din of
Prague, declared: 'These people have no religion at all. It is their entire
desire to parade before the Christians as being more learned than their
brothers. Basically, they are neither Christians nor Jews.' Regarding
Chorin, Rabbi Eliezer of Triesch in Moravia stated: 'We know this rabbi
Aaron Chorin. He is a man of mediocre knowledge in Talmud and
commentaries, and far be it from us to lean on his pronouncements.'
Despite such criticism, these early reformers insisted that Jewish worship
should conform to modern standards. In their opinion, the informality of
the traditional synagogue service was undignified. For this reason they
insisted on greater decorum, unison in prayer, the inclusion of a choir,
hymns and musical responses, and changes in the prayers as well as the
length of services.

From the perspective of both Jewish and Christian avant-garde writers
and thinkers of the period, the rationalism of the Enlightenment was
outmoded. In their view, the Enlightenment was anaemic in comparison
with the Romantic movement. Reacting against the French Revolution as
well as French culture, the proponents of German Romanticism and
nationalism regarded the changes proposed by Jewish reformers as
irrelevant. In their view, no external reform of Judaism would be able to
win respect for Judaism as a vibrant religious tradition.

Nineteenth-century followers of the Romantic movement viewed
subjective religious experience as of primary importance. Such values,
however, were absent from a Jewish religion of reason. Hence, in their
quest to offer a modernized form of Judaism for an enlightened age, the
early reformers failed to satisfy the spiritual aspirations of assimilated
German Jews. Instead, these reformers inadvertently provided the basis for
a critique of traditional Judaism that was later seized upon by anti-Semites.
The destructive impact of their criticism of Torah Judaism and the
traditional Jewish way of life paradoxically intensified antipathy towards
what was increasingly regarded as an outmoded religious tradition.

When Poland was partitioned at the end of the eighteenth century, large
numbers of Jews were absorbed into the Russian empire and confined in
the Pale of Settlement. Determined not to offend the gentile population,
Catherine the Great continued to enforce restrictions on her Jewish
subjects. Despite such a policy, hostility towards Jewish aliens led to further
anti-Jewish measures. In 1799 White Russia was devastated by a famine,

and an official enquiry was initiated to uncover its causes. Gabriel
Derzhavin, the investigator, concluded that:

> The Yids are clever, perceptive, quick-witted, alert, polite, obliging, sober,
> modest, simple, not lascivious, etc., but on the other hand they are
> unpleasant, stinking, lazy, idle, cunning, covetous, pushful, sly, malicious, etc.
> . . . And besides, so many of them look the same, have the same name . . . and
> they all wear a uniform black dress; the memory is befuddled and the
> understanding confused when it is a question of counting them or
> distinguishing them, especially where claims or enquiries are concerned. It is
> difficult to detect the guilty; all present themselves and no one is the right
> man. This must also be an example of their cunning.

In the conclusion of his report, he repeated the traditional charges against
the Jewish community:

> In accordance with these earlier and more recent views on the Yids and varied
> opinions concerning them, I find: their schools are nothing more than a nest
> of superstition and hatred for Christians; the communities are a dangerous
> state within the State, which a well-organized political body is not obliged to
> tolerate; their excommunications are an impenetrable sacrilegious cover for
> the most terrible abuses committed to the detriment of the community.

In light of this view, Derzhavin argued that reform was necessary, and he
advocated that Jews be granted civil status, encouraging the abandonment
of traditional dress, employment in craft and agriculture, and the transfer
of Jews to the steppes of New Russia. In addition, he emphasized the
importance of Western education. Referring to Moses Mendelssohn, he
stated: 'In order to expose the superstition of misguided zealots of his faith,
that is to say the deceivers, he [Mendelssohn] has taught some of his
brethren the pure Jewish language and, by translating the Scriptures into
everyday German, he has made ordinary people read them. They have been
understood, the veil has fallen and the reign of the Talmuds has ended.
Since then, the numbers of erudite Jews, second to none among the most
learned men in Europe, have multiplied on German soil.'

For Derzhavin, it was necessary to establish an educational programme
in which only children up to the age of twelve be allowed to study in Jewish
primary schools (*heders*). Older children would be required to attend

schools in which secular learning would be transmitted by Jewish teachers who were trained in Germany. Later, after Tsar Paul I's assassination in 1801, his successor, Alexander I, established a Committee for the Reorganization of Jewish Life. In 1804 a law was passed that restricted the autonomy of Jewish communities, permitted Jews to attend schools as well as universities, made the study of European languages compulsory, and specified the Pale of Settlement in western Russia as a Jewish area. Following several attempts to drive Jews from the countryside, the Tsar in 1817 initiated a new policy of integrating Jews into the general population by founding a society of Israelite Christians, which extended legal and financial concessions to Jews who had embraced the Christian faith.

Several years later the deportation of Jews from villages began. In 1824 Alexander I died, and was succeeded by Nicholas I who continued the anti-Jewish policies of previous rulers. In 1827 he created a policy of inducting Jewish boys into the Russian army for a twenty-five year period in order to swell the number of converts to Christianity. Nicholas I also deported Jews from villages in certain areas. In the same year they were expelled from Kiev; three years later they were driven from the surrounding province. In 1835 the Russian government instituted a revised code of laws to regulate Jewish settlement in the western border.

To reduce Jewish isolation, the government initiated a policy of educational reform: a Jewish educator, Max Lillenthal, was requested to create a number of reformed Jewish schools in the Pale of Settlement. These institutions were designed to incorporate Western educational methods with a secular curriculum. Lillenthal sought to persuade Jewish leaders that by supporting this project the Jewish community would be able to improve their lot, but when he discovered that the true intention of the tsars was to eradicate Judaism, he left the country. In 1844 these new schools were created, but they attracted only a small enrolment and the Russian government eventually abandoned its plans.

In the same year Nicholas I abolished the *kehillot* and placed Jewry under the authority of the police and the municipal government. Nonetheless, it became impossible for the Russian government to carry out the functions of the *kehillot*, and a Jewish body was created to recruit students for state military service and to collect taxes. Between 1850 and 1851 the government made several attempts to restrict Jewish practices: Jewish dress and men's sidecurls were forbidden, and the ritual shaving of women's hair upon marriage was discouraged. Thus, the various steps towards emancipating the Jewish people became part of a general policy to undermine the traditional Jewish way of life. The programme of the tsars was not designed to liberate Judaism from oppression and persecution, but instead was fuelled by centuries of hostility towards the Jewish people and their way of life.

While many Jews embraced emancipation, such a reaction was not universal. In Comtat-Venaissin, a district of Avignon, some Jews did not want to give up wearing the yellow hat which distinguished them from gentiles. Elsewhere in France there was similar reluctance, as Laumond, the Prefect of the Bas-Rhine, remarked disparagingly concerning Jews in Alsace: 'As for the Hebraic mob, it continues to wallow in the same ignorance and the same lowliness as before. Its religious principles, which in some way separate it from the rest of the nations, and which nothing up till now has been able to eradicate, are an almost insuperable obstacle to the *rapprochement* that the public good would require.' Such Jews, he concluded, are unable to lose the idea that they are foreigners everywhere. In his opinion, such an old prejudice will prevent them from settling permanently for a long time to come.

Despite such opposition, the assimilation of the Jewish population continued. Throughout Europe communal autonomy was abolished, and Jewish educational practices reformed. Jewish children were required to attend school, and later conscripted into the army. As adults they were not subjected to rabbinic authority; freed of former disabilities, they were able to take advantage of widening social opportunities. Within the space of only one or two generations the ideals of emancipation had penetrated all levels of Jewish life, and Jews came to view themselves as equal citizens.

Throughout Europe these changes in Jewish status were noted by both Jews and non-Jews. In France, the Prefect of the Seine remarked: 'It is common knowledge in all Paris that the Jews of that capital, freed from the fetters which have for so long hampered them in the exercise of their industry, with the hope held out of being raised to the rank of other citizens, only took advantage of their first moments of enfranchisement to prove that they were worthy of it. . . . For example, they are to be seen lining up under the colours, cultivating science and the arts, embracing professions, establishing useful institutions, and indulging in speculations distinguished by honour and probity.'

In other countries Jewish emancipation was more limited and as a result alternative routes were followed to assimilation and opportunity. In

Germany, many Jews converted to Christianity in order to further their careers and obtain social advancement. Eduard Gans, for example, embraced the Christian faith so that he could be appointed to a chair of philosophy at the University of Berlin. Even though the writer Heinrich Heine was critical of Gans' decision, he himself later converted in order to register at the Hamburg bar. Such a decision, he stated, was an 'admission ticket to European culture'. Another contemporary figure, Ludwig Borne, also converted, in his case in order to run a newspaper. 'The three drops of water that were administered to me,' he remarked, 'were not even worth the small amount of money they cost me.' According to Rahel Varnhagen-Levin, who herself had become a convert, half the members of the Berlin Jewish community had undergone conversion by 1823.

These Jewish apostates nonetheless remained Jews socially in the eyes of the Christian community. Commenting on this phenomenon, the practising Jew Gabriel Riesser said, 'Believe me, hate like the angel of death can find its man, it can recognize him by whatever name he calls himself.' Although these converts had abandoned their ancestral faith, they could not avoid feelings of guilt as well as admiration for the Jewish way of life. Hence Heine, who had depicted Judaism as 'that misfortune, that family illness of German Jews', declared: 'The Greeks were only beautiful adolescents, the Jews on the other hand were always . . . strong and unyielding, not only in the past, but until today, despite eighteen centuries of persecution and hardship . . . martyrs, who have given the world a God and a code of morality, and who have fought and suffered on all the battlefields of thought.' Similarly, the Alsatian, Alexandre Weill, who had expressed hatred of rabbinic Judaism, stated that 'more ingenuity, more spirit was expended in one day in the Jews' street in Frankfurt than in all the rest of Germany in one year . . . this street represented a civilized life, amidst barbarism, where in an oppressed society, faith, charity, and justice reigned.'

This tension between contempt and deep affection was characteristic of the period. Prior to the Enlightenment, Jews had been denied full citizenship rights, but had nonetheless been able to regulate their own affairs through a range of Jewish organizational structures. In this context Jewish law served as the foundation for communal existence, and the rabbis were able to exercise authority. However, as a result of social and political emancipation, Jewry entered the mainstream of European life, taking on all the responsibilities of citizenship. Consequently, the authority of the rabbinic establishment was undermined, and submission to the authority of the Jewish legal system became voluntary. Emancipation was thus both a blessing and a curse: even though it brought about the amelioration of Jewish daily life, it led to widespread disillusionment with Jewish tradition and culture and thereby provided the background for the emergence of modern anti-Semitism.

In the Christian world the age of Enlightenment stimulated considerable controversy with respect to the position of European Jews. Some theologians envisaged the Jewish nation in terms reminiscent of an earlier age with the Swedish prophetic figure, Emmanuel Swedenborg, for example, arguing that the Jews were an idolatrous people. 'The character of this nation,' he stated, 'is such that, more than the other nations, they worship externals as well as idols, and that they want to know absolutely nothing about internals; in fact, of all the nations, they are the most miserly, and greed like theirs, which consists of loving gold and silver as gold and silver and not for some purpose, is the most worldly affection.'

According to Swedenborg, it would be easier to convert stones than Jews. Because of their hard-heartedness, he believed, the Jewish nation would be deprived of everlasting reward. Rather, Hell would be set aside for this despised nation. Describing Hell as a town, he declared it would be a place where Jews would 'flock, crowding up together; but this town is foul and covered with filth, consequently it is called the defiled Jerusalem. There, they run about in the mud and in filth above their heels, moaning and lamenting.' In Hell they would eat 'cadaverous matter, putrid, excremental, and stercoral, foul and urinous'. Other Jews, he continued, would wander outside the defiled Jerusalem: 'Those are Jews wandering about like that, uttering threats to kill, massacre, burn, roast alive, and this to everyone they meet, even to Jews or friends. From this, I could learn their character, although they dare not show the world what they are.' Other writers such as the occultist Claude de Saint-Martin, issued similar warnings. 'If the Jews were brought back as a national body in this world', he wrote, 'no one could hope for eternal salvation, because the divine circle of the supreme operations would thereby be fulfilled and closed in time.'

Such vituperative language expressed an anti-Semitism evoked in direct response to Jewish emancipation, a sentiment that intensified with the onset of revolution. When Napoleon summoned the Great Sanhedrin, it was widely feared that the Emperor had concluded a pact with the Devil. Thus in 1807 the Holy Synod declared that a proclamation was to be read out in all Russian churches accusing Napoleon of seeking to undermine the Christian faith:

> In order to complete the degradation of the Church, he has convened the Jewish synagogues in France, restored the rabbis to their dignity, and laid the foundations of a new Hebrew Sanhedrin, the same infamous tribunal which once dared to condemn Our Lord and Saviour Jesus Christ to the cross. And now he is daring to bring together all the Jews whom the anger of God had dispersed over the face of the earth, and launch all of them into the destruction of the Church of Christ, in order, Oh unspeakable presumption, greater than any heinous crime, that they should proclaim the Messiah in the person of Napoleon.

In the view of some German theosophists, Napoleon's efforts to enfranchise Jews were perceived as a final struggle between good and evil. In Britain, some French emigrés went so far as to depict Napoleon as the Anti-Christ. In their publication, *L'Ambigu*, they asked: 'Is he [Napoleon] claiming to pass himself off and be acknowledged by them [the Jews] as the Messiah they have waited for, for so long? This, time will tell. Nothing remains for us but to see this Anti-Christ struggle against the eternal decrees of the Divinity: this must be the last act of his diabolical existence.'

Nonetheless, it was widely rumoured that the Jews were seeking world domination through emancipation. As a result, their steps towards assimilation evoked suspicion and fear, with the sadly predictable consequence that outbreaks against Jews took place in August 1819 in Würzburg and spread to other towns and the countryside. Similar acts of violence occurred in Bohemia, Alsace, the Netherlands and Denmark. Travelling rioters, whose cry was 'Hep! Hep!', stirred up the populace against Jews living in their midst. Christians armed with axes and iron bars proceeded to the Jewish quarter and destroyed the synagogue. In Berlin a contemporary account described such violence:

> The excesses which have been committed against the Jews in several towns in Germany have given rise to fear among the Israelites in this capital; there have even been some small scenes here already. A few of the Jews' enemies paid a fair number of ne'er-do-wells to cry 'Hep! Hep' under the windows of the country house of a banker of that nation. An old Israelite pedlar of ribbons and pencils was chased by delinquents in the street which echoed with the

ominous cry; he made the best of it like a man with a sense of humour and continued on his way laughing and even shouting Hep! Hep! incessantly himself.

Having decided to look into a shop and shout inside, the account continues, a woman who was on the threshold struck him, and he then hit her. A policeman then took him to the police station for his own protection. As a result of these incidents and the accompanying atmosphere of menace, many Jews sought refuge in other countries. Hence, even though Jewish emancipation had liberated Jewry from various disabilities, Christian Europe continued to inflict suffering on the Jewish nation as it had done in past ages.

EMANCIPATION AND THE BIRTH OF MODERN ANTI-SEMITISM

At the end of the eighteenth century Jewish life underwent a major transformation as a result of social, economic and political changes. The Enlightenment heralded a new vision of the equality of all human beings, regardless of religion or race. The revolutions in America and France paved the way for Jewish assimilation on an unprecedented scale. In the movement towards Jewish assimilation, Berlin was in the vanguard of such social upheaval. There a number of Jews who had emerged from the Eastern European ghetto were able to live as cultural equals among their Christian neighbours. In the face of opposition from rabbinic authorities, these figures sought to bring about a revolution in Jewish life.

Moses Mendelssohn symbolized the possibility of Jewish acculturation. His translation of the Torah into German, and his commentary on Scripture, were designed to liberate Yiddish-speaking Jews from their cultural and social isolation. Subsequently other emancipated Jews, the Maskilim, similarly promoted a reformation of Jewish educational practices.

Yet, as we have seen, this alteration in Jewish existence did not generate universal tolerance. On the contrary, even Mendelssohn expressed dismay at the intense antipathy of the non-Jewish world. Despite the plea of Christian Wilhelm Dohm for Jewish emancipation, the Christian community was not yet ready to grant Jewry full civic and social equality. Paradoxically, the emancipation that should have brought about a transformation in Jewish life served only to compound the centuries-old hostility towards the Jews. Literary anti-Semites echoed the sentiments of many non-Jews as Jewish emancipation gathered force.

The Lutheran theologian Johann David Michaelis, for example, was a bitter opponent of Jewish emancipation. In his criticism of Dohm's views he accused the Jews of viciousness and dishonesty. They were without honour, he declared. The fact that some Jews no longer observed Jewish customs caused him to remark: 'When I see a Jew disgracing his religion by eating pig, how can I believe in his promise?' Jews, he continued, are worthless as soldiers because of their small stature and also because they refuse to fight on the Sabbath. Further, Jews do not have a religion in the proper sense since Mosaic law stipulates how to act and not what to believe.

The German philosopher Immanuel Kant similarly contended that Judaism is not a religion, but merely a union of a group of people belonging to a particular stock who have formed themselves into a commonwealth under purely political laws. Kant believed that once rid of their 'Judaic spirit' Jewry would be able to mend their ways. At the suggestion of one of his pupils, Lazarus Bendavid, Kant advocated the creation of a Jewish-Christian sect, based on the Torah and the Gospels. Nonetheless, Kant's aim was that Judaism should cease to exist. This would herald the end of the drama of religious evolution and the advent of an era of happiness for all humanity. His disciple Johann Gottlieb Fichte, however, argued that the solution to the Jewish problem consisted in their expulsion from German lands.

In an early work, the German philosopher Hegel compared Jews to non-Jews, concluding that general hostility allowed 'nothing but physical dependence, an animal existence, that can only be secured at someone else's expense, and which the Jews received as their portion'. Such parasitism was characteristic of Jews throughout history: 'All the conditions of the Jewish people, including the wretched abjectly poor and squalid state they are still in today, are nothing other than the consequences and developments of their original destiny – an infinite power which it desperately sought to surmount – a destiny which has maltreated it and will not cease to do so until this people conciliates it by the spirit of beauty, abolishing it as a result of this conciliation.'

For Hegel, the great tragedy of the Jewish people is not Greek in character. 'Hence it can rouse neither terror nor pity, for both of these arise only out of the fate which follows from the inevitable fault of a beautiful character; it can arouse horror alone.' Elsewhere, Hegel repeats in philosophical terms the ancient charge of deicide: 'The Jewish multitude was bound to wreck his [Jesus'] attempt to give them the consciousness of something divine, for faith in something divine, something great, cannot make its home in a dunghill.'

Turning to religious thinkers of the period, the theologian Semler, who is regarded as the founder of historical biblical criticism, protested against the Jewish belief in scriptural authority. 'Because the Jews regard these books as divine and holy,' he wrote, 'is it right to conclude that other people must also consider them divine, or as superior dignity to their own histories and annals?' According to Semler, the Hebrew Bible contains abominable stories, full of threats and curses of other nations. In his view, God could never have made such pronouncements since he is the Lord of all peoples. Semler was also troubled by the traditional doctrine of chosenness. 'For us, for Christians *qua* Christians,' he concluded, 'it is important to see if the spirit of Jesus Christ lives in these books, before regarding them as forming part of Christian teaching.'

Semler's pupil, Friedrich Schleiermacher, who was often a guest at Jewish salons, also wrote denigratingly of Judaism: 'Judaism is long since dead. Those who yet wear its livery are only sitting lamenting beside the imperishable mummy, bewailing its departure and its sad legacy. . . . This faith has long persisted and, like a solitary fruit, after all life has vanished, hangs and dies on the withered stem till the rudest season of the year. The limited point of view allowed this religion, as a religion, but a short duration.'

Such reactions served as the background to the riots of 1819 which began at Würzburg and spread through German towns and countryside. Similar outbursts took place in Bohemia, Alsace, the Netherlands and Denmark, where unknown missionaries travelled through towns and villages, stirring up the population. At the cry of 'Hep! Hep!' rioters armed with axes and iron bars attacked Jewish districts. Synagogues were destroyed as the police turned a blind eye. In several towns, a delegation from the bourgeoisie demanded the expulsion of the Jews.

In a letter to her brother, Rahel Varnhagen-Levin described such public outbursts with sadness and dismay: 'I am infinitely sad as never before. On account of the Jews. They want to keep them; but for torment, for contempt, for swearing at . . . for kicking and throwing downstairs. . . . The hypocritical new love for the Christian religion (may God forgive me for my sins), for the Middle Ages, with its art, poetry and horrors, inflames the people, reminded of old experiences, to the horror to which it can still be inflamed.'

Her husband, however, viewed such events with a degree of equanimity, believing that Jewry would eventually be integrated into society:

The persecution of the Jews in our towns is a horrible phenomenon. The authorities do not show themselves so impressive as in Hamburg. In Heidelberg the town director Pfister is firmly held guilty, in Karlsruhe gentlemen of quality are said to have joined in the attackers' cry of Hep! From the universality of these attacks on the Jews it can be seen that those people are wrong who imagine that our political fragmentation is an obstacle to general popular movements. The greatest unity of the Germans can be recognized in the feelings which they express about their condition. But these assaults on Jews are a beginning of such events which will later bring them all equality of rights with the Christians by way of the people.

Proponents of emancipation thus optimistically predicted the eventual triumph of reason over prejudice. Despite the wave of anti-Jewish sentiment unleashed by the quest for social, political and cultural advancement, these advocates of assimilation continued to press for progressive reform. What they downplayed, however, was the overpowering racist reaction of critics of the Jewish nation. Previously Jews had been viewed as outcasts, shunned by God because of their rejection of Christ. Yet, once they were emancipated and allowed to mix freely in society, the previous religious curse was transformed into a quasi-scientific theory about biological differences between races. In the Middle Ages, conversion was perceived as the solution to the Jewish problem, whereas in modern times the distinction between Jew and gentile was seen as based on inherent racial differences.

In this transformation the Aryan myth symbolized the liberation from church teaching. In 1786, in his *Asiatic Researches*, the Englishman William Jones drew attention to the linguistic affinity that exists between Sanskrit, Greek, Latin, Gothic and Celtic. In his view, the Indian language had pre-eminence. Contemporary philosophy supported such a contention: in 1805 Friedrich Schlegel declared that the Indian language was 'older than the Greek or Latin languages, not to mention German or Persian'; Indian is distinguished, he stated, by its 'depth, clarity, calm, and its philosophical turn'. He also maintained that Indian was 'the oldest of the derived languages'.

During the first decade of the nineteenth century a German philologist, J.C. Adelung, annexed anthropology to his field of research, claiming that

Asia has always been regarded as the cradle of humanity. Comparing Kashmir and Eden, he affirmed: 'Even the people are distinguished above all other Asians. They have nothing of Tartar or Mongol culture, which is characteristic of Tibetans and Chinese; but they are of the finest European forms, and in spirit and wit surpass all Asians.' He then proceeded to tell the story of the first human couple and its descent.

Another writer of this period, Johann-Gottfried Rhode – who appears to have invented the word and concept of 'Aryan' in its modern sense – maintained that the *Zend-Avesta* (the revelation of Zoroaster) was the sacred book of the Medes and Persians, and thus a more reliable source than the other writings of great antiquity. Comparing the Indian with the Jewish revelation, he concluded that Zoroaster was superior to Moses. Mosaism, he contended, was based on miracles, whereas Zoroastrianism rested on the inner strength of truth.

Continuing this theme Gustav Klemm, a popular author of the period, distinguished between an active and a passive race: 'In the meantime another race had matured in the highlands of the Himalayan regions. . . . This tribe did not live in the valleys and plains but in the rough hills, at first a hunting people, then robbing, boldly and arrogantly attacking its passive neighbours.' Similarly, the Christian indologist Lassen described the Aryans as 'the most completely organized, the most enterprising people; it is therefore the youngest the earth only having produced the most perfect species of plants and animals later.' Comparing Aryans to Semites, he continued:

> Among the Caucasian peoples we must award the palm to the Indo-Germans without a doubt. This is not fortuitous but we believe that it springs from their higher and more comprehensive talents. History shows that the Semites do not possess the harmonious balance of all the powers of the soul, in which the Indo-Germans excel.

In the light of such theories, Jews were not viewed as reprehensible because of their religious past as in previous centuries. It was not the crime of deicide that sealed their fate. Rather, their destiny was determined by racial inheritance. Such doctrines, which emerged during the age of the Enlightenment, sowed the seeds of the destructive policies which eventually led to the concentration camps and the gas chambers. Conversion or expulsion offered no solution to the Jewish problem. As we will see, the

Nazis grounded their vision of the future in such racial speculation, insisting that the recovery of Germany would only be possible if the struggle against Jewry were won. In this combat against the forces of evil, Hitler perceived himself as fulfilling a divine directive. Utilizing apocalyptic imagery, he believed the Jews were vermin that must be eliminated from European life if Western civilization were to be rescued and restored.

THIRTEEN

Anti-Semitism in the Nineteenth Century

As Jews increasingly entered into the mainstream of western European life, apologists pressed for the improvement of Jewish life. In England the Prime Minister Benjamin Disraeli, who was himself of Jewish descent, formulated a theory of the Jewish nation that served as the basis for his plan to grant civil rights to British Jewry. His advocacy of Jewish emancipation, however, gave rise to a hostile response from such critics as Robert Knox. A parallel disparagement was an important feature of French life as well, as illustrated by the Damascus Affair during which the President of the French Council sided with French consuls in Damascus who alleged that Jews there had committed ritual murder. Although the matter was peacefully concluded, this traditional Christian charge gave rise to widespread antagonism between gentiles and Jews. In this context the myth of the Wandering Jew, which had played a central role in fostering Judaeophobia in the Middle Ages, again served to highlight the alien nature of Jewry. According to this myth, Jews were destined to wander from country to country as a punishment for rejecting Christ. In a wide range of literature this image was a central feature, stimulating French Judaeophobia. Added to such a charge was the attitude of French socialists, critical of the Jewish establishment. Throughout Germany the advocates of German racism as well as the metaphysical writers of the day were deeply critical of both Jews and Judaism; such hostility reached its climax in the writings of the composer Richard Wagner, whose music paved the way for the Nazi onslaught against the European Jewish community.

EUROPEAN JEWRY

In the eighteenth century Jews in England had a similar status to Catholics and Nonconformists: their only disability consisted in exclusion from political and honorary offices. However, when in 1829 Catholics were granted full civil rights, Jews continued to be denied such privileges. Hence, despite efforts to improve the lot of Jews living in England, their presence continued to cause anxiety, and stereotypes including the image of Shakespeare's Shylock in the *Merchant of Venice*, and Dickens' Fagin in *Oliver Twist* reinforced the negative picture of the Jew.

Anxious to combat such hostility, the Tory politician Benjamin Disraeli formulated a theory of race which became the basis of some of his political views. In his novel *Coningsby*, the doctrine of Semitic superiority, based on purity of race, was formulated by Sidonia, Coningsby's mentor. 'The fact is,' he stated to Lord Coningsby, 'you cannot destroy a pure race of Caucasian organization. It is a physiological fact. . . . And at this moment, in spite of centuries, of tens of centuries, of degradation, the Jewish mind exercises a vast influence on the affairs of Europe. I speak not of their laws, which you still obey; of their literature, with which your minds are saturated; but of the living Hebrew intellect. You never observe a great intellectual movement in Europe in which the Jews do not greatly participate.'

In the light of such attitudes, Disraeli sought to admit Jews to the House of Commons. In a speech of 1847, he declared:

On every sacred day you read to the people the exploits of Jewish heroes, the proofs of Jewish devotion, the brilliant annals of past Jewish magnificence. The Christian Church has covered every kingdom with sacred buildings, and over every altar . . . we find the tables of the Jewish law. Every Sunday – every Lord's day – if you wish to express feelings of praise and thanksgiving to the Most High, or if you wish to find expression of solace in grief, you find both in the words of the Jewish poets. . . . All the early Christians were Jews. The Christian religion was first preached by men who had been Jews until they were converted; every man in the early ages of the Church by whose power, or zeal, or genius, the Christian faith was propagated was a Jew.

Defending Jewish interests, Disraeli continued: 'In exact proportion to your faith ought to be your wish to do this great act of national justice. If you had not forgotten what you owe to this people, if you were grateful for that literature, which for thousands of years has brought you so much instruction and so much consolation to the sons of men, you as Christians would be only too ready to seize the first opportunity of meeting the claims of those who profess this religion.'

Such remarks, however, provoked a hostile response from various writers. Robert Knox in his *The Races of Man*, for example, disputed

Disraeli's proposals. 'A respect for scientific truth,' he wrote, 'forbids me from refuting the romances of Disraeli; it is sufficient merely to observe here that, in the long list of names of distinguished persons who[m] Mr Disraeli has described of Jewish descent, I have not met with a single Jewish trait in their countenance.' Disputing Disraeli's contentions about Jewry, he asked: 'Where are the Jewish farmers, Jewish mechanics, labourers? . . . The real Jew has no ear for music as a race, nor love of science or literature; he invents nothing, pursues no enquiry.' Despite such controversy about the Jewish character, both Disraeli and his opponents advanced theories based on the concept of race, believing race to be a fundamental feature of social and cultural life.

In France, and like their coreligionists in England, Jews were granted full civil rights; as a result, a number of Jewish figures sought to eliminate the last vestiges of Judaeophobia. Pre-eminent among these public figures was the statesman Adolphe Crémieux who praised the advances made by the post-Enlightenment Jewish community. 'Cast your eyes over this France,' he proclaimed, 'the homeland of all liberal feelings. See the Israelites launching into all the honourable careers and distinguishing themselves by all the virtues which make good citizens. . . . Let men cease therefore to make the name of the Jewish nation echo within their boundaries, if indeed the Jews can be regarded as a nation at all since they have the good fortune to be blended into the great family of the French people.'

In this enlightened environment those Jews who were successful had managed to amass great wealth. In the nineteenth century money became the major factor in determining social acceptance as well as esteem. In this milieu the richest Jew, the Austrian consul James de Rothschild, was perceived as the leader of French Jewry. Among his critics, the writer Ludwig Börne sarcastically observed: 'Rothschild has kissed the Pope's hand. . . . Order has at last been restored such as God intended when he created the world. A poor Christian kissed the Pope's feet and a rich Jew kissed his hand. If Rothschild had received his Roman loan at 60 per cent instead of 65 per cent and so had been able to send the Cardinal-Chamberlain 10,000 ducats more, then he would have been allowed to embrace the Holy Father. Would it not be the greatest boon for the world if all kings were chased off their thrones and the Rothschild family installed in their place?'

Such disparagement of Jewry was also voiced when Jews were involved in public scandal. In 1832, when the Duchesse de Berry was betrayed to

Louis Philippe's government by the convert Simon Duetz and arrested, the writer Chateaubriand described Duetz as a traitor: 'Let the descendant of the Great Traitor, let Iscariot into whom Satan had entered, *intravit Satanas in Judam*, say how many pieces of silver he received for the deal.' Again, the novelist Victor Hugo described the apostate Duetz in derogatory terms reminiscent of early ages: 'He is not even a Jew! He is a filthy pagan, a renegade, the disgrace and outcast of the world, a foul apostate, a crooked foreigner.'

During this period the Damascus Affair also inflamed hatred of Jews in France and elsewhere. In 1840, a Capuchin monk, Father Thomas, disappeared in mysterious circumstances in Damascus. Two French consuls, Ratti-Menton and Cochelet, contended that this disappearance was due to the actions of the Jewish community and accused its leaders of ritual murder. False confessions were then obtained through torture. However, some of the accused were Austrian subjects, and the Austrian consuls came to their assistance. This incident aroused intense feelings throughout Europe, and in Syria representatives of England, Russia and Prussia came to the aid of their Austrian colleagues.

In Paris several leaders of the Jewish community, including Adolphe Crémieux and James de Rothschild, were concerned with the plight of the Syrian Jewish community. The President of the Council of Ministers, however, supported the French consuls, and the governmental newspaper *Le Messager* was instructed to assert that the superstitions of oriental Jews endorsed ritual murder; in addition, it encouraged French Jews to refrain from commenting on this matter. The writer Heinrich Heine stated: 'The most distressing thing that the bloody Damascus question has brought to light is the ignorance of eastern affairs which we observe in the French President of the Council of Ministers . . . a glaring ignorance which might one day make him commit the most serious mistakes, when it will no longer be this small bloody question of Syria, but really the major bloody world question, the fatal and inevitable question that we call the Eastern Question which will have to be solved.'

Defending his actions, the President explained to the Chamber of Peers: 'Should I not believe M. Cochelet's words rather than that of a sect which I respect for its energetic efforts to vindicate itself, but which after all is itself a party to the suit?' Endorsed by the President of the Council, the story of the Damascus Affair was publicized by the press, and in Paris only two papers defended the Jews. In other countries, however, public opinion generally supported the Jewish cause. Organizing themselves internationally, a number of Jewish leaders gathered in London to create a common policy. Protesting against the French reaction, Crémieux declared: 'France is against us!' In defence of the Jewish tradition, one of the Jewish leaders, Bernard van Oven, encouraged European rabbis to swear publicly that the Jewish religion does not prescribe human sacrifice. Eventually it was agreed that a mission – composed of Crémieux, the philanthropist Sir Moses Montefiore, and the orientalist Solomon Munk, meet the Sultan and the Viceroy of Egypt, Mehemet Ali. Even though this crisis was peacefully resolved, this event – recalling the medieval charge against Jewry – served as a reminder of the precariousness of Jewish life in the modern world.

Although Jewish life underwent considerable improvement in the nineteenth century, medieval stereotypes of the Jew continued to animate anti-Jewish sentiment. As the *Archives israélites* lamented, contemporary writers continued to perpetuate the image of the Satanic Jew:

> Every one of them at least once in his lifetime is determined to cut himself a doublet in Middle Ages style and, when their imagination runs dry, they knock up a history of the Jews. There is not a novelist, a would-be short story writer, not the most wretched manufacturer of *feuilletons* who has not got a fantastic picture of the Jews of yore in his bag. . . . At the theatre, from Shakespeare to Scribe, in novels, from *Ivanhoe* to Paul de Kock; in the newspapers ever since there have been writers to perpetrate *feuilletons* and a public which is willing to swallow a lengthy daily rigmarole, everywhere in fact, in this world of printed paper . . . crack, a Jew is knocked up for you as an egg would be fried.

Despite such protests, the disparagement of the Jew remained an important literary theme, particularly in connection with the legend of the Wandering Jew. According to this Christian myth, which had spread in Europe from the sixteenth century and gained universal acceptance, the Jewish people were driven from their ancient homeland for having rejected Christ. The Jew, like Cain, is a fugitive, destined to wander from country to country. In their own eyes Jews are blameless. Yet, for Christians they are guilty of the crime of viewing Christ as a criminal and refusing to help him on his way to Calvary. As a ballad of the early nineteenth century explains: 'Churlishly, rebelliously, I said to him irrationally, "Get you gone, criminal, from outside my house, move on, get going for you shame me."' The fault of the Jew lies in his unbelief, the ballad continues, which he regretted, even desiring to become a Christian: 'It was a cruel presumption, which caused my misfortune; if any crime is expiated, I would be too fortunate: I have treated my Saviour too harshly.'

Later, in 1853, Edgar Quinet in *Ahasuérus* depicted the Wandering Jew as a symbol of human suffering. This work was the inspiration for *Le Juif errant, Journal* which proclaimed in the first issue: 'The wandering Jew! at this name, the whole world stops and bows down in terror before the majesty of God: children, peasants, noblewomen. . . . The Wandering Jew, according to the orthodox priest, is the Jewish race, eternally dispersed among the nations, without merging with them, without becoming a sister to them, alone among the peoples of the earth, thus fulfilling the prophecies of the divine curse.'

Influenced by this myth, other authors of the period caricatured Jews. The novelist Victor Hugo, for example, in *Rabbi Manassé ben Israël*, remarked that Jews thirsted for Christian blood: 'Of the two rival parties, what does it matter which succumbs? Christian blood will flow in waves. I hope so anyway.' Again, the poet Lamartine in *Jocelyn*, described the fate of a poor despised Jewish pedlar: 'The poor pedlar died last night. No one wanted to give the planks for his coffin; the blacksmith himself refused a nail. "It's a Jew", he said, "come from I don't know where, an enemy of God whom our land worships and who if he returned, would outrage him again."'

The writer Chateaubriand rejoiced in the perils of those who tortured Christ: 'Happy Jews, crucifix dealers, who rule Christianity today. . . . Ah! If you wanted to change skins with me, if I could at least slide into your strongboxes, rob you of what you have stolen from gilded youth, I would be the happiest of men.'

While such leading literary figures were caricaturing Jewry, anti-Semitism was being promoted by French socialists. Hostile to industrialization, these propagandists blamed Jews for the evils of the modern world. Charles Fourier, for example, in his *Fable of the Jew Iscariot and the Six Christians* attacked Jewish commercialism:

The Jew Iscariot arrives in France with a hundred thousand pounds in capital which he gained from his first bankruptcy: he sets up as a merchant in a town where there are six accredited and respected rival firms. To take away custom from them, Iscariot begins by selling all his goods at cut prices; this is a sure means of attracting the mob; Iscariot's rivals soon start shouting: Iscariot smiles at their complaints and cuts prices even further. Then the people exclaim in admiration: long live competition; long live the Jews, philosophy and fraternity; the price of all goods has fallen since Iscariot arrived; and the public says to the rival firm: 'It is you, gentlemen, who are the real Jews, and who want to make too much money. Iscariot is an honest man, he is content with a modest profit, because his household is not as splendid as ours.' In vain do the old traders point out that Iscariot is a rascal in disguise.

After Fourier's death, his followers continued his verbal assault against the Jewish populace. Hence in *Juifs, rois de l'époque*, Toussenel wrote: 'I call by this despised name of Jew every trader in cash, every unproductive parasite, living off the substance and work of others.' In the view of these socialists, then, the Jew was evil personified. As Pierre Proudhon explained: 'The Jew is by temperament, unproductive, neither agriculturalist nor industrialist, not even a genuine trader. He is an intermediary, always fraudulent and parasitical, who operates in business as in philosophy, by forging, counterfeiting, sharp practices. He only knows the rise and fall of markets, transport risks, uncertainties of returns, hazards of supply and demand. His economic policy is always negative; he is the evil element, Satan, Ahriman, incarnated in the race of Shem.'

Echoing sentiments of previous centuries, Proudhon suggested action chillingly similar to that which would be carried out by the Nazis a century later: 'Jews. Make a provision against that race, which poisons everything, by butting in everywhere, without ever merging with any people. Demand its expulsion from France. Abolish the synagogues, allow them to enter no employment, finally proceed with the abolition of this religion. Not for nothing have the Christians called them deicides. The Jew is the enemy of mankind. That race must be sent back to Asia or exterminated.'

In German society, obsession with racist doctrine resulted in the most pernicious form of Judaeophobia. In particular, the writings of two major proponents of Germano-Christian racism, Ernst Moritz Arndt and Friedrich Ludwig Jahn, perpetuated the myth of the supremacy of the Germanic people. According to Arndt, it is the Germans who possess the divine spark: 'I do not think I am mistaken in stating that the powerful and ardent wild stock called German was the good species into which the divine seed could be implanted to produce the most noble fruits. The Germans and the Latins impregnated and fertilized by them, are the only ones to have made the divine germ flower, thanks to philosophy and theology, and as rulers to animate and guide . . . the surrounding peoples, belonging to foreign species.'

Such German-ness must be protected from contamination, and it was Arndt's desire that the Jews disappear as a separate people. This, he believed, could occur through their conversion to Christianity. 'Experience shows,' he stated, 'that as soon as they abandon their disconcerting laws and become Christian, the peculiarities of the Jewish character and type rapidly grow indistinct and by the second generation it is difficult to recognize the seed of Abraham.' For Jahn too the struggle against foreign blood is a battle of life and death for German society and culture: 'Hybrid animals have no real capacity for reproduction; similarly, mongrel peoples have no national survival of their own . . . he who strives to bring all the noble peoples of the world into one herd runs the risk of ruling over the most despicable outcasts of the human race.'

In the midst of such racial and patriotic sentiment, the Wartburg festival was held in 1817 to commemorate the tricentenary of the Reformation and the tenth anniversary of the Battle of Leipzig. Delegates from fourteen primarily Protestant universities gathered together at Jena to found the United German Student Society. A solemn procession took place, followed by a divine service and an *auto-da-fé* of books and other objects regarded as anti-German. A letter from a Heidelberg student, Richard Rothe, described the event:

The people in Jena want a Christian-German *Burschenschaft* but we had always wanted till then a general one in the strictest sense of the word and we therefore decided to give entry to Jews and foreigners as to anyone else if they had acquired academic rights through matriculation. Thereupon the Germans – there were about twenty of them – flew into a terrible rage. Since then they form a sect in the *Burschenschaft* and at general meetings are mainly distinguished by forming a perpetual opposition. . . . They are not too keen on their studies and act as if they have found the philosopher's stone, and mediate on how they will one day become Germany's saviours and redeemers.

Alongside such patriotic attitudes, which fostered public expression of the most negative assessments of Jewry, German metaphysicians castigated Judaism and the Jewish nation in terms all too reminiscent of previous Christian centuries. The theologian Friedrich Wilhelm Ghillany attempted to expose what he believed to be Jewish cannibalism. According to Ghillany, such cannibalism was evidenced by the ritual murder of Jesus as well as subsequent ritual murders in Jewish history. In the light of such barbarism, he believed that it would be misguided to grant rights to Jews 'who adhere so rigidly to old inhuman prejudices, who regard us as impure, like serfs and dogs, just as their ancestors did, even if they do not flaunt it to our face? It is men such as these who claim full civil rights, the right to exercise functions of government, to become the superiors of Christians, judicial and administrative officers!'

Voicing a similar distaste, the philosopher Ludwig Feuerbach attacked the Jews: 'The Israelites only opened their gastric senses to nature. They only enjoyed nature through their palate. They only become aware of God through the enjoyment of manna. . . . Eating is the most solemn act or even initiation of the Jewish religion. In the act of eating, the Israelite celebrates and renews the act of creation. In eating, man declares nature to be a nullity in itself. When the seventy elders climbed the mountain with Moses, then "they saw the God of Israel. . . . They stayed there before God; they ate and they drank" (Exodus 24:10–11). The sight of the highest being therefore only amused their appetite.'

Arguing in like vein, the Hegelian Arnold Ruge emphasized what he saw as the pernicious influence of Jewry on German society; in the following century, Hitler would use similar imagery in describing the corrupting impact of the Jewish community on German society: 'They are maggots in the cheese of Christianity who are so unutterably comfortable in their reflective and stock-jobbing skin that they believe nothing and precisely for this reason remain Jews.' Another Hegelian, Bruno Bauer, polemicized against Jewish emancipation. In his *Die Judenfrage*, he criticized the Jewish people 'for having made their nest in the powers and interstices of bourgeois society'. The Jews' crime resided in 'not recognizing the purely human development of history, the development of human conscience'.

Joining the ranks of intellectuals from all disciplines, in his social and political writings Karl Marx, himself a Jew, criticized the Jewish influence on bourgeois society. Material concerns, he argued, form the basis of Jewish life:

> The bill of exchange is the real God of the Jew. His God is only an illusory bill
> of exchange. That which is contained in abstract in the Jewish religion –
> contempt for theory, for art, for history, and for man as an end in himself – is

the real, conspicuous standpoint and the virtue of the man of money. . . . The chimerical nationality of the Jew is the nationality of the trader, and above all the financier.

In the nineteenth century the groundswell of German animosity towards the Jews reached its climax in the writings of Richard Wagner. Exiled in Switzerland from 1849 to 1851 he studied Germanic mythology. In his first book, he drew on these studies, presenting an Aryan theory of the origin of humanity: 'Upon this island, i.e. these mountains, we have to seek the cradle of the present Asiatic peoples, as also of those who wandered forth to Europe. Here is the ancestral seat of all religions, of every tongue, of all these nations' kinghood.' Describing the legend of the Niebelungen, he wrote: 'Research has shown the basis of this saga, too, to be of religio-mythic nature: its deepest meaning was the unconscience of the Frankish stem, the soul of its royal race . . . compelling respect.'

For Wagner, the god Wotan is the same as the Christian conception of the Son of God: 'The abstract Highest God of the Germans, Wotan, did not really need to yield place to the God of the Christians; rather could he be completely identified with him . . . for in him was found the striking likeness to Christ himself, the Son of God, that he too died, was mourned and avenged.'

Such a belief served as the background to Wagner's *Das Judentum in der Musik*. In this treatise he stated that the quest to emancipate the Jews is based on idealism rather than personal familiarity with Jewry: 'Even when we strove for emancipation of the Jews, however, we were more the champions of an abstract principle than of a concrete case: just as all our liberalism was not very lucid mental sport – since we went for freedom of the Folk without knowledge of that Folk itself, nay, with a dislike of any genuine contact with it – so our eagerness to level up the rights of Jews was far rather stimulated by a general idea, than by any real sympathy.'

According to Wagner, the Jew is a degenerate element in the social fabric; even those who were emancipated are incapable of making a positive contribution to society. Focusing on his patron the Jewish musician Meyerbeer, Wagner declared: 'Whoever has observed the shameful indifference and absent-mindedness of a Jewish congregation, throughout the musical performance of Divine Service in the Synagogue, may understand why a Jewish opera-composer feels not at all offended by encountering the same thing in a theatre audience, and how he can cheerfully go on labouring for it; for this behaviour, there, must really seem to him less unbecoming than in the House of God. . . . In general, the uninspiring, the truly laughable, is the characteristic mark whereby this famed composer shows his Jewishhood in his music.'

In a later work, *Oper und Drama*, Wagner continued his attack on Meyerbeer. 'As a Jew,' he wrote, 'he owned no mother tongue, no speech inextricably entwined among the sinews of his innermost being: he spoke with precisely the same interest in any modern tongue you chose, and set it to music with no more concern for its idiosyncrasies than the mere question of how far it was ready to be a pliant servitor to Absolute Music.'

His hatred of the Jews became an overwhelming obsession: in 1853 the musician Franz Liszt described to Princess Wittgenstein Wagner's passionate contempt: 'He flung his arms around my neck, then he rolled on the ground, caressing his dog Pepi, and talking nonsense to it, in between spitting on the Jews, who are a generic term with him, in a very broad sense.' Twenty years later the Gobinist Ludwig Schemann presented a more detailed picture of Wagner's deep-seated hatred: 'His laments at the unutterable misery wrought by the Jews against our people culminated in the description of the fate of the German peasant who would soon no longer own a square inch of his own soil. . . . I have never seen him exhibit such a flare-up of holy wrath; after his last words, quite beside himself, he flung himself out into the winter night, and only returned after an interval, when the paroxysm had died down.'

Throughout Wagner's life anti-Semitism was an overarching theme. Thus in 1881 he warned the King of Bavaria about the threat of a Jewish nation: 'I regard the Jewish race as the born enemy of pure humanity and everything that is noble in it; it is certain that we Germans will go under before them, and perhaps I am the last German who knows how to stand up as an art loving man against the Judaism that is already getting control of everything.' In later years such virulent hostility was transformed by the Nazis into racist policy that laid the foundations for the establishment of the killing machinery of the Third Reich.

NINETEENTH-CENTURY RACISM

As we have seen, modern European anti-Semitism was based on attitudes to race – on theories grounded in post-Enlightenment notions about the nature of human society – rather than on religious conviction. No longer were Jews castigated for rejecting Christ; instead, they were viewed as embodying pernicious characteristics that posed a threat to modern civilization. In 1775 the German philosopher Immanuel Kant had argued that blacks and whites are racially distinct. In his view, there were different human races, even though they all belong to a single genus. Such differences, however, are no guide to their respective value. Subsequently, racial theorists disagreed with Kant, insisting that physical and psychological differences between races are an indication of their relative worth. On this basis they constructed racial hierarchies largely founded on physical criteria.

The German theologian Johann Kaspar Lavater, for example, sought to deduce spiritual and psychological characteristics from physiognomy. Similarly, the Dutch anatomist Pieter Camper measured the facial angles of different races and categorized them in terms of physical beauty. The German physician Franz Joseph Gall used cranial measurement to differentiate races in terms of intelligence, moral disposition and beauty. Using a similar method, the German philosopher Christoph Meiners ranked races in terms of beauty or ugliness. In his opinion, fair people are superior to all others, whereas darker individuals are ugly and uncivilized. Arguing along the same lines, the philosopher Carl Gustav Carus postulated that the universe is endowed with a soul which underwent various metamorphoses leading to the creation of human beings. The complexions of the human races, he maintained, reflect their degree of inner illumination.

Parallel with these views, racial anthropological theorists sought to justify European domination of other peoples. Such a doctrine was based on earlier beliefs that ancient German tribesmen who were tall, blue-eyed and blond possessed honourable virtues, convictions that served to promote the belief that Germans were the bearers of civilizations to peoples of an inferior status. In *The World Struggle of the Germans and Slavs* published in 1847, Moritz Wilhelm Heffter maintained that the German drive to the east was a necessary consequence of the superiority of the German nation. Heinrich von Treitschke eulogized the racial struggle against Prussians, Lithuanians and Poles. A form of magic, he believed, had emanated from eastern German soil which had been fertilized by German blood, a belief designed to legitimize the Germanization of Prussia's Polish minority.

In addition to such doctrines, racial theory was buttressed by ideas drawn from various anthropological studies. In *Essai sur la noblesse de France*, published in 1735, Count Henri de Boulainvilliers stressed that the French nobility was descended from Frankish-Germanic invaders whereas townsmen and peasants were the descendants of the ancient Gauls. Such a notion was embraced by ideologists as well as historians of the Restoration. Among those who subscribed to this view was Count Joseph Arthur de Gobineau who asserted that his family was descended from ancient Frankish aristocracy. According to Gobineau, white, yellow and black races were not equal in value. In his opinion, the rise and fall of civilizations were racially determined. All high cultures were created by Aryans; cultures went into decline when the Aryan ruling caste interbred with members of inferior races. When such intermingling occurred, he maintained, rebellions were fomented by the racially inferior groups against the Aryan ruling races. Such insurrections had taken place in ancient Egypt, Greece and Rome. In modern times, the French *ancien régime* was destroyed by a similar revolt.

Alongside such doctrines, modern racism was also supported by various notions derived from Darwinism. In *On the Origin of Species*, Charles Darwin attempted to demonstrate that natural selection was fundamental to the evolution of the human race. According to Darwin, in nature there is a constant struggle for existence. Only those species capable of adaptation are able to survive. Hence, the process of natural selection results in the development of each species. In *The Descent of Man*, he discussed the effects of modern society on this process and argued that selective breeding is necessary to counterbalance the impact of the absence of natural selection.

The application of Darwin's theories to human society was undertaken by a number of writers who pressed for the creation of utopian communities. Francis Galton, for example, embraced the principle of natural selection. In his view, members of the professions as well as healthy members of the middle class should be encouraged to reproduce. However, those who were unable to pass a genetics test should be encouraged to emigrate. As the founder of hereditary health care, which he referred to as eugenics, Galton formulated a programme for improving the human race through genetic regulation. Such ideas applied to mating, education, public health and welfare.

Darwin and Galton's writings were later disseminated in Europe and the United States. In Germany the zoologist Ernst Haeckel sought to promote Darwin's theories, and advanced a new philosophy of life, which he called Monism. This ideology was based on comparative zoology, and was designed to lead to moral perfection. In the *History of Natural Creation*, Haeckel argued that the central European races were the most highly developed; no other peoples could be compared to them physically or intellectually. By virtue of their abilities, they would triumph over all other races and dominate the entire world. However, in order to ensure their ascendancy, selective breeding would be required.

In line with this policy, Haeckel recommended in *The Riddle of Life* that the sick be eliminated from society:

> What profit does humanity derive from the thousands of cripples who are born each year, from the deaf and dumb, from cretins, from those with incurable hereditary defects etc. who are kept alive artificially and then raised to adulthood? . . . What an immense aggregate of suffering and pain these depressing figures represent for the unfortunate sick people themselves, what a fathomless sum of worry and grief for their families, what a loss in terms of private resources and costs to the state for the healthy! How much of this loss and suffering could be obviated if one finally decided to liberate the totally incurable from their indescribable suffering with a dose of morphium.

Similar ideas were found in the writing of the physician Wilhelm Schallmeyer. In his *Heredity and Selection in the Life of Nations: A Study in Political Science on the Basis of the New Biology*, he argued that the state has a responsibility to ensure the healthy character of its people – the birth rate and racial character of the nation must be protected from adverse influences. In his view, child marriages should be encouraged, and earnings-related allowances should be given to mothers. All such measures, he stressed, should be available to anyone examined by a qualified expert in socio-biological science. However, anyone who did not pass should be denied a certificate to marry, and should be isolated and sterilized.

Later in the century, Alfred Ploetz published *The Efficiency of Our Race and the Protection of the Weak*. In his view, the West Aryan or German race was the most civilized, but was being undermined by the increasing protection of the weak in society. In his view, the conception of children should not be haphazard, but instead regulated according to scientific principles. If a deformed child should be born, then a college of physicians should determine if it should be killed. Furthermore, Ploetz argued that only inferior persons should be sent to the front during wartime. Such measures were designed to improve the quality of the race.

Other pioneers of modern eugenics emphasized the decisive impact of genetics on human personality. In their view, it is not possible to improve the capabilities of successive generations through training. Rather, human life is predetermined by its essential make-up – people are composed of positive or negative biological material. In this light such scientists as Alfred Grotjahn, a professor of social hygiene at Berlin University, advocated sterilizing those who were not members of the respectable working classes. These individuals included the insane, the workshy, those with sexually transmitted diseases and alcoholics.

Similar views about race were voiced by a wide range of nineteenth-century thinkers. Although their opinions were not based on scientific evidence, they argued that human society must confront the problem of scarce resources. In 1880, for example, the philosopher Friedrich Nietzsche declared that those who were unfit should be eliminated from society: 'Satisfaction of desire should not be practised so that the race as a whole suffers, i.e. that choice no longer occurs, and that anyone can pair off and produce children. The extinction of many types of people is just as desirable as any form of reproduction.'

In a post-Holocaust world the racial theories of the eighteenth and nineteenth centuries appear preposterous. How could reputable scientists and philosophers have propounded such notions without thought for their disastrous consequences? Cloaked by a veneer of patriotism, the writers we have surveyed sought to provide a justification for European dominance and a policy for subjection and geographical expansion. In advancing doctrines about racial superiority and inferiority, these thinkers came to believe that their views were scientifically grounded and justified by empirical evidence.

Yet, racial anthropology is nothing more than a pseudo-science with no basis in fact. These theorists firmly believed that races can be classified according to strict physical criteria, but such demarcation is exceedingly difficult, if not impossible, to stipulate. As we have seen, these theoreticians held different and conflicting views. And certainly as far as Jewry is concerned, Jews do not constitute a particular racial group; rather, the Jewish community consists of a wide range of physical types with varying genetic backgrounds. There is no such thing as Jewish blood, even though through the centuries Jews have tended to intermarry.

Regarding the systems outlined by racial theorists, there has been no generally accepted system of classification. Some, like Kant, regarded different races as equal because they all belonged to the same genus. Later theorists disagreed: Christoph Meiners believed that it was possible to rank races on the basis of beauty or ugliness. Yet it is obvious that such aesthetic judgements are purely subjective. Adopting a different approach, Carl Gustav Carus advanced metaphysical doctrines about a world soul that evolved into human beings; the complexions of the races, he contended, are reflections of inner illumination. Such belief has no scientific foundation.

Similarly, anthropological theories proposing that Germans are the bearers of a superior culture lack any historical basis. Such figures as Moritz Wilhelm Heffter and Heinrich von Treitschke simply used such a doctrine to justify German expansionism eastward. De Gobineau's conviction that Aryans constitute a superior race and that this justifies inbreeding was also fuelled by the desire to legitimize discriminatory policies. Further, his racial analysis of rebellions that occurred in ancient civilizations lacks any historical foundation.

So, too, those writers who promoted Darwinism were deluded in believing that their views were scientifically grounded. While Darwin's investigation of the natural world was in accord with scientific principles, the application of his studies to human society lacked the same rigour. Hence, Francis Galton's conclusions about natural selection were not based on empirical observation as he implied; his eugenic theories were nothing more than personal proposals for social engineering. Ernst Haeckel's monistic philosophy likewise lacked any scientific basis, and his advocacy of selective breeding was grounded in a particular form of social utilitarianism.

The dangers of giving credence and legitimacy to such pseudo-scientific ideas are now clear: Hitler's quest to rid society of what he believed to be undesirable elements led to mass murder. In his discussion of racism, Hitler emphasized the need for promoting racially selective breeding. Following the view of racial hygienicists, he promoted the victory of the better and stronger. What is required above all is purity of the blood. Repeatedly in *Mein Kampf* and his speeches, Hitler recommended a variety of measures to promote the birth rate of desirable members of German society. In this context, Hitler insisted that Germany could recover only if the struggle against Jewry were won. In advocating the superiority of Aryan blood and the need to protect it from contamination, Hitler and his executioners were convinced that the ends justify the means. The newsreels and photographs of German barbarism in the death camps, however, are a permanent reminder of the consequences of such a policy and a graphic illustration of the inherent immorality of racial and eugenic theories.

FOURTEEN

Jewry in Nineteenth-century Germany, France and Russia

Later in the nineteenth century, the Jewish community continued to suffer prejudice and persecution. In Germany, various racist tracts denigrated Jews, bolstering the formation of political parties that officially embraced anti-Semitic policies. In this context, the investigations of biblical scholars undermined Jewish teaching about the authority of Scripture. Similar hostility towards Jewry was expressed in France by writers such as Chevalier Gougenot des Mousseaux, Edouard Drumont and Jules Soury, and it was such antagonism that provided the background to the Dreyfus Affair. Falsely accused of treason, Dreyfus was sentenced to life imprisonment, but later exonerated. The popular hatred evoked by his trial inspired some Jews, such as Theodor Herzl, to seek to establish a Jewish homeland in Palestine. During this period, Russian Jewry was also subject to widespread hostility, culminating in the pogroms of 1881. Deeply disturbed by this violence, many Jews set off for other lands, while others embarked on a revolutionary struggle for social change. Alarm about such political agitation was intensified by the publication of *The Secret of Judaism* and the fraudulent *Protocols of the Elders of Zion*, which alleged that the Jewish people conspire against society to attain world domination. At the end of the century the revival of the ritual murder charge further inflamed Russian antipathy towards the Jewish community.

THE GROWTH OF JUDAEOPHOBIA
During the second half of the nineteenth century further manifestations of anti-Semitism occurred in Germany and Austria. In 1871 Canon August Rohling, a professor at the Imperial University of Prague, published *The Jew of the Talmud*, based on an earlier work, *Judaism Unmasked*, by Johann Andreas Eisenmenger. This work revived the medieval charge of ritual murder – the twelve ritual murder trials of Jews in German regions held between 1867 and 1914 were largely due to Rohling's influence.

Hostility towards Jewry was also fostered during this period by Wilhelm Marr who is credited with coining the term 'anti-Semitism'. In his *The Victory of Judaism over Germanism*, he lamented that Judaism was victorious in the modern world. Jews, he wrote, 'do not deserve any reproach. They have struggled for 1,800 years against the western world. They have beaten it and subjugated it. We are the losers and it is natural that the winners should shout *Vae victis*. We are so Judaized that we are beyond salvation and a brutal anti-Semitic explosion can only postpone the collapse of our Judaized society, but not prevent it.' Anxious to combat what he perceived as the pernicious influence of the Jewish community, he founded an Anti-Semitic League in 1871. In the magazine *Die Gartenlaube*, Otto Glagau expressed similar fears: 'The Jewish tribe does not work. It exploits the manual or intellectual production of others. This foreign tribe has enslaved the German people. The social question is basically the Jewish question. All the rest is fraud.'

Several years later Adolf Stoecker, chaplain to the imperial court, founded the Christian Socialist Workers' Party, which adopted anti-Semitism as a central feature of its platform. As a consequence, violence erupted in Berlin between 1880 and 1881. During this outbreak mobs attacked Jews in the streets, drove them out of cafés, smashed their shop windows and burned synagogues. At this time Bernhard Förster, Nietzsche's brother-in-law, organized a petition that called for a census of the Jews in Germany and requested their exclusion from the teaching profession.

Such anti-Semitic attitudes gained respectability through the influence of the historian Heinrich Treitschke, and anti-Semitic movements and parties proliferated. In support of such agitation international conferences were held, various fraternities refused to admit Jewish students, and the custom of the student duel was denied to Jews. At the end of the century anti-Semitic tracts began to circulate, yet all these works were overshadowed by the Anglo-German writer Houston Chamberlain's *The Foundations of the Nineteenth Century*. Chamberlain argued that the antiquity and mobility of the Jewish people illustrate the confrontation between superior Aryans and parasitic Semites. Committed to a belief in the racial superiority of the German nation, he wanted Germans to achieve their destiny. Within political circles, similar ideas animated such figures as the leader of the Austrian Christian party, Karl Lueger, who publicly espoused anti-Semitic policies in 1887, with the encouragement of Pope Leo XIII and Cardinal Rampolla. Subsequently, he was elected mayor of Vienna. Later the

Antisemitsche Volkspartei won four seats in the German elections; in 1893, reflecting increased public endorsement of its policies, its presence in the Reichstag increased to sixteen.

The onslaught against Jewry was intensified by the findings of biblical scholars, which undermined the authority of the Scriptures. According to rabbinic Judaism, the Torah (the Five Books of Moses) was revealed by God to Moses on Mt Sinai. This central tenet of the Jewish faith was enshrined in the twelfth-century Jewish philosopher, Moses Maimonides' thirteen principles of the Jewish religion. This tenet holds that the entire text of the Torah, including narrative and law, is infallible. Yet, in the middle of the nineteenth century, two Christian theologians, Karl Heinrich Graf and Julius Wellhausen, challenged this religious dogma. In their view, the Five Books of Moses are composed of four main documents that were later combined by a series of editors into a unified whole. Utilizing this framework, Graf and Wellhausen argued that the problems and discrepancies in the biblical text could be explained on the basis of different traditions in ancient Israel. Subsequently, this hypothesis was modified by other scholars. However, despite the varying interpretations of the textual origins within the Torah, there has been a general acceptance that the Five Books of Moses were not actually written by Moses. Instead, the Torah is understood as a collection of traditions stemming from different times in the history of the nation. Although orthodox Jewish scholars protested against this type of scholarship, referring to such biblical investigation as 'Higher Anti-Semitism', the wide acceptance of this approach called into question one of the central tenets of the Jewish faith.

Turning to events in France, after the Revolution of 1789 French Jews were accused in some quarters of conspiring against western civilization. To defend themselves against such charges the Alliance Israélite Universelle was created in 1860 with headquarters in Paris. Yet, despite such hostility, from 1846 to 1878 under the pontificate of Pius IX most French Catholics and others were largely tolerant of the Jewish population. However, during this period anti-Semitism continued to fester as illustrated by the publication of *Le Juif, le judaïsme et la judaïsation des peuples chrétiens* by Chevalier Gougenot des Mousseaux. Having received the blessing of Pius IX, this tract drew together anti-Jewish allegations concerning the Talmud as well as kabbalistic sources, the activities of the Alliance Israélite Universelle, and a plot allegedly conceived in Italy by a Jewish Mason.

In the view of Gougenot, Jews continually conspire against Christians and encourage revolution. 'This savage code [the Talmud]', he wrote, 'which combines the precepts of hatred and plunder with the doctrine of kabbalistic magic, which professes high idolatry. . . . That is why the Jews will remain unsociable beings until the Talmud is destroyed.' According to Léon Bloy, another writer of this period, 'the Middle Ages had the good sense to isolate in restricted quarters and to compel [Jews] to wear a special attire that allowed everyone to avoid them. When one was forced to deal with this scum it was hidden like a disgrace for which one sought all possible purification. Shame, and the danger of contact, had been the Christian antidote to their pestilence since God wanted to perpetuate this vermin.'

At the end of the nineteenth century the theme of a Jewish conspiracy against Christian society was perpetuated by the Catholic review, *Le Contemporain*, which cited the work of Calixte de Wolski, who regarded the Jews as responsible for the Russian pogroms of this period. According to this author, Jews 'have been pursuing from time immemorial, and by every means, the idea of ruling the earth'. Such a view was based on writings of the Russian convert, Jacob Brafman as well as the forgery, *The Rabbi's Speech*, which was taken from a novel by Hermann Goedsche and incorporated into certain versions of the *Protocols of the Elders of Zion*. In 1882 *Le Revue des questions historiques* relied on a Roman source to state that 'Judaism rules the world, and we must, therefore, conclude either that the Masons have become Jewish or that the Jews have become Masons.' Such a claim was based on the bi-monthly magazine *Civilità cattolica*, which embarked on an anti-Semitic campaign in 1880 that continued until the end of the nineteenth century. During this period such animosity was intensified by the Catholic Eugène Bontoux, founder of the bank Union Générale, who blamed its subsequent bankruptcy on the intrigues of the Rothschilds. This allegation was widely believed, becoming the subject of a number of literary works. The 1880s also witnessed the proliferation of a range of overtly anti-Semitic publications including the periodicals *L'Antijuif* and *L'Antisémitique*.

In 1886 Edouard Drumont's *La France juive* paved the way for a major campaign against French Jews. The first page of this publication linked the Revolution with the Jewish community in France. 'The only one who benefited from the Revolution,' he alleged, 'was the Jew. Everything came from the Jew. Everything returns to the Jew.' Denouncing Jewish emancipation as the cause of the Judaization of France, he contrasted the character of the Semite with the nature of the Aryan: 'Semite, mercantile, greedy, scheming, devious . . . Aryan, enthusiastic, heroic, chivalrous, disinterested, frank, trusting to the point of naiveness. The Semite is earthbound . . . the Aryan is a son of heaven. . . . The Semite sells glasses or grinds lenses like Spinoza, but he does not discover stars in the immensity of heaven.'

As a result of such racist propaganda, various Catholic publications became openly anti-Semitic, and the subject of Jewry became a central preoccupation for novelists and journalists. Thus in 1890 *La Croix* declared itself to be 'the most anti-Semitic newspaper in France'. Philosophical studies also claimed that Jews were an inferior race. As the materialist philosopher Jules Soury stated: 'The product fertilized in the egg of an Aryan or a Semite will reproduce the biological characteristics of the race or the species, body and spirit, as surely as the embryo, the foetus, the young, or the adult of another mammal. Raise a Jew in an Aryan family from birth, and neither the nationality nor the language will modify one atom of the genes of the Jew, and consequently, of the hereditary structure and texture of his tissues and organs.'

As in Germany, a number of ideologists sought to combine socialism and anti-Semitism. Thus at the beginning of 1890 the National Anti-Semitic League of France was formed in Paris under the presidency of Drumont. This movement took to the streets and sought to ally itself with the masses. Within the Chamber of Deputies an anti-Semitic group was formed, and in November 1891 a bill ordering the expulsion of the Jews received thirty-two votes. Again, as in Germany, a number of authors sought to demonstrate the Aryan origin of Jesus. Such attitudes permeated French society during this period, serving as the background to the Dreyfus Affair.

Hostility towards French Jewry reached a climax at the end of the nineteenth century. By this stage more than 300 Jews out of 40,000 served as members of the officer corps, an influx into the military upper echelons that provoked suspicion and mistrust, setting the scene for the Dreyfus Affair, which erupted in the 1890s. In 1892 Alfred Dreyfus had become a captain on the General Staff; two years later a secret memo sent by a French officer to Colonel von Schwartkoppen, the military attaché of the German embassy in Paris, was intercepted and came to the attention of the French Intelligence Service.

Incriminating the innocent Jewish officer by comparing the handwriting on the memo with his, the heads of the Intelligence Service, including Major

H.J. Henry, accused Dreyfus of treason. Tried by a court-martial, Dreyfus was found guilty, sentenced to life imprisonment and demoted in a humiliating public ceremony during which he protested his innocence. Incited by a venomous press, the onlookers attacked Dreyfus and the Jewish community. Later, Dreyfus was exiled to Devil's Island in French Guinea off the coast of South America.

Anxious to clear Dreyfus' name, his brother enlisted the support of the writer Bernard Lazare, who attempted to overturn the verdict. In defence of Dreyfus, Lazare published a pamphlet, *The Truth about the Dreyfus Affair* in November 1886 and sent copies to politicians as well as public figures. At the same time the Intelligence Service seized a letter which Schwartkoppen had written to a French major, Ferdinand Walsin Esterhazy. Lieutenant-Colonel Georges Picquart, the new head of the French Intelligence Service, concluded on the basis of this evidence that the original letter incriminating Dreyfus had in fact been composed by Esterhazy. Major Henry forged further documents to demonstrate that Dreyfus' court-martial had been correct in its judgment, and Picquart was dismissed and dispatched to Africa.

Before departing, Picquart communicated the facts of the case to friends who passed on this information to Auguste Scheurer-Kestner who stated in the Senate that Dreyfus was innocent and accused Esterhazy instead. Even though Prime Minister F.J. Méline was unwilling to accept this testimony, the case became a *cause célèbre*. Subsequently Esterhazy was acquitted, and Picquart punished by sixty days' imprisonment. Nonetheless, on 13 January 1898, the newspaper *L'Aurore* published an open letter by the writer Emile Zola to the President of the Republic entitled: '*J'accuse!*' In this statement those who had denounced Dreyfus were charged with libel. Zola, however, was eventually found guilty of defamation, and officers of the General Staff threatened to resign if Dreyfus were acquitted.

Throughout France anti-Semitic outbreaks occurred, and the Dreyfus Affair became a major public issue. In 1898 a new war minister, Cavaignac, reopened the case. Henry's forgeries were unveiled, and he was arrested. Later he committed suicide. The government then decided to request an annulment of the original verdict and a retrial. During the second trial the army officers continued to repeat their original testimony, and on 9 December 1899 the court-martial concluded that Dreyfus had committed treason and sentenced him to five years' imprisonment because of extenuating circumstances. Even though Dreyfus was eventually granted a pardon by the President of the Republic, he demanded a fresh investigation in 1904. This led to a re-examination of the case, and the court of appeal decreed that the evidence against him was unsubstantiated, and that it was therefore unnecessary to order a further trial.

Not surprisingly, the injustice and public repercussions of the Dreyfus Affair had a powerful impact on world Jewry. In particular the journalist Theodor Herzl, Paris correspondent of the Vienna *Neue Freie Presse*, was deeply affected by the antipathy evoked by the trial. On 5 January 1895 Herzl witnessed the outcry of the mob when Dreyfus was stripped of his rank. Hearing the crowd shout 'Death to the Jews', he came to the conclusion that there was no way that anti-Semitism could be eliminated from Western society. The only solution, he believed, was for the Jewish people to settle in their own country. In the same year he completed a draft of his monumental *The Jewish State*, a work that was initially addressed to the Rothschilds. Herzl was convinced that their capital could only be safeguarded by the creation of a Jewish homeland.

Later Herzl revised this work for the general public. His central thesis was that the Jewish problem could not be solved by assimilation. Jews, he argued, are inevitably marginalized in the countries where they live. 'In vain,' he wrote, 'are we loyal patriots, our loyalty in some places running to extremes; in vain do we make the same sacrifices of life and property as our fellow citizens; in vain do we strive to increase the fame of our native land in science and art, or her wealth by trade and commerce; in countries where we have lived for centuries we are still cried down as strangers.' Only the creation of a Jewish state, he believed, could relieve Jewry of such an insecure existence.

Once the major part of Poland was annexed to Russia at the end of the eighteenth century, Russian authorities became preoccupied with the charge of ritual murder. Even though Derzhavin's investigation had revealed that Jewish law does not permit such a practice, the Damascus Affair of 1840 revived Christian fears. In response the tsar instructed officials to launch an investigation. The folklorist Vladimir Dhal concluded in a report published in 1844 that although ritual murder was not practised by the vast majority of Jews, it did occur among the Hasidim. Later trials for ritual murder occasionally took place. At the same time the former Polish priest Hippolytus Lutostanski published a tract on this subject, which he sent to the future Tsar Alexander III, and the Russian daily *Novoye Vremya* printed a study of ritual murder in the Ukraine.

In the latter half of the nineteenth century, counter-emancipatory tendencies were expressed by a number of Russian writers. Thus in the 1860s the Slavonic theoretician Ivan Aksakov declared: 'The real question is not emancipation of the Jews, but the liberation of the Russians of the south-west from the Jewish yoke.' Subsequently a convert, Jacob Brafman, professor of Hebrew at the Orthodox Seminary of Minsk, wrote a series of articles on Jewish life which were collected into two volumes.

In the *Book of the Kahal*, Brafman described the means by which Jews excluded other religious groups from trade and industry: 'We learn that each Christian landowner is sold by the *kahal* (Jewish community) to a Jew. Yes, sold like an investment, both in his person and in his property. It is not just a way of speaking, but a legal term because the transaction is sealed by a special sales contract. Similarly villages, whole sections with their inhabitants, are bought and sold. Under the cover of our civil laws there exists a radically different legal code, secret and negative, that rules over and subjects to the jurisdiction of the Jews not only the Jews but also the Russians, without their knowledge.' Continuing this diatribe, Brafman further explained the nature of Jewish communal organization in Local and Universal Jewish Brotherhoods: 'The brotherhoods are the major arteries of Jewish society. . . . They link all the Jews scattered over the globe into one powerful and invincible body.'

For many Russian Jews, including the intelligentsia, the Jewish presence was perceived as troublesome and sinister. The writer Feodor Dostoevski, for example, in the summer of 1879 while undergoing his yearly cure for emphysema in Bad Ems, complained about the number of Jews he saw in a letter to Pobyedonostzev, the procurator of the Holy Synod: 'Everything is completely foreign. It's unbearable. It is supposed to last five weeks. And note this. Literally half are Yids. On my way through Berlin I also noticed that Germany, or at least Berlin, has become Judaized.' Responding to this observation, Pobyedonostzev asserted that the Jews had become a dangerous force in Russia as well: 'What you write about the Yids is perfectly correct. They have invaded everything. . . . They are at the root of the Social Democratic movement and tsaricide. They control the press and the stock market. They reduce the masses to financial slavery. They formulate the principles of contemporary science, which tends to dissociate itself from Christianity. . . . And nobody dares say that here the Jews control everything.' At the same time *Novoye Vremya* published selections from Wilhelm Marr's *The Victory of*

Semitism over Germanism; this was followed by the publication of *The Yid is on the March*.

Given such hostility, it was not surprising that when Alexander II was assassinated, Jews were blamed for plotting his death. As a result a pogrom occurred during the Holy Week of 1881 in Elisavetgrad; this was followed by other outbreaks in Kiev, Odessa and elsewhere. The French expert on Russian affairs, Anatole Leroy-Beaulieu, described these events:

> Anti-Jewish riots took place on a set day, almost everywhere in accordance with the same procedure, not to say the same programme. They began with the arrival by train of a gang of troublemakers. Often, on the previous evening posters had been hung accusing the Jews of nihilism and the murder of Emperor Alexander II. To arouse the masses, the agitators read in the streets or cabarets articles from anti-Semitic newspapers . . . the rumour spread that the Tsar had granted three days to pillage Jewish property. In many localities the negligence of the police and the indifference of the officials . . . helped to confirm this legend.

Even though the tsar assured the Jewish community that he would protect them from further violence, he viewed Jewish exploitation of the masses as the cause of this onslaught. Thus in 1882 he issued a series of decrees to protect Christians from abuse: the Pale of Settlement was decreased in size, and Jews were forbidden to settle in the countryside as well as in certain cities. Two years later General Drenteln, Governor-General of the south-western region, closed the vocational school in Zhitomir due to what he perceived as the privileged position of the Jewish community: 'In view of the fact that in the cities and localities of the south-west', he stated, 'the Jews constitute the greatest group of artisans and, consequently, prevent the development of crafts among the native populations exploited by them, a vocational school for which there is no Christian equivalent becomes in Jewish hands an additional weapon for the exploitation of the native population.' Elsewhere, police raids were aimed at reducing their numbers. Defending such a policy, Alexander III declared: 'We must never forget that the Jews crucified Christ and shed his precious blood.'

As a result of the Russian pogroms that occurred in 1881, the Jewish community petitioned the government to legalize emigration, and Jewish periodicals protested against this onslaught against the Jewish populace. A typical example stated: 'When I think how we were treated, how we were taught to love Russia and Russian letters, how we were manoeuvred into introducing the Russian language into our homes, so that now our children know no other, and how nowadays we are hunted and persecuted, my heart is filled with the most corrosive despair.'

In the 1860s, a group of young Jews formed a Zionist organization, Lovers of Zion (*Hoveve Zion*) which promoted settlement in Palestine. Other Jews emigrated elsewhere, primarily to the United States. Concerned about such mass immigration, the US government commissioned a report on the plight of Russian Jews. This document concluded by recommending that there should be a formal protest about persecution in Russia: 'Considering the fact that restrictive measures against the Jews in Russia affect from 5 to 7 million individuals, who are therefore forced to emigrate, and who, for various reasons (mostly individual and religious freedom) choose our country, we have devoted more time to the study of Jewish emigration than any other. . . . Russian emigration is a consequence of official policies. It can be slowed down by an imperial decree or an official order to stop the persecution.'

Even though emigration served as a solution to the problem of anti-Semitism, many young Russian Jews joined the revolutionary struggle. According to Ivan Tolstoy in *Der Antisemitismus in Russland* these young revolutionaries 'after graduating from high school, have acquired the legal right to a university education but are barred from it through administrative prohibitions'. They 'enter practical life deeply frustrated, full of resentment and hatred against authorities who deprive them of their rights. It is these embittered groups who organize and swell the ranks of the revolutionary parties, and the universities, barricaded against their influx, are helpless against their propaganda.'

As time passed Russian hostility towards the Jews intensified due to the publication of tracts that propagated the myth of a Jewish conspiracy aimed at world domination. Following the coronation of Nicholas II in 1895, *The Secret of Judaism* appeared in police files, alleging that in ancient times the doctrine of monotheism was known to a small number of Egyptians who refused to enlighten the masses. Nonetheless, Moses transgressed this ban and passed on such teaching to his people in order to give them an exalted position among the nations. Subsequently, when Christ sought to impart divine knowledge to humanity, the Jews crucified him and were punished as a result. This was the origin of the Jewish plot against the non-Jewish world:

The only method within human limitations that seemed capable of changing the tragic fate of the Jews, punished by God, was to hasten as much as possible the spiritual evolution of the rest of mankind. This premise implies two types of activities: (a) Creative: to contribute to the rapid spread of Christianity throughout the world. (b) Destructive: to undermine at all cost the ethical foundation of Christianity among the believers. This is the programme that became the cornerstone of the whole subsequent history of the Jewish people. . . . How can we help admiring a people that was able to subordinate all its thoughts, passions, enthusiasms, and even every routine detail of its life to a master plan?

In 1905, when the situation appeared to justify the prediction made in this tract, the *Protocols of the Elders of Zion* made its appearance. This forgery was composed at the end of the nineteenth century by an unknown author working for the Russian police. Adapted from an old French political pamphlet by Maurice Joly, it asserted that the leaders of world Jewry control the policies of European states. The aim of this Jewish body is to achieve world power by reducing gentiles to slavery.

Accompanying such charges, the ancient Christian accusation of ritual murder, circulating once more, also aroused hostile feelings towards the Jewish populace. On 20 March 1911 the body of André Luschinsky, a thirteen-year-old boy, was discovered in the suburbs of Kiev. The anti-Semitic press accused the Jews of this murder, and an inquest was conducted. Eventually Mendel Beilis, a foreman in the brickyard near where the body had been found, was accused of the crime. However, the editor of the newspaper *Kievskaya Mysl* launched his own investigation, discovering the true culprits: a gang of thieves who killed the child because they were fearful he would act as a witness against them. Later a trial took place; during the proceedings Father Pranaytis, a Catholic priest who had published a pamphlet on ritual murder, referred to the medieval legend of the punishment of the Jews and its remedy:

The Jewish people was cursed by Moses, who said: 'God will strike you with all the plagues of Egypt.' It is clear that this curse was accomplished since all European Jews have eczema on their posteriors, all Asiatic Jews scabies on their heads, all African Jews boils on their legs, and American Jews a disease of the eyes that drives them insane. The perverse rabbis have found a cure for these diseases. They rub the affected parts with Christian blood. When Jews kill Christians, they respond to a triple motive. First, they satisfy the hatred they bear Christians, and they believe that this crime is a sacrifice pleasing to God. Second, it allows them to perform magical acts. Third, since the rabbis are not sure that the Son of Mary is not the Messiah, they believe that by sprinkling themselves with Christian blood they may find salvation.

ZIONISM AND ASSIMILATION

The events of the nineteenth century illustrated the precariousness of European Jewry. Neither the Reformation nor the Enlightenment had brought about the eradication of Judaeophobia; previous Christian hostility towards the Jewish community had simply been transformed into a modern, secularized anathema founded largely on racial stereotyping. Such anti-Semitism was not fuelled by religious convictions, yet the earlier Christian denigration of Judaism and the inheritance of negative images of Jews provided the basis for hatred and attack.

For some Jews, the problem of Judaeophobia could only be solved through the integration of Jewry into the communities in which they lived. As we have seen, this was the view of Moses Mendelssohn, who sought to overcome the constraints of orthodox ghetto life and enter into the mainstream of European culture as an observant Jew. To bring about such Jewish modernization, Mendelssohn translated the Torah into German so that Jews would be able to learn the language of the countries where they lived. In addition, he oversaw the production of a commentary on Scripture which combined Jewish scholarship with secular learning. Following his example, the *Maskilim* fostered the Jewish Enlightenment which encouraged Jews to forsake medieval patterns of Jewish life and thought. These *Maskilim* also attempted to reform Jewish education by widening the curriculum of Jewish schools, producing textbooks in Hebrew, and publishing literary magazines.

Later, a number of Jewish religious figures sought to bring about the reform of the Jewish tradition. Beginning with Israel Jacobson who founded a secular school for boys in Westphalia in 1801 as well as the first Reform synagogue, Reform Jews promulgated a programme of liturgical as well as religious change. In the middle of the nineteenth century, a series of synods took place to formulate a coherent policy. Although the revolutions of 1848 and their aftermath curtailed the convocation of further Reform synods, rabbis reconvened in 1868 to lay the foundation for a synodal conference of rabbis, scholars and lay leaders. The next year over eighty reform congregations were represented at this synod, and two years later another conference took place where the participants formulated a common statement of the principles of Reform Judaism.

In the United States, Reform leaders also aspired to establish the principles of Reform. At a gathering of Reform leaders in 1885 in Pittsburgh, the Pittsburgh Platform was issued, which set out the basic tenets of the movement. Underlying this declaration was the conviction that religious reform would pave the way for the acceptance and integration of Jewry into society. As the Reformers declared: 'We recognize in Judaism a progressive religion, ever striving to be in accord with the postulates of reason. . . . We acknowledge that the spirit of broad humanity of our age is our ally in the fulfilment of our mission, and therefore we extend the hand of fellowship to all who cooperate with us in the establishment of the reign of truth and righteousness among men.'

However, not all Jews were as optimistic. Faced with continual outbreaks of hostility towards Jews in both Western and Eastern Europe, a growing number of thinkers came to the view that Jews would never be accepted as full citizens in the societies in which they lived. Instead, they argued, Jews must create a homeland in Palestine where they could be secure. The earliest Zionist thinker to embrace this conviction was Moses Hess. Born in Bonn, he later settled in Paris where he was active in socialist circles; from 1842 to 1843 he served as the Paris correspondent of the *Rheinische Zeitung*, edited by Karl Marx. In 1862 he published *Rome and Jerusalem*, a systematic defence of Jewish nationalism.

According to Hess, anti-Jewish sentiment is unavoidable. Progressive Jews believe they can escape from Judaeophobia by recoiling from any Jewish national expression, yet the hatred of Jews is inescapable. No reform of the religion is radical enough to avoid such sentiments, and even conversion to Christianity cannot relieve the Jew of this disability. 'Jewish noses,' he wrote, 'cannot be reformed, and the black, wavy hair of the Jews will not be changed into blond by conversion or straightened out by constant combing.' For Hess, Jews will always remain strangers among the nations: nothing can alter this state of affairs. The only solution to the problem of Jew-hatred is for the Jewish people to come to terms with their national identity.

For Hess, the restoration of Jewish nationalism will not deprive the world of the benefits promoted by Jewish reformers who wish to dissociate themselves from the particularistic dimensions of the faith. On the contrary, the values of universalism would be championed by various aspects of Judaism's national character. Judaism, he contended, is the root of the modern universalist view of life. What is required today, Hess asserted, is for Jewry to regenerate the Jewish nation and to keep alive the hope for the political rebirth of the Jewish people.

According to Hess, a Jewish renaissance is possible once national life reasserts itself in the Holy Land. In the past the creative energies of the people deserted Israel when Jews became ashamed of their nationality. But the holy spirit, he wrote, will again animate Jewry once the nation awakens to a new life. The only question remaining is how it might be possible to stimulate the patriotic sentiments of modern Jewry as well as liberate the Jewish masses by means of this revived national loyalty. This is a formidable challenge, yet Hess contended that it must be overcome. Although he recognized that there could not be a total emigration of world Jewry to Palestine, the existence of a Jewish state would act as a spiritual focus for the Jewish people and for all humanity.

The Russian pogroms of 1881 had a profound impact on another early Zionist, Leon Pinsker, driving him from an espousal of the ideas of the Enlightenment to the determination to create a Jewish homeland. Born in Tomaszów in Russian Poland in 1821, Pinsker attended a Russian high school, studied law in Odessa, and later received a medical degree from the University of Moscow. Upon returning to Odessa, he was appointed to the staff of the local city hospital. After 1860, Pinsker contributed to Jewish weeklies in the Russian language and was active in the Society for the Spread of Culture among the Jews of Russia. However, when Jews were massacred in the pogroms of 1881 he left the society, convinced that a more radical remedy was required to solve the plight of Russian Jewry. In 1882 he published *Autoemancipation*, a tract containing similar themes to those found in Hess's writings. He subsequently became the leader of the new *Hibbat Zion* movement, and in 1884 convened its founding conference.

In *Autoemancipation*, Pinsker asserted that the Jewish problem is as unresolved in the modern world as it was in former times. In essence, this dilemma concerns the unassimilable character of Jewish identity in countries where Jews are in the minority. In such cases there is no basis for mutual respect between Jew and non-Jew. 'The Jewish people,' he wrote, 'has no fatherland of its own, though many motherlands; it has no rallying point, no centre of gravity, no government of its own, no accredited representatives. It is everywhere a guest, and nowhere at home.' This situation is aggravated by the fact that the Jewish people do not feel a need for an independent national existence; yet without such a longing, there is no hope for a solution to Jewish misery.

Among the nations of the world, Pinsker asserted, the Jews are like a nation long since dead: the dead walking among the living. Such an eerie, ghostly existence is unique in history. The fear of the Jewish ghost has been a typical reaction down the centuries, and has paved the way for current Jew-hatred. Over time this prejudice has become entrenched and normalized among all peoples of the world. 'As a psychic aberration,' he wrote, 'it is hereditary; as a disease transmitted for 2,000 years, it is incurable. Such Judaeophobia has generated various charges against the Jewish people: throughout history Jews have been accused of crucifying Jesus, drinking the blood of Christians, poisoning wells, exacting usury, and exploiting peasants. Such accusations are invariably groundless – they were trumped up to quiet the conscience of Jew-baiters. Thus Judaism and anti-Semitism have been inseparable companions through the centuries, and any struggle against this aberration of the human mind is fruitless.'

Unlike other peoples, the Jew is inevitably a stranger. Having no home, he can never be anything but an alien. He is not simply a guest in a foreign country; rather he is more like a beggar and a refugee. The Jews are aliens, he stated, who can have no representatives because they have no fatherland. Because they have none, because their home has no boundaries behind which they can entrench themselves, their misery also has no bounds. It is a mistake, Pinsker continued, to think that the legal emancipation of Jewry will result in social emancipation. This, he believed, is impossible. The isolation of the Jew cannot be removed by any form of official emancipation since the Jew is eternally an alien. In summary, he asserted, 'For the living, the Jew is a dead man; for the natives, an alien and a vagrant; for property holders, a beggar; for the poor, an exploiter and a millionaire; for patriots, a man without a country; for all classes, a hated rival.'

Such natural antagonism between Jew and non-Jew, he argued, has resulted in a variety of reproaches levelled by both parties at one another. From the Jewish side, appeals to justice are frequently made to improve the condition of the Jewish community. In response, non-Jews attempt to justify their negative attitudes by groundless accusations. A more realistic approach, however, would involve the recognition that the Jewish people have no choice but to reconstitute themselves as a separate people in their own homeland.

More than any other figure, Theodor Herzl has become identified with modern secular Zionism. His dismay at the Dreyfus trial led to the publication of *The Jewish State* in which he argued that Jews could never be secure unless they had a homeland of their own. Herzl's analysis of modern Jewish existence was not original, and many of his ideas were prefigured in the writings of Hess and Pinsker, yet what was novel about Herzl's espousal of Zionism was his success in stimulating interest and debate about a Jewish state in the highest diplomatic and political circles.

In his preface to *The Jewish State* Herzl contends that his advocacy of a Jewish homeland is not simply a utopian scheme. On the contrary, his plan is a realistic proposal arising out of the appalling conditions facing Jews living under oppression and facing continual persecution. The plan, he argues, would be impractical if only a single individual were to undertake it. But if many Jews were to agree on its importance its implementation would be entirely feasible. Old prejudices against Jewry, he contended, are ingrained in Western society – assimilation will not act as a cure for the ills that beset the Jewish people. There is only one remedy for the malady of anti-Semitism: the creation of a Jewish commonwealth.

In the conclusion of this work Herzl eloquently expresses the longing of the entire nation for the creation of such a refuge from centuries of suffering: 'What glory awaits the selfless fighters for the cause! Therefore I believe that a wondrous breed of Jews will spring up from the earth. The Maccabees will rise again. Let me repeat once more my opening words: "The Jews who will it shall achieve their state. We shall live at last as free men on our own soil, and in our own homes peacefully die."'

Following the inspiration of these early Zionist leaders, the first Zionist Congress met in 1897; subsequently Herzl cultivated important figures in Turkey, Austria, Germany and Russia to further his plans. In 1902 a British Royal Commission on Alien Immigration was appointed, with Lord Rothschild as one of its members. On 7 July 1902 Herzl appeared before the commission, declaring that further Jewish immigration to Britain should be accepted but that the ultimate solution to the refugee problem was the recognition of the Jews as a people and the finding by them of a legally recognized home.

His appearance before the commission brought Herzl into contact with the Colonial Secretary, Joseph Chamberlain, who subsequently suggested to Herzl that a Jewish homeland could be established in Uganda. Fearful of the plight of Russian Jewry, Herzl was prepared to accept the proposal.

However, when the scheme was presented to the Zionist Congress, a number of Russian delegates who viewed the Uganda Plan as a betrayal of Zionism walked out. At the next congress, Uganda was formally rejected as a place for a national homeland.

At the time of Herzl's death, Zionism had become an established movement, yet it expressed a minority view in the Jewish world. Until the First World War, all branches of Judaism were generally opposed to secular Zionism, and reformers saw no attraction in a Jewish state in the Middle East. The battle between assimilationism and Zionism as competing ideologies continued throughout the twentieth century until the events of the Nazi era appeared to validate the Zionist analysis of the problem of anti-Semitism and its persistence in the modern world.

FIFTEEN

The Early Twentieth Century

In the early part of the twentieth century European Jews became scapegoats for the ills afflicting German society. Protestors raged against the assimilation of German Jewry, and Christian writers fulminated against the influence of Jewish values. Even though Germany prospered after the First World War, millions were unemployed between 1930 and 1933. This situation led to the rise of Nazism with its policies of rabid anti-Semitism. To the east, in Russia, Christian anti-Semites accused Jews of espionage and collaborating with the enemy during the war years. During the Revolution Russian authorities criticized what they perceived as an international Jewish conspiracy; as a result, pogroms took place throughout the country. Following the war a series of forgeries was produced, implicating Jewry with the Revolutionary movement and illustrating the existence of a worldwide Jewish conspiracy. During this period British authors also vilified Jewry for dishonesty as well as revolutionary activities. Similar attitudes existed in France where Jews were criticized for their alleged influence on world affairs as well as their involvement in revolutionary activity. After the war, the publication of the *Protocols of the Elders of Zion* reinforced the Christian myth of international intrigue. Across the Atlantic, in the United States, Jews were similarly blamed for the Russian Revolution; in response, the American Jewish Committee and the Anti-Defamation League were created to protect Jewish interests.

MODERN JUDAEOPHOBIA
Once the the British abandoned their policy of neutrality in 1914, the German Jewish poet Ernst Lissauer wrote 'The Hymn of Hate against England' in which he denounced the British. 'We will hate you with an enduring hatred,' he wrote, 'never is our hatred going to abate. Hatred on the sea, hatred on land, hatred of the head, hatred of the hand, hatred of the blacksmith, hatred of the prince, ferocious hatred of 70 million.' Despite such patriotism, which caused Wilhelm II to decorate the author, a

number of German anti-Semites castigated Lissauer because of his racial origins. Houston Steward Chamberlain, for example, declared that Lissauer belonged to a people who have cultivated hatred through the centuries.

This type of Judaeophobia was characteristic of the age. When the realities of the First World War became evident, the exorbitant costs both in terms of loss of human life and the economic consequences of the reparation requirements of the Treaty of Versailles made Jews the scapegoats for the ills besetting German society. In this environment, the philosopher Max Hilderbert Boehm formulated a bill of indictment in the *Jahrbücher* protesting against Jewish assimilation. In a later article, 'Emancipation as Will to Power in Modern Jewry', he stated: 'Nowadays, they, the cosmopolitan Jews, hold the universe in the palm of their hands, and they have no intention of letting go.' Similarly Dostoevski bewailed the growing power of the Jewish people: 'Like a vast, tightening net, the power of assimilated Jewry stretches over the whole world, and no matter where we set foot, we are caught in it. . . . We must struggle to our last drop of blood against the insidious Judaization of Europe, and especially of Germanism.'

The theme of anti-assimilationism was replicated in the works of other thinkers of the age. Oswald Spengler, in *The Decline of the West*, argued that there can be no understanding between 'Faustian nations' such as Germany, and 'Magian nations', which included Jews:

> Even when the Jews consider themselves members of the host country and share in its destiny, as was the case in most countries in 1914, in reality, they do not live this event as their own destiny, but they side with it, judge it as interested bystanders, and the ultimate meaning of the struggle must for this very reason remain incomprehensible to them. . . . The belief in the inevitability of this mutual misunderstanding leads finally to a frightening hatred, deeply concentrated in the blood, attaching itself to symbolic signs such as race, lifestyle, profession, language, which leads both sides to bloody explosions.

At the conclusion of the First World War, the assembly at Weimar drafted a new constitution that transformed Germany into a federal republic. This new regime faced opposition from both the right and the left. During 1922 to 1923 there was massive inflation in Germany; however, for the next few years greater stability was achieved, and important intellectual and cultural advances were made. This brief period of prosperity was followed by the

Great Depression, when over 6 million were unemployed. As a result the Communists and the Nazis gained considerable support. To cope with this crisis, the government began to rule by presidential decree. After several ineffective conservative coalitions, Field-Marshal Paul von Hindenburg appointed Adolf Hitler as Chancellor of Germany on 30 January 1933.

For Hitler, the Jews were degenerates and parasites. Such a view was the result of deep-seated loathing that had its origins in his early experiences. As he explained in *Mein Kampf*, in Vienna he had become aware of their presence: 'Once, as I was strolling through the inner city, I suddenly encountered an apparition in black caftan and black hair locks. Is this a Jew was my first thought. For, to be sure, they had not looked like that in Linz. I observed this man furtively and cautiously, but the longer I stared at this foreign face, scrutinizing feature for feature, the more my first question assumed a new form: Is this a German?'

For Hitler the Jew could never become a German because he was racially and religiously distinct. The difference between Jews and Germans was so vast as to make the former inherently alien. Comparing Jews with vermin, he wrote: 'Was there any form of filth or profligacy particularly in cultural life, without at least one Jew involved in it? If you cast even cautiously into such an abscess you found, like a maggot in a rotting body, often dazzled by the sudden light – a kike!' The influence of Jews on the press, art, literature and the theatre was pervasive. In addition, he attributed to them responsibility for prostitution and the white slave traffic.

In propounding his opinions, Hitler embraced the belief in a world conspiracy as delineated in the *Protocols of the Elders of Zion*. The Jews, he maintained, seek to dominate world events; in pursuit of this aim a small group of wealthy and influential Jewish figures meet secretly to devise their plans. By inciting social division, the Jew is able to burrow into a healthy society and thereby prepare for the domination of the world. Such logic led Hitler to conclude that the Jew is a personification of Satan who ravages his victims. Convinced that a people's greatness depends upon the purity of its blood, he argued that the German people can only recover its strength by eliminating Jews from its midst and preventing them from polluting its true nature. The German state must breed only the most racially pure specimens to ensure a glorious future.

When war was proclaimed, many Russian Jews declared their allegiance to their country even though the Jewish community had previously been subjected to prejudice and discrimination. Thus in 1914 the Jewish deputy

Friedmann stated to the Duma: 'In spite of the discriminatory legislation that governs us, we have always felt like citizens of Russia, and we are faithful sons of the fatherland. No force on earth can separate the Jews from the fatherland, from this land to which they are bound by ancient links. The Jews are going to defend it, not only out of a sense of duty, but also because of deep affection.'

Despite such expressions of allegiance, Jews were accused of espionage and collaboration with the enemy. Traditional Jewish customs were misinterpreted to support allegations of treason. As one report of the period revealed: 'It is an old Jewish practice to keep in the synagogue of small communities a piece of wire or a rope long enough to surround the whole village on Saturday. When an area is thus roped off, everyone is allowed to carry his usual possessions on Saturday, that is to say, the day of rest. According to a convention of Jewish law, a city surrounded by a rope is considered a courtyard. The soldiers, not understanding the function of that rope, believe that its function was to telephone the enemy.'

Given such suspicion of Jewish motives, it was not uncommon for Russian officers to encourage hatred of Jewry, attitudes reflected, for example, in the instructions given by Lieutenant-General Zhdanovitch, commander of the First Infantry Brigade: 'During the present patriotic war all the numerous nationalities that settled in Russia, with the exception of the Yids, have united so thoroughly that national differences have been completely forgotten. The Yids could have taken advantage of this exceptional, historical moment to restore the reputation of their people, to give proof of their human dignity, and to obtain equal rights, since they claim to be the object of unfair treatment.'

These, however, were not Jewish aspirations. Instead, Zhdanovitch stated, 'Russian Yids exhausted every trick to keep from participating in the defence of the homeland. Anger and hatred will then find an outlet infinitely more dangerous for them than the risks that they run by fulfilling their military obligations, and popular resentment will turn not only against those who through their criminal behaviour helped the enemy but also against their relatives and innocent children.'

Determined to denigrate Russian Jewry, the authorities invoked the spectre of an international Jewish conspiracy. When the Revolution of 1917 occurred, pogroms took place in the provincial cities and elsewhere. In Ekaterinodar a 'Slavic Group' was formed to carry out an anti-Semitic campaign in the countryside, and the Ukraine witnessed widespread anti-

Jewish activity. Alarmed by such an outburst of hostility, the regional prosecutor of Petrograd stressed the need for an anti-pogrom law. 'According to our information,' he wrote, 'there is a growing incitement to riots in the markets and other gathering places of the public. It is in Vitebsk and Petrograd that the calls for pogroms are the loudest. The pogromists insist that the Jews control the militia, the Soviets, and the District Dumas, and threaten to assassinate certain political figures.' In response, the Soviets accused the counter-revolutionaries of prejudice: 'This anti-Jewish militancy, often marked by radical rallying cries, constitutes an enormous danger, not only for the Jewish people, but also for the whole revolutionary movement, for it threatens to drown in blood the whole cause of the liberation of the people, and cover the revolutionary movement with an indelible shame.'

In the view of many Russians, the Jews were responsible for the revolutionary struggle. In addition, influential Jewish capitalists were seen as playing a central role in these historical events. In a series of forgeries, it was claimed that the Bolsheviks were controlled by a Rhenish-Westphalian syndicate through the agency of the Jewish banker Max Warburg and the Bolshevik Jew Fürstenberg. Convinced of their authenticity, the American government published these documents in 1918 under the title *The German-Bolshevik Conspiracy*. It was further alleged that the tsar and his family had been murdered on the order of the Jew Jacob Sverdlov and under the direction of the Jews Yurovsk and Goloshtshekin. As the British military attaché, General Alfred Knox, explained: 'There were two camps in the local soviet. One wanted to save the royal family. The other was directed by five Jews, two of whom were adamantly in favour of the murder.' As a result, an anti-Jewish crusade was initiated by the White armies.

In the aftermath of the First World War, a number of forgeries were circulated to implicate the Jews with revolutionary movement activities and to illustrate the existence of a worldwide Jewish conspiracy. In an alleged secret report of the French government, for example, a list of Communist leaders – all of whom except Lenin were Jews – described their plans for universal Zionist domination: 'The Jews have already secured the formal recognition of a Jewish state in Palestine. They have also succeeded in organizing a Jewish republic in Germany and Austro-Hungary. These are but the first steps towards the future domination of the world by the Jews, but it is not their last attempt.'

In another forgery, *The Report of Comrade Rappaport*, the Zionist manipulation of the Russian masses was described: 'After the fiasco of national cooperation, Ukrainian nationalism lost its economic base. The discount banks run by our comrades Nazert, Gloss, Fischer, Krauss, and Spindler play the major role in this case. The Russian landowning class, frivolous and stupid, will follow us like sheep going to the slaughter. As representative of the Poale Zion, I must acknowledge to my great satisfaction that our party and the Bund have become centres of activity manipulating the immense flock of Russian sheep.' Likewise, the most important forgery of this period, the *Protocols of the Elders of Zion*, was circulated by propagandists and further intensified fears of Jewish influence. After the defeat of the White armies, Russian emigrés publicized this document in the West, thereby fomenting further hostility towards Jewry.

The British public was highly critical of the French during the Dreyfus Affair. However, with the coronation of Edward VII in 1901, attitudes began to change. The king's banker, Ernest Cassel, was a German Jew, and British officials sought to undermine his projects, particularly when he travelled to Constantinople to reorganize the Ottoman Empire's finances. Between 1911 and 1912 a journalistic campaign was launched which alleged that the Turkish revolution was the result of a Zionist conspiracy.

Additional unrest was brought about by the Marconi Affair which concerned two leading Jewish politicians, Rufus Isaacs, the Attorney General, and Herbert Samuels, the first non-Christian member of a British Cabinet. In 1912 Lloyd George and other liberals were accused of mishandling funds, as the magazine *Eyewitness* reported: 'Isaacs' brother is the president of the Marconi Company. Isaacs and Samuels have privately arranged to have the British people pay the Marconi Company a considerable sum of money through the intermediary of Samuels, and for Isaacs' benefit.'

Even though the Jews involved in this affair were cleared by a parliamentary commission of enquiry, the scandal had a significant impact on British attitudes. In the wake of these events the writer Rudyard Kipling dedicated a hymn of hate to the affair. Based on the biblical story about Naaman's servant Gehazi, who is portrayed in the Book of Kings as a greedy and crafty figure punished with leprosy for his deceit, the poem was intended to illustrate the cunning of these Jewish politicians.

Such hostile attitudes were exacerbated by a large influx of Jews from Eastern Europe to London; in 1902 the Bishop of Stepney compared these immigrants to a conquering army that would 'eat the Christians out of house and home'. With the onset of war, suspicions were raised about these foreigners. In 1915 the sinking of the *Lusitania* led to further Judaeophobia. According to *The Times*, this war crime was caused by a Jew Albert Ballin, Wilhelm II's courtier, and in the wake of such media outcry and the fears engendered a campaign was initiated to strip Sir Ernest Cassel of both his citizenship and titles. In response the London Jewish newspapers complained about describing all Jews as Germans. Despite this protest, the British dailies and weeklies continued to incite racial hatred.

The English writer and critic G.K. Chesterton in *The New Witness*, for example, invoked the medieval image of ritual murder to fuel anti-Semitism. A Mr Thompson in *The Clarion* maintained that the 'Prussians, like the Jews, came from a tiny, rocky and arid land, and they, too, conquered the place in the sun through robbery.' The Prussians, he continued, are like the Jews; they have a tribal God whose principles are based on the fear he inspires. In the *National Review*, Leo Maxse argued that the international Jew, having been informed of the departure of Lord Kitchener for Russia, informed the German High Command. This Jew, he stated, was a miserable, calculating creature without king or homeland.

Similar animosity was expressed by leading political figures. Despite his support for the creation of a Jewish homeland, Lord Balfour, for example, complained to his mistress about a leading Jewish family:

In Brighton, at the Sassoons, I met Rosebery, Devonshire, and H. Farquhar. We found out, to our profound indignation, that we had been invited under false pretences. The Prince of Wales had dedicated a hospital in the morning, and he stayed at Reuben Sassoon's until Monday. The two evenings, we were forced to attend a long, hot and pompous dinner, crowded with innumerable Sassoon young ladies. Although I have no prejudices against the race (far from it) I began to understand the point of view of those who are opposed to foreign immigration!

Echoing similar sentiments, Lord Cecil commented that the enthusiasm of Chaim Weizmann 'overshadowed his rather repulsive, even sordid, physique'. Joseph Chamberlain commented to the Italian minister of foreign affairs that he despised the Jews. 'They are all physical cowards,' he stated. Reporting on the events taking place in Russia, the British press accused the Jews of playing a leading role in the Revolution. Thus *The Times* reported that the soviet leadership was composed of Jewish partisans: 'The Petrograd soviet is an organism accredited only by itself, composed of idealists, theoreticians, and anarchists . . . most of the time typical international Jews, and including no soldiers or workers. A few of them are known to be in the pay of the Germans.'

Commenting on these events, the *Morning Post* reported:

> From the very beginning, German influence in the soviet was barely disguised. Some time ago, we published a list of the members of this remarkable council who thought it useful to change names, and the number was considerable. These conspirators were obviously Russian Jews of German extraction, and we fear that it will be said that Russian Jews betrayed Russia. It used to be said that the Spanish Jews had been expelled from Spain because they opened the gates to the Moors. Indeed, it would be unfortunate for the Jews of the entire world if it could be said that Russian Jews have opened the gates of Russia to the Germans.

Such allegations led to widespread hostility towards Jewry, and in 1918 the *Herald* reported numerous outbreaks of violence:

> Our attention has been called to the terrorism practised against the Jews and foreigners in some parts of East London. We are informed that all kinds of mean persecutions prevail, that men with long beards are insulted in the streets by having their beards pulled, that shopkeepers are obliged to submit to what is nothing more nor less than organized blackmail. . . . This kind of thing is directly traceable to the free distribution of incitements, which the police allow to be circulated, and to the venomous attacks on foreigners appearing in the yellow press.

Following the war, the distribution of the *Protocols of the Elders of Zion* evoked considerable controversy. On 8 May 1920, *The Times* raised questions about its authenticity in terms that suggested that a secret international body might indeed exist: 'What is this *Protocols*? Is it authentic? Did a gang of criminals really prepare such a project and gloat over their exposition? Is it a forgery? If so, whence comes the uncanny note of prophecy, prophecy in part fulfilled, in part far gone in the way of fulfilment? Have we been struggling these tragic years to blow up and exterminate the secret German organization of world domination only to find beneath it another more dangerous because more secret?'

Even though Jews were generally accepted in the United States, the traditional stereotype of the Jew continued to play a significant role in the perception of the Jewish community. As thousands of immigrants poured into the country, discrimination became a feature of American life. In 1876, for example, a hotel in New Jersey announced in New York newspapers that it would not admit Jews. In the next year the hotelier John Hilton refused to let the millionaire Joseph Seligman stay in his resort in Saratoga. By the end of the century such discrimination extended to country clubs and Masonic lodges as well as to colleges and universities.

In response, a number of prominent Jews protested publicly against such intolerance. When, for example, the librarian Melvil Dewey established a club in New York that excluded Jews, several important Jewish figures complained to the state:

> More than 750,000 Jews reside in this state. The majority are taxpayers who fulfil their obligations for the maintenance of state institutions and the payment of salaries of state employees, including Mr Melvil Dewey as head librarian. They are proud of this state and its administration. They strive to raise its cultural level, to facilitate education, and to promote the arts, science, and literature. They have worked for the cause of education as much as any other group of citizens in this community. They, therefore, feel they have the right to demand that a man, as a public official representing the whole population of the state, be prohibited as a state employee from showing the vile prejudice to which a man can stoop.

It was such antipathy that had led the Jewish community to create organizations to protect their interests, such as the American Jewish Committee and the Anti-Defamation League.

In the quest to defend and protect the rights of American Jews, the American Jewish Committee fought successfully against attempts to limit Jewish immigration; on the international scene it pressurized the Russian government to issue entry visas to Americans of Jewish descent. In addition, the American Jewish Committee attempted to ensure that Jews be fully accepted as Americans, an undertaking needed to counter the views of writers such as Madison Grant who continued to maintain in *The Passing of the Great Race* that the Jews posed a threat to the American population.

Once America entered the First World War, Jews were seen as participants in international conspiracy. Thus the report *Bolshevism and Judaism*, written by a Russian refugee who had served as an official of the Ministry of Justice, which appeared in November 1918 asserted that the decision to overthrow the tsar had been taken in the Jewish section of New York on 14 February 1916 by a revolutionary group headed by one Jacob Schiff. Quoting a section of the *Protocols of the Elders of Zion*, this report stated that the Elders were persuaded that they could stop any rebellion of the '*goyim*'. The report also listed thirty-one Russian Jewish leaders, excluding Lenin, who ruled Russia. The fears evoked by these allegations were compounded by a succession of strikes in the United States in 1919, including that of the garment workers, most of whom were Jewish. In response, the Citizens' Committees and Patriotic Organizations prospered.

Even though the Russian Revolution was welcomed by a number of Americans, most Americans abhorred Communism. In their view, the Jews had been responsible for the course of events, with some witnesses even maintaining that the ringleaders of the revolution were Jews from New York. Hence in a conversation with American senators, the Revd George A. Simons of the English Methodist Church in Russia stated that the Bolshevik movement was aided by American Jews. 'We were told,' he stated, 'that hundreds of agitators who had followed Trotsky-Bronstein came from the East Side of New York. I was surprised to find a great number of these men going up and down the Nevski. Some of them, when they learned that I was the American minister in Petrograd, stopped me and seemed happy to find someone who spoke English. But their bad English showed that they were not real Americans. Some came to visit me. We were struck by the prominence, from the beginning, of the Yiddish element in this affair, and it soon became evident that half the agitators were Yiddish. . . . I am firmly convinced that this business is Jewish.'

Such allegations encouraged American patriots to defend their country from the influence of Jewry. After a trip to the United States during this period, Hilaire Belloc reported:

[In Great Britain] a certain proportion of Jews had become generally necessary to the ruling circles. Nothing of the sort in the United States. The Jews are barely admitted in major country clubs, and most of the time they are barred. Their talents are rarely used on the General Staff of the army. They have no real civic standing. They are excluded from I don't know how many hotels. As I have just stated, the major country clubs refuse to admit them. The universities, particularly Harvard, have openly organized their defences against the invasion of Jewish students.

In literary circles a number of writers commented on the evil influence of Jewry. Hence, in the American F. Scott Fitzgerald's *The Beautiful and the Damned*, the character Antony Patch describes the Jewish impact on life in New York: 'Down in a tall, busy street he read a dozen Jewish names on a line of stores. In the door of each stood a dark, little man watching the passers by with intent eyes, eyes gleaming with suspicion, with pride, with clarity, with cupidity, with comprehension. New York – he could not dissociate it now from the slow upward creep of this people. The little stores, growing, expanding, consolidating, moving, watched over with hawk's eyes and a bee's attention to detail.'

The most vehement American opponent of Jews during this period was the prominent industrialist Henry Ford, who in an interview recalled the origin of his contempt: 'On the ship there were two very prominent Jews. We hadn't travelled two hundred miles [when] these Jews started telling me about the power of the Jewish race and the way they manipulated the world through their control of the gold supply. The Jews, and only the Jews, could stop the war. I refused to believe this, and I told them so. They went into details to describe how the Jews controlled, and how they owned the money.' Having uncovered this scheme, Ford felt compelled to share his observations. On 22 May 1920, the *Dearborn Independent*, which Ford owned, denounced the economic power of the Jewish community. Later, Ford's newspaper began to print sections of the *Protocols of the Elders of Zion*, and an American version of this forgery was published in 1921. At the same time a protest against such slurs was launched by leading American figures including Presidents Taft, Wilson and Harding. Nonetheless, anti-Jewish feeling continued to fester beneath the surface of American life.

Even though French Jews had defended their country during the First World War, anti-Jewish sentiment persisted during this period, As elsewhere, the Russian Revolution was perceived in France as having been instigated by Jewish activists. Hence in July 1917 when the Bosheviks sought to gain power, Jews were accused by *La Libre Parole* for their role in these events: 'It is impossible to understand anything about the great tremors that are tearing society apart if we neglect the Jewish factor. . . . Austro-Boche or Franco-German Jews will raise the flag of Israel over the ruins of the vanquished.'

Just before the triumph of the revolutionary forces, *L'Heure* accused Jews of plotting against the tsar: 'Even those who are not anti-Semitic cannot help making a small observation on the composition of the Petrograd society and the background of its members. The real name of Chernov, the former minister of agriculture, who is now Kerensky's bitterest opponent, is Feldman. The real name of Steklov, the well-known author of Order Number One to the Russian army, the one that abolished discipline, is Nahinkes, German Jew. . . . As for Lenin, everyone knows that his name is Zederblum.'

Once the Bolsheviks prevailed, the French press blamed the Jews for the revolution. As Maurice Barrès commented: 'Russia is disappearing because it is infested with Jews.' The politician Georges Clemenceau similarly attacked the Jews for their involvement: 'without patriotism, how can there be a homeland?' he asked. He continued:

What is a people that no longer has a homeland? Alas, we can see it in this mob of German Jews who, unable to keep the land of their ancestors, appeared at the instigation of their brothers in Germany to derussify Russia, whose first reaction was savage pogroms, the supreme aggravation of all barbarisms. One must not kill, for killing is not an answer. Among others, before and after him, the Nazarene proved it. It is sufficient not to be led, that is, misled, by the suggestions of a people that once was great, but now shows itself incapable of creating this homeland that its atavistic concepts considered secondary, the way the fox of the fable convinced others to disdain an appendage of which it had been deprived.

During 1918 condemnation of Jewry intensified. Jewish Bolshevism was seen as a threat to national stability, and Zionism was interpreted as posing a danger to the Christian world. Thus in March 1919 *La Documentation catholique* argued that the Jewish claim to universal domination does not prevent Jews from pursuing the reconstruction of their own kingdom. Several months later this publication proposed a series of remedies for the Jewish threat:

We must create a public opinion in Christian countries. . . . We must echo the moving complaint of the Holy Father: we must speak to these Christian nations of the Christian ideal, of the disgrace of allowing the cradle of their religion to fall under the domination of the Jews, whether disguised or not.

A second remedy . . . persuade the peasants not to sell their land to the Jews by pointing out that this land will increase in value. A bank that would give mortgages . . . would be extremely helpful. Finally (I ought to say, above all), union between Christians and Muslims is required as an essential salvation.

The following year *Le Petit Parisien* reported on events taking place in Russia: 'It would be easy to see the organization of the great Asiatic crusade against the British. The Jew Braunstein [*sic*], known as Trotsky, surrounded by his Semitic or oriental cabal, dreams of becoming the Napoleon of the East. He is the undisputed head of the immense international secret society that aspires to overthrow European civilization and expel the British from their possessions in Asia.'

Commenting on world affairs, the reporter Albert Londres stated in *L'Excelsior*: 'The proletarians are led by the nose. Who rules, then? The activities of socialist conventions, the grimy exiles, the moles of the world's libraries, wasting their youth on books dealing with pauperism to find ways to cope with their material needs, the Siberians, the Mongolians, the Armenians, the Asiatics, and in the labyrinths of hallways, in the police stations, under the wastepaper baskets, the king: the Jew. Ah! the charming little massacre that is brewing on the horizon.'

Nor did this verbal barrage against the Jews let up in following years. In 1921 Roger Lambelin proclaimed in *Le règne d'Isräel chez les Anglo-Saxons* that Jewry was determined to prevail over those among whom they lived. 'The documents I have consulted,' he claimed, 'the examination of English, American and Jewish newspapers and periodicals, testimonies gathered in Egypt and Palestine, and data furnished by reliably informed correspondents on certain Jewish manoeuvres, have put me in a position to follow rather closely the steps towards the creation of Jewish rule over the Anglo-Saxons.' Other observers claimed that the Judaeo-German conspiracy had increased its hold on power. Thus André Chéradame observed: 'The people of the Entente are caught in the formidable pincers held by pro-German leaders. The first branch of this pincer is represented by the international financial activities of the Judaeo-German syndicate operating on the upper strata of the countries of the Entente to recruit accomplices through corruption. The second batch is represented by the activities of the Bolsheviks or Socialists of Bolshevik leanings acting on the labouring classes of the Allied countries.' Such attitudes served as the background for the rise of Nazism and the systematic extermination of European Jewry.

THE EVOLUTION OF MODERN ANTI-SEMITISM

As we have seen, traditional hostilities towards Jews were based on religious convictions; such attitudes persisted through the Reformation into modern times. Yet, the conditions that transformed such sentiments into racial hatred were the consequence of social, economic and political change. Previously European society was based on a feudal order; with industrialization, however, this hierarchical structure was radically altered, causing anxiety, dislocation and resentment. While socialists proclaimed the virtues of revolution, conservatives sought to strengthen pre-capitalist institutions and preserve the old order.

In the years following the revolutions of 1848, traditionalists blamed the Jews for the political upheavals that had spread throughout Europe. Anxious to return to previous patterns of social life, various political parties and interest groups targeted liberalism as the cause of social disruption. In their view, Jewish emancipation was the primary cause of social change. By the 1890s, anti-modernism was widely embraced as the only ideology which could prevent further upheaval. In espousing such a view, conservatives glorified the past, nurturing the collective memory of a Golden Age that celebrated discipline, peace and order.

From the middle of the nineteenth century, Jews had been granted civil rights in all German states, including the Austrian monarchy, yet such a policy inadvertently unleashed fierce opposition towards the Jewish population. Even though many Jews prospered, they faced numerous social and political barriers. It was widely recognized that few would be able to become civil servants, teachers, professors, judges or officers in the military. In time, however, Jews came to play an increasingly important role in economic affairs and had attained prominence in newspaper publishing and the retail trade.

A new stage of anti-Semitism occurred following the financial crash of 1873. In the wake of this event, severe economic dislocation took place, and Jews were blamed for the ensuing social upheaval. Word spread that the crash had been caused by Jews or 'Jew-like' Germans. In the opinion of some journalists, such social tumult was the result of the rupture of the bonds between master and apprentice. To combat such pressures, theorists extolled opposition to the Jews as a precondition to the restructuring of society. According to some Christians, a return to traditional values was imperative.

As we have seen, writers and publicists of this period ranged from ultra-conservatives to bohemians. Repeatedly they emphasized that Jews were infecting or taking over various aspects of German cultural and economic life. In the 1870s the use of the term 'anti-Semitism' by Wilhelm Marr crystallized this process. His book, *The Victory of Judaism over Germanism* became a best-seller: in this diatribe, he alleged that the Jewish victory over European society permeated all aspects of modern life. Germans, he argued, had become jewified: the Jews had won not with armies, but with their indomitable spirit, which infected every aspect of contemporary German life. Even though he dismissed medieval charges against the Jews, he insisted that Jewishness was determined by racial descent. The League of Anti-Semites which he founded sought to unite Germans against the pernicious influence of Jewry. In the view of its supporters, Jews should be excluded from teaching, the judiciary and other civic positions.

A number of significant political figures exploited anti-Semitism to their advantage. Pre-eminent among these politicians was the Imperial Chancellor and first minister of the Crown, Otto von Bismarck, who argued that Jews posed a threat to Christian society. Unlike Bismarck, who simply used anti-Semitism for his own purposes, the court chaplain to the German emperor, Adolf Stoecker, was ideologically committed to Jew-hatred. In 1878 he founded the Christian Social Party, which was widely popular with middle- and lower-middle-class audiences. Before gatherings of the faithful, he denounced Jews as materialists and enemies of the state.

Even though Stoecker claimed he was not preaching Jew-hatred, he implied that Jews deserve to be despised because of their hard-heartedness. In his view, with the coming of Christ, the Jews had fulfilled their role in history; hence Judaism had been nullified by Christianity. A more extreme position was adopted by Eugen Dühring, an economist and philosopher who argued in *The Jewish Question as a Question of Race, Morals and Culture*, that Jews had no right to exist at all. Another influential figure of this period was Heinrich von Treitschke who regarded the Jewish people as the root of all misfortune: 'Year after year,' he wrote, 'out of the inexhaustible Polish cradle there streams over our eastern border a host of hustling, pants-peddling youths, whose children and children's children will some day command Germany's stock exchanges and newspapers.' In his *German History in the Nineteenth Century*, he described Jews in the most negative terms.

In the 1880s, such antipathy served as the background for the emergence of a number of political parties dedicated to solving the Jewish problem. Even though they adopted differing ideologies, these agreed on the need to prohibit Jewish immigration and exclude Jews from positions of authority. Standing on platforms combining nationalism, racism and conservatism, these patriots advocated a return to traditional German values. In 1893 these anti-Semitic political parties won 16 out of 400 seats in the Reichstag. In advocating Jew-hatred these parties sought to recruit to their ranks and garner the votes of small-town dwellers as well as rural inhabitants. Alongside these political organizations, extra-parliamentary pressure groups such as the Agrarian League also embraced anti-Semitic attitudes. Founded in 1893, the Agrarian League represented the interests of impoverished nobility who sought to safeguard what they deemed historical and organic German purity from infection by Jewish aliens.

Chamberlain's *The Foundations of the Nineteenth Century* echoed such anti-Semitic attitudes. According to Chamberlain, humanity is divided into distinct races. In his view, the struggle and interaction between these races has served as the propelling force of history. The book's main theme is the destructive influence of the Jews, and the creative impact of the Aryan race. For Chamberlain, the Jew is identified with predatory economic activity and unearned wealth. In his opinion, the Jew threatens to destroy civilization and culture; the Aryan, on the other hand, is capable of contributing to art and science. This work, which focuses on the Aryan teachings of Christ, provided a basis for national Volkish rebirth.

In Habsburg Austria anti-Semitism was also pervasive throughout the nineteenth century, and capitalism was identified with the Jew; as a result, Jew-hatred became an anti-modernist reaction against the impact of capitalism. The Austrian Christian Social Party, for example, defended Austrian traditionalism, glorifying the pre-industrial world. Peasants were identified with the Volk, whereas the industrial way of life was the result of the pernicious influence of Jewry. In this context the image of the modern industrial order was contrasted with the familiar patterns of traditional rural life. Throughout this period, anti-Semitism flourished in a range of parties, including the Slavic nationalists, the Pan-Germans and the Christian Socialists. Figures such as Georg Ritter von Schönerer and Karl Lueger championed traditional values against the liberal principles of those who were seen as destroying European civilization.

Unlike Western Europe, the world of Eastern Europe had not been affected by the social, political and economic features of Western liberalism, nor had hostility to Jews been associated with racial theories. Yet, former patterns of anti-Semitism continued into the nineteenth century. By the turn

In 1848 the liberals offered voting rights to all inhabitants regardless of religion. The city dwellers reacted by attacking the Jewish population of Pressburg, Hungary. The lithograph is by Bachman Hochman. *(Beth Hatefutsoth Photo Archive, Tel Aviv)*

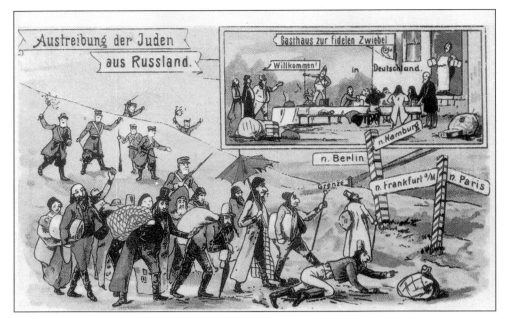

This postcard illustrates the dispersal of the Jews once they were expelled from Russia. *(Jewish Images/photo courtesy Beth Hatefutsoth Photo Archive, Tel Aviv)*

A Tunisian or Algerian postcard depicting the ceremony of circumcision as a barbaric act, 1900s. *(The Gross family collection/photo courtesy Beth Hatefutsoth Photo Archive, Tel Aviv)*

An anti-Semitic caricature of Alfred Dreyfus. He is seen as a dragon with serpents, stabbed with a dagger bearing the words 'the Traitor'. The drawing was published in *Musée de l'horreur*, no. 6, c. 1894. *(Beth Hatefutsoth Photo Archive, Tel Aviv)*

Verlag: A. Braib, Plauen i. V. Gesetzl. gesch.

28./II. 10.

Der Schnorrer
oder
Der neueingewanderte Staatsbürger

The beggar (or recent immigrant). This German postcard shows a new citizen from Eastern Europe, and was posted in Frankfurt in 1910. *(Beth Hatefutsoth Photo Archive, Tel Aviv)*

The SS forced Jews to walk through the streets of Munich with their heads shaved. This man is carrying a placard with the words: 'I will never complain to the police again.' The photograph dates from 1933. *(Photo 146/71/6/1, Bundesarchiv Koblenz)*

Louis Cohn's shop in Landsberg, Germany, at the time of the April 1933 boycott. The graffiti reads 'Don't buy from Jews'. *(Beth Hatefutsoth Photo Archive, Tel Aviv)*

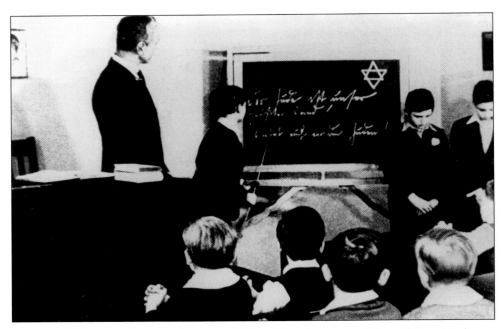

Two Jewish boys have been made to stand facing their classmates. A Star of David is drawn on the blackboard and the legend reads: 'The Jew is our greatest enemy! Beware of the Jews!' This was an Austrian classroom in 1938, when the country was annexed by Germany. *(Copyright © Topham Picturepoint)*

Anti-Jewish graffiti covers the synagogue at Nijmegen (south-east Netherlands) in 1941. *(Collection Jewish Historical Museum, Amsterdam)*

Nazi soldiers cutting off the sidelocks of a Hasidic Jew, Poland, *c.* 1941. *(Beth Hatefutsoth Photo Archive, Tel Aviv)*

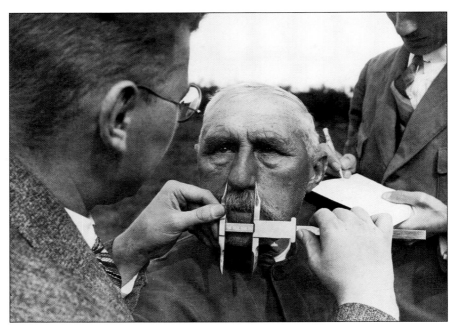

A man having his nose measured by the authorities, in accordance with the 'anthropometric' system of determining 'Aryanism'. *(Courtesy of Ullsteinbild)*

This Egyptian cartoon depicts Israel in the form of the 'ugly Jew', with the word 'racism' written on his clothing. Israel's racism is also suggested by the 'mass destruction weapon' on which he is leaning. *(Al-Gomhouriya, 28 February 1998/Israel Government Press Office)*

of the century Russia contained over 5 million Jews, nearly half the world's Jewish population. In the Middle Ages, Jews had been expelled, and even itinerant Jewish merchants had been banned until the eighteenth century. However, with the annexation of vast Polish and Lithuanian territories, nearly a million Jews came under Russian rule. Confined to the Pale, Russian Jews were vilified by the ferociously anti-Semitic Orthodox Church.

In general the tsars sought to maximize the benefit of the Jewish community to Russian society while at the same time minimizing the danger they posed to the peasantry, with the result that frequent attempts were made to assimilate this vast population. Alexander I encouraged assimilation in the hope that it would bring about the disappearance of Jewry; Nicholas I instituted military conscription assuming that it would bring about the total integration of Jews into the general populace. Alexander II, however, sought to utilize Jewish resources, and thereby encourage the participation of Jews in the intellectual and cultural life of Russia. Some Jews converted to Christianity; others remained loyal to the Jewish faith while pursuing the opportunities opening up for engineers and entrepreneurs in Siberia and the Caucasus. In some cases Jewish children attended university and subsequently joined an urban elite.

Many Russians perceived Jews as constituting a danger to society because of their modernist attitudes. In this milieu, the Russian intelligentsia sought to save the real Russia from Jewry, identifying Jews as the hated adversary and the embodiment of the changes they detested. For some the image of the Jew as the champion of capitalism was the source of anxiety and fear. By the late 1860s anti-Semitism had become a policy of the Russian autocracy, especially the police; frequently it served as a safety valve and outlet for social discontent. When Alexander II was assassinated in 1881, violent action was taken by Jew-haters and the Jewish question gained national prominence. The commission established by Alexander III blamed these disturbances on Jewish exploitation. In 1882 the government issued a series of regulations that restricted the economic activities of Jews, narrowed the boundaries of the Pale, and deprived Jews of their rights of residence in villages. In the period between 1881 and the end of the civil wars of the Bolshevik Revolution there were three major waves of pogroms: 1881–2; 1903–6; 1918–20. These outbursts were fuelled by Jew-hatred combined with fear of the perceived pernicious influence of Jewry on Russian society.

In France, anti-Semitism was rooted in the Christian past. Even though the Enlightenment had undermined the Christian foundation of Judaeophobia, the theological basis was replaced by a secular perspective. Paradoxically, the Enlightenment reinforced prejudices against the Jews. Such figures as the humanist historian Jules Michelet maintained that the influence of the Judaeo-Christian tradition had to be curtailed in the modern world. Ernst Renan sought to liberalize and humanize Jesus and the Christian tradition. In his view, Christianity is a religion of spiritual love in contrast to the tradition from which it sprung; according to Renan, Judaism was burdened by the legalism of the past. Other writers associated Jews with capitalism and its corrupting influence on the nation. In this environment the Catholic Church fostered Jew-hatred, insisting that the emancipation of Jewry was an evil to be resisted. Between 1870 and 1894 one-third of all anti-Semitic books published in France were written by Catholic priests. During this period a semi-official Vatican publication *Civilità Cattolica* publicized purported cases of ritual murder, providing lists of victims and coverage of new cases.

With the influx of immigrants to Paris from Alsace as well as German lands, Jews increasingly came to be associated with the vices of capitalism. Critics continually complained that the economic transformation of French life led to the erosion of traditional values. As a consequence, reactionaries extolled the merits of pre-industrial society. Such figures as Alphonse Toussenel idealized the past as unspoiled. In *The Jews: King of the Epoch*, he blamed the Jews for the ills afflicting society. In his view, Jewish bankers and financiers were a pernicious influence. The French forests, he declared, had been destroyed by the Rothschild railroads. It was time, he believed, to seize the country back from the grip of the tribe of Satan. In a similar vein, Pierre Joseph Proudhon described the Jews as the race that poisons everything.

According to Edouard-Adolphe Drumont in *La France juive*, the Revolution had benefited only the Jews. Contrasting the Semite and the Aryan, he described Jews as greedy, grasping and scheming. Aryans, on the other hand, were the true founders of French civilization. Aryans were creative and noble; Jews were hook-nosed, with huge ears, soft hands, and arms of unequal length. They were diseased and cunning, determined to subjugate the Aryan race. Such hostility toward French Jewry was intensified by the Dreyfus Affair which gave anti-Semitism in France a particular prominence. In the eyes of many French citizens, Dreyfus' treason appeared as the latest example of Jewish conspiracies against the French nation. In 1898 violent demonstrations took place throughout the country as mobs screamed: 'Death to the Jews!' The fury unleashed by these events was the background to the growth of Fascism in the 1930s and the emergence of Nazi collaborators during the Vichy regime. Arguably, the strength of such anti-Semitic sentiments enabled French officials to collaborate with the Nazi deportation of Jews to the death camps.

As we have seen, rabid anti-Semitism was not confined to Europe. In the New World, hostility to Jews was engendered by commercial and industrial expansion in the middle of the nineteenth century. Over this period American literature repeatedly described Jews in the most unsavoury terms.The migration of millions of Jews to America between 1880 and 1914 engendered suspicion and fear of Jewish foreigners. The case of Leo Frank symbolized growing antipathy towards the Jewish presence on American soil. In 1913 Frank, a Jewish factory superintendent in Atlanta, Georgia, was accused of brutally murdering a thirteen-year-old girl. He was tried, found guilty and sentenced to death. After numerous appeals, the state governor commuted the sentence to life imprisonment. However, in the summer of 1915 a mob broke into the prison and hanged him from a tree.

After the First World War, racism combined with the alleged connection between Jewish interests and Bolshevism evoked fury against the Jewish community. Pre-eminent among modern US anti-Semites Henry Ford, in his newspaper the *Dearborn Independent*, launched a ferocious campaign against Jews until 1927, attacking and blaming them for the evils afflicting American society. With the hardships experienced by millions during the Depression, anti-Semitism became increasingly virulent. The aviator Charles Lindberg glamorized pro-Nazi attitudes, while Father Charles Coughlin attacked Jews in radio broadcasts. As the Nazis' plan of extermination for European Jewry gathered momentum, anti-Semitism in America intensified despite US determination to win the war.

SIXTEEN

Anti-Semitism and Zionism

Under the leadership of Theodor Herzl the first Zionist Congress took place in August 1897; subsequently Herzl engaged in extensive negotiations with political leaders throughout the world. By the time Herzl died, Zionism had become an organized movement and Zionists continued to press for the creation of a Jewish homeland. In time the British government approved of such a plan, although Britain insisted that the rights of the Arabs be safeguarded. After the First World War, Herbert Samuels was appointed High Commissioner in Palestine to oversee this policy, but he met with considerable resistance from the Zionists who did not wish to appease the Arab populace. Although the British government initially allowed free immigration to Palestine, this policy was superseded by increased restrictions on the number of Jews allowed in. In May 1939 a White Paper was published which limited the number of immigrants to 75,000 over the next five years. This policy evoked widespread Jewish resistance, and the Jewish military forces engaged in conflict with the British. Throughout this period, Jews in Palestine continually faced Arab hostility to Zionist aspirations, giving rise to a new form of anti-Semitism fuelled by political resentment.

JEWISH SETTLEMENT IN PALESTINE
Herzl, the guiding force of the Zionist movement, was determined to solve the problem of anti-Semitism, and advocated the creation of a Jewish homeland where Jews would be able to live fully and achieve their potential in every sphere. While he and others agitated for the creation of a Jewish state in Palestine, Jewish immigrants founded a variety of settlements and institutions in the Holy Land. By the middle of the nineteenth century approximately 10,000 Jews lived in Palestine. Following pogroms in Russia in the 1880s members of *Hovevei Zion* emigrated to Palestine where they established farms and villages. During the First *Aliyah*, from 1882 to 1903, about 25,000 Jews reached Palestine.

In the ensuing years, immigration continued and a wide variety of Jewish institutions were established to serve the needs of these settlers. By 1914 there were approximately 90,000 Jews living in the Holy Land, of whom 75,000 were immigrants. Anxious about the influx of Jewish settlers, the Arab population began to engage in political activity. Two Jerusalem Arabs were elected to the Ottoman Parliament in Constantinople as anti-Zionists. In response, in the summer of 1914 the Turkish government imposed strict measures to curtail Jewish immigration. Later, when Turkey entered the First World War on the side of the Central Powers, France and Russia became Turkey's enemies. As a result, the Jews of Palestine suffered great hardships as food supplies dwindled and the Turkish government came to regard the Jewish population with hostility, because large numbers of Jewish immigrants were Russian in origin.

The Turkish military commander, Jemal Pasha, sought to quell both Jewish and Arab national sentiment. In Beirut and Jerusalem several Arab leaders were hanged, and some 18,000 Jews were expelled or fled from Palestine to Alexandria. In addition, Jews known to have been active in Zionist circles, including Arthur Ruppin, head of the Palestine Office of the Zionist Executive, were expelled from the country. In response to these developments, the Jaffa Group, consisting of a number of Jewish fighters, was established to defend Jewish settlements in Palestine.

With the outbreak of war, a number of Zionists were anxious to establish a Jewish legion to fight alongside the Allies against the Turks. It was the aim of this group to participate in the liberation of Palestine from Turkish control and to convince the Allies of the need for a Jewish homeland. Foremost among these Zionists, Vladimir Jabotinsky, a Russian correspondent of a Moscow newspaper who had travelled to Egypt in December 1914, encouraged Zionists there to join in political and military alliance with the British, French and Russians against the Germans and Turks.

Another major Jewish figure in this campaign was Joseph Trumpeldor, a veteran of the Russo-Japanese war of 1904–5. Strongly in favour of a Jewish military force, he joined with Jabotinsky in an effort to persuade the British government to create a Jewish defence force, the Zion Mule Corps, to serve on the Gallipoli Peninsula, where an Anglo-French force had landed. Although the Allied offensive at Gallipoli was unsuccessful, the efforts of the Zion Mule Corps were appreciated by the British, an outcome that encouraged the Allies to include Jewish troops in the conquest of

Palestine. Yet, as the war intensified, Turkish troops were successful in keeping the British out of the country.

Throughout the war, the defence of the outlying settlements in the north was a priority. In 1916 Kibbutz Kfar Giladi was established by members of Ha-Shomer to guard the northern settlements against Arab attack. In Tel Aviv a committee headed by Meir Dizengoff, head of the local Israel council, was created to help those suffering in the war. Like other Jews, he was expelled by the Turks and sent to Damascus, where he remained until liberated by the British in 1918. During this period, a spy ring worked behind Turkish lines, known as Nili; it had been set up in Palestine to support the British. One of this faction, Aaron Aaronsohn, was instrumental in the quest to persuade the British government to allow Jews to create a national home in Palestine.

After more than a year of negotiations between the Zionists and the British government, the Balfour Declaration was signed. Such a solution to the Jewish problem was in line with the British aspiration of defeating Turkey and becoming the major power in the Middle East. In a letter from the British Foreign Secretary, Arthur Balfour, to Lord Rothschild, dated 2 November 1917, the British government resolved to create a National Home for the Jews in Palestine in a resolution that brought rejoicing throughout the Jewish world. In Odessa some 200,000 Jews followed Menachem Ussishkin, the founder of the Hebrew Teachers' Federation in Palestine, and his colleagues in a motor-car in a massive procession. However, in the United States, David Ben-Gurion, the future Prime Minister of Israel, was more reserved. Britain, he declared, had not given back Palestine to the Jewish people. The British had made a magnanimous gesture in recognizing the right of the Jewish population to their own country. But it was only the Jewish people, he emphasized, who could bring about the creation of a Jewish state.

Within a month of the Balfour Declaration coming into force, the British had driven the Turkish forces from Jerusalem and only the northern half of Palestine remained in Turkish hands. Following this victory, it became possible for Zionists to work with the British in establishing a Jewish National Home as promised by the Balfour Declaration. As a result of the war, the entire population of Palestine, including Jews, Muslims and Christians, had suffered considerably. The total population had fallen from about 800,000 in 1914 to about 640,000, consisting of about 512,000 Muslims, 66,000 Jews and 61,000 Christians.

In order to ensure that a Jewish National Home would be established in Palestine a Jewish delegation addressed the Paris Peace Conference on 27 February 1919. After listening to impassioned speeches by the delegates, the conference agreed to grant the Palestine Mandate to Great Britain, and accepted the need to establish a Jewish homeland there as outlined by the Balfour Declaration.

In the meantime Jewish settlements in Upper Galilee were caught up in the conflict between local Arabs and the French authorities who controlled the area following the war. Subsequently, the territory was transferred to Britain, yet Arabs continued to attack the Jewish population. In response, Joseph Trumpeldor led the defence of these northern settlements. On 1 January 1920 he began to fortify Tel Hai; two months later this settlement was attacked by armed Bedouin. Wounded in this conflict, Trumpeldor died along with five other Jewish settlers.

On 30 June 1920 Sir Herbert Samuel arrived in Palestine as High Commissioner and Commander in Chief. Although Samuel was an ardent Zionist, he believed that Jews would be able to live harmoniously with the Arab population. In August 1920 Samuel authorized a Land Transfer Ordinance that made it possible for Zionists to acquire land; in September an Immigration Ordinance opened Palestine to legal immigration for those who obtained visas from the Zionist organization. Initially Samuel sought to reconcile Arabs to these measures by pardoning the ringleaders of the Arab riots of 1920, including Hajj Amin al-Husseini, and creating an Advisory Council with an Arab majority in the official membership. Such actions, however, did not pacify the Arab community.

In January 1921 responsibility for the administration of Palestine was transferred from the Foreign Office to the Colonial Office under Winston Churchill. In March 1921 Churchill convened a conference of senior British officials in the Middle East in Cairo in order to reach a settlement with the leaders of Arab nationalism. A focus of Arab resentment was the increasing number of Jews who had entered Palestine. By April 1921 nearly 10,000 Jews had come into the country under Samuel's Immigration Ordinance. Added to Arab fears about Zionist aspirations was the dispute about the election of the Grand Mufti of Jerusalem. Previously the post of Mufti was of little significance, since the sultan served as both the supreme religious and temporal leader of the Muslim population. However, once the country was dominated by the British, the Grand Mufti became the supreme representative of Muslim Arabs.

Once the post of Grand Mufti became vacant, it was to be filled according to Ottoman procedures. An election took place in mid-April 1921, and Hajj Amin al-Husseini came fourth despite his notoriety as the principal instigator of the anti-Jewish riots of Easter 1920. Hajj Amin and his followers, however, declared that the elections had been rigged by the Jews in order to have a pro-Zionist Mufti. Even though Samuel's major advisor on Arab affairs, Ernest Richmond, encouraged him to invalidate the elections, Samuel made no decision.

While this matter remained unresolved, further anti-Jewish riots occurred on 1 May in Jaffa. Jewish shops and a shelter for immigrants were attacked – 27 Jews and 3 Arabs were killed and 104 Jews and 34 Arabs wounded. In the next few days, rioting spread to other coastal centres. By 7 May, 47 Jews had been killed and 146 wounded, with 48 Arabs killed and 73 wounded.

In order to calm Arab passions, Samuel introduced a temporary suspension of immigration and agreed to Richmond's recommendation about the election of the Grand Mufti. One of the three Arabs who had been elected was encouraged to stand down, and on 8 May Hajj Amin was appointed Grand Mufti of Jerusalem. The Jewish community was incensed. In the same year the military sought to subvert the Balfour Declaration. At the end of June, General Sir Walter Congreve, commander of British forces in the Middle East, went to London and argued against the Zionist cause.

In October Congreve issued a circular to officers under his command that supported the Arabs. Shortly after this letter was sent, Arabs in Jerusalem attacked Jews who were celebrating the fourth anniversary of the Balfour Declaration. Five Jews and three Arabs were killed. At Christmas 1921, after receiving a copy of Congreve's circular, Churchill resolved that the Air Ministry should assume responsibility for the defence of Palestine, and a squadron of the Air Force was stationed in the area and a British gendarmerie established.

During the years 1920–1 there were grave doubts about the possibility of creating a Jewish National Home as proposed by Balfour. Even though Samuel intended to establish representative institutions in Palestine, the Jewish population was fearful of such an endeavour since Jews composed only 11 per cent of Palestine's population. In such conditions, it appeared certain that the Arabs would constitute the majority in any institution that was established. Samuel and Churchill, however, envisaged the creation of a Middle East Federation, of which the Jewish National Home would be a part. Although there was some support for this notion in Jewish circles, the Jewish population of Palestine was bitterly opposed.

Despite such resistance, Samuel initially set up a nominated Advisory Council in October 1920 with a majority of Arab notables among its unofficial membership. After the May 1921 riots, he proposed that the Advisory Council be elected as a step towards self-government. At the same time, Samuel asserted that the Balfour Declaration did not imply that a Jewish government would be formed to rule over the Muslim and Christian majority. Rather, he insisted that the British government would never impose a policy that would be contrary to the religious, political and economic interests of those living in Palestine. In August 1921 an Arab delegation went to London to meet British officials; because the Arabs were not able to secure an assembly with legislative and executive powers, to control immigration and receive a repudiation of the Balfour Declaration, they turned down the offer of an elected assembly.

Despite the Arab rejection of a representative body, Samuel and Churchill were not deterred from their plans for Palestine. Once the League of Nations Council meeting in London on 24 July 1922 passed the Mandate for Palestine, the British government proposed a Palestinian Constitution, which established a Legislative Council. Even though such an assembly would have had an Arab majority, the Palestinian Constitution was accepted by the Jewish population. However, the Arabs adamantly rejected such a plan at a Palestinian Arab Congress in Nablus.

Undeterred by the Arab reaction, the British proceeded with elections. The Palestinian Arab Executive, elected by the Nablus Congress, decided on a boycott that effectively undermined the Legislative Council. Samuel then sought to reconstitute an Advisory Council and establish an Arab agency – both of these bodies were similarly rejected by the Arab representatives, who had adopted a policy of non-cooperation as long as the Balfour Declaration remained in force. The British government, however, was unable to overcome this impasse, since the Balfour Declaration was enshrined in the Palestine Mandate.

With the fall of the British government in 1922, the Arabs hoped to influence the new administration, which had not been responsible for the Balfour Declaration. However, neither the British government of Bonar Law nor any future government had any intention of repudiating the Palestine Mandate. As far as the Zionists were concerned, Arab non-cooperation suited their purposes. They had accepted the Palestine

Constitution, and thereby became partners in the quest to find a solution to the problems of the Middle East. The Arabs, on the other hand, remained intractable in their opposition to the creation of a Jewish homeland as envisaged by the Balfour Declaration and the Mandate.

Samuel's lack of success in creating representative institutions meant that Palestine had to be ruled by the High Commissioner and his officials without any consultation with Jewish and Arab representative bodies. As a consequence, both Jews and Arabs were compelled to create their own institutions. In the last year of Samuel's administration, there was a massive increase in Jewish immigration to Palestine, largely because of deteriorating conditions in Eastern Europe. From 1920 to 1923 approximately 8,000 Jews a year had settled in the Holy Land. In 1924 the rate increased to about 13,000; by 1925 it was over 33,000. Such an influx of Jewish settlers – referred to as the Fourth *Aliyah* – resulted in a significant increase of Jews residing in Jerusalem, Haifa and Tel Aviv. Surprisingly, this did not give rise to public demonstrations as had occurred only a few years previously.

With the retirement of Samuel in June 1925 and the appointment of Baron Plumer of Messines as High Commissioner, the British were anxious to ensure that the Mandate was upheld. According to Plumer, the commitment to a Jewish National Home was not inconsistent with the establishment of peace and order in Palestine. Unlike Samuel, Plumer did not seek to found representative assemblies, nor to reconcile Jewish and Arab aspirations. Instead, he was anxious to ensure that peace reigned in the land. Among Jews in the diaspora, Plumer's period in office marked a positive step towards settlement; it appeared that the Arab population had accepted the implications of the Balfour Declaration.

Within Palestine, however, the Jews continued to be aware of Arab hostility. Inside the country two conflicting approaches to the Arab problem emerged during this period. On the one hand, some Jews believed that a form of reconciliation might be possible. A number of Zionists, for example, founded *Berit Shalom* (Covenant of Peace), which aimed to achieve peace with the Arabs through the granting of various concessions leading to the establishment of a bi-national state, but this approach received little support from either Arabs or Jews.

The second approach was more pragmatic: within the Jewish community in Palestine a number of influential Zionists maintained that Arab hostility was inevitable and would eventually lead to armed conflict. The main proponent of such a view was Vladimir Jabotinsky, who had reached this conclusion as a result of his role in the defence of Jews living in Jerusalem during the riots of April 1920. According to Jabotinsky and others, it was impossible to bridge the gap between Jewish and Arab intentions; instead, the two communities should be isolated from one another. In the turbulent period of 1920–2, such a policy was widely accepted, but under Plumer's firm control conflict between the two communities was suppressed.

After the massive immigration from Poland and Russia in 1925, relatively few Jews arrived in Palestine. Between 1926 and 1931, the Jewish population increased from 149,640 to 174,606. At the same time, the Arab population increased from 675,450 to 759,700. Given such figures, it looked unlikely that there could ever be a Jewish majority in the land. Added to this difficulty, the Jewish community faced severe economic hardship in the late 1920s. At the end of 1928, Plumer retired from his office as High Commissioner – and within a month the Arab population attacked the Jewish community.

On the eve of Yom Kippur in September 1928, a police officer and the District Commissioner of Jerusalem took a walk around the Old City of Jerusalem and saw that Jews had placed a screen to separate men and women at prayers near the Wailing Wall. On the following day the police disrupted the prayer service and removed the screen. Furious with this decision, the Jewish population was incensed with the British. Such was the mood of the country when Sir John Chancellor arrived in Palestine. Intent on following previous policy, Chancellor announced that he would consider creating a legislative council. This suggestion was supported by Arab leaders who now believed that by participating in representative institutions they would be able to control immigration to Palestine.

At this time there was a change in Whitehall in London; the Conservative government fell and was replaced by a Labour administration. Britain was now governed by those who had no past links with the Balfour Declaration. In June 1929 an agreement was reached that the proposed legislative council would consist of ten Muslims, three Jews and two Christians. The Grand Mufti, however, had other plans. In his view the Holy Places in Palestine were under threat from the Jewish population. Following the Yom Kippur incident, he initiated a campaign against the Jews in mosques and the press.

In August a further incident inflamed Arab–Jewish hatred. A Jewish boy kicked a ball into an Arab garden and in the ensuing fight he was killed. After the boy's funeral, a Zionist demonstration took place at the Wall. This was followed by a sermon from the Mufti in the Mosque of Al-Aqsa.

On 22–23 August, large crowds of Arab peasants made their way to Jerusalem armed with clubs and knives. The Chief of Police in Jerusalem did not have enough men to disarm this mob, and the Jewish community was severely attacked in Jerusalem and later in other Jewish centres. In this conflict, 133 Jews were killed and 339 wounded, and 110 Arabs were killed and 232 wounded by reinforced police. Subsequently, six Arabs were killed in a Jewish counter-attack near Tel Aviv. It now appeared that full-scale confrontation between Jews and Arabs was inevitable.

The hostility between Jews and Arabs led to a reorganization of the Haganah. Supporters of military force emphasized that the Haganah had saved the Jewish communities of Jerusalem, Tel Aviv and Haifa from mass destruction; others were critical of its efforts. As a consequence, a major restructuring of the Haganah took place. This, however, did not avert a split in its ranks. The political leadership of those who seceded was furnished by the Betar, an activist movement founded in 1923 in Riga, Latvia, under the influence of Vladimir Jabotinsky.

In 1931 a group of Haganah members left the organization in protest against its policies and joined forces with Betar. The first Betar congress took place in 1931 in Danzig, where Jabotinsky was elected head of the movement. Rejecting the Histadrut and Haganah policy of self-restraint, Betar adopted retaliation as its strategy in dealing with the Arabs. From 1929 the politics of the Jewish community in Palestine was divided between the Histadrut–Haganah movement led by David Ben-Gurion and the right-wing Revisionist movement led by Jabotinsky.

Among the Arabs the events of 1929 led to increased support for the Grand Mufti. In Palestine and throughout the Arab world, the Grand Mufti was seen as the leading figure in the struggle against the Zionist threat. In British circles, it became clear that a Jewish National Home was impossible because of the Arab reaction. Anxious to protect Jewish interests, Chaim Weizmann went to London to meet Lord Passfield, who insisted that mass immigration to Palestine would be impossible. Such a policy was subsequently enshrined in two Royal Commissions and a White Paper.

Concerned about the implications of government policy, Weizmann resigned as president of the Zionist Organization; this decision highlighted his view that the Balfour Declaration had been betrayed by the British. When the White Paper was debated in the House of Commons in November 1930, it was widely criticized. On 13 February 1931 the Prime Minister read to the House a letter he had written to Weizmann in which he emphasized that the Mandate had an obligation to facilitate Jewish immigration to Palestine without jeopardizing the rights of all sections of the population. Among the Arabs, this communication became known as the 'Black Letter'.

Despite this success, many Zionists were not satisfied. They had hoped for a new White Paper, rather than a letter. Having resigned as the president of the Zionist Organization over the White Paper, Weizmann was eclipsed by Jabotinsky at the Seventeenth Zionist Congress in Basle in June–July 1931. During the session Weizmann was rebuked by the congress for his statement in an interview that he had no sympathy with the demand for a Jewish majority in Palestine. This internal conflict within the Zionist Organization, however, was overshadowed by the rise of Nazism and the succession of Adolf Hitler as the Chancellor of the German Reich in January 1933.

From 1933 the Zionists and the Nazis cooperated in the emigration of Jews from Nazi Germany to Palestine. In Palestine, Jabotinsky and his colleagues denounced such arrangements because they violated the boycott against German goods. At the Eighteenth Zionist Congress held in Prague in August–September 1933, this issue was debated. Jabotinsky called for a worldwide boycott of Germany, but the majority were not in favour of such action. The transfer arrangements that allowed German Jews to settle in Palestine were defended, and the boycott resolution was not put to a vote. Undeterred by this setback, the Revisionists continued to attack this policy and sought to impose their own boycott.

During this period the immigration policy of the Mandatory power was relatively liberal, yet the number of those without capital who were allowed to immigrate was severely restricted. Such a policy was justified on the basis of the ability of the country's economy to absorb such migrants. Nonetheless, between 1933 and 1939 a significant amount of Jewish capital was imported into the country. As a result, the Jewish community in Palestine was far wealthier than at any other time in its history, and the notion of a Jewish state became more plausible.

Due to the influx of new immigrants, the Arab population became increasingly agitated. Not only were the Jews viewed as enemies of the Arab cause, but the British also came under attack. In Palestine, the conflict between Jews and Arabs intensified. In a terrorist operation, Sheikh Izz al-Din al-Qassam and his followers were surrounded and killed. As a martyr to the Arab cause, al-Qassam's death put pressure on Hajj Amin to launch a Muslim revolt. On 15 April 1934 a group of armed Arabs took two Jews off a bus in the Nablus mountains and killed them; two days later members of the nationalist Haganah, the parent body of the Irgun, murdered two Arabs in retaliation. Following these events, Arab demonstrations took place in Jaffa, Nablus and elsewhere throughout the country.

The shift from an anti-Jewish to an anti-British stance was not a simple option for Hajj Amin. If he complied with this policy, he risked losing his power as head of the Supreme Muslim Council, which was appointed by the British. However, if he failed to comply, he might forfeit his prestige as the leader of Muslim nationalism. As a result, he acceded to the demands of the young militants by becoming head of the Higher Arab Committee. Because this was a lawful body, such a position was reconcilable with his leadership of the Supreme Muslim Council.

Throughout June this council encouraged Muslims to join in the rebellion. The Jews, they argued, aimed at reconstructing a Jewish Temple in place of the Mosque al-Aqsa. Having refused Muslim demands, Britain was perceived as supporting the Jewish people in this quest. During the summer the revolt spread throughout the country. In June attacks took place along the roads and against the Haifa–Lyddah railway line with the first major conflict between British troops and Arab forces occurring near Tulkarm. During the next two months, clashes continued and were accompanied by a general strike. Although British forces defended themselves, there was no concerted attempt to repress this revolt. Any political solution to the conflict required concessions to Arab demands. During this period three Arab princes, Abdul Aziz Ibn Saud, King of Saudia Arabia, Ghazi, King of Iraq, and Abdullah of Transjordan became involved in the Mandatory government. All three detested Zionism and saw that personal political gains could be made from their participation in the affairs of Palestine.

In the quest to stem the Arab revolt, the British hoped the Arab princes would encourage the rebels to desist. Yet because the Arab fighters perceived their struggle against the British as a holy war, they were undeterred by such foreign intervention. In the meantime, the British had created the Peel Commission, which was empowered to look into the roots of the Palestinian question. By 1937 the British had assembled a large military force in Palestine and decided to impose martial law on the country. Both the Higher Arab Committee and the Foreign Office did not wish it to appear that the rebels had accepted defeat. Hence, the Arab princes were encouraged to issue a joint appeal for public order, which the Higher Arab Committee would accept.

When this appeal was made, the Higher Arab Committee published a manifesto urging the rebels to abandon their strike as well as to desist from public disorder. In November the 1936 the Royal Commission, headed by Lord Peel, arrived in Palestine. In July 1937 the Peel Commission published its report. It declared that the Palestinian problem was insoluble for it arose within the narrow bounds of a small country in which approximately one million Arabs were in conflict against 40,000 Jews. Since in its view neither group could justly rule over all of Palestine, the commission concluded that the country should be partitioned. In this light the commission recommended that the Palestine Mandate should be terminated and replaced by a Treaty System, and a new Mandate for the Holy Places be established. Further, it suggested that a Treaty of Alliance should be negotiated between the government of Transjordan and the Arabs of Palestine, representing an expanded Transjordan, and that the Zionist Organization should be responsible for the Jewish state. The commission assigned to the Jewish state a coastal strip from the south of Jaffa to the north of Gaza along with Galilee from the sea to the Syrian border. Jerusalem, with a corridor to the sea, was to be placed under the new Mandate; the remainder of the country was to be the new Arab state.

Even though this scheme was endorsed by the British government, it was strongly opposed by the Palestinian Arabs. On the Jewish side Weizmann and Ben-Gurion favoured the principle of partition because it would have created a Jewish homeland. Under their influence, the Twentieth Zionist Congress held in Zurich in August 1937 approved the plan, and the Zionist Executive was authorized to negotiate with the Mandatory power for the purpose of ascertaining the British terms for the proposed establishment of a Jewish National Home.

In the summer of 1937 the Arab revolt, which had been suspended during the deliberations of the Peel Commission, was renewed following a meeting of nationalists in Syria. During this period Lewis Andrews, acting District Commissioner of Galilee, was murdered. Despite the Higher Arab Committee's condemnation of this act, Hajj Amin was removed as head of this body and warrants were issued for the arrest of its members. Fleeing to Lebanon, Hajj Amin was given asylum by the French.

These events led to a full-scale revolt that lasted until the end of 1938 and was severely repressed by the British government. At this time steps were taken towards abandoning the partition plan. In December 1937 the Prime Minister, Neville Chamberlain, supported the Foreign Office, which opposed partition as well as the creation of a Jewish state. Despite such a shift in policy, the British sought the support of the Jewish community in Palestine in repressing the Arab uprising.

In Palestine a section of the Jewish youth joined the National Military Organization, Irgun Tzevai Leumi, which was opposed to the Haganah policy of self-restraint. In June 1938 the British hanged a young Revisionist for attacking an Arab bus; in retaliation, the Irgun exploded landmines in Haifa, killing 74 people and wounding another 129. This act was condemned by both Zionist and Haganah leaders. On 17 September 1938 partition was reaffirmed by the League of Nations, and the British appeared to be committed to the Jewish state because of their repression of the Arab revolt. Although little official Arab response to such action was made outside Palestine, hostility to Jews living in Arab lands was widespread.

In November the British government officially confirmed its intention to abandon the policy of partition and invited the governments of Iraq and Egypt to help prepare for a London conference on the future of Palestine. This gathering was held in St James's Palace and was attended by representatives of five Arab countries as well as a Palestinian delegation, the Zionist Executive and the British. The three bodies of delegates did not meet together; instead, the British met separately with the Arabs, and similarly with the Jews.

At one of the joint meetings between Zionists and leaders of the Arab states, Aly Maher of Egypt appealed to the Zionists to limit immigration. Although Weizmann was prepared to consider this appeal, Ben-Gurion and the rest of the delegation fervently supported the policy of Jewish immigration to Palestine. On 17 March 1939, the conference ended without any agreement between the various parties. In May, a further White Paper was published which ruled out partition and the creation of a Jewish state. However, it decreed that a Palestinian state be created within ten years, and that after five years Jewish immigration would not be allowed unless approved by the Palestinian Arabs. Despite this anti-Jewish bias, the White Paper allowed for a further 75,000 Jews to settle in Palestine within a five-year period, and stipulated that the sanctioning of an independent Palestinian state depended on adequate safeguards for the Jewish community.

In effect the White Paper endorsed a double veto: the Arabs were empowered to block the growth of a Jewish National Home, whereas the Jews could prevent the Arabs from having an independent state. Anxious to avert this change in policy, the Jews contested the legality of the White Paper. In its report to the Council of the League, the Permanent Mandates Commission stated that the White Paper was not in accord with the interpretation that the commission had placed upon the Palestine Mandate. Under Article 27 of the Mandate, the council's consent was required for any change in its terms. The outbreak of war, however, meant that the council never met to debate this issue. Such a change of policy was profoundly disturbing to the Jewish community in Palestine. The Zionists perceived that Britain had abandoned the principle of the Balfour Declaration. For many Zionists, it had become clear that force was now required to oppose the White Paper; previously, the Arab community had rebelled against British rule, now the White Paper had reversed the situation. A Jewish revolt had begun.

THE ZIONISTS AND THE ARABS

In the eyes of the Arab world, Zionism is a racist doctrine and Jews have no entitlement to Palestine. Until the middle of the twentieth century, Arab critics point out, there had not been a Jewish majority in Palestine for eighteen hundred years. Hence, the immigration of hundreds of thousands of Jews to the Holy Land was a tragedy, involving the destruction and dispersal of a settled, indigenous population. In Arab eyes, Jews had no right to colonize an inhabited land at the very time when the rest of the world was divesting itself of colonialism. Even though the yearning to return to a spiritual homeland has animated Jewish consciousness through the centuries, Arab opponents stress that this does not justify Zionist activity over the last hundred years.

In historical terms, the Arab argument continues, the Jewish nation were not the only people to have been conquered, defeated and dispersed. The history of the world is one of endless conquests and migrations over the centuries. Palestine could easily have accommodated a significant number of settlers if they had come in moderate numbers to live alongside the indigenous population and developed organically as a community. A great deal of land was acquired by Jews legitimately, but the purchase of land did not give them the right to create a Jewish state in Palestine.

In previous centuries the Ottoman Empire, of which Palestine formed a part, had provided a refuge for Jews fleeing from persecution. Yet for Arabs there is a fundamental difference between the scale of immigration represented by those seeking refuge from persecution, and the calculated usurpation of an inhabited land. In this context, the Balfour Declaration had no legal status since Palestine did not belong to Britain, nor did the British government have any legal authority in Palestine. Moreover, the Jewish people had no juristic personality in international law; they were not a legal entity and thus could not be party to an agreement in international law.

In *Palestine and the Law*, the Arab scholar Musa Mazzawi points out that international law has spent centuries ridding itself of provisions based on religion and ethnicity. Thus, the Balfour Declaration lacks legal authority. The British simply did not have any legal justification for offering a defined religious/ethnic group the right to establish a state within Palestine. The Balfour Declaration gained its *de facto* legal effect when the Mandate, incorporating the policies of the Declaration, was imposed on Palestine. At this time the Palestinian people did not choose to be governed by the British, rather they had British rule imposed on them. Jews were represented in the British government, whereas Palestinians were merely a subject population carved up according to the interests of Britain and France.

So runs the Arab critique of the intervention of the British in the history of modern Palestine. Israel is perceived as an apartheid state, embodying ethnic and religious discrimination. Here then is a new form of Judaeophobia, political in character yet rooted in inherited stereotypical images of the past. Yet from a Jewish point of view such arguments overlook the historical circumstances giving rise to Jewish aspirations for a homeland. As we have noted, through the centuries Jews have continually been subject to persecution. Since the emergence of Christianity as the dominant religion of Europe, the Jewish community has been repeatedly attacked. As we have seen, secular Zionists were unified in their contention that the Jewish people would never be able to overcome anti-Semitism unless they had a state of their own.

Hence, in *Rome and Jerusalem*, Moses Hess argued that Jews will inevitably be regarded as strangers among the nations. In his view, the restoration of Jewish nationalism is the only bulwark against Jew-hatred. Similarly, in *Autoemancipation*, Leon Pinsker stressed that the Jewish problem is as unresolved in modern society as it was in ancient times. In essence, he wrote, this dilemma concerns the unassimilable character of Jewish identity in countries where Jews are in the minority. In a similar vein, the father of modern Israel, Theodor Herzl, wrote in *The Jewish State* that the plan for a Jewish state is a realistic proposal arising out of the terrible conditions facing Jews living under oppression and persecution.

Zionists contend that the events of the Second World War demonstrate the validity of these early Zionist reflections on the future of the Jewish nation. Although German Jews were assimilated into German life and made a major contribution to the country, Hitler and his executioners embarked on a campaign to rid Germany and Europe of the Jewish population. Arguably, the onslaught against European Jewry, one of the most horrific chapters in modern history, provides sufficient moral grounds for the Jewish quest to obtain a foothold in their ancient homeland. In attempting to persuade the British of the justice of their cause, Zionists recounted the terrible legacy of anti-Semitism as it evolved through the ages. The Jews had been oppressed simply because of their faith. They constituted a small, vulnerable minority in alien cultures. In the face of rising anti-Jewish agitation, particularly in Eastern Europe, these Zionist pioneers championed the establishment of a Jewish homeland to safeguard the lives of their coreligionsts.

Inevitably Jews turned to those in power to attain this objective; there was initially no resort to arms. Rather, Herzl and the leaders of the Zionist movement sought to secure a homeland for the Jewish nation through appropriate legal and political channels. Repeatedly Herzl appealed to those in control of Palestine and Zionist leaders around 1900 continued this policy. What was required was the legitimate, legally recognized acquisition of territory in the Middle East; such was the Zionist quest from the inception of the movement until its realization through the authority of the United Nations. In no way did Jews seek to undermine the legal or political framework of the nation states with whom they dealt.

Turning to the events following the First World War, Arab critics argue that the Churchill White Paper of 1922 was a betrayal of the interests of the Palestinian people. The British attempted to satisfy all the parties involved in this conflict, but in fact provided the basis for the displacement of the native population. While Arabs were protesting against both the Balfour Declaration and the White Paper, Jews were steadily buying land, promoting agriculture, building schools and developing social organizations.

From a Zionist perspective, however, the Churchill White Paper offered a reasonable solution to the conflict between Jews and Arabs. Recognizing the case for a Jewish homeland in Palestine, the British government was determined to uphold the Balfour Declaration. In the view of the British government, the Jewish people had the right to live in the Holy Land – they were not there on sufferance.

Nevertheless, the British were determined not to oppress the Palestinian population. The Churchill White Paper asserts that the British government did not aim to transform Palestine into a Jewish state. Nor did the British seek the disappearance or subordination of the Arab population, language or culture. Further, the British wished to ensure that immigration into Palestine would not exceed the capacity of the country.

These were not empty aspirations. On the contrary, the British sought to provide a framework for peaceful coexistence between Arabs and Jews. The most significant paragraphs of this document emphasize the British quest to satisfy Jewish and Arab aims:

> Nor have they [the British government] at any time contemplated, as appears to be feared by the Arab Delegation, the disappearance or the subordination of the Arabic population, language or culture in Palestine. They would draw attention to the fact that the terms of the declaration referred to do not contemplate that Palestine as a whole should be converted into a Jewish National Home, but that such a Home should be founded in Palestine. . . .
>
> So far as the Jewish population in Palestine are concerned, it appears that some among them are apprehensive that His Majesty's Government may depart from the policy embodied in the Declaration of 1917. It is necessary, therefore, once more to affirm that these fears are unfounded, and that the Declaration, reaffirmed by the Conference of the Principal Allied Powers at San Remo and again in the Treaty of Sèvres, is not susceptible of change. . . .

In effect the main principles of the White Paper were as follows:

1. His Majesty's Government affirms the declaration of November 1917, which is not susceptible of change.
2. A Jewish National Home will be founded in Palestine. The Jewish people will be in Palestine as of right not on sufferance, but His Majesty's Government has no such aim in view as that Palestine should become as Jewish as England is English.

3. Nor do His Majesty's Government contemplate the disappearance or subordination of the Arab population, language or culture.
4. Status of all citizens of Palestine will be Palestinian. No section of the population will have any other status in the eyes of the law.
5. His Majesty's Government intended to foster the establishment of full measures of self-government in Palestine and as the next step a legislative council with the majority of elected members will be set up immediately.
6. The special position of the Zionist executive does not entitle it to share in any degree in the government of the country.
7. Immigration will not exceed the economic capacity of the country at the time to absorb new arrivals.
8. The committee of elected members of the legislative council will confer with the administration upon matters relating to the regulation of immigration.
9. Any religious community or considerable section of the population claiming that terms of the Mandate are not being fulfilled will have the right of appeal to the League of Nations.

Despite Arab protests, the Churchill White Paper sought to achieve a solution to the problem of Jewish settlement and immigration while at the same time recognizing the legitimate concerns of the Arab community. At this stage there was every reason for both Jews and Arabs to accept the conditions of this statement, and work together in the quest for peace and harmony. Yet this was not to be the case; instead the Arab population remained adamant: Palestine was for the Palestinians.

Seeking to fulfil the terms of the White Paper, Samuel promoted the issue of the legislative council. But, on returning from London, the Palestinian delegates at their conference rejected the concept of a legislative council. According to Zionists, such determination to subvert the aims of the British was a tragedy, with far-reaching consequences for the Middle East. If a legislative body consisting of both Arabs and Jews had been created in 1922, there would have been a possibility for harmonious coexistence between Jews and Arabs, and the violent outbreaks of the early part of the twentieth century could have been avoided.

Undeterred by the Arab reaction, the British staged elections. But, as we have seen, these were boycotted, thereby undermining the legislative council. Determined to implement British policy, Samuel sought to reconstitute an advisory council and create an Arab agency. Again, both of these bodies were rejected by the Arabs, who had embarked on a policy of non-cooperation as long as the British government supported the Balfour Declaration. These were fatal errors on the road to peace. Zionists stress that it was not the Jews who were intransigent, but the Arabs who clung tenaciously to their determination to protect Palestine from a Jewish presence. Political aspirations thus became the basis for the development of virulent anti-Jewish attitudes that erupted into full-scale violence in the ensuing decades.

Repeatedly the Grand Mufti encouraged the Arab population to rise up against Jewish settlers; later, he sided with the Nazis against the Jews. After Hitler acceded to power, Hajj Amin joined forces with the Nazis and planned a boycott against the Jews. After escaping from Palestine, he went to Syria, Iraq and Italy, eventually moving to Berlin where he supported pro-Axis propaganda, organized Muslim SS troops from Bosnia, and collaborated with Berlin intelligence. On 28 November 1941 in a meeting with Hitler, he thanked the Führer for his support of the Arab cause. According to Hajj Amin, the Arabs were the natural allies of Germany against the British, the Jews and the Communists. Zionism thus ushered in a new era of anti-Jewish hostility: in the quest to escape from the anti-Semitism of the past, a new political form of Judaeophobia emerged in the Arab world.

SEVENTEEN

The Rise of Nazism

Following its defeat in the First World War, the German nation experienced humiliation, economic disruption and cultural disorder. Longing for a return to past glories, Conservatives sought to restructure society along traditional lines. In these circumstances, the German Workers' Party advanced extreme nationalist policies as well as anti-Semitic attitudes. Under Hitler's influence, this party, renamed the National Socialist German Workers' Party or Nazi Party, quickly became a major force in German life. As the Nazis increased their control of the state, steps were quickly taken to ensure that Hitler would be able to rule without opposition, and that the Jewish population in Germany would be subject to an increasing series of restrictions depriving them of their fundamental rights. This onslaught against the Jewish community culminated in *Kristallnacht*, 9/10 November 1938, when German Jews were subject to a massive attack on their property.

NAZISM

The Nazi Party emerged in the aftermath of the First World War. After four years of conflict, the Allied armies conquered the German nation and amid the ensuing political instability, Kaiser Wilhelm fled to Holland. Intent on punishing Germany, the Allies formulated a peace treaty that stripped the German nation of all power. By agreeing to the terms of this document, the German representatives were accused of betrayal, and many Germans never forgave them for their actions. Within three years the leader of the delegation, Matthias Erzberger, was assassinated.

After the war the Weimar government consisted of an elected legislature (the Reichstag) along with a president (who was in essence a figurehead standing above day to day affairs). Following national elections, the president appointed the leader of the majority party in the Reichstag as chancellor; it was the chancellor's responsibility to form a Cabinet from his colleagues. However, because political parties were often unable to form a majority, governments consisted of coalitions of various parties.

Post-1918, the major parties ranged across the political spectrum with the Communists, Marxists and radical socialists on the left; centrist parties embracing more moderate policies; and, on the right, ultra-nationalists, Nazis and fascists who pressed for the creation of a totalitarian dictatorship. In the right's view, it was necessary that a single political party govern to ensure the maintenance of a strong and prosperous nation.

Exploiting the political and economic instability of this period, the Nazis sought to bring order back to society. From 1919 to 1924 the party was based in Munich and Bavaria where it attracted a variety of members from among extreme right-wing groups of ex-soldiers, anti-Communists and tsarist emigrés. On 7 November 1923, the major leaders of Bavaria's right-wing organizations, including Hitler, planned a putsch. The next evening a large gathering assembled at a beer hall in Munich to listen to a major address by the State Commissioner. Just before 8 p.m. Hitler arrived. As the State Commissioner was speaking, a group of SA men (*Sturmabteilung*; the Nazi terrorist militia) armed with pistols and machine guns burst into the main hall while other SA troops cordoned off the building.

Hitler and his men then mounted the speaker's platform and announced that a national revolution had broken out all over Germany. Military units, however, put down this revolt and Hitler and his fellow conspirators were arrested. Taken to the fortress of Landsberg am Lech, Hitler was eventually tried and convicted of high treason. From 11 November 1923 to 20 December 1924, he served time for this crime along with other Nazi conspirators, and composed the first volume of *Mein Kampf*. During this period the Nazi Party began to disintegrate. However, when Hitler returned to Munich he was determined to rebuild it.

After numerous setbacks the Nazis became the largest political party in Germany, and on 30 January 1933 Hitler was appointed Chancellor of the German Republic. As Chancellor, his first act was to persuade the president, Paul von Hindenburg, and the Cabinet to dissolve the Reichstag and institute new elections in the hope that the Nazis would achieve a majority. Germany, he declared, was on the verge of a new awakening. On 4 February, Hindenburg signed a decree under Article 48 that enabled police to prohibit public meetings and suppress subversive literature; this law was directed primarily against Communists and Socialists as well as other opponents of the NSDAP.

On 27 February 1933 the Reichstag was set on fire, and a Dutch Communist, Marinus van der Lubbe, was discovered in the building. The

Communists were blamed for the burning of the Reichstag, and several days later Hindenburg signed a number of emergency decrees, which inadvertently led to the dissolution of the Constitution. Designed to prevent further Communist acts of subversion, these edicts suspended freedom of speech, press and assembly as well as the freedom from invasion of privacy and house search. In order to protect public order, the death penalty was imposed for various crimes.

In the days before the election, the Nazi Party swamped voters with propaganda, alleging that only by voting for the Nazis would a Communist revolution be thwarted. Despite such efforts, the NSDAP failed to win a majority. As a result, the NSDAP was compelled to enter into a nationalist coalition with the DNVP (German National People's Party). After the elections, the Nazis increased the attacks on their opponents. The SA, numbering 400,000, intensified their assault against Communists, Socialists, trade unionists and Jews.

Prior to the opening of the Reichstag, the Cabinet approved an Enabling Act which gave the government dictatorial powers. With this Act in place, the Nazis were able to pass laws without the consent of Parliament, even though this constituted a violation of the Constitution. Hence, from the beginning of Hitler's chancellorship, democratic procedures were overturned, and parliamentary authority was discarded in favour of dictatorial control.

Empowered to act independently, the Nazis were now able to initiate a campaign of harassment against German Jewry. In the manifesto of 1920, the party had stated:

> Only nationals can be citizens of the State. Only persons of German blood can be nationals, regardless of religious affiliation. No Jew can therefore be a German national.

In the past attempts had been made to incite the German people to embrace such a policy. These early attempts had largely failed, but with the power of the Enabling Act, Hitler was able to introduce legislation that would isolate German Jewry from public life.

On 1 April 1933 the Nazis proclaimed a boycott against Jewish shops, businesses and professional services. Prior to the boycott, the NSDAP leaders issued instructions for this protest: all party units were to form local boycott committees. At the meeting of the Cabinet Hitler explained that an organized boycott was necessary to control popular opposition to the Jewish populace; to calm those in the Cabinet who feared adverse public opinion, he stated that the boycott would last only one day. The party's instructions were to avoid violence.

In the event, the boycott lasted three days: Storm Troopers were stationed outside Jewish businesses with pickets that read: 'Don't buy from Jews!' In addition, anti-Jewish slogans were written on the windows of stores, and customers were verbally and physically abused. Some Jews reacted to such acts of terror with defiant pride. Robert Weltsch, for example, the editor of a Zionist publication, called on his coreligionists to remain loyal to their community and heritage.

This assault against Jewry was followed on 7 April 1933 by the first anti-Jewish law, the Restoration of the Professional Civil Service Act, which eliminated Jews and political opponents of the Nazi regime from the civil service. Hindenburg's objections to this law were met in a paragraph that exempted officials who had already been employed as civil servants on or before 1 August 1914, or who had fought at the front for Germany or her allies during the First World War, or whose fathers or sons had been killed in action. On the same day another law cancelled the admission of lawyers of non-Aryan descent to the bar and denied permission to those already admitted to practise law.

This legislation was followed by similar steps that excluded Jews from the positions of lay assessors, jurors and commercial judges, patent lawyers, panel doctors in state social-insurance institutions, dentists and dental technicians associated with these institutions. On 21 April a law was promulgated banning Jewish ritual slaughter. Several days later the Law against the Overcrowding of German Schools and Institutions of Higher Learning limited the number of non-Aryan students.

On 6 May the Law for the Restoration of the Professional Civil Service was extended to honorary professors, university lecturers and notaries. On 10 May a campaign against disaffected writers, academics and intellectuals was initiated. A public burning of un-German literature was organized in Berlin: all books written or published by Jews or those that dealt sympathetically with the Jewish tradition were consigned to the flames. On 14 July a law was passed that cancelled the citizenship of any German who had been naturalized after 1918.

This was followed on 28 September by the enactment of a law forbidding the employment by government authorities of non-Aryans or of those married to them. On 29 September the Hereditary Farm Act was passed. This declared that only those farmers who could prove that their ancestors had no Jewish blood as far back as 1800 could inherit farm property. In addition, the Reich Chamber of Culture was established, which aimed to bring all the country's cultural activities under control. The result of such legislation was the elimination of all non-Aryans from German cultural life.

Such segregation was facilitated through a decree promulgated on 11 April which defined a non-Aryan as anyone who was descended from non-Aryans, especially Jewish, parents or grandparents; such descent was categorized as non-Aryan even if only one parent or grandparent was non-Aryan, especially if the person was of the Jewish faith. Thus, in cases of racial ambiguity, religious affiliation was crucial. In cases of uncertainty, it was necessary to obtain an opinion from the expert on racial research who was attached to the Reich Ministry of the Interior.

The legal campaign of exclusion mounted against the Jewish community culminated in the Nuremberg Laws that redefined German citizenship, prohibited the pollution of the race, and required couples to undergo medical examinations before marriage. On 14–15 September representatives of the Ministry of the Interior drafted various bills that were approved by Hitler, who then instructed the ministry to prepare a basic Reich citizenship law. At the Nuremberg Rally these laws were adopted, radically affecting the status of German Jews. On the final day a session of the Reichstag took place that ratified new legislation concerning the Reich Citizenship Law. This Law for the Protection of German Blood and Honour was designed to protect the German nation from racial impurity:

> Entirely convinced that the purity of German blood is essential to the further existence of the German people, and inspired by uncompromising determination to safeguard the future of the German nation, the Reichstag has unanimously adopted the following law, which is promulgated herewith:
>
> I. 1. A subject of the State is a person who belongs to the protective union of the German Reich, and who therefore has particular obligations to the Reich.
>   2. The status of the subject is acquired in accordance with the provisions of the Reich and State Law of Citizenship.
> II. 1. A citizen of the Reich is that subject only who is of German or kindred blood and who, through his conduct, shows that he is both desirous and fit to serve the German people and Reich faithfully.

2. The right to citizenship is acquired by the granting of Reich citizenship papers.
3. Only the citizen of the Reich enjoys full political rights in accordance with the provisions of the laws.

III.   The Reich Minister of the Interior in conjunction with the Deputy Führer will issue the legal and administrative decrees for carrying out and supplementing this law.

The belief that Jews were at least marginally protected as second-class citizens under the new legislation proved to be an illusion. During this period Wilhelm Frick, Minister of the Interior, dismissed servants who were descended from three or four grandparents who were full Jews. In the weeks following Nuremberg, state officials discussed the question of how to define Jewishness. On 14 November 1935 the First Supplementary Decree of the Reich Citizenship Law listed a series of regulations regarding Jewish status.

On 27 October 1938, Hitler expelled 18,000 Jews living in Germany who had been born in the former Polish provinces of the Russian empire. One of these Jews was Zindel Grynszpan who had been born in Radomsko in Russian Poland in 1886. Since 1911 he had resided with his family in Hanover. When Zindel Grynszpan sent a postcard to his son in Paris, the young man went to the German Embassy in Paris and shot the first German official he encountered, Ernst von Rath. Hitler and Nazi leaders denounced this act as part of a Jewish conspiracy; it sparked a wave of violence against the entire German Jewish community. Fires were lit throughout the country, and Jewish buildings were set on fire and demolished.

In towns and villages sacred objects, including Torah scrolls, prayerbooks and rabbinic texts, were thrown on bonfires. In addition, synagogues were demolished – for this reason, this Nazi onslaught was called *Kristallnacht* (night of broken glass). Not surprisingly, this event provoked vehement protests from abroad, and German goods were increasingly boycotted. The damage to property was estimated at approximately 25 million marks. It appears that Hitler in collaboration with Goebbels decided to use this incident as an opportunity to intensify action against the Jewish population. On 10 November 1938 Göring, Hitler and Goebbels discussed the technicalities of this new policy and two days later Göring convened a conference specifically to discuss this issue. Opening this meeting Göring explained that he had received a letter written by Bormann, the chief of staff of the Führer's deputy, on the order of the Führer, requesting that the Jewish question be resolved. The problem, he stressed, was economic in character.

If Jewish shops were destroyed, insurance companies would be compelled to cover the damage. At this point Goebbels intervened, urging that Jews should be eliminated from any positions in public life that might cause further provocations. What was necessary at this stage was for the Reich Ministry of Transport to decree that Jews and Germans must be separated from one another when travelling on trains. After debating the practicality of such legislation, Goebbels further recommended that there should be a law which barred Jews from German beaches, resorts and parks. In addition, he recommended that Jewish children should be removed from German schools.

The cost of *Kristallnacht* was borne partly by insurance companies and partly by the Jewish community. On 12 November Göring promulgated the Decree for the Restoration of the Street Scene in Relation to Jewish Business Premises:

> All damage which was inflicted on Jewish businesses and dwellings on 9 and 10 November 1938 as a result of the national indignation about the rabble-rousing propaganda of international Jewry against National Socialist Germany must at once be repaired by the Jewish proprietors of the Jewish businesses and dwellings affected. Insurance claims by Jews of German nationality will be confiscated for the benefit of the Reich.

At the same time Göring sought to assist the rearmament programme by utilizing Jewish funds to increase the Reich's resources. On 12 November he issued a Decree Concerning Reparations from Jews of German Nationality:

> The hostile attitude of the Jews towards the German people and Reich which does not shrink even from cowardly murders, demands decisive resistance and heavy reparation. . . . I therefore announce the following: 1. The Jews of German nationality are required to pay a contribution of RM 1 billion to the German Reich. A Jew can no longer be an employer within the meaning of the Law on the Organization of National Labour of 20 January 1934.

In addition, the law excluded Jews from German economic life:

I. 1. From 1 January 1939 the running of retail shops, mail-order houses and the practice of independent trades are forbidden to Jews.
   2. Moreover, Jews are forbidden from the same date to offer goods and services in markets of all kinds, fairs, or exhibitions or to advertise them or accept orders for them.
   3. Jewish shops which operate in violation of this order will be closed down by the police.
II. 1. No Jew can any longer be manager of an establishment as defined by the Law on the Organization of National Labour of 20 January 1934.
   2. If a Jew is a leading employee in a business concern he may be dismissed at six weeks' notice. After the expiration of this period, all claims of employees derived from the denounced contract become invalid, especially claims for retirement or redundancy pay.
III. 1. No Jew can be a member of a cooperative society.
   2. Jewish members of cooperatives lose their membership from 21 December 1938.

Following such legislation, further steps were taken to exclude Jews from public life. On 28 December 1938 Göring issued a decree concerning the Führer's decisions about the Jewish problem:

1.   Housing of Jews
1(a) The law for the protection of tenants is not, as a rule, to be abrogated for the Jews. On the contrary, it is desired, if possible, to proceed in particular cases in such a way that the Jews are quartered together in separate houses in so far as housing conditions will allow.
2.   Use of sleeping and dining cars is to be forbidden to the Jews.
3.   Only the use of certain public establishments is to be prohibited to the Jews. In this category belong the hotels and restaurants visited especially by party members. The use of bathing establishments, certain public places, bathing resorts, etc., can be prohibited to Jews.

A further section of this law introduced new restrictions in the case of intermarriages based on the criteria of the children's religious affiliation and which spouse was the Jewish partner in the marriage.

For the German population, *Kristallnacht* symbolically represented the power of the state against the enemy within. But for the Nazis there were more sinister motives. The destruction of Jewish property during the Night of Broken Glass provided an opportunity to ensure that Jews would no longer participate in the economic life of the country. The aim of the meeting convened by Göring on 12 November was to take all necessary measures to eliminate Jews from the German economy – all this was to be done for the good of the Reich.

On 2 September 1939 the Nazis invaded Poland and 2 million Jews came under German domination. In this attack Polish Jews suffered like their fellow compatriots. Yet the conquest of Poland resulted in the massacre of Polish Jewry and the eventual extermination of Eastern European Jewry in the Nazi drive for land in the east. Aware of the dangers of invasion, Polish Jews sought to flee from the German onslaught and thousands set out on foot, in carts and in waggons to find safety.

Once German troops entered a town or city, they confiscated Jewish property and businesses. Jewish shops were ordered to be opened so that looting could take place. In large manufacturing centres, goods were confiscated. In small communities Jews were compelled to hand over valuables at the threat of death. Hostages were also taken to ensure the extortion of vast sums of money from Jewish communities. Throughout the country, the Nazis burned down synagogues, and pogroms became commonplace. Violence and massacres occurred everywhere.

From mid-November 1939 Jews in Poland were prevented from working in government offices, travelling by train, buying or selling to Aryans, going to an Aryan doctor or having an Aryan patient. In these conditions, life became intolerable. Wherever Jews lived, they were subject to continual harassment. David Wdowinski, for example, the head of the psychiatric department of the Czyste Street hospital in Warsaw, recalled that a truck with German officers and civilians drove up to one of the apartments where Jews were living:

> There they demanded money, jewels, goods and food. They shut women up in one room and men in another. They stole everything they could lay their hands on and ordered the men to load it on to the trucks, to the accompaniment of kicks and beatings. The women were searched individually for anything that they might have hidden. But they were still unsatisfied with their loot. At the point of guns they forced the women and young girls to undress and they performed gynaecological examinations on each of them. And even this was not enough. They forced the women and girls to get up on the tables and jump to the floor with legs straddled.

'Maybe something will fall out. One never knows how deep the Jewish swindlers can hide their jewels.'

During this period hundreds of Polish synagogues were demolished and sacred texts violated. As an eye-witness to the destruction of books in the Talmudic Academy of Lublin recalled:

> We threw the huge Talmudic library out of the building and carried the books to the market place, where we set fire to them. The fire lasted twenty hours. The Lublin Jews assembled around and wept bitterly, almost silencing us with their cries. We summoned the military band, and with joyful shouts the soldiers drowned out the sounds of the Jewish cries.

Throughout the month of November, Germans demanded Jewish labour for work brigades. Treating Jewry like cattle, the Germans regarded these individuals as less than human. As one of the victims remarked: 'Truly we are cattle in the eyes of the Nazis. When they supervise Jewish workers they hold a whip in their hands. All are beaten unmercifully.' Such acts, he continued, 'are enough to drive you crazy. Sometimes we are ashamed to look at one another. And worse than this, we have begun to look upon ourselves as "inferior beings", lacking God's image.'

Later in the month Hans Frank ordered the creation of Jewish councils in every Jewish community located within the sphere of the General Government; these bodies were to consist of twenty-four members where there was a population of over 10,000 Jews, and twelve members in smaller communities. As Reinhardt Heydrich instructed, these bodies were to assume responsibility for the internal organization of Jewry within the General Government. One of the central aims of the Nazi plan was to impoverish Polish Jewry; repeatedly, the Jewish community was ordered to pay large sums to the occupying forces.

On 11 December Jews living within the General Government were made liable to two years' forced labour with a possible extension. In consequence, numerous tasks were created for Jews deported to labour camps including clearing swamps, paving roads and constructing buildings. On 13 December the SS headquarters in Poznan decreed that all Jews still living in the western regions of Poland which had been annexed to Germany were to be shot. Those expelled from these lands generally went to Warsaw and Lodz, whose Jewish population had swelled to over

10 million. There the assault against Jewry continued without restraint. In his diary for 16 December 1939, Chaim Kaplan noted that Jewish girls were forced to

> clean a latrine – to remove excrement and clean it. But they received no utensils. To their question 'With what?' the Nazis replied 'With your blouses.' The girls removed their blouses and cleaned the excrement with them. When the job was done they received the reward: the Nazis wrapped their faces in the blouses, filthy with the remains of excrement and laughed uproariously.

By mid-December, the Jewish population in the General Government area numbered between 2,500,000 and 3,500,000 Jews. In the view of Frank, there appeared to be no solution to the Jewish problem. 'We cannot shoot 2,500,000 Jews,' he wrote, 'neither can we poison them. We shall have to take steps, however, designed to extirpate them in some way – and this will be done.' In line with this policy, Jews were forced to work in labour camps throughout Poland. Although the purpose of such camps was to force Jews to engage in physical labour, they also served as a means of humiliating and torturing Jewish victims.

In committing such crimes the Nazis believed they were acting in accordance with the principle of *Lebensraum*. Jews in Poland, they maintained, constituted a biologically undesirable population. Terror, torture and slaughter were acceptable given the quest to rid Europe of parasites, which threatened the purity of the race. Such a policy was implicit in Hitler's speech to the Reichstag on 30 January 1939, the anniversary of his appointment as Reich Chancellor when he prophesied the extermination of European Jewry:

> Today I will once more be a prophet: if the international Jewish financiers in and outside Europe should succeed in plunging the nations once more into a world war, then the result will not be the Bolshevizing of the earth, and thus the victory of Jewry, but the annihilation of the Jewish race in Europe.

Convinced that German *Lebensraum* required more land in the east, Hitler launched an offensive against Russia on 22 June 1941. Hitler had amassed 600,000 motorized vehicles, 3,580 tanks, 7,148 artillery pieces and 2,740 aeroplanes on the Russian frontier. In addition, the German army was supported by 12 Rumanian divisions, 18 Finnish divisions, 3 Hungarian divisions, and 2½ Slovakian divisions. Later these forces were joined by 3 Italian divisions, and a Spanish division. Adopting the pattern of earlier campaigns, Hitler launched a surprise assault by the Luftwaffe. This airborne attack was followed by a second wave of attacks on civilians by special extermination squads, the *Einsatzgruppen* (killing battalions).

According to Hitler, the Russian people were sub-human and their country was a Bolshevized wasteland; in his view, Russians were destined to become slaves to a superior people. Their subjugation was a task allocated to Himmler and four *Einsatzgruppen*. In pursuing this aim, Himmler and Heydrich had given orders that all Jews, Asiatic inferiors, Communist functionaries and gypsies should be murdered. In a series of decrees, Hitler ensured that this policy could be undertaken without any possibility of prosecution for those who complied. A guideline issued by the German High Command before the attack stated that ruthless and energetic measures should be taken against Bolshevik agitators, guerrillas, saboteurs and Jews.

In this onslaught the SS *Einsatzgruppen* acted in close association with the army. Each *Einsatzgruppe* was composed of between 600 and 1,000 men; the lower ranks contained Gestapo, criminal police, order police, Waffen-SS and various specialists. The leaders, however, were carefully selected, largely from the Security Service. These forces followed directly behind the invading troops. On 2 July 1941, Heydrich issued written instructions to the four Higher SS and Police Leaders who had been appointed with special responsibility for the operations of the *Einsatzgruppen*.

Although Heydrich referred only to the execution of Jews in the service of the party or the state, it appears that he was intent on the extermination of all Russian Jews when he addressed the *Einsatzgruppen* commanders on 17 June 1941. In any event, in the course of the war the *Einsatzgruppen* came to interpret their task as the extermination of the entire Jewish population. In this onslaught, an attempt was made to encourage Russian non-Jews to initiate pogroms against the local Jews.

A typical example of the horrors that took place throughout Russia occurred in the city of Lvov shortly after the German invasion. At the beginning of the German occupation, Ukrainian mobs murdered Jews wherever they were found. A witness to this slaughter recalled the scene in the yard of a police station where more than 5,000 Jews had been gathered:

Thousands of men were lying here in rows. They lay on their bellies, their faces buried in the sand. Around the perimeter of the field searchlights and machine guns had been set up. Among them I caught sight of German officers standing about. We were ordered to lie flat like the others. We were pushed and shoved brutally, this way and that. My father was separated from me, and I heard him calling out in despair: 'Let me stay with my son! I want to die with my son!' Nobody took any notice of him.

Now that we were all lying still, there was a hush that lasted for a moment or two. Then the 'game' started. We could hear the sound of a man, clearly one of us, stumbling awkwardly around, chased and beaten by another as he went. At last the pursued collapsed out of sheer exhaustion. He was told to rise. Blows were rained down upon him until he dragged himself to his feet again and tried to run forward. He fell to the ground again and hadn't the strength to get up. When the pursuers were at last satisfied that the incessant blows had rendered him unable to stir, let alone run, they called a halt and left him there. Now it was the turn of the second victim. He received the same treatment. . . .

Thoughts raced in disorder and confusion through my mind. I was so exhausted that I fell asleep. Not even the agonizing screams, the sound of savage blows, or the continual trampling on our bodies could prevent me any longer from sinking into oblivion. . . .

The welcome state of unconsciousness passed all too quickly. I came to, and was startled by a painful stab of dazzling light. Powerful searchlights were focused on us. We sat up, one beside the other, so close that we could not stir. Directly in front of me sat two men with shattered skulls. Through the mess of bone and hair I could see the very brains. We whispered to them. We nudged them. But they did not stir. They just sat there, propped up, bulging eyes staring ahead. They were quite dead.

Throughout the Soviet Union mass executions of Jews became commonplace. A harrowing account of such atrocities was given at the Nuremberg Trials by a German builder:

The people who had got off the lorries – men, women and children of all ages – had to undress on the orders of an SS man who was carrying a riding or dog whip in his hand. They had to place their clothing on separate piles for shoes, clothing and underwear. I saw a pile of shoes containing approximately 800–1,000 pairs, and great heaps of underwear and clothing. Without weeping or crying out these people undressed and stood together in family groups, embracing each other and saying goodbye while waiting for a sign from another SS man who stood on the edge of the ditch and also had a whip. During the quarter of an hour in which I stood near the ditch, I did not hear a single complaint or a plea for mercy. I watched a family of about eight, a man and a woman, both about 50 years old, with their children of about 1, 8, and 10, as well as two grown-up daughters of about 20 to 24. An old woman with snow-white hair held a 1-year-old child in her arms, singing to it and tickling it. The child squeaked with delight. The married couple looked on with tears in their eyes. The father held the 10-year-old boy by the hand speaking softly to him. The boy was struggling to hold back his tears. . . .

I walked around the mound and stood in front of the huge grave. The bodies were lying so tightly packed together that only their heads showed, from almost all of which blood ran down over their shoulders. Some were still moving. Others raised their hands and turned their heads to show that they were still alive. The ditch was already three-quarters full. I estimate that it already held about a thousand bodies. I turned my eyes towards the man doing the shooting. He was an SS man; he sat, legs swinging, on the edge of the ditch. He had an automatic rifle resting on his knees. . . . The people, completely naked, climbed down steps which had been cut into the clay wall of the ditch, stumbled over the heads of those lying there and stopped at the spot indicated by the SS man. They lay down on top of the dead or wounded; some stroked those still living and spoke quietly to them. Then I heard a series of rifle shots. I looked into the ditch and saw the bodies contorting or, the heads already inert, sinking on the corpses beneath. Blood flowed from the napes of their necks.

THE RISE OF NAZISM

How can one account for the incredible success of the Nazi Party? From its beginnings as a tiny splinter party, it grew to become the major factor in German political life. There is no question that Hitler was the driving force behind its growth and ultimate victory. From the start of its development Hitler played a fundamental role. When he joined the party as a board member in September 1919, he became responsible for recruitment and propaganda. Disconcerted by the chaotic character of the party, Hitler was determined to institute discipline within the ranks. After only three months, he recommended a series of changes aimed at broadening the base of the party.

For Hitler, the NSDAP was more than a political party: it represented the hope for a new civilization based on race. Once he was sworn in as chancellor, it became possible for the Nazis to put their ideology into practice. At the core of Nazi social policy was the quest to rid Germany of a Jewish presence. The emergence of political anti-Semitism was a response to social and intellectual developments within Germany in the pre-war period. By the 1930s the Jewish community had become an easy target for the discontent and disorientation felt by many Germans in the wake of rapid industrialization and urbanization. Within German society, Jews were easily identifiable, and much resented because of their relative success and affluence. By 1933, for example, Jews composed more than 16 per cent of lawyers, 10 per cent of doctors and 5 per cent of editors and writers even though they constituted less than 1 per cent of the population.

From 1933 the assault against Jewry was gradual, and the early forms of persecution gave no indication of what was to follow. For many ordinary Germans, such agitation was no more than the Jews deserved. And, once the Nazis were firmly entrenched, any form of opposition – either from within the Jewish community or from sympathetic non-Jews – became totally impractical. Paradoxically, in such an environment of hatred and fear, it became possible for many Germans to harbour anti-Semitic sentiments while retaining positive relationships with individual Jews.

During this period, culminating in the promulgation of the Nuremberg Laws, the Jewish population came under increasing assault. Year by year their civil rights were undermined, and German Jewry was compelled to create its own institutional structure. Under such circumstances, many Jews emigrated although a substantial number remained. Of the 525,000 Jews residing in Germany when Hitler became chancellor, approximately a third left the country before *Kristallnacht*, and another third left during the following ten months. Compared with other Jewish communities, Germany Jewry was fortunate. Nearly 3 million Polish Jews were killed by German troops and over 700,000 Russian Jews died in the Nazi onslaught. Some 400,000 Jews in Hungary were murdered, and in Austria, approximately half of the Jewish population of 200,000 perished.

Comparatively, then, German Jews did not suffer the same fate as other European communities. Yet why was there a reluctance to leave the country once the Nazis had attained power? Initially many Jews believed it would be possible to achieve some form of *rapprochement* with Hitler. In the first weeks of his chancellorship, Hitler sought to mollify non-Nazi conservatives and moderates while ridding the country of all left-wing opposition. As a group, German Jews desired peace and stability and Hitler's vision of a *Volksgemeinschaft* under Nazi leadership offered the possibilities of a strong and united Reich.

With the exception of Jewish Communists and Socialists, German Jewry believed that it would be possible to continue to prosper under Nazism just as Italian Jews had survived Mussolini's rule. Various Jewish groups embraced the notion of national renewal; others found in the ascendancy of Nazism the framework for economic regeneration. Those repelled by street fighting and sporadic violence looked to strong rule as necessary for social stability. Other assimilated and patriotic Jews looked to Hitler to restore Germany to its place among the nations. Liberals, on the other hand, believed that the Nazis would eventually adopt a more reasonable political stance. The Zionists, too, believed that Nazism would encourage a return to the Holy Land. Such aspirations, however, were quickly undermined by anti-Jewish legislation. And rather than encourage foreign protest against their plight, Jewish leaders feared Nazi reprisals.

For some Jews, the assault against German Jewry was not perceived as a calamity, but rather an opportunity for Jewish self-discovery and revival. The Zionist journalist Robert Weltsch responded to the boycott against Jewish shops with the article 'Wear the Yellow Badge with Pride', in which he encouraged Jews to affirm their Jewishness. Other Jews simply hoped that Hitler would adopt a more moderate course. The Jewish establishment, as represented by Leo Baeck, the head of the Reichsvertretung, called for community help. In his view, educational and social facilities would enable the Jewish community to withstand this assault.

Initially adopting a policy of appeasement, Baeck and others engaged in dialogue with the government. In May 1933 Baeck declared that German Jews should join with the Nazis in rejecting Communism and accept that the renewal of Germany was a desirable goal. Such a strategy, however, failed to alter Nazi aspirations; in consequence, Jewish leaders sought to improve German Jewish life. What was needed, they believed, was a cohesive and self-supporting community that would encompass all Jews regardless of religious affiliation. Unity, they believed, was their only weapon against government directives.

For Baeck and others, emigration could only save a small segment of the Jewish population. Only very few Jews had the desire to leave Germany and few had the resources to establish a new life abroad. Moreover, the practical difficulties of relocating half a million Jews were overwhelming. Leaving Germany was a solution only for younger Jews or those who were politically suspect. Hence, the only conceivable response to Nazi persecution was to find some form of accommodation with Nazism. In Baeck's view, Jewish unity was fundamental to ensure that members of the community would not engage in internal dispute. In the light of the public response to Weltsch's call for Jewish renewal, Jewish leaders advocated the creation of a central Jewish organization composed of representatives of the various factions within German Jewry.

With the Nazi definition of Jewishness, it became clear that there was no means of escaping the Nazi assault against Jewry. For many Jews ambivalence about emigrating increased. The fear about loss of work or arrest gave way to consideration about ways to endure the Nazi regime. As the bonds of unity became greater, many Jews found it increasingly difficult to contemplate leaving Germany. Such feelings of uncertainty were aggravated after the April 1933 boycott. In addition, the Law for the Restoration of the Professional Civil Service was not as devastating as had been feared. Only about 25,000 families were affected, leaving approximately 200,000 Jews who were engaged in business unscathed. Moreover, the fact that this law stipulated that those who had begun their careers before 1918, who had fought in the army, or whose fathers or sons had been killed in battle, were exempt enabled many Jews to keep their jobs.

Some Jews came to the conclusion that Hitler might leave the community alone; indeed, he might even recognize that Germany needed its Jewish population. Possibly the Nazis might not stay in power long. Speculation of this nature served as a deterrent to emigration. Leaving Germany was a final act – perhaps it would not be necessary after all. At this stage it was difficult to forsake Germany, and there was a general reluctance to depart. Tragically, such hesitation was intensified by the fact that a number of Jewish emigrés who had fled abroad returned to Germany now that the Nazi revolution seemed to have ebbed.

During this confusing period the energies of the Jewish establishment were directed towards preserving and strengthening German Jewry. Figures like Baeck, who was privately convinced that Jews in Germany had no future, nonetheless sought to console the Jewish community. In a lecture given at a Munich synagogue in April 1934, he declared that Jews should not break the endless chain of generations any more than they could sever their links to God. Repeatedly Baeck called upon German Jewry to unite to face the Nazi menace.

A year after Hitler's seizure of power, only one tenth of the Jewish population had departed. Most Jews were reluctant to leave, believing that the Nazi onslaught had reached its zenith. Even though they were hemmed in by over three hundred laws and regulations restricting Jewish life, many continued to hope for better times. Although Jews ceased to have equal rights with German Aryan citizens, the majority retained their means of livelihood. In addition, the community under threat had drawn closer, and took comfort from such contact. What was required, many believed, was forbearance in the face of continuing hostility.

A sizeable number of Jews believed that by withdrawing from German public life it would be possible to avoid further degradation. Yet such appeasement and retreat did not bear fruit. The vast majority clung to the belief that the law would restrain the Nazis. Urging restraint, Baeck continued to console the community for its loss and sought to persuade Jewry to engage in communal activities that would bind Jews closer together, advice given in the expectation that despondent Jews would be able to find a common purpose.

The Night of the Long Knives, however, brought about a crisis of confidence. The violence of this event coupled with Hindenburg's death led to despair. Appeasement of the Nazis no longer seemed a viable option. Nonetheless, many Jews believed that life could go on. However, such ill-founded optimism was shattered by the promulgation of the Nuremberg Laws. Through such legislation the Nazi Party had made its intention clear: Jews were to be denied their full political rights as citizens. The Nuremberg Laws meant in effect that Jews would no longer be able to look to German law or the courts for protection. To safeguard the purity of German blood, Jews were to be kept apart from their neighbours.

Paradoxically, the reaction of the German Jewish community was divided. The Jewish establishment immediately issued a blueprint for Jewish life in the light of these new laws. It was now possible, they believed, for the Jewish community to develop along independent lines with its own institutions. Writing to Hitler, the Reichsvertretung's leaders asked for their organization to be given official recognition. Other Jews, however, saw the Nuremberg Laws as the final nail in the coffin of Jewish life in Germany. There was no turning back, they believed; what was required now was emigration to Palestine before it was too late.

The Nazi onslaught against Jewry was exported with the attack on Poland. From the beginning the German invasion was not an ordinary conquest. Rather, soldiers displayed an utterly callous disregard for the lives of those whom they encountered. In the view of those who lived during this period, the brutality of the Nazis was overwhelming. Wilhelm Moses, for example, who served in a regular army transport during the invasion, recalled that as he drove through a Polish village, an SS German regimental brass band played as seven or eight victims hung from the gallows. The tongues of these victims were hanging out, and their faces were blue and green. Subsequently Moses and his truck were confiscated by the SS, and he was ordered to transport Polish Jews from one SS unit to another. When he was told by the Jews that they would be killed, he asked:

'Well, who said that they are going to kill you?'
'But of course they will kill us, they killed the others too, my mother, my father, my children have all been killed. They will kill us, too!'
'Well, are you Jews?' asked Herr Moses.
'Yes, we are Jews,' they replied.
'What could I do?' says Herr Moses. 'I am a tortured person. As a German, I can only tell you that I was ashamed of everything that had happened. And I no longer felt German. . . .
I had already got to the point where I said, "If a bullet were to hit me, I would no longer have to be ashamed to say that I'm German, later, once the war is over."'

The activities of the *Einsatzgruppen* in Russia marked a new stage in the assault against the European Jewish community. Previously Jews had been persecuted, deported, ghettoized, and worked to death. However, there had been no policy of mass murder. The killing squads, however, set the scene for a new approach to the Jewish problem. No doubt the decision to exterminate Jewry emerged gradually as the Nazis came to realize that they had no coherent plan for what to do with the millions of Jews living in the east.

EIGHTEEN

The Holocaust

The Nazi persecution of the Jewish people proceeded in stages, from prejudice and discrimination to annihilation. In this sequence of events, the Wannsee Conference, held in a villa outside Berlin, marked the final stage of the process. The result of the conference was the official adoption of the Final Solution to the Jewish problem. In the war against the Soviet Union, the *Einsatzgruppen* had systematically murdered Jews wherever they were found. Following Wannsee, the decision to exterminate Jews became a central feature of Nazi policy. Unrestrained by moral compunction, this assault against Jewry was facilitated by the creation of death camps in which innocent victims were gassed. This task was to be carried out bravely in the quest to create an Aryan civilization that would endure for over a thousand years. Men, women and children were to be killed so that no future generation would pollute the race. This was a life and death struggle between the German people and sub-human, corrupting elements of society.

ONSLAUGHT AGAINST THE JEWS
Having embarked on the task of deporting Jews to their destination in the east, Germany was confronted with the practical problem of defining criteria for those who were to be transported. In addition, the process of uprooting thousands of people from their homes, transporting them during wartime, and relocating them in new dwellings became a major logistical problem. What was required was a coordinated system. To resolve these dilemmas, Heydrich invited a group of senior officials to a conference to discuss this issue.

The Wannsee Conference took place on 20 January 1942. The minutes, prepared by Adolf Eichmann, record the nature of the discussion:

> The chief of the Security Police and SD, SS *Obergruppenführer* Heydrich, began by announcing his appointment by the Reich Marshal as the person

responsible for the preparation of the final solution of the European Jewish question and pointed out that this meeting was being held to achieve clarity on basic questions. The Reich Marshal's wish that he should be sent a draft on the organizational, technical and material matters regarding the final solution of the European Jewish question made it necessary that all central authorities directly concerned with these questions should deal with them together in advance so as to ensure the coordination of the lines to be taken.

The Chief of the Security Police and SD then gave a brief review of the struggle that had been waged hitherto against these opponents. The basic elements were:

(a)　The exclusion of the Jews from the individual spheres of German life. (b) The exclusion of the Jews from the living space of the German people. In pursuit of these efforts, the acceleration of the emigration of Jews from the Reich territory was increased and systematically adopted as provisionally the only feasible solution. . . .

The evacuation of the Jews to the east has now emerged, with the prior permission of the Führer, as a further possible solution instead of emigration. These actions, however, must be regarded only as an alternative solution, but already the practical experience is being gathered which is of great importance to the coming final solution of the Jewish question. . . .

In pursuance of the final solution, the Jews will be conscripted for labour in the east under appropriate supervision. Large labour gangs will be formed from those fit for work, with the sexes separated and they will be sent to these areas for road construction and undoubtedly a large number of them will drop out through natural wastage. The remainder who survive – and they will certainly be those who have the greatest powers of endurance – will have to be dealt with accordingly. For, if released, they would, as a natural selection of the fittest, form a germ cell from which the Jewish race could regenerate itself.

The minutes of the Wannsee Conference were circulated to a wide range of government departments and SS head offices – the language used was designed to disguise the true intentions of those gathered at the conference. As is clear from the interrogation of Adolf Eichmann by the Israelis in 1960, the Final Solution of the Jewish problem was understood by the participants at the conference as referring to extermination:

What I know is that the gentlemen sat together, and then in very blunt terms –
not in the language that I had to use in the minutes, but in very blunt terms –
they talked about the matter without any circumlocution. I certainly could not
have remembered that if I had not recalled saying to myself at the time: look,
just look at Stuckart, who was always regarded as a legal pedant, punctilious
and fussy, and now what a different tone! The language being used here was
very unlegalistic. I should say that this is the only thing from all this that has
still stuck clearly in my mind. . . . The talk was of killing, elimination and
annihilation.

In the months that followed, the Nazis rounded up Jews for deportation
to their deaths. Aware of their eventual fate, these innocent victims sought
to hide or escape from their oppressors. 'We tremble at the mention of
Lublin,' Chaim Kaplan wrote in his diary. 'Our blood turns to ice when we
listen to tales told by refugees from the city. Even before they arrived in the
Warsaw Ghetto, the rumours reaching us were so frightful that we thought
they came from totally unreliable sources.'

The first extermination site, Chelmno, was created in December 1941 in
the woods 40 miles north-west of Lodz. This was not strictly a camp, but a
site equipped with mobile vans that used exhaust fumes. Belzec, Sobibor
and Treblinka, on the other hand, were solely death centres with no
organizational link to the concentration camp system. Approximately
225,000 Jews were killed in Chelmno; 250,000 in Sobibor; 600,000 in
Belzec; and 974,000 in Treblinka. At Majdanek about 200,000 died
including about 60,000 Jews. In Auschwitz more than one million were
murdered.

Belzec, Sobibor and Treblinka were located on several hectares of land
with an area set off for the guards' barracks, and the camp administration
centre. The reception area, including a railway ramp and disrobing
barracks and storeroom sheds, was located nearby. There was a narrow
passage leading from the reception area to the annihilation facilities. This
path was bordered on both sides by barbed wire covered with brushwood.
At the start of the path or further on, there was a barracks for shaving
prisoners' hair. The annihilation area was surrounded by 6-foot-high
fences, and the gas chambers were disguised as showers.

Initially no camp had more than three gas chambers. In the summer of
1942 Sobibor and Belzec increased their number to six, and Treblinka had
ten. At Treblinka a ceremonial curtain taken from a synagogue was hung

with the inscription: 'This is the gate through which the righteous enter.' Each factory was equipped with a diesel engine that emitted exhaust fumes into the gas chambers. The dead were then put on rail waggons that were pulled to a grave by Jewish *Kommandos*. From 1942, however, bodies were dug up and burned on massive grills; the ashes and remains of bones were then dumped into empty graves about 10 metres deep and covered with sand and refuse.

Those who worked in the camps were recruited from the euthanasia programme, which was instituted by the Nazis in 1939 to eliminate the mentally ill and handicapped by gassing. The senior officials in each camp consisted of between 20 and 40 German SS officers and non-commissioned officers. The guard personnel consisted of units of Ukrainians and ethnic Germans. In Treblinka the staff numbered between 90 and 120; at Sobibor it was about 90. These guards went on patrols, took up positions in watchtowers, supervised Jewish *Kommandos*, and served as sentries at the ramp and along the path to the gas chambers.

Majdanek and Auschwitz were part of the central concentration camp administration; as a result, there was no need to bring in extra staff from the outside. A large number of Majdanek personnel were recruited from Buchenwald to construct the camp, but because there was a constant lack of supplies the camp was subject to permanent improvisation. For some time Soviet prisoners of war as well as Jewish and non-Jewish Poles were shot. In July 1942, however, a small crematorium was built and in September a gassing facility. Later, three gas chambers were constructed. In September 1943 the mass shootings were replaced by gassing. New arrivals were usually confined to barracks, to await selection. On 3 November 1943, when the gas chambers ceased functioning, all Jews in the camp were killed in a major massacre.

The largest death facility was built at Auschwitz; this was done because of the increasing number of transports and overcrowding in the camps. The first gassings took place in September 1941 in the basement of Block 11 in the main camp. Subsequently, the morgue near the crematorium was used as a gas chamber. In 1942 operations were shifted to Birkenau where two farmhouses were converted into gas chambers. Corpses were then transported by rail to pits about several hundred metres away where they were buried. In the autumn of 1942, they were exhumed and burned. In July 1942 work began on four large death facilities, which came into operation from March to June 1943. Each of these centres had disrobing rooms, gas chambers and furnaces.

In order to function properly, the organization of the death camps had to be highly efficient. After selection, prisoners were taken to the disrobing rooms. Simultaneously, the ovens were ignited in the crematoria and wood was piled up next to the burning pits. Victims were informed that after showering they would be given their clothing or told they would have warm soup. After handing over their valuables, they were moved in groups divided by sex through the passage to the gas chambers. When the first groups were pushed into the gas chambers, the *Kommandos* were already bringing clothing to the sorting site and packing it for shipment.

A Ukrainian assistant then turned on the motor. In cases where it did not start, victims stood sometimes for half an hour. At Auschwitz, prisoners noticed that the shower heads were fake. Lights were turned off, and the executioner who wore a gas mask shook Zyklon B crystals into shafts; after fifteen minutes all had been killed. Fans were then turned on to clear the gas chamber. The door was unbolted, and members of the *Sonderkommando* hosed down the corpses and took them out. The members of the transport *Kommando* then hauled the dead to the freight elevator or the morgue where dentists pulled the gold teeth and fillings from the jaws and barbers cut off their hair. The bodies were then put into crematoria.

This process ensured that while those who had been murdered were being burned, the next group was gassed. In this fashion, killing became a mechanized function of the camps. Gassing and cremation became stages in an efficient series of murderous acts. To facilitate the smooth operation of the death camps, deception became a central feature of the Nazi onslaught. Victims were kept ignorant of the consequences of following orders on their arrival at the camps. Trees surrounded the crematoria, and innocent signs were put up so that the final stop appeared to be a normal station. In Sobibor special barracks were constructed for baggage; in Treblinka prisoners were instructed to deposit their documents and valuables. In disrobing rooms, numbers were put up for clothes and deportees were told to remember the number so they would find their belongings after showering. In Sobibor an SS squad leader wore a white doctor's coat and explained that hygienic measures were necessary before entering the camp.

Yet, despite these measures, victims were often aware of what lay ahead. At Treblinka, for example, new arrivals were able to see masses of decomposing bodies. As a consequence, many suffered nervous collapse. After one arrival of a transport from Bialystok, one woman who had been told about the death camps ran screaming from group to group. Initially she was not believed, but eventally the inmates began to panic and were eventually pacified by reassuring words and the appearance of armed SS sentries and their dogs.

The SS used repeated violence against the victims. Deportees were compelled to hurry and struck by blows; the sick were dragged from the trains and thrown with the dead on to waggons. In some cases bloodhounds were released on the ramp and hesitant prisoners were dragged away. At Sobibor some of the guards grabbed small children left behind in the boxcars and smashed their skulls against the walls. At Auschwitz, the SS frequently herded victims immediately on arrival into the gas chambers. Any form of resistance was dealt with severely. In the view of the SS, all inmates were doomed, and therefore could be killed without restraint.

The effectiveness of the death camps was further facilitated by the use of the Jewish *Sonderkommandos*. These Jews were compelled to participate in the murder of fellow Jews and the cremation of the dead. Dentists, barbers, corpse bearers, stokers and gravediggers performed the most appalling tasks out of fear of death. These inmates were allowed to live so that they could dispose of the other Jews. Such individuals were chosen during selection. In Sobibor, new arrivals were received by the station *Kommando* dressed in uniform; another *Kommando* group took their possessions; another sorted and packed items. At Treblinka, a Jewish *Kommando* was made up of goldsmiths, jewellers and bank clerks. In most cases corpse workers in the extermination camps consisted of about 150 workers who were housed in separate barracks – their job was to empty the gas chambers, examine the orifices of victims in the search for valuables, extract gold from their teeth and stack the dead in pits. Another group – the forest *Kommando* – was responsible for chopping down wood and bringing it to the camp for burning in the crematoria.

In Auschwitz the first *Sonderkommando* group consisted of about 80 prisoners; it was responsible for burying victims gassed in bunkers 1 and 2. This was liquidated in August 1942. The second *Sonderkommando* group was made up of about 150 to 300 members; it was responsible for exhuming corpses buried until November 1942 and burning them. On

3 December 1942, gravediggers were gassed in the crematorium of the main camp. The SS then recruited workers in the men's camp, isolating them in bunker 11. Subsequently, young men were selected on arrival without being processed for admission. From mid-1944 the *Sonderkommando* was housed in the crematorium itself.

The horrors of the camps have been described by both victims and perpetrators. At his trial, Adolf Eichmann recalled his visit to Chelmno to witness the gassing of Jews:

> There was a room – if I remember correctly – perhaps five times as large as this one. Perhaps it was only four times as big as the one I am sitting in now. And Jews were inside. They were to strip and then a truck arrived when the doors opened, and the van pulled up at a hut. The naked Jews were to enter. Then the van was making for an open pit. The doors were flung open and corpses were cast out as if they were animals – some beasts. They were hurled into the ditch.

The man chosen by Christian Wirth, the person in charge of the gas chambers at Belzec, to organize the death camp at Sobibor was Franz Stangl; subsequently he recalled his first trip to Belzec:

> The smell was everywhere. Wirth wasn't in his office; they said he was up in the camp. I asked whether I should go up there and they said, 'I wouldn't if I were you – he's mad with fury. It isn't healthy to be near him.' I asked what was the matter. The man I was talking to said that one of the pits had overflowed. They had put too many corpses in it and putrefaction had progressed too fast, so that the liquid underneath had pushed the bodies on top up and over and the corpses had rolled down the hill.

Another visitor, Kurt Gerstein, recalled the smell of the camp and the terrifying scene of new arrivals.

> Next morning, shortly before seven, I was told: 'the first transport will arrive in ten minutes. . . . Behind the barred hatches stared the horribly pale and frightened faces of children, their eyes full of the fear of death. . . . The train arrives: 200 Ukrainians fling open the doors and chase the people out of the waggons with their leather whips. Instructions come from a large loudspeaker: 'Undress completely, including artificial limbs, spectacles. . . .

Give your valuables up at the counter without receiving a ticket or receipt.'. . . Then the women and girls have to go to the hairdressers who, with two or three snips of the scissors, cut off their hair. . . . Then the procession starts to move. . . . The chambers fill up. . . . People are treading on each other's toes. 700–800 in an area of 25 square metres, in 45 cubic metres! The SS push them in as far as possible. The doors shut; in the meantime, the others are waiting outside in the open, naked. . . . After 28 minutes, only a few are still alive. At last, after 32 minutes, they are all dead. Men from the work detail open the wooden doors from the other side. Even though they are Jews, they have been promised their freedom and a small percentage of all the valuables which are found as a reward for their frightful duty. The dead stand like basalt pillars pressed together in the chambers. There is no room to fall or even to lean over. Even in death one can tell which are the families. They are holding hands in death and it is difficult to tear them apart to empty the chambers for the next batch. The corpses are thrown out wet with sweat and urine, smeared with excrement and menstrual blood on their legs. The corpses of children fly through the air. There is no time. The riding whips of the Ukrainians whistle down on the work details. Two dozen dentists open mouths with hooks and look for gold. . . . Some of the workers check genitals and anus for gold, diamonds and valuables.

Horrific scenes of murder were described by other witnesses. At Auschwitz a German surgeon watched as Jews from France were killed:

When the transport with people who were destined to be gassed arrived at the railway ramp, the SS officers selected from the new arrivals, persons fit to work, while the rest – old people, all children, women with children in their arms and other persons not deemed fit to work – were loaded on to lorries and driven to the gas chambers.

I used to follow behind the transports till we reached the bunker. There people were first driven into the barrack huts where the victims undressed and then went naked to the gas chambers. Very often no incidents occurred, as the SS men kept the people quiet, maintaining that they were to bathe and be deloused.

After driving all of them into the gas chamber, the door was closed and an SS man in a gas-mask threw the contents of a Zyklon tin through an opening in the side wall. The shouting and screaming of the victims could be heard through the opening and it was clear they were fighting for their lives.

In their quest to carry out the Final Solution, SS doctors played a central role in the functioning of the camps. Rather than engage in direct medical work, their function was to carry out the Nazi project of racial segregation and mass extermination. When Jewish prisoners arrived, these doctors performed initial large-scale selections. These were undertaken according to a fixed pattern: old and debilitated people, children and women with children were chosen to be sent to the gas chamber. Young adults, on the other hand, were allowed to survive, at least for a short time. After this selection took place, the presiding doctor with a medical technician was driven in an SS vehicle usually marked with a red cross. As leader of his team, the doctor had responsibility for carrying out the killing programme. In addition, it was up to him to allow twenty minutes or so to pass before the doors of the gas chamber could be opened and bodies removed.

SS doctors also engaged in two other types of selection. Jewish inmates were ordered to line up at short notice to make room for arrivals from new transports. In other selections individuals who were viewed as significantly ill or who required more than two or three weeks for recovery were sent to the gas chambers. This process was influenced by the euthanasia programme in which those who were judged as lacking worth for society were eliminated. In addition, racial ideology provided the rationalization for such wanton killing. Himmler's vision of ridding the Reich of biological pollution served as the justification for those who participated in such actions. In his view:

> Jews are the eternal enemies of the German people and must be exterminated. All Jews within our grasp are to be destroyed without exception, now, during the war. If we do not succeed in destroying the biological substance of the Jews, the Jews will some day destroy the German people.

Embracing such racial theories, Nazi doctors called forth an absolute conception of good and evil as a justification for their actions. As one Nazi doctor explained:

> Precisely because they were convinced of the justness . . . or of the National-Socialist 'world blessing' and that the Jews are the root evil of the world – precisely because they were so convinced of it did they believe, or were strengthened, that the Jews, even existentially, had to be absolutely exterminated.

To those who arrived at the camp, the role of the SS doctors was not always apparent. Amid mass confusion, deportees did not realize that doctors were carrying out a selection. As one victim explained:

> We arrived at night. . . . Because you arrived at night, you saw miles of lights
> – and the fire from the . . . crematoria. And then screaming and the whistles
> and the 'Out, out!', and the uniformed men and the SS with the dogs, and the
> stripped prisoners. . . . They separated you and then lined up everybody in
> fives . . . and there were two men standing. . . . On one side was the doctor,
> one was Mengele . . . and on the other side was the *Arbeitsführer*, which was
> the . . . man in charge of the work *Kommando*.

For the SS doctors such selections were simply part of concentration camp life. Whatever reservations they might initially have had, they soon came to view their role as a regular job. In addition, doctors were responsible for various technical aspects of the gas chambers. In particular, they were preoccupied with the technical problem of burning large numbers of corpses.

Paralleling selections for the gas chambers, inmates were killed by phenol injections. At Auschwitz from September 1941 this technique was used when patients became debilitated or a medical block was overcrowded. In addition to such activities, SS doctors also participated in various types of experimental research. A typical example was witnessed by Dr Miklos Nyiszli from among the Lodz ghetto Jews who reached Birkenau in August 1944:

> When the convoys arrived Dr Mengele espied, among those lined up for
> selection, a hunchbacked man about 50 years old. He was not alone; standing
> beside him was a tall, handsome boy of fifteen or sixteen. The latter, however,
> had a deformed right foot, which had been corrected by an apparatus made of
> a metal plate and an orthopaedic, thick-soled shoe. They were father and son.
>
> Dr Mengele thought he had discovered, in the persons of the hunchback
> father and his lame son, a sovereign example to demonstrate his theory of the
> Jewish race's degeneracy. . . . Scarcely half an hour later SS Quartermaster
> Sergeant Mussfeld appeared with four *Sonderkommando* men. They took the
> two prisoners into the furnace room and had them undress. Then the
> *Obergruppenführer*'s revolver cracked twice. Father and son were stretched
> out on the concrete covered with blood, dead.

Later in the day Dr Mengele arrived and ordered that the bodies of the father and the son be boiled in water so that flesh could be removed from their bones. When this was completed, the laboratory assistant took up the bones of the skeletons and placed them on the work table. The skeletons were subsequently transported to the Anthropological Museum in Berlin.

Other examples of Mengele's cruelty were recorded by survivors – at Auschwitz over a thousand medical experiments were carried out on Jews whom Mengele took from the barracks. Following his arrival in May 1943, Mengele joined other SS officers and doctors in selecting victims for experimentation. From May 1943 to March 1944 he took part in sixty-four selections of deportees at the railway station, and also played an important role in at least thirty-one selections in the camp infirmary. Among those who were chosen for medical research were more than fifteen hundred Jewish inmates.

One of the survivors recalled that when she and her sister arrived at Birkenau, 'children were having their heads beaten in like poultry by SS men with gun butts, and some were being thrown into a smoking pit. I was confused: I thought that this was some sort of animal kingdom or perhaps I was already in Hell'. Mengele's interest in these twins was genetic: he wanted to know why their eyes were brown and their mother's were blue. Forced to live in a cage for ten days, their eyes were injected with a burning liquid. In Auschwitz, she continued, she had entered a laboratory where she was confronted by a collection of human eyes used in experiments of which she, her sister and her mother were a part.

In Block 28 an experimental area was created for various types of research. There Jewish inmates were taken to have toxic substances rubbed into their arms and legs – this procedure caused areas to become severely infected and produced extensive abscesses. The purpose of these experiments was to gather information that would help recognize attempts by those who deliberately created such responses in order to avoid military service. A second type of experiment involved the application of lead acetate to various parts of the body: this caused painful burns as well as discoloration. After such experiments were undertaken, specimens were sent to laboratories for investigation, and photographs were taken to provide records of the conditions caused. A final type of experiment required ingestion of a powder in order to study the symptoms of liver damage. Such research was undertaken in accordance with Himmler's interest in liver disease and jaundice.

By September 1942 the German armies had conquered most of Europe, yet, as mass killing continued, resistance increased. On 24 September the Jews of the White Russian town of Korzec set the ghetto on fire, and a number of Jews established a partisan band. On 25 September in Kaluszyn near Warsaw, the chairman of the Jewish Council in Lukow near Lublin collected money from Jews assembled in the main square in the hope that he could use the funds to ransom the Jewish community. But when he found that the deportation would take place, he shouted: 'Here is your payment for our trip, you bloody tyrant.' Tearing the money into shreds, he struck the German supervisor and was shot on the spot by the Ukrainian guards. In the same month a former Jewish soldier in the Polish army who was being held with several hundred other prisoners in Lublin escaped with seventeen Jews, forming a small partisan group.

In the Warsaw Ghetto, the Jewish Fighting Organization prepared itself for action. On 29 October 1942 a member of the organization killed the commander of the Jewish police in the ghetto. In the Bialystok ghetto resistance was also taking place with the assistance of German soldiers from whom they obtained weapons. Near Cracow six members of the Jewish Fighting Organization fled to the forests armed with pistols and a knife, but were betrayed by local peasants. The next month the Jewish Fighting Organization in Cracow sabotaged railway lines, raided a German clothing store, and killed several Germans. In Marcinkance the chairman of the Jewish Council called out to the Jews who had been brought to the railway station: 'Fellow Jews, everybody run for his life. All is lost!' As the Jews ran towards the ghetto fence, attacking the guards, over one hundred were shot.

In November 1942 Polish Jews who had managed to escape the deportation to Treblinka established a small group to protect those Jews who went into hiding. The news of executions in the labour camps in December encouraged plans for resistance in Warsaw. As an eye-witness to these events recorded:

> The community wants the enemy to pay dearly. . . . They will attack them with knives, sticks, carbolic acid; they will not allow themselves to be seized in the streets, because now they know that the labour camp these days means death.

In the labour camp at Krustzyna near Radom Jews decided to resist with knives and fists in December 1942. When they were ordered to gather together, they attacked the guards. Three weeks later 400 Jews in the Kopernik camp in Minsk Mazowiecki barricaded themselves into the buildings and resisted the oppressors with sticks, stones and bricks. On 22 December 1942 in Cracow, the Jewish Fighting Organization attacked a café frequented by the SS and the Gestapo. In Czestochowa on 4 January 1943 members of the Jewish Fighting Organization wounded the German commander.

On 19 April 1943 German troops entered the Warsaw Ghetto determined to transport Jews to Treblinka. While they did not expect any resistance, preparations had been made in the ghetto by Jews who sought to defend themselves. Pistols and grenades had been obtained; those who had no weapons armed themselves with sticks, bottles and lengths of pipe. As German troops entered the ghetto, the Jews attacked. One of those who witnessed the battle, Zivia Lubetkin, recounted the events which took place:

> All of a sudden they started entering the ghetto, thousands armed as if they were going to the front against Russia. And we, what were our arms? The arms we had – we had a revolver, a grenade and a whole group had two guns, and some bombs, home-made, prepared in a very primitive way. We had to light it by matches, and Molotov bottles. It was strange to see those twenty men and women, Jewish men and women, standing up against the enemy army glad and merry, because we knew that their end will come. We know that they will conquer us first, but to know that for our lives they would pay a high price.

According to Lubetkin, the Germans were initially repulsed by this small fighting force:

> When the Germans came up to our posts and marched by and we threw those hand grenades and bombs, and saw German blood pouring over the streets of Warsaw, and after we saw so much Jewish blood running in the streets of Warsaw before that, there was rejoicing. The tomorrow did not worry us. The rejoicing amongst Jewish fighters was great and, see the wonder and the miracle, those German heroes retreated, afraid and terrorized from the Jewish bombs and hand grenades, home-made.

Reports of the resistance in Warsaw spread throughout Europe; nonetheless, pressure against the Jews continued. When the Red Army

advanced on the Eastern Front, the Nazis decided to dig up the corpses of
Jews and burn them. On 15 June at the Janowska death pits in Lvov Jewish
labourers were compelled to dig up those who had been killed and extract
gold teeth and rings. An eye-witness later recalled:

> The fire crackles and sizzles. Some of the bodies in the fire have their hands
> extended. It looks as if they are pleading to be taken out. Many bodies are
> lying around with open mouths. Could they be trying to say: 'We are your
> own mothers, fathers, who raised you and took care of you. Now you are
> burning us.' If they could have spoken maybe they would have said this, but
> they are forbidden to talk too – they are guarded. Maybe they would forgive
> us. They know that we are being forced to do this by the same murderers that
> killed them. We are under their whips and machine guns.

The pace of murder was unrelenting. At Birkenau on Christmas Day
1943 Jewish women who had been starving were brought from the
barracks. The victims knew they were going to the gas chambers and tried
to escape. According to an account of this incident, when the lorry motors
started a terrible noise arose – the death cry of thousands of young women.
As they struggled to escape, a rabbi's son cried out: 'God show them your
power – this is against you.' When nothing happened, the boy cried out:
'There is no God.'

As the months passed, Jews continued to be subjected to equally terrible
events. In Kovno several thousand children were rounded up, driven off in
trucks and murdered. As an observer of this action related:

> I saw shattered scenes. It was near the hospital. I saw automobiles which
> from time to time would approach mothers with children or children who
> were on their own. In the back of them two Germans with rifles would be
> going as if they were escorting criminals. They would toss the children in the
> automobile. I saw mothers screaming. A mother whose three children had
> been taken away – she went up to this automobile and shouted at the
> German, 'Give me the children,' and he said, 'You may have one.' And she
> went up into that automobile and all three children looked at her and
> stretched out their hands. Of course, all of them wanted to go with their
> mother, and the mother didn't know which child to select and she went down
> alone, and she left the car.

DENYING THE HOLOCAUST

Despite the mass of evidence, a number of revisionist historians have been adamant that the Holocaust never took place. In their view, the attempt to annihilate the Jewish people did not occur. Further, they insist that if either side was guilty during the Second World War, it was not the Germans; rather the real crimes against humanity were committed by the Americans, Russians, British and French. In their view, the Jewish community has perpetrated the myth of the Holocaust for their own purposes. Such a twisted interpretation of history thus constitutes a further onslaught against Jewry in contemporary society.

An early proponent of Holocaust denial was Maurice Bardèche who was highly critical of Allied war propaganda. In *Nuremberg or the Promised Land*, he argued that some of the evidence regarding the concentration camps was falsified. In his view, many of the deaths that took place in the camps were the result of starvation and illness. Further, he maintained that the term 'Final Solution' referred to the transfer of Jews to ghettos in the east. According to Bardèche, the Jews were responsible for the war by supporting the Treaty of Versailles. In addition, he maintained that German soldiers were not culpable for following orders – Nazi Germany was intent on overcoming the Communist threat. Further, he alleged that the Nuremberg Trials were a scandal since they punished Germany for seeking to defeat Stalin. Finally, in his view, the Allied bombing policy was the major crime of the war.

A second figure who contributed to this early debate was Paul Rassinier, a former Communist who had been deported to Buchenwald. In *Le Passage de la ligne*, he attempted to demonstrate that survivors' claims about the Nazis were not reliable. In this and subsequent works Rassinier maintained that survivors exaggerated what had happened to them. It was not the SS who were responsible for atrocities in the camps, but rather inmates who were in charge of the camps. Although he admitted that extermination did take place, he alleged that this was not the official policy of the Nazis. According to Rassinier, the Nazis were not evil; rather they acted as benefactors of those who had been deported. Their intention in rounding up Jews and transferring them to the east was to protect such individuals by removing them from areas where they could be attacked.

In a later work, *The Drama of European Jewry*, Rassinier asserted that the alleged genocide of European Jewry was a myth. The gas chambers, he claimed, were an invention of Zionists. Further, he maintained that former

Nazis falsely claimed that they had committed crimes against Jews so that they would receive lenient treatment. He also stressed that the testimonies of Nazi leaders tried for war crimes should be discounted because they were testifying under the threat of death, and they therefore confessed what was most likely to save their lives.

In Rassinier's view, those responsible for such falsification were the Zionists who were aided by Jewish historians and institutions that conducted research on the Holocaust. Such fraud was motivated by the Jewish desire for gain; those who perpetrated the genocide hoax wished to ensure that Germany would pay remunerations to Israel. In this way Israel had swindled Germany with the assistance of Jewish scholars and researchers. Turning to Hitler, Rassinier was intent on demonstrating that, despite contradictory evidence, the Führer had no intention of destroying the Jewish population of Europe.

In the United States, a number of writers argued along similar lines. In 1952, W.D. Herrstrom stated in *Bible News Flashes* that 5 million illegal aliens, including many Jews who resided on American soil, were survivors of the Holocaust who were reported to have perished under the Nazi regime. Another writer of this era, Harry Elmer Barnes, claimed that the Allies were responsible for the Second World War. In his view, Hitler's actions were necessary to rectify the injustices of the Versailles treaty. It was not Hitler's inhumanity, but rather his benevolence, that led to his downfall. Hitler did not launch an aggressive attack on Poland; rather he sought to avoid war. It was the British who were responsible for the outbreak of war on the Eastern and Western Fronts. Hitler did not instigate the conflict, but was forced into war by the actions of the British.

Later Barnes became increasingly absorbed by claims about German atrocities. In *Revisionism and Brainwashing*, he was critical of the lack of opposition to atrocity stories and anxious to demonstrate that the Allies had waged a brutal and inhumane assault against Germany. Supportive of Rassinier's writing, he believed that such accounts were fabrications produced by Jews for their own ends. Following the Eichmann trial, Barnes attacked the media for its sensationalism about the Nazis. The gas chambers, he asserted, were postwar inventions, concocted by historians and others.

Arguing along similar lines, Austin J. App in the late 1950s maintained that less than 6 million Jews died during the Nazi regime. A defender of Nazi Germany, he later formulated eight axioms in the *Six Million Swindle* that have served as the guiding principles of Holocaust denial:

1. Emigration, never annihilation, was the Reich's plan for solving Germany's Jewish problem.
2. 'Absolutely no Jews were gassed in any concentration camps in Germany, and evidence is piling up that none were gassed in Auschwitz.' The Hitler gas chambers never existed. The gassing installations in Auschwitz were really crematoria for cremating corpses of those who had died from a variety of causes.
3. The majority of Jews who disappeared and remained unaccounted for did so in Soviet, not German, control.
4. The majority of Jews who supposedly died while in German hands were, in fact, subversives, partisans, spies, saboteurs, and criminals or victims of unfortunate but internationally legal reprisals.
5. If there existed the slightest likelihood that the Nazis had really murdered 6 million Jews, world Jewry would demand subsidies to conduct research on the topic and Israel would open its archives to historians.
6. The Jews and the media who exploit this figure have failed to offer even a shred of evidence to prove it.
7. It is the accusers, not the accused, who must provide the burden of proof to substantiate the 6 million figure.
8. The fact that Jewish scholars themselves have 'ridiculous' discrepancies in their calculations of the number of victims constitutes firm evidence that there is no scientific proof to this accusation.

Neo-fascist groups were also anxious to promote Holocaust denial. In 1974 a short pamphlet, *Did Six Million Really Die? The Truth at Last*, was published by Richard Harwood, the pseudonym of Richard Verrall of the British National Front. Based on the *Myth of Six Million*, this work contended that Jews have used the Holocaust myth to protect the Jewish faith and weaken other people's quest for self-preservation. According to Harwood, the Jewish people have manipulated historical events to serve their own ends.

Holocaust denial was promoted later in the 1970s by Arthur Butz, a professor of electrical engineering at Northwestern University. In *The Hoax of the Twentieth Century*, Butz argued that the Jewish people had perpetrated the hoax of the Holocaust to further Zionism. In Butz's opinion, the Holocaust myth was promoted by a conspiratorial group of Zionists who were intent on gaining sympathy and support for Israel. Banding together, Jews worldwide had used their considerable power to foster the belief that millions of Jews died at the hands of the Nazis.

In the early 1980s the Canadian government accused Ernst Zundel, a German citizen living in Canada, of promoting anti-Semitism through false documents about the Holocaust. During the trial, the prosecution maintained that Zundel was an ardent racist and anti-Semite. Found guilty in 1985, he was sentenced to fifteen months in prison, but this was overturned on appeal. There followed a second trial in 1988. Anxious to be of assistance, Robert Faurisson, infamous for his views about the gas chambers, went to Canada to help Zundel and his lawyers. According to Faurisson, the apparatus in the camp was too small and primitive to have functioned as gas chambers.

Joining in Zundel's defence, the historian David Irving, who later unsuccessfully brought a libel suit against the scholar Deborah Lipstadt for defamation of his credentials as a historian, together with Faurisson, solicited the help of Fred A. Leuchter who believed that it was impossible for the Germans to have gassed the Jews. After visiting Auschwitz and Majdanek, Leuchter argued on the basis of fragments from these sites that execution chambers did not exist during the Nazi era. His findings are contained in *The Leuchter Report: An Engineering Report on the Alleged Execution Gas Chambers at Auschwitz, Birkenau and Majdanek, Poland.*

There are, however, serious difficulties with this wide range of revisionist interpretations of the Nazi era. The most glaring difficulty is the Holocaust deniers' refusal to accept the mass of evidence about the evils of the Third Reich. Given that similar testimonies were provided by both Jews and non-Jews, such eye-witness accounts appear to constitute incontrovertible evidence about the victimization of those deported to the camps.

With regard to the gas chambers, Holocaust deniers repeatedly call for proof of the existence of such facilities. Yet they systematically dismiss the reliability of all accounts, whether given by Jews who claim to have witnessed such killing operations or first-hand testimony by the SS. Such refusal is based on the paradoxical conviction that because these accounts corroborate one another, they are likely to be fabrications. Further, Holocaust deniers refuse to accept extensive research such as that undertaken by Jean-Claude Pressac. On a research trip to Auschwitz in 1979 Pressac examined photographs, documents and work orders regarding the construction of gas chambers. On further visits, he discovered additional documents. Since the publication of his study of the gas chambers in 1989, he has investigated archives in the former Soviet Union where he has discovered additional material.

Pressac's findings demonstrate the falsehood of the Holocaust deniers' claim that there is no documentary evidence regarding the existence of the gas chambers. His investigation revealed that an inventory of equipment for Crematorium III included one gas-tight door and fourteen showers. The drawings for these showers revealed that the shower heads were not connected to water pipes. Further, a letter of 29 January 1943 from SS Captain Bischoff, head of the Auschwitz Waffen-SS, to an SS major general in Berlin, referred to the gassing cellar. Added to this evidence was a time-sheet in which a civilian worker had recorded that a room in the western part of Crematorium IV was a *Gaskammer*.

Pressac also discovered an order made in February 1943 by the Waffen-SS and Police Central Construction Management for twelve gas-tight doors for Crematoria IV and V. In March a time-sheet submitted by the contractors referred to a concrete floor in a gas chamber. Moreover, a telegram of 26 February 1943 sent by an SS officer to one of the firms hired for the construction of a gas chamber requested the use of ten gas detectors. In the same month a civilian employee working on Crematorium II referred to modifying the air extraction system of the undressing cellar II. In the same letter he asked about the possibility of preheating the areas to be used as the gas chamber. Another letter of March signed by SS Major Bischoff referred to an order for a gas door for Crematorium II. Finally, an inventory for Crematorium II contained a reference to a gas-tight door. All this material constitutes documentary evidence supporting the existence of gas chambers in the camps, the type of proof demanded by Holocaust deniers.

Given the existence of such material, it might be thought that Holocaust deniers, particularly those who describe themselves as historians of the Third Reich, would have abandoned their position. Yet this conclusion overlooks the fact that Holocaust denial is in many cases politically motivated and the result of rabid Judaeophobia. The founder of the Institute of Historical Research, Willis Carto, was the founder of Liberty Lobby, an ultra-right-wing organization. According to the Anti-Defamation League, the Liberty Lobby is at the helm of a publishing complex that has propagated anti-Jewish propaganda for decades. Willis Carto's political vision was based on contempt for Jews, the belief that the government needs to protect the racial heritage of the United States, and the conviction that there currently exists a conspiracy to undermine the Western world.

Other figures advocating Holocaust denial share similar ideas. In a variety of writings as well as at his libel trial, David Irving advocated a revisionist approach to understanding the nature of the Third Reich. According to Professor Lipstadt in *Denying the Holocaust* such attitudes are one of the greatest dangers in the modern world:

If Holocaust denial has demonstrated anything, it is the fragility of memory, truth, reason and history. The deniers' campaign has been carefully designed to take advantage of these vulnerabilities. . . . Right-wing nationalist groups in Germany, Italy, Austria, France, Norway, Hungary, Brazil, Slovakia and a broad array of other countries, including the United States, have adopted Holocaust denial as a standard facet of their propaganda. Whereas these groups once justified the murder of the Jews, now they deny it. Once they argued that something quite beneficial to the world happened at Auschwitz. Now they insist nothing did. Their anti-Semitism is often so virulent that the logical conclusion of their argument is that though Hitler did not murder the Jews, he should have.

NINETEEN

Anti-Semitism in the Postwar Period

After the end of the Second World War, Germany expressed little remorse for the events of the Nazi regime. Instead, most Germans continued to harbour anti-Semitic attitudes. Even though the radical left was critical of Fascism, there was little sympathy for Jewry. Such attitudes were also found in postwar Austria where a number of ex-Nazis were rehabilitated. Similar antipathy was expressed in Britain where neo-Nazis and ultra-right-wing groups maintained that a worldwide Jewish conspiracy sought to dominate modern society. In the United States, anti-Semitism intensified, largely as a result of the conflict between American Jews and the black community. French hostility towards Jews led to the condemnation of Zionism, attacks on Jewish property and the resurgence of a nationalist party. Poland, too, witnessed the rise of anti-Semitism despite the absence of a sizeable Jewish population. In Russia, hostility towards Jews has similarly resurfaced in the last few decades.

MODERN JUDAEOPHOBIA

Due to the war, Ashkenazi Jewry largely disappeared from German soil, and the crimes committed against Germany's Jewish community did not evoke either guilt or remorse. Between 1946 and 1947 opinion polls revealed widespread indifference to the plight of Jewry. Hence in 1947 three-quarters of all Germans believed the Jews to belong to another race. In the following year, 41 per cent of the population continued to approve the Nazi seizure of power. By 1952, 88 per cent declared that they bore no responsibility for the Nazi era.

From the late 1960s the German new left has reacted to what it views as the philosemitism of the conservative establishment. Even though anti-fascist and anti-capitalist in orientation, these reactionaries have criticized Israel for its policies concerning the Palestinians. Hence when the Green Party Euro MP Brigitte Heinrich was refused entry to Israel in 1984, she stated: 'The genocide of the Jews created the psychological prerequisites for setting up Israel as an internationally recognized state. The expulsion of the Palestinians is therefore indirectly the result of the Nazi persecution of the Jews. . . . For the same reason that we – the generation which did not experience National Socialism – do not reject the moral guilt of our people for killing millions of Jews, we cannot keep silent about Israeli expansionist policy, occupation of foreign territories by Israeli troops, the repressive measures in the occupied territories.'

According to the radical left, Israel's attitudes are similar to those of the Third Reich. The play *Garbage, the City and Death* by Rainer Werner Fassbinder, for example, portrays a rich Jewish speculator who despoils Frankfurt, and anti-Semitic stereotypes are among the characters. In 1985 the controversy surrounding the Bitburg affair exemplified the lack of concern with Jewish sensitivities: Chancellor Kohl requested that President Reagan pay homage to the German war dead at Bitburg cemetery where the Waffen SS were buried.

Open hostility towards Jews has also been expressed. Thus, the Bavarian deputy Hermann Fellner from the Christian Social Union attacked Jewish survivors who were seeking compensation from a German firm. In North-Rhine Westphalia the mayor claimed that the only way to solve his budget deficit would be to kill a few rich Jews. Again, the local chairman of the Christian Youth Union claimed that Israel had made the democratic constitutional state responsible for the murder of Jews under the Nazis. In the 1980s anti-Jewish sentiment was widely manifest. According to the researches of Werner Bergman, 6 to 7 million Germans could be classified as holding anti-Semitic views with approximately 2 million of that number being characterized as hard-core anti-Semites. With the unification of Germany, the emphasis on the continuities of German history and national pride has overshadowed the Jewish question.

In postwar Austria, anti-Semitism continues to fester beneath the surface of political life. By 1949 a considerable number of Austrian ex-Nazis had been re-enfranchised; from 1955 a number of prominent National Socialists had been fully integrated into political life, and the Socialists and Catholic conservatives competed for the former Nazi vote. In this context even the election of a Jewish-born socialist, Bruno Kreisky, as chancellor did not eliminate anti-Jewish hostility. Such attitudes surfaced when the former Secretary General of the United Nations, Kurt Waldheim, was criticized for his activities during the war: the campaign against him provoked a backlash of anti-Semitism, and it was widely believed that international Jews based on the east coast of the United States had manipulated the media to defame his character.

At the end of the war antipathy towards the Jews in Britain increased as a result of the Anglo-Zionist conflict over Palestine, and pro-Arab attitudes in the Foreign and Colonial Office affected decision-making. Nonetheless, in postwar Britain a considerable number of Jews became affluent, taking on prominent positions in both the professions and the business world. During the Thatcher years Anglo-Jewry became steadily more conservative and several Jewish figures were included in the Cabinet. Such attitudes were also mirrored in the religious establishment, and the former chief rabbi, Lord Jakobovits, frequently espoused views in harmony with the Tory government.

Despite the general prosperity of the Jewish community, anti-Semitism continued to fester in English life. From the 1970s neo-Nazi and ultra-right-wing groups espoused conspiracy theories. The National Front, for example, has supported Fascism and racial bigotry. Its anti-Semitic publication, *Holocaust News*, for example, seeks to illustrate that the murder of European Jewry did not take place. Such attitudes have been supported by revisionist historians like David Irving. As a result of such theories, Jewish cemeteries have been attacked, anti-Semitic graffiti has proliferated, and assaults on Orthodox Jews in north London have taken place.

As in the United Kingdom, so in America Jews also achieved substantial prosperity in the 1950s and 1960s. By the 1970s many Jews reached the upper ranks of American society. Yet, in the 1980s a sizeable number of Jews believed that anti-Semitism was on the increase, due to resentment of Jewish political power and the growing antagonism between blacks and Jews. In the 1960s tensions between the black and Jewish communities led to the creation of a Third-World ideology among blacks; this struggle was linked at home with the exploitation of non-white peoples in other lands. In this context, the black social activist Malcolm X described Jews as expropriators: 'Jews who with the help of Christians in America and Europe,' he stated, 'drove our Muslim brothers out of their homes where they had been settled for centuries, and took over the land for themselves.'

According to Malcolm X, American aid to Israel was stolen from the pockets of black taxpayers to support aggression against the Third World. Further, Jewish businessmen in Harlem were viewed as colonialists who exploited the blacks, just as Western colonialists had previously violated the peoples of Africa and Asia. Several years later the Black Panther Party equated racism with Israeli policies. Eventually this anti-Jewish stance became a central motif of the presidential campaign of Reverend Jesse Jackson who referred to Jews as 'Hymies' and New York as 'Hymie-town'; his unwillingness to distance himself from the anti-Semitic black leader Louis Farrakhan, the leader of the Nation of Islam, caused considerable consternation in the American Jewish community. This black separatist movement, which originated in the back streets of Chicago, converted a significant number of the black population to Islam.

Farrakhan himself has described Hitler as a great man and Judaism as a 'gutter religion'. In August 1984 he told a UN correspondents' meeting that 'President Reagan and Walter Mondale absolutely bow down to the strength of the Jewish lobby'. On another occasion, he stated that 'There seems to be an unwritten law that Israel and Jews cannot be criticized, particularly by blacks.' A publication of the Nation of Islam, *The Final Call*, declared in a 1984 issue: 'Two thousand years have not changed the Jews, nor has it changed God's condemnation of them from the mouth of one of his righteous servants. Then it was Jesus, today it is Minister Farrakhan.'

Farrakhan's anti-Jewish attitudes, which were rooted in the 1950s Black Muslim faith of Elijah Muhammad, have been overlaid by leftish national ideologies, Third Worldism, support for the PLO, and the acceptance of funds from Colonel Qaddafi of Libya. In the 1980s a survey revealed that Jews in America believed that blacks were more anti-Semitic than any other group in the United States including Catholics, fundamentalist Christians, big business and the State Department. According to recent research, 37 per cent of blacks as opposed to 20 per cent of whites are anti-Semitic. Even though less than half of black anti-Semites are more anti-Jewish than anti-white, anti-Semitism in the black community appears to increase with economic interaction with Jews. Alleged exploitation by Jewish merchants, landlords and employers of blacks has been the cause of considerable friction between both communities. In addition, blacks are resentful if they are forced into positions below those of Jewish professionals. Tensions between the new black middle class and affluent Jews have also exacerbated community relations. Further, it appears that anti-Semitism increases with the educational level of blacks. Among those who are college educated, ideological commitment serves as the basis for virulent clashes between blacks and Jews.

Paradoxically, the anti-Jewish policies of Farrakhan have attracted the support of hate groups and individuals, from the Californian racist Tom Metzger and the Liberty Lobby founder Willis Cato to neo-Nazis and members of the Ku Klux Klan. Meetings have taken place between left-wing black nationalists and right-wing racists, condemning Jews as a destructive force in modern life. Such attitudes are shared by a number of US Christian conservative fundamentalists who continue to accuse Jews of killing Christ.

Following the war, French Jews ceased to have confidence in the French state due to its activities during the war: under its auspices thousands of Jews died in labour camps; French gendarmes pursued Jews and crowded them into cattle trucks that transported them to the death camps. In addition, identity cards were stamped with the word 'Juif' as the press denounced the Jewish community. Such actions were barely acknowledged in French historical accounts of the war, and it was commonly believed that Marshal Pétain helped protect Jews despite the legislation directed against them. Further, the French government and judiciary sought to obstruct the trials of French officials such as Maurice Papan, the former Gaullist minister and Paris prefect of police who was instrumental in deporting Jews from Bordeaux. Another figure who was allowed to go free was the prominent banker Réné Bousquet who served as secretary-general of the Vichy police and coordinated the deportation of Jews from the Free Zone.

Another legacy of the Vichy past was the personality cult of Marshal Pétain among the supporters of the National Front that circulated anti-Semitic literature, advocated a revisionist interpretation of the events of the Second World War, and inflamed anti-Jewish sentiment and contempt for Israel. Such anti-Jewish sentiment was the theme of Jean-Paul Sartre's study of anti-Semitism in his *Réflexions sur la Question Juive*. Pondering the silence of his compatriots regarding Jews at the end of the war, he stated:

Today those Jews whom the Germans did not deport or murder are coming back to their homes. Many were among the first members of the Resistance; others had sons or cousins in Leclerc's army. Now all France rejoices in the streets. . . . Do we say nothing about the Jews? Do we give a thought to those who died in the gas chambers at Lublin? Not a word. Not a line in the newspapers. That is because we must not irritate the anti-Semites.

Such determination not to discuss the plight of Jewry continued for twenty years after the war. By the mid-1950s over half of those who identified with the right claimed that Jews were not authentically French. Another poll in the mid-1960s revealed that 20 per cent of the population were anti-Semitic in orientation. After the Six Day War in 1967, the French President Charles de Gaulle referred to Jews as an arrogant, elitist and domineering group. These views evoked the image of Jewish power and domination and encouraged suspicion about Jewish loyalties. During this period the Jewish commentator Raymond Aron claimed that de Gaulle was making anti-Semitism respectable, yet the president was simply expressing a traditional prejudice against Jews that was deeply rooted in the French psyche.

During this period the Communist Party also expressed neo-Stalinist hostility to Zionism. In the 1970s the left-wing media created new themes to manipulate public opinion – Zionism was equated with racism and Nazism, and Israel was perceived as a terrorist state seeking the genocide of the Palestinians. Leftish French Catholics amplified these views, expressing contempt for Jewish xenophobia and exclusivism. By the time of the 1982 war in Lebanon, anti-Jewish discourse had become widespread, combining elements of Christianity, Marxism and Third Worldism. Added to these trends in French society, the emergence of Muslim fundamentalism among North African Arab immigrants further inflamed hostility towards the Jews and Judaism.

In this climate of anti-Jewish sentiment a bomb exploded outside a Paris synagogue in 1980 which was possibly the work of Palestinian terrorists or neo-Nazis. This was followed by a series of attacks on synagogues, schools and other Jewish institutions. An opinion poll taken at the time revealed that over half of the respondents believed that anti-Semitism had become widespread. The 1982 terrorist assault on a Jewish delicatessen in the rue des Rosiers caused six deaths and twenty-four injuries. Simultaneously Jewish graves were desecrated throughout France, resulting in the attack that took place at Carpentras on 9 May 1990: thirty-four graves were damaged or destroyed and a corpse was exhumed and impaled on an umbrella. This desecration was followed by other anti-Semitic incidents throughout the country, ending in a Paris protest by prominent Jews as well as Christians and Muslims.

Despite such public outrage at these anti-Semitic assaults, a number of French citizens were attracted to the radical policies of Jean-Marie Le Pen, who attacked what he perceived as *L'Internationale juive* as well as Jewish control of the media. Publications of the National Front as well as the radical right have advanced revisionist histories of the war, denigrated Jewish politicians and journalists, and accused French Jewry of dual loyalty. Such figures as Roman-Marie, a deputy of the European Parliament, have publicly endorsed the conspiratorial theories expressed in the *Protocols of the Elders of Zion*. As a result of all these activities, the myth of the demonic Jew continues to haunt contemporary French life.

Even though some Poles sought to save Jews from the Nazi onslaught, most remained passive in the face of the German attack. In the years following the Second World War thousands of Poles perished in the Polish Civil War including over a thousand Jews who were killed in anti-Semitic campaigns. A number of these assaults were carried out by the anti-Communist underground who were convinced that Jews were betraying the Poles to the Soviet occupying forces.

During this period a pogrom took place in Kielce where forty Jews were killed and over seventy-five wounded. This attack, which was provoked by a blood libel charge, reflected the unstable atmosphere of the country. Right-wing activists and Catholic bishops viewed this massacre as the consequence of Jewish provocation; others insisted that Communists were responsible for the attack in order to discredit their rivals as well as fascist anti-Semites. The Communists, on the other hand, declared that the attack was the work of ultra-nationalists. Whatever the case, massive emigration ensued.

Those who remained in Poland were determined to create a classless, Communist society. Within the country a number of Jews including Jakob Berman, Hilary Minc and Roman Zambrowski attained important positions of power within the party, the security services and in economic planning. These individuals were widely despised by the populace both as Jews and as servants of the Communist regime. In 1956 these Jewish Stalinists became scapegoats – on a visit to Warsaw, Nikita Khrushchev recommended that they be purged from the party so as to restore its popularity.

In the late 1950s when President Gomulka rose to power, Polish politics became more nationalistic and anti-Semitism, which had previously been suppressed, was integrated into a neo-Stalinist version of Polish xenophobia. By the early 1960s Jews were beginning to be removed from high positions in the party, state government and the civilian and military security services. Senior officers of Jewish origin came under surveillance, and a card index for Polish Jewry was compiled. By the time of the Six Day War in 1967 plans were formulated to purge Jews from all positions of influence.

During this period a campaign of anti-Zionism was initiated and a witchhunt of Jews took place in 1968; this event forced the majority of Jews to emigrate. In the political struggle between two Communist factions – those of Gomulka and General Moczar – the latter appealed to Polish nationalism, anti-Russian sentiment, and anti-Semitism, attracting young members of the party as well as those who belonged to the Veterans Association. In this campaign Gomulka's followers proposed an even more nationalist Communism, devoid of Jewish cosmopolitanism and Marxist revisionism.

Gomulka as party leader advocated anti-Semitism: on 16 June 1967 he accused Polish Jews of launching an anti-Soviet campaign, working as agents of Western imperialism, and propagating Zionism. As a consequence, Jews were removed from the foreign ministry and other government departments, the universities, the press and party schools. In addition, those individuals who had been lifelong Communists were viewed as cosmopolitans and aliens. Further, international Zionism was accused of inciting students during the anti-government protests of November 1968.

During this period Jews were also accused of Trotskyism and Social-Democratic revisionism. In an essay of 1968 the Polish Communist Party theorist Andrzej Werblan stated that it was necessary to correct the ethnic imbalance in government policy. This was essential because, he believed, no society is able to tolerate excessive participation of the national minority in the elite of power, particularly in the organs of national defence, security, propaganda and representation abroad.

Werblan's claim was followed by a campaign against Zionism and world Jewry. Initiated by Moczar and supported by the PAX organization of the pre-war Polish Catholic Fascist Buleslaw Piasecki, this attack led to a mass exodus of those Jews who had remained in Poland. However, despite the disappearance of Polish Jews, anti-Semitism continued as a vital factor in Polish political life. In 1980 to 1981 the Communists sought to discredit Solidarity, the Polish trade union movement, and the dissident organization KOR. In the Communist press Jews were accused of influencing Solidarity, and anti-Semitic pamphlets caricatured the Solidarity advisor Bronislaw Gieremek as a Hasidic Jew. A number of labour activists were also falsely accused of being Jewish. In the elections of 1990 the liberal Catholic Prime Minister, Tadeusz Mazowiecki, was accused of being a crypto-Jew and his government was depicted as being controlled by Jews rather than real Poles.

Such anti-Semitic attitudes were largely fed by previous Christian hostility towards the Jewish community. Many Polish peasants continued to believe in the blood libel accusation; even university students tended to accept the validity of negative Jewish stereotypes. Such opinions were reinforced by the pronouncements of Cardinal Jozef Glemp, the Primate of Poland, who attacked Jewish reservations about the creation of a Carmelite monastery at Auschwitz. Paradoxically, virulent anti-Semitism continued to flourish despite the absence of Jews in Poland.

Following the Second World War, there was renewed suspicion of Russian Jews, and accusations were made about Jewish nationalism as well as rootless cosmopolitanism. In this milieu Nazi anti-Jewish propaganda had a powerful impact on many sections of the Soviet population, particularly in the Ukraine, Belorussia and the Baltic states. As the Cold War intensified, Stalin sought to isolate the USSR from the West and promote a cult of Russian nationalism. In this environment, Jewish Stalinists in eastern European countries expressed loyalty to Moscow, yet they were nonetheless sacrificed in show trials – Communists of Jewish origin were branded as crypto-Zionist traitors.

In the USSR Jewish cultural organizations were eliminated in 1948. Yiddish writers and Jewish artists were arrested and sent to concentration camps in Siberia. Several years later Soviet Yiddish intellectuals were executed or allowed to die in prison. During this period nine doctors – including six Jews – were charged with attempting to poison the Soviet leadership under the direction of Western intelligence organizations and the American Distribution Committee. As a consequence, Jews were expelled from various institutions and assaulted in the streets and schools.

Although Stalin's successors dismissed the accusations against the doctors, they did not attempt to curtail Soviet anti-Semitism. In 1956 Khrushchev condemned Stalin's policies in a report to the Twentieth Party Congress; however, he did not denounce Stalin's policy towards Jews. Instead, he criticized Yevgeny Yevtushenko for drawing attention to anti-Jewish attitudes in his poem 'Babi Yar'. Under Khrushchev's regime atheistic campaigns were relaunched, and Judaism was presented in negative terms. At this time the Ukrainian writer Trofim Kychko published a tract, *Judaism without Embellishment*, which mirrored the anti-Jewish attitudes of the period.

By the 1960s Jews had been removed from the Diplomatic and Foreign Services, leading positions in the army, and important Communist posts. Further, they were unrepresented in Soviet institutions and universities. In 1967 the Six Day War led to an official anti-Jewish policy that continued for two decades: Judaism was portrayed as a criminal religion that advanced an ideology of racial superiority. Hence, during a debate on the Middle East at the United Nations Security Council in 1971, the Soviet ambassador claimed that Zionism is fascist and racist: 'The chosen people,' he asked, 'is that not racism?' 'What is the difference,' he asked, 'between Zionism and Fascism, if the essence of the ideology is racism, hatred towards other peoples? The chosen people. The people elected by God. Where in the second half of the twentieth century does one hear of anyone advocating this criminally absurd theory of the superiority of one race and one people over others?'

During this period, books by anti-Zionists were published, criticizing the Jewish notion of chosenness. Vladimir Begun in *Creeping Counter-Revolution*, for example, argued that Zionist aspirations are based on the Torah, which he caricatured as a textbook of bloodthirstiness, hypocrisy, treason and moral degeneracy. In his view, Zionism had become the central ideology of Jewish bankers in their struggle for world domination, a view reminiscent of the malicious claims promulgated in the forged *Protocols of the Elders of Zion*. Later anti-Zionists became popular lecturers for the nationalist Pamyat organization, and the proliferation of their writings revived latent hostility towards Jews. In addition to such semi-official propaganda, there was an outpouring of novels, essays and pamphlets which portrayed Jews as responsible for undermining Russian life.

Under Gorbachev, chauvinist anti-Semitism flourished, particularly within Pamyat, which spearheaded the Movement for the Restoration of Monuments of Russian Culture, and the Russian Republic Culture Fund. Other organizations with similar attitudes included the Patriot Society, Otchestvo in Novosibirsk, and Rossy in St Petersburg. Publications promoting anti-Semitism included *Nash Sovremenik*, the journal of the Union of Writers of the Russian Republic, *Molodaya Gvardiya*, the Komsomol literary monthly, the weekly *Nedelya*, and the newspaper *Sovietskaya Rossiya*. Among the ranks of those who supported Pamyat were intellectuals whose ideology was grounded in their disillusionment with Communism. Advancing the values of patriotism and traditionalism, they attacked what they perceived as the destructive influences of Western cosmopolitanism.

In *Russophobia*, for example, Igor Shafarevich argued that the Jews seek to destroy the Christian as well as natural foundations of Russian life. This new wave of national loyalty reaffirmed the Stalinist myth of rootless cosmopolitanism. Symbolic of this new movement was an event that occurred in January 1990 when members of Pamyat besieged the Moscow Writers' Club shouting: 'You dirty Jewish mongrels, you're not writers! Get out to Israel! Now we are masters of the country and neither the Party, nor the KGB, nor the militia are going to help you! Next time we'll come with machine guns!' The paradox of the period of glasnost was that it unleashed fury against the Jewish community despite its liberalizing aspirations.

ANTI-SEMITISM IN MODERN TIMES

After the murder of 6 million Jews at the hands of the Nazis it might have been expected that the dangers of anti-Semitism would have been realized. Yet, as we have seen, this has not been the case. In Europe and elsewhere, hostility towards Jews has continued unabated. In Germany immediately following the war, opinion polls revealed that the German populace continued to harbour deep-seated prejudice against Jewry. The majority declared they would not marry a Jew, and in a later poll a third of the respondents evaluated Hitler positively and a similar proportion stated that anti-Semitism was caused principally by Jewish characteristics. In another poll taken at the same time 37 per cent of the population believed it would be better for Germany not to have any Jews.

After the war, many ex-Nazis were employed by the military government, and academics with a Nazi record, German judges who had enforced Nazi law, and former Nazis in various positions of power retained their positions. Only a small number of Nazis were tried in the courts – the vast majority went free. In later years the Nazi past was repressed as much as possible, and the establishment of the Federal Republic was viewed as a new beginning for the German nation. In the 1960s the German new left denounced Israel for its policies towards the Palestinians and demonized Zionists. In their view, those who had previously been persecuted had become persecutors once they were empowered in their own country.

With the resurgence of pride in German national identity and the return to normality in the 1980s, anti-Jewish sentiment has increased. Public opinion polls have revealed that many Germans still regard Jews as devious and greedy, and consider that they are ruthless in exploiting the Nazi past for personal gain and support of Israel. Paradoxically, anti-Semitism has flourished in the absence of a sizeable Jewish population; such hostility is based on stereotypes deeply entrenched in the national consciousness as well as on unresolved conflicts concerning Germany's recent past. In the new united Germany, the Jewish question continues to haunt the present as it did the first half of the last century.

Similarly, as we noted, Austria has witnessed the persistence of anti-Jewish attitudes. The de-Nazification of the country was superficial, and by 1949 most ex-Nazis had been re-enfranchised. In this context the Socialists and the Catholic Conservatives competed for the former Nazi vote. Even though Bruno Kreisky, a Jewish-born socialist, became chancellor in 1970, this did not bring about a fundamental change in perception. Kreisky himself continued to employ anti-Semitic discourse, and his Cabinet contained three former Nazis. As chancellor, Kreisky sought to discredit Simon Wiesenthal, the Austrian Nazi-hunter, whom he labelled a 'Jewish fascist'. When Kurt Waldheim, former General Secretary of the United Nations, was attacked for his Nazi past, latent Judaeophobia that had previously inhibited the articulation of anti-Jewish prejudice was openly expressed.

In Eastern Europe similar attitudes prevailed. In Poland those Jews who remained after the war were committed to creating a new classless order based on Communist principles. Some Jews became important figures in the government, but were widely detested. During October 1956 the Jewish Stalinists became a scapegoat for the ills afflicting society. Once Gomulka came to power after 1957, Polish nationalism became a central feature of Communist ideology, stressing the Polishness of the country. Even though anti-Semitism had been viewed by Communists as a reactionary response, it was incorporated into a neo-Stalinist variant of Polish chauvinism.

From the early 1960s Jews were slowly being removed from the party leadership: senior officials of Jewish origin were under surveillance, and an index of Polish Jewry was being prepared. The anti-Semitic campaign that began in 1967–8 eventually forced two-thirds of Polish Jews to emigrate. In the 1980s a renewed attack on Polish Jewry took place as part of the campaign to discredit Solidarity and the dissident organization KOR. The Communist press charged that KOR activists who served Jewish interests were influencing Solidarity. With the collapse of Communism in Poland,

Lech Walesa appealed to anti-Jewish feelings. During this period anti-Jewish stereotypes and animosities were reactivated.

In Russia a similar resurgence of Jew-hatred occurred in the postwar period. As we saw, the years between 1948 and 1953 witnessed a campaign against Russian Jewry: Jewish nationalism and rootless cosmopolitanism were regarded as characteristic of the Jewish population. During the Cold War Stalin sought to seal the USSR off from all Westernizing influences, and the Jews became a scapegoat for his policies. In various show-trials leading Communists of Jewish origin were labelled 'crypto-Zionist' traitors, and many famous Jewish authors were secretly executed or allowed to die in prison.

Although Khrushchev later denounced Stalin's policies, he consciously omitted such crimes from his list of criticisms. As we noted, his attack on the Russian poet Yevgeny Yevtushenko for referring to Soviet anti-Semitism in his poem 'Babi Yar' illustrated his contempt for Jews and Judaism. During this period Khrushchev initiated the Soviet alliance with Nasser and the Arab world as part of a Third-World strategy based on a condemnation of Israel and Zionism. By the 1960s, Jews had been largely eliminated from leading positions in the government, and their numbers in the academic and professional elite had diminished since the 1930s.

The ongoing conflict in the Middle East also significantly affected Soviet attitudes to Jews worldwide. The Six Day War of 1967 provoked an anti-Jewish campaign. Even though the State of Israel was the object of such criticism, Judaism was castigated as a morally deficient religious tradition that promoted racial superiority and hatred. At the UN Security Council, Zionism was described by the Soviet ambassador as fascist and racist. Such contempt was reflected in a variety of books, which denounced the Jewish concept of chosenness and castigated Jewish religious texts. According to Vladimir Begun in *Creeping Counter-Revolution*, Zionist gangsterism was based on the Torah. In addition, he argued that Jewish capitalists and businessmen were behind the monk Rasputin who had dominated the tsarist court. According to Begun and others, Zionism had become the policy of the Jewish banking world in its quest for world supremacy. Later ultra-nationalist organizations have sought to promote anti-Jewish attitudes. Disillusioned with Communism, they advance patriotism and traditional values and have attacked the destructive influence of Western cosmopolitanism that is epitomized for them by Jewish interests.

It might be expected that in the United States anti-Semitism would have disappeared in the postwar years. This, however, has not been the case. In 1938 opinion polls demonstrated that antipathy towards Jews was widespread: 41 per cent agreed that Jews had too much power in the country; by 1945, this figure had risen to 58 per cent despite the war against Germany. In the view of many Americans, Jews were greedy and dishonest. During this period a number of pollsters pointed out that the Jews were regarded as one of the greatest threats to American society.

After the Second World War, anti-Semitism began to decline. With the economic success of the 1950s and 1960s, the position of Jews improved enormously. By the 1970s and 1980s a significant number of Jews were concentrated in the upper ranks of the professions. As a consequence, Jews no longer felt defensive and powerless. During this period, a number of American Jewish organizations successfully combated educational and social discrimination, thereby diminishing the impact of anti-Semitic propaganda. However, it was generally acknowledged that there had been a rise in anti-Jewish hostility in the black community. In the mid-1960s, the emergence of the struggle of American blacks against the discriminatory and repressive features of American society provoked bitter disputes between black and Jewish leaders.

As we have noted, in 1964 the black nationalist leader Malcolm X castigated Jews in America and Europe for their pro-Israel stance. Together with other militants, he argued that US aid to Israel was used for its aggression against the Third World. In his opinion, such financial support was taken from the needy black community at home to help support the Jewish cause in the Middle East. Jewish business in Harlem, he suggested, was conducted by colonialists who were intent on exploiting the black community just as Western colonialists had done in previous centuries. After 1967 the rhetoric of the Black Panthers identified Zionism with racism and fascism.

The effects of radical Third World ideology were manifest in the 1984 presidential campaign of Jesse Jackson who adopted an anti-Israeli and pro-Palestinian platform. More recently, the black leader of the Nation of Islam, Louis Farrakhan, has been outspoken in his condemnation of Jews and Judaism. Born in 1933, Farrakhan joined the Nation of Islam in 1955, eventually becoming its leader. Within the movement, he has advanced the cause of blacks in America, encouraging them to achieve social and economic advances. In 1991 he reintroduced the Three Year Economic

Programme to establish an economic base for the development of blacks through business ventures. As part of the major thrust for political empowerment of the black community, he formed a coalition of religious, civic and political organizations to represent the voice of the disenfranchised.

The Nation of Islam advocates black separatism along with some of the practices and beliefs of Islam. One of its main goals is for blacks to attain self-sufficiency. Farrakhan, however, has frequently been criticized as a racist and is widely regarded as anti-Semitic. Both the Nation of Islam and Farrakhan have a long, well-documented record of hate-filled and anti-Semitic rhetoric. Over the years, Nation of Islam ministers and representatives have regularly expressed anti-Semitic, anti-white, anti-homosexual and anti-Catholic sentiments in their speeches. Furthermore, the official organ of the movement, *The Final Call*, reflects the anti-Semitism of Farrakhan and his organization.

In a speech delivered in 1991, Farrakhan argued that he does not hate Jews. 'I want to tell all of you I have never been anti-Semitic,' he stated.

> I have never been a hater of Jews, nor am I now that, but I discovered in my tussle with them that they were on me because I had the nerve to pull the cover off some deceitful practices that they practice on us and on others. And so they tried to make me the worst black man in history. When they did that, some Muslims in the Nation rose up to defend me and went into libraries and did research and compiled a manuscript of over 300 pages from their own writings not from us. And not one scholar that we quote is an anti-Semite. Here are Jewish rabbis, Jewish scholars, Jewish writers. They document their own hand in the slave trade.

Continuing this catalogue of crimes, Farrakhan points out that 'they tell us how they supplied smallpox to General Amherst to send the blankets among the Native Americans – it's all here. I'm going to send this to every Jewish person that has attacked me.'

In a number of interviews in 1997 Farrakhan focused on the problems of blacks in America, seeking to project himself as a concerned mainstream black leader. Most of the interviewers, however, focused on the issue of anti-Semitism. Discussing dialogue with Jews on the TV programme *Fox News Sunday* on 30 March, Farrakhan stated: 'Are you afraid of the truth that is in my mouth? If you can defeat what I believe is truth, you have no problem with me. I'll apologize to you before the entire world.' On *Meet the Press* on 14 April, Farrakhan reaffirmed his beliefs about Jewish control and conspiracy. 'I believe,' he said, 'that for the small numbers of Jewish people in the United States, they exercise a tremendous amount of influence in the affairs of government. . . . Yes, they exercise extraordinary control, and black people will never be free in this country until they are free of that kind of control.' At the same time, he also insinuated that Jewish bankers financed Hitler.

Interviewed several months later on the same programme, Farrakhan was asked why he would not apologize for his past statements, such as referring to Jews as 'bloodsuckers' and alleging that the Jews had dominated the slave trade in the colonial period. 'I want to sit down and dialogue with members of the Jewish community,' he stated, ' with no preconditions. That demand for me to apologize comes out of an arrogance that makes one feel that if I am critical of Jewish behaviour relative to Black people, that all of a sudden I have to apologize for being critical.'

Responding to the attack on the World Trade Center on 11 September 2001, Farrakhan spoke of the tragedy of this event. Yet, at the same time, he condemned Israel for its treatment of the Palestinian people:

The Palestinians believe they have sustained injustice since 1948. Whether you agree or disagree, from their point of view, they have not had justice. They have cried out in every forum for the redress of their grievances and justice has not come. They live in refugee camps, are scattered throughout the world and every day they live with the horror of what they suffer. So more and more minds become imbalanced to the degree that life has no more meaning, for there is no joy in being free if there is no justice. Joy is the result of justice. Out of despair and hopelessness and waking up everyday without the joy of justice, this is what causes children to strap themselves to bombs. They care nothing for their lives, and they care nothing for the lives of others.

Seeking to explain the reaction of Palestinians to this tragedy, he went on: 'Some Palestinians danced in the streets, not because they have no feeling for American life. They danced because they wanted America to feel what they feel, what they have lived with.' Cautioning America on the possibility of further violence, he stressed the need to solve the problem of the Middle East. Insistent that America alter its foreign policy, he declared: 'A better foreign policy of America would defeat terrorism forever in the world.

I hope that President Bush and those with him will turn this tragedy into the triumph of right over wrong, of good over evil, of justice over injustice, and let not the blood of those who died be shed in vain.'

We can thus see that in the modern world the scourge of anti-Semitism has not disappeared, despite the terrors of the Holocaust. Instead, throughout Western and Eastern Europe and extending to the United States, the flames of Judaeophobia have been kept alive. Anti-Semitism lurks furtively in the world at large. In the wake of the wars, instability and uprisings in the Middle East, Muslims today carry the banner of anti-Semitism and constitute a constant threat to Jewish survival. According to a recent survey, while rightists continue to harass Jews in Europe and elsewhere, violent attacks are perpetrated by Muslim extremists. For example, the only anti-Semitic terrorist act in Europe during 1995 was carried out not by skinheads but by an Algerian fundamentalist group. Muslims from South Africa to Argentina to Sweden outscore the right in terms of the reach of their anti-Semitic rhetoric and actions.

The same pattern holds true for the United States. Explicit, virulent anti-Semitism, such as that stemming from the Nation of Islam, has become increasingly pervasive. The influence of the Nation of Islam is far more extensive than that of right-wing groups because of its organizational network. Unlike the Ku Klux Klan, it has an organized paramilitary force in dozens of cities. It regularly packs thousands of listeners into arenas where they are exposed to virulent attacks on the Jewish community. As a result, American blacks speak in overtly anti-Semitic terms hardly found elsewhere in the West.

TWENTY

Modern Arab Jew-hatred

Although the British government was initially favourable to the creation of a Jewish homeland in Palestine, its policy changed due to Arab pressure. In May 1939 a White Paper was published that limited the number of immigrants to 75,000 over the next five years and none thereafter, except with Arab permission. Such a stance evoked widespread Jewish resistance. After a campaign of terror, Britain handed over the Palestinian problem to the United Nations. On 29 November 1947 a recommendation that there be both an Arab and a Jewish state was passed by the UN General Assembly. Immediately the Arabs began to attack Jewish settlements, and the Jews were forced to defend their new state. On 14 May 1948, Prime Minister David Ben-Gurion read out the Scroll of Independence in the Tel Aviv Museum. In subsequent years Arabs and Jews have repeatedly engaged in battle, and this conflict has given rise to rabid Arab anti-Semitism.

DEVELOPMENTS IN PALESTINE

Despite the change in British policy, the Higher Arab Committee that met in Beirut rejected the White Paper of 1939. Hence, the British ruled in Palestine without the consent of either Jews or Arabs. From the Jewish side, immigration became the overriding concern in light of the Nazi threat. In response the British terminated their relationship with the Haganah and increased their efforts to police entry into Palestine. Bitterly critical of such actions, the Jewish Agency repudiated the Mandatory policy limiting immigration, and a number of Revisionists insisted on the need for retaliation.

During this period the Twenty-First Zionist Congress met in Geneva on 16–26 August 1939 and declared its opposition to the policy of the White Paper. At the Congress, Ben-Gurion stated that the White Paper created a vacuum in Palestine, which would have to be filled by the Jewish community itself. The Jews, he claimed, should act as though they were an independent state. During the Congress, Hitler announced the Nazi-Soviet pact. Aware of the implications for European Jewry, the delegates vowed to press Jewish interests in Palestine and to ensure that Germany be defeated in the war.

Before the end of 1941, 10,881 soldiers enlisted in the British forces serving in Palestine; by the end of 1942, approximately 18,000 were serving in the military. Owing to this increase in numbers, the Jews pressed for the creation of large Jewish units. Fearful of Arab resentment, the British refused. In Palestine, the Yishuv supported the British in the war effort. Not only did the Irgun suspend its pre-war terrorist activities, but a pro-British spirit became the dominant attitude of Jews living in the Holy Land. Inevitably, however, such a *rapprochement* between the Irgun and the British gave rise to serious misgivings.

A section of the Irgun headed by Avraham Stern, known as Lehi or the Stern Gang, made an offer to Hitler to assist in the conquest of Palestine in exchange for the transfer of the Jews of Europe. In the early years of the war, Ben-Gurion was the dominant figure in the Yishuv; with Irgun and Lehi on the margin. After the events of May 1940, Ben-Gurion focused on defeating the Germans rather than overturning the White Paper. Victory over Hitler, he believed, had become the key issue. Now that Churchill had replaced Chamberlain, the Yishuv believed that the White Paper would be discarded. Yet, once Italy entered the war, the British believed that the policy of restricting immigration should continue so as not to antagonize the Arabs. At the same time, the Nazi conquests increased the need for Jews to have a safe haven in the Middle East.

During this period, the British feared that the Arabs under the influence of Hajj Amin, who was living in exile, might again stage a revolt. In October 1939 the Grand Mufti left Beirut for Baghdad where he was greeted as a hero. Working on behalf of a pro-Axis war effort which culminated in a coup headed by Rashid Ali, he issued a *fatwah* (an official ruling) on 9 May 1941 that was broadcast over Iraqi and Axis radios. Proclaiming *jihad* (holy war) against the British, he declared that they had profaned the al-Aqsa Mosque and had been waging a war against Iran.

Escaping from Baghdad along with Rashid Ali, he fled to Teheran; however, when the Soviet and British forces occupied Iran in September 1941, the Mufti made his way to Berlin. On 21 November 1941, Hitler received the Mufti, who told the Führer about his struggle with the Jewish people. Hitler stated that he was not at present prepared to help the Arabs in this conflict; such cooperation could not take place until the defeat of Russia. When German forces reached the southern Caucasus, he stated, then the hour of Arab liberation would have arrived.

In November 1942 a group of Palestinian citizens was permitted to leave Poland and return to Palestine; they brought news of the Nazi onslaught against the Jews. In December this report was confirmed by the Allied governments. In a speech at the Berlin Sports Palace on 30 September 1942, Hitler recalled a prophecy he had made three years earlier that if Jewry were to start a world war in order to eliminate Aryans from Europe, it would be the Jews who would be eliminated instead.

During this period a number of Jews were helped to escape from Europe by the United Rescue Committee. This body represented all factions in the Yishuv and worked together with the Jewish underground operating in Europe. In 1943–4 Haganah volunteers were parachuted into the Balkans to collect military evidence and to aid in this escape work. Through their actions about 10,000 people were able to emigrate to Palestine. Within the Yishuv, however, the Allies' apparent indifference to the plight of European Jewry as well as Britain's support of limited immigration caused considerable frustration.

The election of a Labour government after the war appeared to offer hope to the Zionist cause. Repeatedly, the Labour Party had shown its opposition to the White Paper, and in 1944 and 1945 it expressed its commitment to the creation of a Jewish National Home as well as to unlimited immigration to Palestine. Nonetheless, when US President Truman indicated his wish that the British government lift the White Paper's restrictions on Jewish immigration, the new Prime Minister, Clement Attlee, sent back an ambiguous response. Truman continued to apply pressure on the British, and in August 1945 he sent Attlee a report on the conditions of 100,000 Jewish survivors of the concentration camps who were now housed in camps in Germany and Austria.

In reply Attlee stated that the Jews had little more to complain about than many other peoples who were compelled to endure such conditions and should not receive favourable treatment. By September it became apparent that the Labour Party would not alter the restrictions of the White Paper, and only a limited number of Jews would be allowed into Palestine. Bitterly opposed to such a stance Ben-Gurion warned that Jews would fight against Britain if such attitudes prevailed. On 1 October, Ben-Gurion sent a telegram instructing the Haganah to instigate armed uprisings against

British forces. Subsequently, the Haganah issued daily broadcasts over its illegal Voice of Israel radio station. Simultaneously the Haganah re-established links with the Irgun and Lehi. On 31 October 1945 the Palestine railway system was blown up, an act of defiance defended by all segments of the Yishuv.

In May 1946 the Anglo-American Committee of Inquiry recommended that Palestine become a bi-national state with the immediate admission of 100,000 Jews, a proposal welcomed by Truman. In a statement to the House of Commons, Attlee declared that Britain would not implement this recommendation unless the United States was prepared to share the added military and financial responsibilities. The next month Ernest Bevin explained to the Labour Party Conference that the reason the Americans were anxious that Jews immigrate to Palestine was because the United States did not itself want to absorb so many new immigrants. During the same month the Attlee government authorized the High Commissioner, Sir Alan Cunningham, to carry out searches in the main Jewish centres. As a consequence thousands of Jews were arrested, including members of the Jewish Agency. Although the Agency had previously condemned acts of terrorism, it had refused to cooperate with the authorities against the Irgun and Lehi.

By the end of June, Britain had resolved to suspend such disciplinary action even though it had not disarmed the Haganah. Such a change in policy was a result of pressure applied by American Jews on public opinion regarding the postwar loan to Britain that was before Congress. A prominent American Zionist, Dr Abba Hillel Silver, had urged Jews to ask their congressman whether the United States should make a loan to Britain given its policies in Palestine. Under such pressure, the British reversed their policy towards the Jewish Agency and the Haganah. At the end of July the Irgun blew up the government offices in the King David Hotel, killing about eighty British, Jewish and Arab civil servants and wounding about seventy others. A four day curfew was imposed and the British carried out intensive searches.

In the Muslim world, pressure was initially applied on Britain through agitation against American investment in Arab lands. Yet when it became clear that such actions would adversely affect Arab interests, the plan to impose Arab sanctions in support of the Palestinian cause disintegrated. Nonetheless, the Arab states were anxious to help the Palestinian cause. In May the Mufti arrived in Cairo. Although he was not allowed to travel to Palestine, he was able to influence Arab affairs in Palestine through the Higher Executive Committee. This body was supported by the Arab states, and with British encouragement had formed the Arab League. At a conference with the British in London in September, the Arab nations demanded that an independent Arab state be created in Palestine no later than 31 December 1948.

From 1947 the political climate in Britain underwent a transformation. For some time the opposition had urged that the Mandate be rescinded. With the failure of the London talks, Churchill urged that the United Nations take over control of Palestine. On 18 February 1947, the British government announced that it had no power under the Mandate to determine whether Palestine belonged to the Arabs or the Jews. As a consequence, the only course open was to submit the problem to the United Nations. To facilitate this transition, Britain requested that a Special Session of the General Assembly be convened to consider this issue.

This meeting, which took place from 28 April to 15 May 1947, resolved to set up an investigative eleven-member body – the United Nations Special Committee on Palestine (UNSCOP) – which was to report by the autumn. During the summer, members of the Special Committee went to Palestine. On the day they arrived a British military court sentenced three members of the Irgun to death. Although the committee appealed against this decree, its plea was ignored. The Irgun then captured two British sergeants on 12 July and threatened to kill them if the British carried out these sentences.

At the end of the month the Irgun members were executed; in retaliation the Irgun hanged the two sergeants. This event evoked widespread antipathy towards Zionism in Britain, and British troops in Tel Aviv rioted. Five Jews were killed, but no one was ever charged for these murders. During this period of unrest Jewish refugees continued to flood into Palestine. On 31 August UNSCOP completed its report, recommending the end of the British Mandate. A majority report recommended that Palestine be partitioned into an Arab and a Jewish state with an international zone to administer the Holy Places. The British expressed disdain for the report, and the Arabs were bitterly opposed. On 17 October 1947, the British government made it clear that it would not accept responsibility for the enforcement of such a settlement. On 29 November the UN General Assembly formally considered the report: 33 delegates voted in favour; 13 were opposed; including the 11 Muslim states. There were 10 abstentions. A two-thirds majority had thus been achieved.

In December the British indicated that they would continue to rule Palestine until 15 May 1948. The Mandate would then come to an end. In the remaining months British forces would be used only in self-defence; this meant that they would not intervene in any conflict between Arab and Jew. In November the Jewish population was subjected to a number of attacks. These were followed by retaliation against the Arabs in which both the Haganah and the Irgun played a role. In these new circumstances the policy of self-restraint was abandoned. In April 1948 the Irgun attacked Deir Yassin, an Arab village near Jerusalem, killing 107 citizens, an onslaught that led to the flight of the Arab population from areas with large Jewish populations. By mid-May about 300,000 Arabs had fled, seeking refuge in neighbouring countries. In retaliation for this massacre, the Arabs ambushed a medical convoy, killing seventy-five doctors, nurses, teachers and students.

During this period Weizmann was lobbying in Washington attempting to persuade President Truman of the need for a Jewish state. Despite the threat of Arab attack, on 14 May 1948 in Tel Aviv, Ben-Gurion and other leaders put their signatures to Israel's Declaration of Independence. The document opened by describing the Land of Israel as the birthplace of the Jewish people, and looked back to the Jewish past. It went on to explain that the Jewish people had prayed and hoped for their return to the land of their ancestors, and strove in every generation to re-establish themselves in their ancient homeland. In recent times they had returned as pioneers and defenders and had created a thriving community.

Recounting the stages of historical development, the Declaration emphasized the destruction of European Jewry under the Nazi regime and the urgency of creating a Jewish nation. Through the partition resolution of 1947, the United Nations had recognized the right of the Jewish people to establish their own state, which would henceforth be known as the State of Israel. This Jewish state, the Declaration concluded, would be open for immigration and would be based on freedom, justice and peace as envisaged by the prophets of Israel. To Israel's Arab neighbours the state extended an offer of peace and good neighbourliness, and to Jews living in the diaspora it appealed for support.

Following Arab attacks against Israel on 11 June 1948 a truce was concluded, but in the next month conflict broke out and the Israelis seized Lydda, Ramleh and Nazareth as well as large areas beyond the partition frontiers. Within ten days the Arabs agreed to another truce, but outbreaks of hostility continued. In mid-October the Israelis attempted to open the road to the Negev settlements and took Beersheba. On 12 January 1949 armistice talks took place in Rhodes and an armistice was later signed by Egypt, Lebanon, Transjordan and Syria. These events created the ongoing Arab-Palestinian problem with 656,000 Arab inhabitants fleeing Israeli-held territories: 280,000 to the West Bank; 70,000 to Transjordan; 100,000 to Lebanon; 4,000 to Iraq; 75,000 to Syria; 7,000 to Egypt; and 190,000 to the Gaza Strip.

On the basis of the 1949 armistice, the Israelis sought agreement on the boundaries of the Jewish state. The Arabs, however, refused to consider this proposal; instead, they insisted that Israel return to the 1947 partition lines without giving any formal recognition to the new state. Further, despite the concluding of the armistice, fedayeen bands continued to attack Israeli citizens, and boycotts and blockades sought to injure Israel's economy. After King Abdullah was assassinated on 20 June 1951, a military junta ousted the Egyptian monarchy and on February 1954 President Gemal Abdul Nasser gained control of the country. From September 1955, the Soviet bloc supplied weapons to the Arabs, and this encouraged Nasser to take steps against the Jewish state. From 1956 he denied Israeli ships access to the Gulf of Aqaba (they had already been prevented from using the Suez Canal). In April 1956 he signed a pact with Saudi Arabia and Yemen, and in July he seized the Suez Canal. Fearing Arab intentions, Israel launched a pre-emptive strike on 29 October, and in the war that followed Israel captured all of Sinai as well as Gaza, and opened a sea route to Aqaba.

At the end of the Sinai War Israel undertook to withdraw from Sinai as long as Egypt did not remilitarize it and UN forces formed a protective *cordon sanitaire*. This arrangement endured for ten years, but attacks continued. In 1967 Nasser launched another offensive, and on 15 May he moved 100,000 men and armour into Sinai and expelled the UN army. On 22 May he blockaded Aqaba; several days later King Hussein of Jordan signed a military agreement in Cairo. On the same day Iraqi forces took up positions in Jordan. In the face of this Arab threat, Israel launched a strike on 5 June, destroying the Egyptian air force on the ground. On 7 June the Israeli army took the Old City, thereby making Jerusalem its capital. On the next day the Israeli forces occupied the entire Left Bank, and during the next few days captured the Golan Heights and reoccupied Sinai.

Despite such a crushing defeat against such numerically superior odds, the Six Day War did not bring security to the Jewish state. Nasser's successor President Anwar Sadat expelled Egypt's Soviet military advisers in July 1972, cancelled the country's political and military alliance with other

Arab states, and together with Syria attacked Israel on Yom Kippur, 6 October 1973. With surprise on their side, at the outbreak of war the Egyptians and the Syrians broke through Israeli defences, but by 9 October the Syrian advance had been repelled. On 10 October US President Richard Nixon began an airlift of advanced weapons to Israel; two days later the Israelis engaged in a counter-attack on Egypt and moved towards victory. On 24 October a cease-fire came into operation.

Later, after the Israeli Labour coalition lost the May 1977 election and handed over power to the Likud headed by Menahem Begin, Sadat offered to negotiate peace terms with Israel. On 5 September 1978 at the American presidential home Camp David, the process of reaching such an agreement began and was completed thirteen days later (although another six months were required before a detailed treaty was formulated). The treaty specified that Egypt would recognize Israel's right to exist and provide secure guarantees for her southern border. In return Israel would hand over Sinai. In addition she would undertake to negotiate away much of the West Bank and make concessions over Jerusalem as long as a complementary treaty was agreed with the Palestinians and other Arab countries. This latter step, however, was never taken: the proposal was rejected by the Palestinian Arabs. This meant that Israel was left with the responsibility for overseeing Arab occupied territories.

In the years that followed, Arab influence grew immeasurably, due to Arab control of oil in the Middle East. As the price of oil increased, Arab revenue provided huge sums for the purchase of armaments. At the UN the Arab world exerted its power, and in 1975, the General Assembly passed a resolution equating Zionism with racism. Further, Yasser Arafat, the leader of the Palestine Liberation Organization (PLO), was accorded head of government status by the UN. Fearing the growing threat of Palestinian influence and terrorism, Israel launched an advance into southern Lebanon in June 1982, destroying PLO bases. This Israeli onslaught and subsequent occupation served as the background to the killing of Muslim refugees by Christian Falangist Arabs in the Sabra and Shatilla camps on 16 September 1982. Throughout the world this atrocity was portrayed as Israel's fault. In response to this criticism, the Israeli government ordered an independent inquiry that placed some blame on the Israeli Minister of Defence, Ariel Sharon, for not having prevented the massacre.

After the Israeli conquests during the Yom Kippur War, the State of Israel took control of the Occupied Territories. In the following years the

Palestinians staged demonstrations, strikes and riots against Israeli rule. By 1987 the Palestinians in the West Bank and Gaza were largely young educated people who had benefited from formal education. Yet despite such educational advances, they suffered from limited job expectations and this situation led to political radicalism. Such frustration came to a head on 9 December 1987 in Jabaliya, the most militant of the Gaza refugee camps. An Israeli patrol was trapped there during a protest about the death of four Jabaliya residents who had been killed in a road accident the previous day. The soldiers shot their way out, killing one youth and wounding ten others. This event provoked riots throughout the Occupied Territories. By January 1989 the Israeli Defence Forces declared that 352 Palestinians had died, more than 4,300 were wounded and 25,600 arrested. In addition, 200 Arab homes had been sealed or demolished. As hostilities increased, the *intifada* (resistance) demonstrated that occupying the West Bank and the Gaza Strip would pose a perpetual problem.

The Jewish state was unprepared for such a situation, and the army was forced to improvise. As time passed, the *intifada* became resilient and its tactics changed to ambushes, small-scale conflicts and selective strikes. In addition, modern technologies of communications – including radio, fax and photocopying – were used to apply pressure on the Israelis. In the view of many observers, this uprising had transformed the Palestinian people. Thus Dr Eyad Sarraj, the Arab director of mental health services in the Gaza Strip, declared:

> The uprising has dramatically transformed the Palestinian self-image. They have regained their self-respect. They feel they have scored a significant victory over the Israelis. For the first time they feel equal, even more powerful. The national identity has been strengthened and sharpened; there is a new cohesion. A high level of aspiration is replacing hopelessness. People are now talking of an end of the occupation as a matter of fact.

Again, Dr Ali Kleibo, an anthropologist at the University of Bethlehem, emphasized that the *intifada* was being used to change the nature of Palestinian existence:

> People are using it to question the traditional institutions of Palestinian life, be it the educational system, the importance of community action (something that has never happened before), the reorganization of the village into an

educational, political and economic unit that goes beyond the *hamula* [extended family]. The level of solidarity that you see now never existed before. We are totally involved in questioning relations that before seemed sacrosanct, that appeared to us as absolute. The system is being reshuffled – with the Israelis, with our village, with our family, the whole system. And we are the ones who are reshuffling it.

Despite having such a profound impact on the fabric of Palestinian life and attitudes, the *intifada* created tensions within the Palestinian community. As the resistance developed, Islamic revivalism spread from the Gaza Strip to the West Bank and Jerusalem and posed a serious threat to secular Palestinian nationalism. Such a division was aggravated with the PLO who endorsed a two-stage solution to the Palestinian problem, a policy that was bitterly condemned by fundamentalists. Hamas, the Islamic Resistance Movement, insisted on the goal of a Muslim Palestine stretching from the Mediterranean to the Jordan. Clause 11 of its manifesto declared:

The Islamic Resistance Movement believes that all the land of Palestine is sacred to Islam, through all the generations and forever, and it is forbidden to abandon it or part of it, or to yield it or part of it. No Arab state individually has the right, nor do all of the Arab states collectively, nor does any king or president individually, nor do all the kings and presidents collectively. No organization individually has the right, nor do all the organizations collectively, whether they are Palestinian or Arab.

Yasser Arafat, however, adopted a more pragmatic approach and abandoned such maximalist formulations of the Palestinian position in favour of a policy that took into account the reality of Israel's existence.

From the Israeli side, the Israeli Defence Forces viewed the *intifada* in the context of Israel's relationship with its Palestinian neighbours and the world in general. As a result, General Shomron ruled out the use of massive force in dealing with this issue. 'The *intifada*,' he stated, 'will end at some point.' But the question remains what legacy it will leave. 'I am saying,' he claimed, 'that therefore do not think that we have an interest in causing a great deal of suffering, even though we can do so the moment we take such a decision.' Similarly, Brigadier-General Zvi Poleg, who took over as commander of the Israeli Defence Forces in the Gaza Strip in 1988, stressed that the *intifada* was not a war. 'I'm a military commander,' he declared, 'but you must be able to see a number of aspects of the problem, and not just see it through the gunsights, because you're working with human beings. If a local person gets hurt, gets killed, you must first of all remember that he is a human being. He was born to live. So if there's no absolute need to shoot, don't.'

Despite such a stance, the *intifada* was generally regarded as more than a local skirmish, and throughout the world Israelis were considered guilty of brutality. As a result, there was a growing feeling that Israel should abandon the Occupied Territories. Thus a poll conducted by Professor Elihu Katz, Director of the Hebrew University's Israel Institute of Applied Social Research, in January 1989 revealed considerable sympathy for the idea of a Palestinian state.

On 2 August 1990 the Iraqi leader Saddam Hussein decided to invade Kuwait. Joining with the United States, Israel demanded Iraq's withdrawal from Kuwait. On 17 January 1991 a coalition of Allied forces attacked the Iraqi army in Kuwait. Israel was encouraged not to participate in this conflict. Although there was resistance among leading figures in the government, Israel complied despite Iraq's use of Scud missiles against the country. When Saddam was defeated, the population of Israel was deeply relieved.

Nevertheless the *intifada* continued. Throughout 1991 attacks on Jews and Palestinian collaborators intensified. By September, 1,225 Arabs had died, of whom 697 had been killed by Israeli forces; the others were killed by fellow Arabs. In addition, thirteen Israeli soldiers had been killed by Arabs. Israel was determined not to recognize the PLO. Hence, when Ezer Weizman met with Arafat in Vienna, he was sacked by Samir. Yet, through James Baker's intervention, it was agreed that the Palestinians would be represented by people from the Occupied Territories who would form a joint Jordanian–Palestinian delegation.

In October the Madrid Conference opened with Presidents Bush and Gorbachev as the main speakers. Israel was represented by Prime Minister Yitzhak Shamir, and the Arab states by their foreign ministers. In December another conference took place in Washington dealing with the procedures for future talks. Israel insisted it was not willing to discuss territorial concessions; rather it desired to focus on Palestinian autonomy. The Palestinians, however, were not content with such a limitation on their aspirations. After these talks, Jews and Arabs met in a number of cities to explore various practical issues.

Such collaborative ventures were interrupted by the Israeli elections, in which Labour became the largest party; forming an alliance with the left-wing party Meretz and the Arab Democratic Party. The religious party Shas, too, joined the coalition. As Prime Minister Yitzhak Rabin was committed to continuing the peace process as well as the absorption of Russian immigrants into the country. Seeking to extend the agenda beyond the subjects discussed at Madrid and Washington, Rabin stated that the Israeli government would propose a continuation of the talks based on the framework of the Madrid Conference. Aware of Palestinian suffering in previous decades, Rabin proposed a form of Palestinian self-government in the West Bank and Gaza Strip.

On 19 July 1992 James Baker arrived in the Middle East to seek a solution to the conflict between Israel and its neighbours. Two days later Rabin went to Cairo to renew negotiations for a peace settlement. The next month he travelled to the United States to meet President Bush. In September Shimon Peres, acting foreign minister, met Prime Minister John Major in London. Despite these steps, tensions mounted in the West Bank and Jerusalem during November and December. These efforts to renew the peace process only served to inflame the feelings of members of Hamas and Islamic Jihad who were bitterly opposed to compromise.

Against a background of continuing violence, talks between Israel and the PLO began on 20 January 1993. At a villa outside Oslo representatives met for three days. At the meeting several PLO delegates submitted proposals involving the Israeli withdrawal from the Gaza Strip, a mini-Marshall Plan for the West Bank and Gaza to inject much-needed funds, and economic cooperation between Israel and the Palestinian authorities. On 11 February the Oslo talks continued, and a draft declaration of principles was drawn up as well as a paper establishing guidelines for a regional Marshall Plan. Between 20 and 22 March secret meetings took place in Oslo from which it seemed that an accord between Israel and the PLO might emerge. On 13 September 1993 a ceremony took place in Washington with Yitzhak Rabin and Yasser Arafat as the main representatives. In the following months Israel and the PLO engaged in active negotiations for an Israeli withdrawal from the West Bank and the Gaza Strip.

As these steps were being taken towards peace, on 25 February 1994 an Israeli gunman, Baruch Goldstein, opened fire on Palestinian Arabs inside the main mosque in Hebron, killing twenty-five people. As a result of this massacre, Arafat broke off negotiations with Israel, but after several weeks of pressure the talks were resumed. Discontented Palestinians, however, actively sought to undermine the peace process. Despite repeated acts of violence, the Oslo II agreement was signed in September 1995. In response, the opposition parties denounced Rabin, calling him a traitor to his country, an accusation repeated at a rally held on 28 October. The next week Rabin and Peres appeared at a rally in Tel Aviv in support of the peace process; as Rabin left the platform at the end of the rally he was shot dead by a religious Jew, Yigal Amir.

Although Peres and Rabin had been adamant that terrorism would not be allowed to undermine the peace process, the opposition parties unleashed a frenzied campaign against the Oslo Accords. In the midst of such uncertainty about government policy, Peres called an election, and Benjamin Netanyahu was elected Prime Minister. Unable to achieve the type of cooperation with Palestinian authorities attained by Rabin and Peres, Netanyahu further exacerbated relations with the Palestinians by opening the exit of an ancient tunnel that ran under the Old City next to the Temple Mount.

In October 1998 Prime Minister Netanyahu and Yasser Arafat met in Washington to discuss the peace process. After prolonged argument, Israel and the Palestinians agreed to embark on a new stage of cooperation. According to the Wye Agreement, Israel would effect a further West Bank redeployment, involving 27.2 per cent of the Occupied Territories. Of this area, 13 per cent would pass from Israeli occupation to Palestinian civil control. The remaining 14.2 per cent, which was previously under joint Israel-Palestinian Authority control, would come under direct Palestinian rule.

Despite the conciliatory steps taken by the new Prime Minister Ehud Barak, elected in the summer of 1999, the events that took place in September and October 2000 merely aggravated tensions between Israelis and Palestinians. On 28 September Israel's hard-line leader Ariel Sharon angered Palestinians by visiting a Jerusalem shrine sacred to Jews and Muslims, an act widely perceived as deliberate provocation. Dozens of police and several Palestinians were injured in the ensuing riots. Subsequently, clashes erupted in the West Bank and the Gaza Strip. This outburst was followed by increased conflict, Barak called for an election and Ariel Sharon became Prime Minister. As the conflict continued, a terrorist attack was launched against the United States on 11 September

2001 resulting in the destruction of the Twin Towers of the World Trade Center in New York.

The next month, the United States mounted a bombing campaign against the Taliban in Afghanistan after their refusal to hand over the terrorist Osama bin Laden who was held responsible for this outrage. As the US bombing campaign intensified, Muslims in Pakistan and elsewhere protested, accusing the United States of launching an attack against Islam. As the war continued, Osama bin Laden in repeated television interviews denounced the United States and Israel. In April 2002 the Israeli onslaught against Palestinians in the Occupied Territories further intensified Arab hostility towards world Jewry.

JEWS, ARABS AND THE FUTURE

As we have seen, the partition plan proposed by the British as a solution to the problem of Jewish-Arab conflict was constantly resisted by the Palestinians. At the Arab Summit in Bludanan in Syria before the Second World War, five resolutions were formulated that rejected the notion of a Jewish National Home, repudiated the Balfour Declaration, agitated for restriction of Jewish immigration and called for the recognition of Palestinian sovereignty over the land. Such determination later served as the basis for rejecting the 1939 White Paper in which the British made various concessions to the Palestinian population. Throughout this period the Arab community was unwilling to negotiate over any of the issues facing those living in the Holy Land. Jews, on the other hand, continually sought to find a solution to the problems confronting the native population while retaining their conviction that a Jewish National Home must be established in the land of their ancestors.

In May 1947 the United Nations Special Committee on Palestine (UNSCOP) was created and given responsibility to report by the autumn on the future of Palestine. During the summer members of UNSCOP went to the Holy Land. On 31 August UNSCOP recommended the end of the British Mandate. A majority report advocated that Palestine be partitioned into an Arab and a Jewish state with an international zone for the Holy Places. On 29 November the General Assembly formally considered the report, and thirty-three delegates voted in favour. Thirteen delegates were opposed and ten abstained.

The British resolved to continue their rule in Palestine until 15 May 1948. On the 14th Ben-Gurion and other leaders signed Israel's Declaration of Independence. As we have seen, this document described the Land of Israel as the birthplace of the Jewish nation and went on to explain that the Jewish people had long prayed for their return to the land of their ancestors. The Declaration further emphasized the destruction of European Jewry by the Nazis and the need for a Jewish state. The Declaration stated that the United Nations had accepted the right of the Jewish people to establish their own country, which would be open for immigration. It was hoped that the Arabs of Israel would be active participants in this newly founded nation on the basis of equal citizenship rights.

The consequence, however, was an attack on Israel by the surrounding Arab nations. Arab countries simply disregarded the authority of the United Nations, and instead of seeking peace with the Jews in their midst, subjected them to a ferocious onslaught. From a Zionist perspective, such an attack was a violation of international agreements and international law. Zionists contend that the Arabs were aware of the massacre of European Jewry during the Second World War, and therefore should have been conscious of the need for Jews to protect themselves from further attack. The Zionist cause was based on the recognition that Jews had been and no doubt would continue to be regarded as aliens in countries where they constituted a minority. By creating a Jewish commonwealth in the Holy Land, the Jewish people sought to defend themselves from future hostility.

Arguably the Palestinians who fled from their homes during this conflict could have been spared this tragedy if their fellow Arabs had accepted the authority of the United Nations. By rejecting the majority decision to partition Palestine, the Arab nations had placed themselves outside the fundamental democratic process on which the United Nations is based. Since the creation of Israel over fifty years ago, Arab nations have repeatedly denied Israel's right to exist. As we have noted, hatred and bloodshed have been the result of such intransigence. While Jews have sought peace with their neighbours, the Arabs have waged war.

Throughout the twentieth century, Arab opposition to Jews was based on the belief that their land was taken from them by the Jewish community. Zionists emphasize that land was purchased from Palestinian and non-Palestinian landowners under Ottoman rule. This, they argue, was a legitimate transaction. The tracts of land obtained before the State of Israel was created were purchased legally. Even though the mass of the Palestinian population was not involved in this transaction, this was a proper business venture, quite different from the seizure of land following the War of Independence.

As we have seen, more than half a million Arab refugees fled from Israeli territory after the War of Independence. Most of these refugees went to Jordan, and others escaped to the Gaza Strip. Given the antagonism of the Arabs to the Jewish state, it is understandable that the Israeli government was opposed to their return. In June 1938 Ben-Gurion stated to his Cabinet that those who took up arms against the Jewish nation would have to bear the consequences.

One of the results of the war was Israel's determination to protect itself from further aggression. It is not surprising, therefore, that the Israelis took steps to restrict the activities of Palestinian refugees living in their midst. Although Israel's Declaration of Independence guarantees social and political equality for all its citizens, Israelis were ambivalent about the Arab population of the country. As events proved, the Arabs in Israel constituted a real threat to the stability of the country. Ben-Gurion was right that they were a dangerous presence.

For this reason the Jewish state took steps to control Arab agitators. Article 125 of the Emergency Regulations of 1949 granted military governors the power to declare access to any place or area forbidden. Under this provision, many Arab villages were designated as closed areas; no one was permitted to move without a permit. Further, Bedouin in the Negev were subjected to similar provisions. Other powers granted to the Israeli government included the right to banish, restrict the residence of or detain Arabs without trial. The justification for such regulations was state security.

Given the events of the Second World War, it is understandable that the Israeli government was determined to protect the Jewish state at all costs. The main objective of this policy was to ensure that any form of Arab insurrection would be thwarted and that the Arab population was controlled. Many Arabs were prepared to accommodate themselves to such conditions, but Arab youth protested. Of particular concern was the confiscation of Arab land under the Absentees Property Law of 1950 as well as the loss of Arab influence in the area.

Israel's policies, however, are in Jewish eyes totally comprehensible. Throughout its history, the country has been besieged by Arab nations intent on driving Jews from the land. More recently the *intifada* has sought to undermine and prevent Israeli control of its Arab inhabitants. Repeatedly Israel was determined to defend itself from its enemies. Its actions, including the attack on a nuclear reactor in Iraq and the attempt to drive the PLO out of Lebanon, have been dictated by such policies. Surrounded by its foes, isolated from external support, the Jewish nation has continually sought to safeguard itself from aggression.

In the last few years the Oslo agreement provided a framework for negotiation between Israelis and Palestinians even though Israel remained in charge of East Jerusalem, the settlements, sovereignty and the economy of the country. Although Palestinians were to be allowed limited autonomy in the Gaza Strip and Jericho with regard to health, internal security, education, the postal services and tourism, Israel retained control over foreign affairs and overall security. In the West Bank, Israel would be the dominant partner. But with the election of the hardline Benjamin Netanyahu, the Oslo plan was derailed.

Yet, the victory of the Labour Party in the 1999 elections promised hope for a Middle East solution. The Sharm al-Shaykh agreement signed on 5 September 1999 provided for Israeli withdrawal from the Palestinian areas, the release of prisoners, security passages, the construction of the Port of Gaza, and a final settlement. It appears that Barak was anxious to grant even further autonomy to the Palestinians. Nonetheless, the election of Ariel Sharon as Prime Minister has yet again raised serious doubts about a possible solution to this continuing conflict.

This ongoing struggle between Israel and the Palestinians has intensified Arab anti-Semitism and led to the destruction of Jewish communities in Arab lands. Throughout the Arab world, Jews are continually vilified – as a consequence, the Zionist aspiration to solve the problem of anti-Semitism by creating a Jewish state in the Middle East has proved an illusion. In modern times the Arab community has become the greatest proponent of anti-Jewish attitudes, and has transformed the demonic image of the Jew to suit its own purposes.

As we have noted, during the last fifty years a vast quantity of anti-Semitic literature has been published in Muslim countries utilizing religious as well as racial motifs. Some of this literature, such as Hitler's *Mein Kampf*, Henry Ford's *International Jew* and the *Protocols of the Elders of Zion*, has been translated into Arabic and is widely available. Other writings have exploited stereotypical images of the Jew inherited from the past. In all cases, these negative depictions of Jewry have been reinterpreted to express Arab antipathy towards Jews: repeatedly the Jew is portrayed as an evil force determined to corrupt and exploit the society in which he lives.

In addition, Jews are presented as forming a global conspiracy intent on dominating world affairs.

Typical of such diatribes against the Jewish community is the tract *Holy War and Victory* written by Abd al-Halim Mahmoud, the former Rector of Cairo's al-Azhar University. In his view, the struggle for Islam is depicted as a struggle against Satan:

> Among Satan's friends – indeed his best friends in our age – are the Jews. They have laid down a plan for undermining humanity, religiously and ethically. They have begun their work to implement this plan with their money and their propaganda. They have falsified knowledge, exploited the pens of writers and bought minds in their quest for the ruination of humanity.

Such denunciations of Jewry parallels medieval polemics, as does the repeated allegation that Jews carry out acts of ritual murder. Thus in December 1984 the President of the World Muslim Congress, Dr Ma'ruf al-Dawalibi claimed to quote the Talmud at the UN Centre for Human Rights' Seminar alleging that it is necessary for Jews to drink the blood of non-Jews. 'If a Jew does not drink every year the blood of a non-Jewish man,' he stated, 'then he will be damned for all eternity.' In his view, the Talmud asserts that the whole world is the property of Israel including the wealth, blood and souls of gentiles. Another Muslim authority, Damil Safan in his *Jews: History and Doctrine* argued that there have been numerous cases of blood libel which have gone unnoted in history.

As a result of such perceptions, many fundamentalist Muslims are intent on carrying out a *jihad* against the Jewish community. Such intransigence, reflected in the proclamations of Osama bin Laden and other Arab reactionaries throughout the world, highlights the ongoing presence of Jew-hatred in contemporary society. As humanity's most persistent hatred, anti-Semitism continues to flourish in the modern world. Nearly 4,000 years of antipathy towards Jews has not diminished despite the determination of the Jewish people to free itself from the scourge of prejudice and misunderstanding. Even though the Jewish people are now empowered in their own country, Jewish security is as imperilled as it was in previous centuries. In a world now faced with the very real threat of mass destruction, the flames of such hostility continue to burn bright, with the threat of Jewish extermination as great as ever.

Select Bibliography

Almog, Shmuel (ed.), *Antisemitism through the Ages* [Oxford 1988]

Arendt, Hannah, *Antisemitism* [New York 1968]

Bauer, Yehuda, *A History of the Holocaust* [New York 1982]

Bayfield, Tony and Braybrooke, Marcus (eds), *Dialogue with a Difference* [London 1992]

Berger, David (ed.), *History and Hate: The Dimensions of Anti-Semitism* [Philadelphia 1986]

Blech, Arthur, *Anti-Semitism: The Guilt of Jews and Christians* [New York 1994]

Bodansky, Yossef, *Islamic Anti-Semitism as a Political Instrument* [Houston 1999]

Braham, Randolf L., *The Origins of the Holocaust: Christian Anti-Semitism* [Boulder 1986]

Braiterman, Zachary, *(God) after Auschwitz* [Princeton, NJ 1998]

Browning, Christopher, *The Path to Genocide* [Cambridge 1992]

Burleigh, Michael and Wipperman, Wolfgang, *The Racial State: Germany 1933–1945* [Cambridge 1994]

Burrin, Philippe, *Hitler and the Jews* [London 1994]

Cargas, Henry James, *Shadows of Auschwitz* [New York 1990]

Carmichel, Joel, *The Satanizing of the Jews* [New York 1992]

Cohen, Arthur A., *Tremendum* [New York 1981]

Cohen, Jeremy, *The Friars and the Jews: Evolution of Medieval Anti-Judaism* [Ithaca 1982]

Cohen, Norman, *Warrant for Genocide* [London 1970]

Cohn-Sherbok, Dan, *The Crucified Jew* [London 1992]

Colijn, C. Jan and Littell, Marcia Sachs (eds), *Confronting the Holocaust* [Lanham, MD 1997]

Curtis, Michael (ed.), *Antisemitism in the Contemporary World* [Boulder 1986]

Cutler, Alan Harris, *The Jew as Ally of the Muslim. Medieval Roots of Modern Anti-Semitism* [Notre Dame 1986]

Davies, A.T. (ed.), *Antisemitism and the Foundations of Christianity* [New York 1979]

Dawidowicz, Lucy S., *The War against the Jews* [New York 1985]

Dinnerstein, Leonard, *Uneasy at Home: Antisemitism and the American Experience* [New York 1987]

Dobkowski, Michael N., *The Tarnished Dream. The Basis of American Anti-Semitism* [Westport, CT 1979]

Dundes, Alan (ed.), *The Blood Libel Legend* [Madison 1991]

Eichmann Trial, April–May 1961; Testimony of Eichmann, Adolf (session 10), Zivia Lubetkin (session 25), Dr Aharon Peretz (session 28)

Eliach, Yaffa, *Hasidic Tales of the Holocaust* [Oxford 1982]

Esposito, John (ed.), *Voices of Resurgent Islam* [New York 1981]

Ettinger, Shmuel, *Antisemitism in the Modern Age* [Tel Aviv 1978]

Fein, Helen (ed.), *The Persisting Question. Sociological Perspectives and Social Contexts of Modern Antisemitism* [Berlin 1987]

Fiddes, Paul, *The Creative Suffering of God* [Oxford 1998]

Finzi, Roberto, *Anti-Semitism* [Gloucestershire 1999]

Fiorenza, Elisabeth Schussler and Tracy, David (eds), *The Holocaust as Interruption* [Edinburgh 1994]

Fischer, Klaus, *The History of an Obsession: German Judaeophobia and the Holocaust*

Flannery, Edward H., *The Anguish of the Jews* [New York 1985]

Fleischner, Eva (ed.), *Auschwitz: Beginning of a New Era?* [New York 1977]

Fogel, Yehezkel, *I Will Be Sanctified* [Northvale, NJ 1998)

Forster, A. and Epstein, B., *The New Anti-Semitism* [New York 1974]

Freedman, Theodore (ed.), *Anti-Semitism in the Soviet Union, its Roots and Consequences* [New York 1984]

Friedlander, Albert (ed.), *Out of the Whirlwind* [New York 1976]

Gager, John, *The Origins of Antisemitism: Attitudes towards Judaism in Pagan and Christian Antiquity* [Oxford 1985]

Gerber, David, *Anti-Semitism in American History* [Urbana 1986]

Gilbert, Martin, *The Holocaust* [London 1987]

Gilman, Sander and Katz, Steven T. (eds), *Anti-Semitism in Times of Crisis* [New York 1991]

Glassman, Bernard, *Anti-Semitic Stereotypes without Jews: Images of Jews in England 1290–1700* [Detroit 1973]

Goldberg, Michael, *Why Should Jews Survive?* [Oxford 1995]

Goldhagen, Daniel J., *Hitler's Willing Executioners. Ordinary Germans and the Holocaust* [New York 1996]

Graml, H., *Antisemitism in the Third Reich* [Oxford 1982]

Gross, John, *Shylock: A Legend and its Legacy* [New York 1992]

Grosser, Paul E., *Anti-Semitism, Causes and Effects* [New York 1983]

Hargrove, Katherine T. (ed.), *Seeds of Reconciliation* [North Richmond Hills, TX 1996]

Harkabi, Y., *Arab Attitudes to Israel* [Jerusalem 1937]

Harrelson, Walter and Falk, Randall, *Jews and Christians* [Nashville 1990]

Hay, Malcolm, *The Roots of Christian Anti-Semitism* [New York 1981]

Haynes, Stephen R. and Roth, John K., *The Death of God Movement and the Holocaust* [Westport, CT 1999]

Hilberg, Raul, *The Destruction of the European Jews* [Chicago 1967]

Hirsch, H. and Spiro, J.D., *Persistent Prejudice: Perspectives on Anti-Semitism* [Fairfax, VA 1988]

Holmes, Colin, *Anti-Semitism in British Society, 1876–1939* [New York 1979]

Isaac, Jules, *Genese de l'Antisemitisme* [Paris 1956]

Isaac, Jules, *Has Anti-Semitism Roots in Christianity?* [New York 1961]

Isaac, Jules, *The Teaching of Contempt: Christian Roots of Anti-Semitism* [New York 1964]

Jacobs, Steven, *Rethinking Jewish Faith* [Albany, NY 1994]

Jaher, Frederic Cople, *A Scapegoat in the New Wilderness: The Origins and Rise of Anti-Semitism in America* [Cambridge 1994]

Johnson, Nels, *Islam and the Politics of Meaning in Palestinian Nationalism* [London 1982]

Katz, J., *From Prejudice to Destruction, 1700–1933* [Cambridge, MA 1980]

Katz, J., *The Darker Side of Genius: Richard Wagner's Antisemitism* [London 1986]

Katz, Steven T., *The Holocaust in Historical Contexts* [New York 1994]

Kaufman, John, *Jew Hatred: Anti-Semitism, Anti-Sexuality and Mythology in Christianity* [New York 2001]

Keith, Graham, *Hatred without a Cause* [Falmouth 1997]

Klein, Charlotte, *Anti-Judaism in Christian Theology* [London 1975]

Korey, William, *The Soviet Cage: Anti-Semitism in Russia* [New York 1973]

Kushner, Tony, *The Persistence of Prejudice: Anti-Semitism in British Society during the Second World War* [Manchester 1989]

Langmuir, Gavin, *Toward a Definition of Antisemitism* [Berkeley 1996]

Langmuir, Gavin, *History, Religion and Antisemitism* [Berkeley 1990]

Leaman, Oliver, *Evil and Suffering in Jewish Philosophy* [Cambridge 1995]

Lee, Albert, *Henry Ford and the Jews* [New York 1980]

Levine, Hillel, *Economic Origins of Antisemitism. Poland and Its Jews in the Early Modern Period* [New Haven 1975]

Levinger, Lee, *Anti-Semitism Without Jews: Communist Eastern Europe* [New York 1971]

Levy, Richard (ed.), *Antisemitism in the Modern World. An Anthology of Texts* [Lexington, MA 1991]

Lewis, Bernard, *Islam in History: Ideas, Men and Events in the Middle East* [London 1973]

Lewis, Bernard, *Semites and Antisemites: an Inquiry into Conflict and Prejudice* [New York 1986]

Lifton, Robert Jay, *The Nazi Doctors* [New York 1986]

Lindemann, Albert, *Anti-Semitism before the Holocaust* [New York 2000]

Lipstadt, Deborah, *Denying the Holocaust: The Growing Assault on Truth and Memory* [New York 1993]

Littell, Franklin, *Crucifixion of the Jews* [New York 1975]

Littell, Franklin H. and Locke, Herbert G. (eds), *The German Church Struggle and the Holocaust* [Lampeter 1990]

Litvinoff, B., *The Burning Bush: Antisemitism and World Jewry* [London 1989]

Maccoby, Hyam, *Judas Iscariot and the Myth of Jewish Evil* [New York 1992]

McGarry, Michael, *Christology after Auschwitz* [New York 1993]

Maduro, Otto, *Judaism, Christianity and Liberation* [Maryknoll 1991]

Mehlman, Jeffrey, *Legacies of Antisemitism in France* [Minneapolis 1983]

Memmi, Albert, *Jews and Arabs* [Chicago 1975]

Mendes-Flohr, Paul R. and Reinharz, Jehuda (eds), *The Jew in the Modern World* [New York 1995]

Mitchell, R.P., *The Society of the Muslim Brothers* [London 1969]

Montefiore, Hugh, *On Being a Jewish Christian* [London 1998]

Morais, Vamberto, *A Short History of Anti-Semitism* [New York 1976]

Morgan, Michael, *Jewish Thought of Emil Fackenheim* [Detroit 1987]

Mosse, G., *Towards the Final Solution, A History of European Racism* [New York 1978]

Nettler, Ronald, *Past Trials and Present Tribulations: A Muslim Fundamentalist's View of the Jews* [Oxford 1987]

Nicholls, William, *Christian Anti-Semitism* [Northvale, NJ]

Niewyk, Donald L., *Socialist, Anti-Semite and Jew* [Baton Rouge 1971]

Noakes, J. and Pridham, G. (eds), *Nazism 1919–1945* [Exeter 1995]

Nyiszli, Miklos, *Auschwitz: A Doctor's Eye-witness Account* [London 1973]

Oberman, Heiko A., *The Roots of Antisemitism in the Age of Renaissance and Reformation* [Philadelphia 1984]

Oppenheim, Michael, *Speaking/Writing of God* [Albany, NY 1997]

Opsahl, Paul and Tannenbaum, Marc H., *Speaking of God Today* [Philadelphia 1994]

Oxaal, I. *et al.* (eds), *Jews, Antisemitism and Culture in Vienna* [London 1987]

Parkes, James, *Antisemitism* [London 1963]

Patterson, David, *Sun Turned to Darkness* [Syracuse, NY 1998]

Peck, Abraham (ed.), *Jews and Christians after the Holocaust* [Philadelphia 1982]

Pinson, Koppel S. (ed.), *Essays on Antisemitism* [New York 1942]

Poliakov, Léon, *The History of Anti-Semitism*, vol. 1 [London 1974], vol. 2 [London 1974], vol. 3 [London, 1975], vol. 4 [Oxford 1985]

Pulzer, P.G.J., *The Rise of Political Antisemitism in Germany and Austria* [London 1988]

Quinley, Harold and Clock, Charles, *Anti-Semitism in America* [New Brunswick 1983]

Rittner, Carol and Roth, John (eds), *From the Unthinkable to the Unavoidable* [London 1997]

Rose, Paul, *Revolutionary Antisemitism in Germany from Kant to Wagner* [Princeton 1990]

Rubenstein, Richard L. and Roth, John K., *Approaches to Auschwitz* [London 1987]

Rubenstein, W.D. and H., *Philosemitism* [London 1999]

Ruether, Rosemary Radford, *Faith and Fratricide* [New York 1974]

Schafer, Peter, *Judaeophobia* [Cambridge, MA 1998]

Seidel, Gill, *The Holocaust Denial: Antisemitism, Racism and the New Right* [London 1986]

Shain, Milton, *Antisemitism* [London 1998]

Solomon, Norman, *Judaism and World Religion* [London 1990]

Stelman, Lionel, *Paths to Genocide: Antisemitism in Western History* [Basingstoke 1998]

Stillman, Norman A., *The Jews of Arab Lands: A History and Source Book* [Philadelphia 1979]

Telushkin, Joseph and Dennis Prager, *Why the Jews: The Reason for Antisemitism* [New York 1983]

Trachtenberg, Joshua, *The Devil and the Jews* [New Haven 1943]

Trachtenberg, Joshua, *Jewish Magic and Superstition* [New York 1961]

Valentine, Hugo, *Anti-Semitism* [London 1936]

Weinberg, Meyer, *Because They Were Jews: A History of Anti-Semitism* [New York 1986]

Weinrich, Max, *Hitler's Professors* [New York 1946]

Wells, Leon Weliczker, *The Janowska Road* [New York 1970]

Wistrich, Robert, *Antisemitism: The Longest Hatred* [London 1991]

Wistrich, Robert, *Between Redemption and Perdition: Modern Antisemitism and Jewish Identity* [London 1990]

Ye'or Bat, *The Dhimmi* [London 1985]

Index